Gardening Success with Difficult Soils

GARDENING SUCCESS
WITH DIFFICULT SOILS

Limestone,
Alkaline
Clay,
and
Caliche

SCOTT OGDEN

Taylor Publishing Company
Dallas, Texas

Published by
Taylor Publishing Company
1550 West Mockingbird Lane
Dallas, TX 75235

Designed by Whitehead & Whitehead

Library of Congress Cataloging-in-Publication Data

Ogden, Scott.
    Gardening success with difficult soils : limestone, alkaline clay,
and caliche / Scott Ogden.
        p. cm.
    Includes index.
    ISBN 0-87833-741-5 : $17.95
    1. Gardens, Limestone—Southwestern States. 2. Gardens, Chalk—
Southwestern States. 3. Gardening—Southwestern States.
4. Problem soils—Southwestern States. 5. Gardens, Limestone.
6. Gardens, Chalk. I. Title.
SB426.043 1992
635.9'55—dc20   91–33679
                                                          CIP

Printed in the United States of America

10 9 8 7 6 5 4 3 2 1

For My Parents

CONTENTS

PREFACE and ACKNOWLEDGMENTS

Learning to garden on the limy soils of Texas has presented an absorbing challenge to me since childhood, and lessons learned of plant successes and failures continue to fascinate me today. By fortune (good, bad, or indifferent) most of my gardening experience has passed the tests of heavy, calcareous soils and a brutally hot summer climate. These conditions are typical in much of Texas, my home, but are familiar to gardeners elsewhere as well.

As it happens, the regional problems of gardening in Texas (difficult soil and a troublesome, extreme climate) pose some of the most common complaints of gardeners everywhere. The harsh conditions of Texas, therefore, serve as a model for gardeners in many areas of North America, particularly the arid Southwest, the hot, humid Southeast, and the windswept prairies of the Midwest. Although the majority of the plants discussed in this volume are included with the South-central U.S. in mind, many of the same varieties may be found thriving in gardens of the Rocky Mountain West, California, Florida, or on the hillsides of New England.

There is a certain unity to gardens built on limestone or limy subsoil, wherever they occur, and the same groups of plants follow such soils into many differing climates. Gardeners on lime comprise a unique community, and frequently share the joys of plants that are passed by or ignored by gardeners on acid lands. The range of attractive lime-loving plants is far from exhausted, and assiduous exchange and experimentation will no doubt widen the palette of lime-tolerant garden subjects for years to come.

Encouragement and assistance from several gardening friends has helped to guide me throughout this effort. In particular, Paul Cox, supervisor of the San Antonio Botanical Center, was quick and generous to offer his wide horticultural experience, wit, and wisdom. The San Antonio Botanical Center also graciously shared some of the beautiful slides in their collection.

To Tim Mills, William C. Welch, Raydon Alexander, and L. A. Demartino, Jr. I give thanks for their insightful reviews and comments. In acknowledging their contributions I also hasten to dissociate these able thinkers from anything reckless or foggily-conceived in what I have written.

James David and the extraordinary gardening community represented by the staff and clientele of Gardens on West Thirty-fifth Street in Austin were a constant and unselfish source of inspiration, advice, and information.

Generous gardeners such as Lynn Lowrey, Margaret Kane, and Thad Howard supported the very foundations of my horticultural experience. Without their cheerful sharing far less, if any, of my understanding as a gardener might have been reached. Joe Toquigny and Manuel Flores also sponsored my gardening efforts and shared their wisdom and enthusiasms.

I wish to thank Neil Sperry for his tireless encouragement, particularly through *Gardens and More* magazine, in which my fledgling adventures in garden writing were permitted to flower.

My mother, Joyce Ogden, provided her able artistry for the delineation of the calcareous soils map. Jimmi Leaverton helped with some of the "herbarium" style photography and layout. Barbara Herritt helped me troubleshoot with my word processor problems.

My wife, Seresa, offered encouragement and common sense when I strayed off course, and entertained our two children while I wrote. Without her tolerance both my garden and this writing could scarcely have come to fruition.

SCOTT OGDEN
New Braunfels, Texas
July, 1991

INTRODUCTION

A great deal of the beauty projected by any garden derives from the health and vigor of the inhabitants. This in turn depends largely upon the adaptability of individual plants to local soils and climate. Every garden region has parameters that restrict choices to a greater or lesser extent. Sometimes, as in the case of countries dominated by extreme cold or aridity, environments are so severe that to garden at all is a challenge. Although less obvious to the untrained eye, the underlying geology of a region also exerts a profound effect on the plants growing on the local soils. Nowhere is this more evident than on limestone, chalk, and the limy clay soils and rocky *caliche* formations that derive from calcareous rocks.

The great forests of southeastern America come to an abrupt halt where they abut the black waxy lands of the Texas prairies. Here the limy soils exclude many of the plants adapted to the old South, in part through a compacted internal structure that favors the deep, fibrous roots of prairie grasses over those of most woody plants, but also through an alkaline soil chemistry that restricts the availability of many minerals essential for plant growth.

When settlers moving westward from the Southern states first broke the prairie sod to establish gardens on these limy grounds they brought with them the favorite flowers of their homelands. Crape myrtles, roses, lilacs, peaches, and a variety of bulbs came to the limestone regions with these early pioneers. Although these plants were among the more successful colonizers of the new gardens of the Southwest, other favorites of Southern gardens failed. Azaleas, camellias, gardenias, and dogwoods perished on the drought-prone, alkaline prairies unless provided with special care and coddling seldom available on the frontier. Thomas Afleck, a nineteenth-century nurseryman of Mississippi and Texas, recommended Cherokee roses (*Rosa laevigata*) for hedging in the Southern gardens of 1869, but lamented that they did not "thrive well on the upland prairies of Texas and least so on the strong hog-wallow soils or those strongly impregnated with lime."

In essence these early prairie gardens were diminished transplants of their Southern forbears, constructed from the reduced ranks of the garden plants of eastern America. Nineteenth-century nurserymen offered an extraordinary array of plants for the gardens of the settlers. Yet, many of the varieties successful in other sections were poorly suited to limy ground. This was a true instance of natural selection and survival of the fittest, for only the strongest-growing plants were able to establish themselves on the difficult prairie clays and chalky limestone uplands.

This new land was rich in unusual and attractive plants, however, and possessed a whole realm of prairie wildflowers unknown to the gardens of the Southeast. Gradually, gardeners began to adopt these Southwestern natives into their gardens, as well as a host of plants brought in by early immigrants from around the world.

Gardeners bring with them the love of plant varieties grown in their former homelands. Just as in the days of the early pioneers, today's gardeners on lime often attempt to grow plants brought from other parts of the country. When cultural heritage clashes with prairie clay, the harsh climate and difficult soil will most often determine success or failure. Many gardeners on these troublesome limestone soils have experienced the frustration of helplessly watching beautiful plants perish. But by trying new varieties gardeners learn about their gardens and participate in the same adventure begun by the pioneers of the last century: to build a vision of paradise on the limy hills and plains.

By their very natures many gardeners cherish most what is difficult to cultivate, and seek wherever possible to widen the range of plants in their gardens. Gardens on the limestone heartlands have benefited greatly by the many plants introduced from other parts of the world. Yet, along with the booming growth of cities in recent decades there has also come a loss of sensitivity to the distinctive character of the limestone regions. Gardens need to help restore a sense of place, while at the same time exploring fully the wonderful palette of the botanical world.

It is intelligent experimentation that allows gardeners slowly to unlock the secrets of climate and soil, and to create gardens that are memorable and lasting expressions of beauty. To succeed in this effort, would-be gardeners on lime must garner all the information and experience available, lest they endlessly repeat the mistakes of the early pioneers. Limy-soil gardens suffer mightily from the cultural domination and traditions brought from other sections of America. This must be recognized and resisted if gardens on limy ground are to reach their full potential. Yet, with these challenges comes a promise of reward, for by facing the unique problems of gardening on calcareous soils, gardeners may create something truly original and worthwhile.

CHAPTER ONE

Legacy of the Chalk Age

The Nature of Calcareous Soils

Black soils convey an image of richness and fertility to most gardeners, and the hopeful immigrant into an area underlain by limestone looks with gladness on the dark-colored earth that covers the hills and prairies. It's not until the shovel stubbornly sinks in the backyard that the new resident realizes that all may not be well with this soil. Instead of the hoped-for crumbly loam, the average gardener on calcareous (limy) soil inherits sticky black clay that clings to shovels and shoes and dries into bricklike clods. Gardeners on the shallow soils of limestone uplands find only a little of this intractable clay mixed with lots of lime rubble, a discouraging condition grudgingly referred to as *caliche*. So much for the reputation of dark-colored earths!

These heavy black clays and rubbly limestone soils present some of the greatest challenges a gardener may face. Like clay soils everywhere, the black earths that form over limestone hold much of their richness chemically trapped on the surface of the clay particles. Although most clay molecules may be envisioned as tiny sheets or plates, the unusual mineral that dominates limy blackland clays is more readily likened to an accordion, for it has the capacity to expand and absorb water and minerals within its platelike structure. The result of this arrangement is readily apparent in the tremendous shrinkage and expansion displayed by these prairie soils. Due to the tiny clay mineral particles called calcium montmorillonite, these soils have a well-earned reputation for changing overnight from boggy saturated clay-muck to dry, deeply cracked adobe. As they dry out in late summer, these limy clays develop cracks over three feet deep and show evidence of movement at even greater depths.

Such soils are uncommon, but form in response to a warm, semiarid climate with summer rainfall and underlying calcareous rocks. Limestones, chalks, and marls (limy claystones) may be found in many regions, but especially characterize parts of Texas. The calcareous sediments of this section extend in a broad arc from the Red River south through Dallas-Fort Worth to Austin, San Antonio and westward through the Texas Hill Country. Like the layers of chalk which form the famous white cliffs of Dover, these calcareous sediments were laid down between sixty and one hundred million years ago during the Cretaceous era or Chalk Age.

Through most of this period warm shallow seas covered large areas of the earth.

Along with mosasaurs, ammonites, reef-building clams, and other exotic forms of life, billions of tiny one-celled plants and animals swarmed in the tropical lagoons of the Chalk Age seas. In this halcyon environment countless generations of these creatures contributed their limy shells to the sediments collecting on the bottom of the ocean. Like a steady rain falling over the millennia these accumulated and coalesced into the various layers that would become limestones, chalks, and marls.

Although soil scientists would no doubt regard it as reckless oversimplification, the calcareous soils that form over these sediments may be divided into two broad groups: shallow soils which develop over uplands such as the Edwards Plateau and parts of the Grand Prairie, and deeper clay soils typical of the Blackland Prairie. The shallow soils usually form over relatively hard, lower Cretaceous limestones, while the deeper clays most often derive from fairly soft chalks and marls of the upper Cretaceous. The critical difference between these soil types seems to be the greater portion of undissolved lime rock, or calcium carbonate, that remains in the soils of the uplands, for this helps to moderate expansiveness and internal compaction and may slightly increase the alkalinity of these thinner soils as compared to the deep earths of the Blackland Prairie. In some areas, however, as where soils form over the ancient reef deposits of the Edwards limestone, magnesium-bearing dolomite in the lower Cretaceous rocks may allow near neutral soils to develop.

Garden Chemistry

Gardeners concern themselves with this geology and soil chemistry, as well as other properties such as soil texture and pore space, because of the vital influence these conditions have when one is selecting plants to establish and thrive on limy ground. Many plants are known to be lime-hating (calcifuge), while others have the reputation of being lime-friendly (calcicole). The underlying factor that often determines this difference is a plant's range of tolerance for the soil's pH, or degree of acidity or alkalinity. Chemists determine this rating for soils by measuring the concentration of hydrogen ions, a figure that is expressed on a scale where neutral is 7, representing a concentration of one in ten million or $1:10^7$. A lower pH is considered acid, while a higher pH rates as alkaline.

The effects of pH on soils and the plants that grow in them are complex, but, as a generalization, the availability of elements such as iron decreases as soils become more alkaline. To gardeners on lime this usually means that the beautiful green plant recently purchased at the nursery and planted in the backyard next to the swimming pool has turned a bright chartreuse yellow! This condition, known technically as chlorosis, is the familiar bane of all gardens on alkaline land and results from the plant's inability to absorb the minerals necessary to form chloroplasts, or green cells.

These cells are the organs that green plants use to harness the energy of the sun for food production. Through a chemical miracle called photosynthesis plants use sunlight to transform water taken up by the roots and carbon dioxide absorbed by the leaves into sugars and starches, with oxygen as a by-product. Molecules of chlorophyll trap the sun's energy and provide power for this reaction, and it is this substance that fills the chloroplasts and gives the green color to plant leaves and stems. Without this green pigment, plants slowly starve to death.

When plants are unable to take up the necessary minerals to form chlorophyll molecules, their newly formed leaves begin to take on a characteristic yellowing or discoloration that varies depending on the mineral that is missing and the severity of the shortage. Iron or zinc deficiencies often produce yellowish leaves with darker green veins, while shortages of magnesium may induce just the opposite color pattern. In advanced or severe cases the leaves of chlorotic plants may turn purplish or develop puckering and distortion before turning brown and dying.

Gardeners can distinguish these symptoms from other types of leaf yellowing because chlorosis generally affects only the recent growth of plants and is most pronounced on tender new leaves. Although commonly a result of the plant's too-large appetite for minerals that are in short supply, chlorosis may also be brought about by other environmental stresses such as soil compaction or extremes of temperature. Prompt applications of epsom salts (magnesium sulfate) may save chlorotic plants, and a variety of mineral products that help correct this condition are available at nurseries. Sometimes a chemical boost of this kind is all that is needed to set a plant right, and it may thrive thereafter without additional treatment.

Because calcareous soils derive from lime-rich sediments they include an abundance of basic minerals. In many areas this practically guarantees the development of alkaline soil conditions. The lime-rich soils of Texas commonly vary from a mildly alkaline pH near 7.4 up to 8.4 or higher. Where high rainfall leaches away lime, as on the eastern blacklands near Paris, Texas, or where locally abundant minerals counteract the effect of calcium, some soils may approach neutral or slightly acid conditions at the surface. Even in these areas subsoils generally remain limy, and gardeners over limestone must often deal with irrigation waters that are decidedly alkaline as well.

Standard horticultural practice recommends lowering a high pH through the addition of sulfur, a technique that can be reasonably effective in some alkaline soils. Because of the unusual calcium montmorillonite in the black earths that form in the soils of warm climates, this method has little value in areas such as Texas. The tiny molecules of clay have an almost inexhaustible capacity to absorb such chemicals, and the oft-recommended gypsum used in other regions to lighten heavy soils, likewise, quickly neutralizes with little lasting effect. Soil-improving chemicals offer scant assistance for these calcareous soils, and gardeners must look elsewhere to find help for their plants.

In the last two hundred years agricultural science has attempted to unravel the details of how plants get their food and which minerals they require for growth. Early researchers analyzed the tissues of plants to see what they contained, finding mostly carbon, hydrogen, and oxygen absorbed from the air and water. But they also found nitrogen, phosphorus, potassium, calcium, and magnesium, which the plants obtained from the soil. The first three are the most common elements used by plants and are the ones included in most "balanced" or "complete" fertilizers today. Nitrogen was found to increase plant vigor and promote green leaves, while phosphorus aided flowering and fruiting, and potassium proved important to root growth. In practice the beneficial effects of these nutrients are to some extent interdependent and therefore manufactured fertilizers generally add these elements together. Later research identified six more plant foods—iron, manganese, boron, copper, zinc, and molybdenum—which occur in much smaller quantities than the five primary elements. In modern parlance these are known as "micro-nutrients" or trace elements, while the major elements are referred to as "macro-nutrients."

By applying fertilizers containing these essential macro- and micro-nutrients, agriculturalists discovered that they could grow plants even in sterile soilless media, a common practice in nursery production today. Likewise, the chemical limitations of alkaline soils could for a time be overcome if the plants received the essential nutrients directly from the fertilizers. As with the natural soil elements, however, under alkaline conditions the plant foods soon bound to the minerals in the soil and were rendered unavailable. What was needed was a way to keep the fertilizers, especially iron, zinc, and manganese, in a chemically available form.

The technique eventually developed by chemists to accomplish this feat is known as chelation, and modern fertilizers make available a range of nutrients in chelated forms. Iron, zinc, and manganese are commonly supplied to plants growing on alkaline lands through the use of these special fertilizers, which hold these elements in a type of chemical vise, protecting them from theft by the soil, while making them available to the plant roots. For much the same reason many fertilizers are prepared in special pellets, often with a coating of sulfur, so that the fertilizer elements will have the best chance to be absorbed by the plants before the alkaline chemistry of the soil renders them valueless. These carefully designed fertilizers sound like miracles of modern chemistry, and they are. But the methods they employ come from imitating the behavior of one of the oldest fertilizers known to humankind: manure!

The Vital Humus

Manure, dried grass, fallen leaves, and other animal and plant refuse are the original sources of food for all plants, supplying the same macro- and micro-nutrients that modern chemical fertilizers attempt to deliver. These natural sources of plant foods offer their elements through a slow process of decay and decomposition, yielding nitrogen fertilizer along the way and humus, a partially decayed spongy vegetable matter, as an end result. It is this last substance, the humus, that functions like the chelated fertilizers, making plant foods available in otherwise infertile alkaline land. Moreover, humus and the population of soil organisms it supports are the agents which over time convert sterile rock into life-supporting soil. By its very definition a fertile soil is a soil with an abundant presence of this partially decayed organic residue.

Humus has another role in soils, however, that exceeds in importance even its value as a long-term fertilizer. This crumbly brown fresh-smelling substance familiar as the litter on the forest floor or as the end product of the gardener's compost pile acts like chemical glue on the tiny particles of clay. A sort of organic slime binds the clay minerals together into larger crumbs of soil, a process that vastly increases the availability of soil moisture and essential plant foods. With an abundant supply of humus even heavy alkaline clays remain open and friable, and thus are able to absorb erratic rains and feed them back to plants as needed. Pore space in the soil remains large and the air required by most plant roots to metabolize and absorb soil nutrients is readily available.

Take away the humus, however, and everything goes wrong. The clay particles line up shoulder to shoulder, admitting neither air nor water. Heavy spring rains puddle on the surface and run off as if the earth were an asphalt roadway. Plants struggle in the ensuing summer's drought, and leaves yellow as oxygen-starved roots fail to deliver the vital elements to the growing plants. The dying soil shrivels and contracts, forming deep cracks as it dries into lifeless adobe.

It was just this deteriorated soil condition that faced Texas farmers in the early years of this century. In the late 1800s the limy clays of the blacklands had been plowed up to create farmland, and the pioneers found soils so rich they thought they would produce crops indefinitely. The newfound prosperity of this era was evident in the substantial homes constructed by nineteenth-century plantation owners. In the ruthless ignorance of frontier agriculture these farmers used up the organic wealth created by centuries of deep-rooted prairie grasses, whose decayed leaves, stems, and roots had developed one of the richest soils west of the Mississippi. By the time they passed the farms on to their sons and daughters the reduced yields were supporting families in shotgun houses instead of Victorian mansions.

Cyrus Longworth Lundell, a botanist with a flair for meso-American archaeology, grew up on a cotton farm and knew firsthand the deteriorating state of Texas agriculture. His early career as a field botanist in southern Mexico introduced him to the ancient Maya civilization and he made a special study of these Indians and their agriculture. He came to believe that the collapse of this once great culture was brought on by depletion of the soils of the ancient Maya region, which, like the blacklands of Texas, are dark earths formed over calcareous rock. The warm climate of southern Mexico with its abundant summer rainfall quickly decomposed organic matter and used up the soil humus. The principle responsible for this—expressing the relationship between soil temperature and moisture—and for the formation of humus is known as Lang's Rain Factor, and it decrees that humus tends to accumulate in the soils of cool, wet regions, but disappears quickly in the soils of warm climates; in arid regions it hardly forms at all.

In 1944 Lundell and other concerned scientists organized the Texas Research Foundation at Renner, Texas to find a way to save the failing farms of the Texas blacklands and to develop a system of agriculture compatible with the Texas soil and climate. These researchers used the full armament of modern agricultural science to determine the needs of these alkaline soils and, after twenty years of testing, developed farming methods to help restore and maintain the fertility of the Blackland Prairies. The findings of this unique organization are valuable for all who garden on calcareous soils, and offer special insight into limy grounds and the requirements of plants grown upon them.

As Lundell had suspected, when researchers compared the exhausted soils of Texas farms with the soils of virgin prairie, they found that organic matter, and, consequently, available soil minerals such as nitrogen and phosphorus, as well as capillary pore space and soil structure, had markedly declined. Just as in Mexico, the warm Texas climate and calcareous soils encouraged an active population of soil microorganisms that speedily consumed all available humus. Crop rotation experiments determined that the blackland soils digested about two tons of vegetable residue per acre each season. For the home gardener this translates into about a pound of dry straw for each square yard of garden space, and that's just the amount needed annually to maintain the status quo! These researchers learned that to improve the organic content and fertility of these soils required still more vegetable matter and manure (usually with supplements of nitrogen and phosphorus as well) and not just as a one-time effort, but continuously.

Sir Albert Howard, whom many revere as the first pioneer of organic gardening, published his *Agricultural Testament* in 1940. Like the scientists at Texas Research Foundation, this student of tropical agriculture dreamed of creating a system of renewable farming that would improve and maintain the fertility of the soil, and he founded the Institute of Plant Industry at Indore, India to pursue this goal. Unlike Lundell and his colleagues, Sir Albert eschewed the use of commercial fertilizers and relied on abundant human labor to help deliver the crucial manures and composts to the growing crops. Although the differing philosophies of the two groups led them to different conclusions and recommendations, both the Texas scientists and Sir Albert recognized the value of soil humus and the need to return organic matter to the soil. It is fascinating to realize that the heavy soils of central India which concerned Sir Albert and inspired his organic method are one of the few examples around the world of soils similar to those of the Texas blacklands. Thus two foci of agricultural research on opposite sides of the globe began with the need to cultivate these difficult calcareous earths successfully.

Whether a gardener chooses to use chemical fertilizers or relies on natural manures and composts, the critical message of these researchers is that calcareous soils must be fed, and fed often, in order to maintain their fertility. Few gardeners today have access to enough fresh manures and composts (or the necessary labor to spread them) to rely solely on these excellent sources of plant food. Yet without a modicum of humus even the most powerful chemical fertilizers will fight a losing battle to feed the plants in our gardens, and much of their value will be wasted, remaining locked in the alkaline clay minerals. Calcareous soils are crying for organic food; like the parents of open-mouthed nestlings, as gardeners we are charged to see that they get enough.

Meeting the Needs of Limy Garden Soil

One of Sir Albert's contributions to horticulture was the perfection of a method for composting vegetable and animal refuse, and this is a tried and true means to obtain humus. The compost pile is one of the gardener's reliable assets in the campaign to add organic matter to limy soils, and even a small garden should set aside space for this invaluable material. All manner of leaves, grass clippings, tender shoots, shredded paper, kitchen scraps, and other organic remains may be thrown on the pile. (Most animal refuse and oils should be left out; fish remains are acceptable, but should be turned in promptly.) Manure or, if this is unavailable, nitrogen fertilizer may be added to speed the decay process. Some gardeners construct boxlike enclosures to house the decomposing vegetation, but all that is really needed is a reasonably well ventilated heap and patience. The best assurance of ventilation is frequent forking and turning of the pile, and in a warm climate only a few weeks or months are needed to yield the desired result: crumbly brown humus. Since the collection of compostable debris is generally an ongoing activity, most gardeners find a second pile an asset, so that accumulation may continue while the first heap is ripening.

The unfortunate reality for most gardeners on lime is that the average well-run compost heap only delivers enough humus for a few patches of vegetables. (Remember the two tons of hay per acre calcareous soils may consume annually and picture a compost pile big enough to provide it!) Limy soils demand continual additions of organic matter, yet it seems unrealistic to provide this solely through spreading compost and manure. Fortunately, gardeners on alkaline clay and limestone soils have more options at their disposal.

Sir Frederick Stern, who in 1956 received knighthood in reward for his services to horticulture, constructed the most famous of all gardens on calcareous soils on the chalk downs of southern England. Sir Frederick was fascinated with the natural abilities of certain plants to grow on the chalky soil of his estate and reported the results of his years of experimentation in the classic, A Chalk Garden. Because he wished to test which varieties would naturally succeed on the downland soils, he imitated the natural manuring of the earth by spreading mulches of uncomposted leaves over his garden beds. This technique of annual mulching allowed Sir Frederick gradually to build up the soil of his estate and eventually reclaim the land of a former quarry, which became his famous "chalk pit garden."

Just like Sir Frederick, gardeners on limy soils in other regions can improve and build the fertility of their garden soils by imitating the natural cycle of plant growth and decay with frequent additions of mulches. Covering flower beds with organic debris not only provides an *in situ* compost heap, but improves the moisture-holding capacity of the earth as well. A mulch of leaves or shredded plant remains reduces the warm summer temperatures of soils, slowing down the breakdown of organic matter and encouraging the accumulation of vital humus. Like the natural coverings of dried prairie grasses that once built the rich soils of chalk downs and grasslands, a continuously renewed surface mulch can, over time, build a fertile topsoil from even the poorest limy substrate.

Different types of mulches offer varying nutritional values as they decompose, and so are more or less suited to this use. The determining factor in most cases is the ratio of carbon to nitrogen in the vegetation, for this affects the speed with which it decomposes and the quantity of plant foods released during decay. Mulches with relatively low C/N ratios, such as fresh grass clippings, decompose quickly and may actually provide more nutrients than equivalent amounts of compost and manure. Shredded bark and tree leaves are slower to rot down and have less food value, but make their effects on the soil apparent over a long period.

Oxygen is required by the soil bacteria and fungi to complete the decay process properly, and gardeners should take care to leave mulches on the soil surface until decomposition is complete. If dug in too soon, this otherwise valuable source of plant food will actually steal nitrogen from the soil, for without the crucial atmosphere anaerobic composting will begin and the soil microbes will compete with garden plants for food. If left on the surface as in nature no such detrimental effects should result.

In practice, a mix of tender green leaves as well as woody plant remains and available manure and compost offers the necessary material for earthworms and other soil organisms to mix with heavy clays and chalky rubble. Just as in the compost pile, modest additions of chemical nitrogen and superphosphate can also be included to help speed the process of decay and soil improvement. Autumn rakings and fresh leaves in the form of lawn mowings are available to most gardeners at no cost, and tree-trimming services are often grateful to find a home for their chipped and shredded prunings. Fresh hay is a clean, inexpensive, and underappreciated mulching material that is easy to obtain from local feed stores, and convenient to spread around the garden. Most nurseries and garden centers sell shredded and composted pine bark, and this may be available in bulk as well as by the bag.

All of these and a variety of other vegetable wastes such as pecan and rice hulls, cotton bolls, and so on will help to improve the soil when applied as mulches. (The popular peat moss available at garden centers dries out too quickly to make an appropriate mulch, although it functions as an acceptable, but expensive and short-lived, soil amendment.) Whatever the choice of mulching materials, gardeners on calcareous soil must always bear in mind this admonition: to watch and do nothing to cover exposed bare earth constitutes an unforgivable sin, for without a renewing source of organic matter the soil will exhaust its supply of humus.

Vegetable and flower beds that will be replanted each season can take advantage of a special type of mulch that grows on site. This is the technique of "green manuring," a garden practice with a history dating to the Chou Dynasty of ancient China (1110 to 250 B.C.). These early agriculturalists discovered that various green grasses and legumes would enrich the soil for their crops if they were plowed under before spring planting. Why certain plants worked better than others presumably remained a mystery to these farmers, but the value of green manures was known to the ancient Romans as well. (In Book I of *The Georgics* Virgil advises farmers to "plant your golden corn where grew the bean, the slender vetch or the fragile stalks of bitter lupin.") We now know that these helpful plants have associations with nitrogen-fixing bacteria that allow them to obtain this element directly from the soil air. Because their roots develop special swollen nodules to house these bacteria, members of the pea family, or legumes, are the best known nitrogen-fixing plants, but other herbs and grasses, and even shrubs such as elaeagnus and wax myrtle have this capacity as well.

Green manures, or "cover crops," are usually planted in the fall to grow through the cool, moist winter months, and then mown down or turned under before spring or summer planting. Elbon rye, oats, hubam sweet clover, and alfalfa are some of the plants that make effective cool-season crops for green manuring on alkaline land. Rye grasses in particular also help to reduce certain soil pests such as nematodes, and their fibrous roots break up the heavy prairie soil. Gardens especially benefit from a rotation of these plants, which disrupts the life cycles of various pests and soil pathogens at the same time that soil is being improved. Southern peas such as blackeyes and crowders, and hairy indigo may be used as soil-building summer covers where gardens will be filled with vegetables or flowers in the cool parts of the year. For gardeners who can afford to wait a season or two, these green manure crops offer the ideal means to improve the soil of a new flower bed at minimal expense.

Preparing the Ground

Mulches and green manures benefit calcareous soils surprisingly quickly, and generous applications of nitrogen-rich leaves soon have a noticeable effect. The ground ceases heaving and cracking and displays an improved tilth and a thriving population of earthworms as evidence of success. Yet, however valuable these additions may be on established beds, they prove impractical when it comes to new plantings. A cartful of prospective garden inhabitants, fresh from the nursery and irresistibly full of flower, are already unloading from the tailgate of the car before most gardeners are sure where they will be planted. Even those whose restrained plantings follow their landscape schemes with the precision of a military drill need a method to prepare new beds from scratch without waiting for the earthworms and other soil creatures to do their work.

The solution requires a good shovel (or better still, a border fork) and a few hours of hard physical labor. Traditional gardeners rely on the technique called double trenching to provide a home for their cherished plants, and for long-lasting success there is no substitute for these old-fashioned double-dug beds. First the gardener removes one shovel layer, and then the layer below, taking care to keep the top spit separate from the bottom. Then, starting with the bottom layer, manure, compost and other rough vegetable matter are incorporated into an equal volume of the clay subsoil. A complete fertilizer and sulfur or epsom salts (magnesium sulfate) may be added at this time to help give the soil a good start and moderate the alkaline pH. Replacing the top spit, the gardener repeats the process, incorporating more manure and compost, and finishes by jacketing the bed with a layer of mulch. This is hard, backbreaking work, and gardeners will be well advised to moisten the ground a few days before beginning such a chore. Nevertheless, this is the quickest and most effective means to prepare a fertile bed and the benefits can last the lifetime of the garden.

Where soils are reasonably well drained and sufficiently deep, this double digging is a worthwhile effort. But many calcareous soils are shallow and full of lime rock, and prairie clays are frequently so poorly drained that any excavation is susceptible to seasonal waterlogging. Sometimes, if the chalky limestone is sufficiently soft, it may be broken up with a pick and the drainage and soil depth improved enough to create a bed even in the shallowest soils. But where the underlying rock forms an impermeable hardpan, or the heavy clays lack adequate internal drainage, it is probably better to build up than dig down.

Raised flower beds are the conventional answer to most of the garden problems of these soils and they have the additional attraction of placing the garden plants on stage where they can be better appreciated and enjoyed. A rise of six to eight inches is usually sufficient to correct most drainage problems, but more is welcome and will be appreciated by the plants where it can be arranged. The simplest raised beds are constructed in the same way as the double-dug beds described above, by amending the existing topsoil. Instead of returning the soil to its position in the ground, however, the gardener then piles it high in the desired area for the new planting. Since the process of mixing the organic materials into the clay soils more than doubles the volume of earth in a new bed, even traditional double digging usually results in some rise to the level of soil, and it is probably best for all garden beds to take advantage of this with a modest rise.

More radical bed preparation may bring in completely new earth to construct the raised beds, and on shallow rocky ground this may be the only way to obtain a sufficient depth of soil to grow vegetables and other favorite plants. When new soil is brought in to the garden there is an opportunity to obtain neutral or slightly acid materials that will broaden the range of potential garden inhabitants. Calcifuge plants such as azaleas and camellias may be planted in acid beds of pine bark or peat, while many bulbs may benefit from the fast drainage offered by beds of sand, and roses may receive their preferred neutral loam. As soon as the new soils arrive, however, they initiate a slow mingling with the local rock and earth, as well as the generally lime-rich irrigation waters, so that the pH begins to rise. Periodic treatments of acidifying sulfur or epsom salts and careful watering with collected rainwater will be necessary if these special beds are to retain their favorable chemistry. This kind of extraordinary effort soon taxes the limits of most gardeners' pocketbooks, if not their backs, for in essence this is container gardening on a grand scale.

Lime-loving Plants

Salvation comes with the realization that an enormous variety of plants will grow without these extensive efforts. While raised or double-dug beds offer the most generous environments we can reasonably provide in our gardens, many plants will put up with much less. Some even prefer it. The legumes we use as green manures are a case in point: the facility these plants have for obtaining nitrogen on humus-poor alkaline soils prepares them to grow in just our conditions.

Another example is the bluebonnet, the state flower of Texas, which traditionally has resisted attempts to bring it into cultivation. This native member of the pea family is especially adapted to poor, calcareous soils. It *needs* lean, droughty conditions in order to thrive, and usually fails in the garden because of overgenerous treatment. Ironically, the bluebonnet's botanical name, *Lupinus*, which in Latin means "wolf," refers to the ancient belief that these plants stole the fertility of the soil. As we now know, it is the poor, infertile soil that allows these plants to grow in the first place, and their nitrogen-fixing roots that enable them to begin the long natural succession of plants that eventually builds back the richness of the earth.

Limestones, chalks, and marls, and the calcareous soils they yield, occur all around the world, and wherever they are found they support lime-loving flora. All of the varied habitats associated with limy soils, from dry chalky bluffs to soggy prairie wallows in alkaline clay, have their own special groups of plants uniquely suited to perform under these conditions. Many of the most beautiful of the world's garden plants grow naturally on these calcareous soils and promise to thrive in gardens on alkaline land. Indeed, there are so many attractive plants suitable for limy grounds that the effort often expended by gardeners to cultivate difficult calcifuge azaleas, gardenias, and others hardly seems justified.

Many of the gardens of the ancient world developed in countries with limy soils, and much garden heritage is based on successfully growing lime-loving plants on calcareous grounds. Ancient Persia, considered by many to be the birthplace of western garden traditions, as well as Greece, Italy, Spain, central France, and southern England, evolved their famous gardens on limestone soils and depended on lime-loving plants. Unknown gardeners of the old civilizations of China, India and Egypt helped to introduce lime-tolerant plants which remain in cultivation to this day.

Remarkably, what is arguably the oldest of all cultivated garden flowers, the madonna lily, *Lilium candidum,* is one of the few of its genus to prefer limestone soils. This is perhaps the earliest example of a long tradition among gardeners on lime of seeking out and introducing those special and unusual plants that, unlike their near kin, thrive on limy ground.

One of the great pleasures of gardening on calcareous soil is the never-ending search for these varieties of lime-tolerant plants. This challenge was accepted by Sir Frederick Stern at his garden in Highdown, and the plant varieties that he successfully introduced and shared now benefit many gardens constructed on lime. Sir Frederick noted that many plant genera that are otherwise calcifuge may include one or two members that naturally occur upon and, thus, tolerate lime. Often a lime-hating American tree such as the fringe tree (*Chionanthus virginicus*) will have an oriental counterpart (in this case the Chinese fringe tree, *Chionanthus retusus*) that succeeds on lime. In this way, members of plant groups usually considered to be calcifuge may be represented in gardens on calcareous soil.

If lime-loving plants may be said to share a common characteristic, it is their frequently coarse, vigorous root structure. Whether on light, chalky soils or heavy clays, the most successful varieties seem to possess these tough root systems, and this may be used as a guide to evaluate potential varieties for trial on limy grounds. When offered a choice between similar plants, gardeners on lime should choose the most vigorous types, as they promise the greatest chance of success. Dwarf or slow-growing plant varieties should usually be avoided unless they are known to do well in other gardens in the region.

Gardening on Lime

The gardener on limestone or limy clay soil need not covet so-called "optimal" neutral or slightly acid soils. By improving the soil with periodic mulches of organic materials and incorporating compost, most problems of plant nutrition and soil structure may be overcome. As long as healthy amounts of humus are maintained in the soil little additional fertilizer will be needed, and what is added will work most efficiently. With this attention to the soil our gardens will support an impressive variety of plants.

For those who long for the forbidden beauty and the challenge of true lime-hating azaleas, hydrangeas and others, modern chemistry provides the necessary means to defeat nature. By constructing acid beds of raised peat or pine bark, the gardener may overcome the alkaline soils and accomplish the seemingly impossible. At least for a time, acid-loving plants may successfully be grown on limy ground.

By calling upon centuries of tradition, gardeners on lime can find and select plants suitable for the garden, and, by sharing with others, increase the diversity of plant varieties at their disposal. By paying close attention to the various habitats afforded by lime and chalk soils and carefully providing similar situations, gardens on calcareous soil may take advantage of the full array of lime-loving plants. Through intelligent experimentation, new and unusual varieties suitable for limy ground will come to light, and plant groups previously believed to be lime-hating will enter our gardens. With a knowledge and awareness of the soil, and the needs of the plants grown upon it, gardeners will be ready to explore the limits that their climate will allow.

CHAPTER TWO

Climate at the Crossroads

Here the winds play an important part. The soft breezes from the Gulf are counterbalanced by the icy blizzards from the Rockies, intermingled with the fierce heat-blasts from the arid desert regions. Each controls a special section, yet wields its influence over all.
— Marian Price Scruggs, *Gardening in the Southwest*, 1932

Weather Patterns on the Limestone Heartlands

A sense of openness and change pervades and characterizes the climate of the North American interior, and this is a region where many calcareous garden soils can be found. Residents of the heartland have a keen awareness of the exposed positions they occupy on the North American continent and the frustrating unpredictability of weather conditions. Powerful fronts advance over this vast landscape with alarming suddenness, changing torrid heat to biting cold, and turning drought to deluge. The quick-changing meteorology of the region presents such a confusing picture that folk wisdom brags: "There is no climate, only weather!"

Yet, as difficult as this region's climate is to understand and predict, gardeners strive to grasp its peculiarities and nuances. They depend on an intimate knowledge of weather patterns to plan and develop their plantings, and to evaluate garden plants for adaptability to the local regime. Gardeners seek out plants to endure and perform under trying conditions, and use their familiarity with the seasonal weather routine to position each plant in the garden where it will have the greatest chance of success. When necessary, gardeners may attempt to modify the climate to accommodate and protect their plants. Together with the calcareous soils of this region, the distinctive nature of climate limits the choice of plantings and determines the nature of gardens.

Regions of lime soil occupy strategic positions in south-central North America that experience weather influences from all points of the compass. The continental air mass that dominates the Great Plains provides bodies of cold, high pressure air that bring low winter temperatures. Warm surface waters of the Gulf of Mexico give rise to moist subtropical air that helps to moderate this cold and supply humidity and precipitation, sometimes in the form of hurricanes.

The Pacific Ocean also plays an important role in determining this climate, and cool Pacific fronts frequently dominate fall and winter weather. When the Pacific air mass passes over the highlands of central Mexico and drops suddenly onto the plains to the north it may heat up and produce hot, dry blasts. This effect is analogous to the chinooks of the Northwest or the Santa Anna winds of southern California, and occurs most commonly in early spring.

All of these weather forces combine to produce the succession of brutally cold "northers," rain-bearing "gully-washers," and searing summer heat and drought that visit gardens in this region each year. The interplay of differing temperatures, humidities, and air pressures from these various influences produces an "anecdotal" climate more easily characterized by its extremes than by its mean conditions. Regions of calcareous soil such as the Blackland Prairies and Edwards Plateau experienced severe drought, averaging only half normal rainfall in 1956, yet received near record rainfall in 1957. Likewise, the relatively mild winters of 1984–88 were framed by the devastating freezes of December, 1983 and 1989. Record heat spells such as the summer of 1980, which brought three months of temperatures over 100° F to this area, are yet another example of the extremes which afflict the region with regrettable frequency.

The climate that dominates these limestone heartlands is a transitional one, uniting the humid subtropical Southeast with the arid Southwest, and receiving regular visits of dry windy cold from the Midwest as well. This transition zone coincides with the generally north-south trending belts of calcareous soils to reinforce the distinctive nature of the environment. Average annual precipitation across the limestones of central Texas ranges from forty-five inches at Paris to twenty-eight inches at San Antonio. Yet, because of the properties of the calcareous soils of this region, much of the spring rainfall received in the northeast is ineffective and runs off the heavy clay soils, while the porous limestones of the western Hill Country act as a summertime reservoir of moisture for the plants growing upon them. In this way the calcareous soils buffer the changeable climate of the region and, despite differences in rainfall from east to west, provide similar environments for growing plants.

A fundamental constant of climate in much of this area is the intense and unrelenting heat of summer. More than any single weather factor, this influences the choice of plants for gardens. The remarkable aspect of this summer heat is not the high point reached at 3:30 each afternoon, though this can be formidable, but the failure of the thermometer to fall sufficiently in the evening. It is these relatively high night temperatures that distinguish the torrid Texas summer from the hot-summer climates of the Great Plains or the desert Southwest. The peculiar blend of comparatively high summer humidity with semiarid weather conditions produces one of the hottest places in North America. Like the tropical deciduous forests and chaparrals that dominate low elevations in neighboring Mexico, the limestone regions of Texas belong to the *tierra caliente*, the hot land, and many of the hardy trees and shrubs of eastern American gardens fail or give only limited value because of this long hot season.

The Garden Year on the Limestone Heartlands

A typical growing season on the calcareous soils of this region begins in early March as the cold fronts coming down from the Great Plains and across the West from the Pacific gradually give way to warm, moist air from the Gulf of Mexico. This is not a steady change, but a tug of war between opposing forces that makes spring weather erratic and unpredictable. Average dates for last frosts vary from about March 23 at Dallas to

March 6 at Austin and San Antonio, but gardens remain at risk from late freezes well into April. Spring is frequently a false season, with warm humid spells of weather occurring as early as February. Precocious flowering shrubs, trees and bulbs put out confidently, only to be brutally revisited by cold weather from the north. This, too, is a season for unusual blasts of hot dry air drawn up from the south in advance of approaching cold fronts. Withering southwest winds often abruptly halt the spring displays of daffodils, azaleas, and others.

By April the warm Gulf air usually dominates conditions, and cold fronts arriving from the north and west generate thunderstorms. With abundant rainfall and moderating temperatures this is one of the most reliably rewarding times for gardens. From early April to the end of May a great rush of flowers come into bloom and a variety of ornamental trees, shrubs, and climbing roses give their best displays of the year.

High temperatures in early June signal the beginning of the long, hot summer, and when evening lows fail to drop below 70° F many plants enter a period of dormancy. Rainfall received at this time of year goes a long way toward moderating temperatures, and the life-supporting summer thunderstorms not only provide the necessary moisture to keep plants growing, but also can deliver significant quantities of readily absorbed nitrogen fertilizer dissolved from the electrified atmosphere. As soon as rains fall off, however, the intense heat of the summer quickly saps the moisture from plants and soils, and a long-lasting Southwestern siesta begins. The characteristic feature of all western landscapes, dry brown grass, comes to dominate the limy prairies and uplands.

High summer is a difficult time for many garden plants on lime, for not only heat, but punishing drought generally affects these lands. The porous nature of the underlying limestones and the high capillarity of the clay soils invariably wicks away moisture, making it difficult or impossible to keep garden soils from drying out, especially on the chalky uplands. Successful plants for the summer garden must be able to endure and perform both with abundant heat and with limited water.

Because of the relative proximity of the Gulf of Mexico, limestone soil regions near Austin and San Antonio are spared some of the brutality of this season. High humidity, especially at night, affords a moderating influence and often produces morning clouds that shield south-central Texas gardens from the sun. Many of the flowers that continue to bloom in the summer take advantage of this by opening fresh blossoms each morning, wilting in the afternoon as the clouds burn off and the full heat of the day bears down on the gardens below.

North Texas has no such buffer, however, and in years of low rainfall summer humidity may drop to near desert conditions. Cloudless blue skies are the rule for several weeks each summer, and there is little relief for plants or people. Growing conditions remain harsh until the advent of cooling late summer and fall thunderstorms.

If fall rains are generous and come early, as sometimes happens when tropical storms influence the weather, the period between early September and the first frosts of autumn can be an especially rewarding time of year for gardens. Even when the rains come late or stingily, the mild dry air that characterizes this season makes it a pleasant time to garden and suits the needs of many flowers. Cool Pacific fronts move in and combine with warm humid air from the Gulf of Mexico to produce the best growing weather of the year. Early fall rains bring a subtropical aspect to the climate that gradually yields to the sunny Mediterranean feel of Indian summer. A variety of late-blooming bulbs and perennials perform in this period and everblooming roses reach their finest form and quality.

The first frosts of autumn occur about November 13 at Dallas and November 26 at Austin and San Antonio, usually following passage of the earliest high-pressure cold fronts of the continental air mass. Cold dry air from the Great Plains pushes southward, lowering humidity, and as night falls the warmth of the day radiates into the cloudless evening sky. This radiation cooling is characteristic of fall and winter weather over much of the limestone region and short-lived early morning freezes account for much of the time garden plants spend below the freezing point. These nighttime radiation frosts are especially hard on still windless nights, and because chilly air sinks like a pool of water, these freezes are more severe in gardens on low-lying land in hollows or valleys.

Where early frosts are undesirable gardeners delay their killing effect by throwing barriers over their plants and garden beds in order to help hold in the warmth of the earth at night. Sheets of cloth or plastic or old pots turned over the plants are sufficient to stop most light freezes, and large live oak trees provide natural frost barriers for many gardens. Gardens on windy hilltops from which cold air drains safely away to the valley below may escape frost well into fall or winter, and a lucky gardener with a southerly aspect may have a growing season a month longer than a neighbor in a shady frost hollow. Daytime temperatures are often 30 degrees warmer than nighttime lows at this season, and many winter-growing flowers such as annual phloxes, poppies, pansies, narcissi, and lycorises make active growth, while loquats (*Eriobotrya japonica*) and silverberry (*Elaeagnus* × *ebbengii*) scent the autumn air with fragrant flowers.

The northers intensify as winter progresses and from late December through February gardens remain at risk of severe cold. Winter freezes often last more than twenty-four hours and the measures that succeeded in preventing nighttime radiation frosts in the early fall prove insufficient to prevent these stronger chills from penetrating and freezing the garden. Frigid air moves across the prairies, suddenly dropping temperatures and bringing with it cruel biting winds. The result for garden plants can be devastating, depending on the type of plant and its degree of dormancy and hardening to winter cold. It is not only the severity of freezing temperatures that causes damage but also the suddenness of their arrival. Average winter lows vary from 20° F at San Antonio to 10° F near Dallas, but unusually cold years may deliver temperatures from 0 to − 10° F across the same region.

Broadleaved evergreens and spring-blooming shrubs suffer particularly during these events and even relatively mild freezes cause tremendous damage if plants are not fully dormant. Many varieties that perform well in equally cold but more temperate climates fail in the erratic and unpredictable cold waves that punctuate the winter. In many cases the moisture-holding properties of the limestone soils provide an added stress during these sudden cold snaps. For this reason the climate zone maps found in much nursery and garden literature create confusion about plant hardiness in this area and offer little assistance when evaluating new or unfamiliar plants.

Catastrophes

If the capricious weather patterns of typical winters in this territory fail to thwart the gardener's efforts, about once in a decade an unusually severe norther will blow in to ravage plantings. There is no reasonable way to prepare for these periodic disasters except to remind oneself that, after all, plants, like other living things, are mortal and therefore are not meant to live forever. When the big freeze ("blue norther," "Siberian express," "Alberta clipper") comes to town it may bring with it freezing rains or snows that damage trees and evergreens by breaking limbs and splitting bark. More commonly, the combined forces of several successive fronts push temperatures to unreasonably low levels that result in death or damage to any plant not fully dormant and hardened to the cold, dry winds. Often plants that have made valuable contributions to gardens and have thrived for years will nonetheless perish in these once-in-a-decade cold snaps. Such periodic spells greatly limit the choice of hardy broadleaved evergreens and place special value on those varieties whose vigor allows them to resprout and grow when a particularly cold year kills them back to ground level.

There is another long-term aspect to the climates on these calcareous soils that few residents recognize: periodic chronic drought. Because the population of this region has more than doubled since the last round of the drought cycle ended in 1957, many are unaware of the consequences of a major dry spell. In December of 1956, 244 of Texas' 254 counties were classified as disaster areas; the Medina River and Medina Lake near San Antonio were dry, as were Comal Springs and the Comal River at New Braunfels. Although Dallas had completed the dam for what is now Lake Lewisville some years earlier, the land behind it remained dry and the city was forced to pipe salt-laden water from the Red River to supply its needs. Throughout the blacklands and the Edwards Plateau region the preceding six years of drought had decimated the native vegetation and a large percentage of the trees, particularly those less than ten inches in diameter, perished during this period. In gardens the salty water available for irrigation killed all but the most tolerant trees and shrubs.

The Gardener's Strategies

Both the short- and long-term vicissitudes of this climate can create tough circumstances for plants, and a large part of garden planning in this region depends on modifying conditions to suit a wide variety of trees, shrubs, and flowers. Since the area displays a transitional climate that at various times of the year resembles the hot lowlands of the tropics, the sun-drenched lands surrounding the Mediterranean, or the windswept prairies of the Midwest, successful gardens use plants adapted to each of these environments to make the most of the varying seasons. Because spring is a brief and unpredictable time of year in this part of the country, wise gardeners avoid overloading their plantings with the spring-blooming trees, shrubs, and perennials that dominate gardening in most of North America. Plants that perform during the long hot summer season, and those that take advantage of mild, sunny fall weather offer the greatest value, and any well-planned garden on the limestone heartland devotes most of its space to plants that will enliven these seasons.

Climate modification begins with the recognition of small-scale variations. Even the smallest gardens offer a series of microclimates around the house or grounds that favor various plants and enable a wider variety to be grown. East-facing walls or fences offer choice gardening sites on many properties, as these areas experience less of the intense heat of the afternoon sun and generally receive some protection from the cold winter blasts that approach from the northwest. Roses, daylilies, and other favorite flowers whose blooming seasons are cut short by the early heat of the summer may continue in flower on these sheltered walls long after more exposed plantings have finished.

North walls offer a mix of challenge and opportunity, for these areas are shady for much of the year and often poorly drained and waterlogged, and they receive the full brunt of cold winter winds unless sheltered by large trees or windbreaks of tall evergreens.

In many new gardens north foundation walls beneath the overhang of the roof provide the only all-day shade and one of the few places to grow such popular shade-lovers as *Aucuba japonica, Impatiens sultana,* Japanese maple (*Acer palmatum*), river fern (*Thelypteris kunthii*), or Venus' maidenhair fern (*Adiantum capillus-veneris*). This is the spot to try the early-flowering deciduous *Magnolia* × *soulangeana* cultivars, for on warmer sites they are sure to come into bloom in midwinter and may be damaged or killed by late freezes. Where no protective overhang exists or where walls or fences are built with a northwesterly aspect, brutally hot afternoon sun may reach in to create an especially extreme environment. Such situations are best given over to tough evergreens such as nandina, mahonia, or holly, and truly hardy perennials and flowering shrubs.

Intense summer heat limits plant choices for south exposures, but because these areas receive light and warmth from the winter sun and shelter from cold north winds, they encourage many subtropical plants that might fail on more exposed sites. Windmill palms, oleanders, pomegranates, figs, crinums, and spider lilies (*Hymenocallis* spp.) are some of the warmth-loving plants that do well at the foot of a south-facing wall. This is also a choice aspect for late-blooming perennials like firebush (*Hamelia patens*), yellow bells (*Tecoma stans*), cigar flower (*Cuphea micropetala*), purple bush sage (*Salvia leucantha*), and Mexican marigold (*Tagetes lucida*), for frosts come late in such positions and afford gardeners an opportunity to enjoy these flowers well into the fall.

West-facing walls experience tremendous heat, and receive some of the worst winter cold as well. Dry country natives such as century plant (*Agave neomexicana*), Spanish bayonet (*Yucca* spp.), Texas mountain laurel (*Sophora secundiflora*), bird of paradise shrub (*Caesalpinia gilliesii*) and ceniza (*Leucophyllum* spp.) make the most of the reflected light and strong sun provided by these walls. A good deal of the cold-hardiness of these desert plants depends on proper hardening and ripening of summer growth, and this type of sunny western exposure helps to prepare the plants for winter and affords them a congenial home in gardens where they might otherwise freeze. Autumn foliage color often matures better in strong western light as well and smoke tree (*Cotinus obovatus*), purple crape myrtle (*Lagerstroemia indica* 'Catawba'), red-leaf barberry (*Berberis thunbergii* 'Atropurpurea'), and creeping plumbago (*Ceratostigma plumbaginoides*) put on vibrant fall displays in such positions.

Handling the Hydrology

With the erratic rainfall patterns experienced on these calcareous soils, moisture levels move from surfeit to deficit and back again each year, and one of the most important garden tactics is the adjustment of this water supply to meet the needs of the plants. Since modern homes often have no gutters, roof runoff may greatly increase effective rainfall for plants located near foundations, and astute gardeners take advantage of this extra moisture to grow water-loving plants in these areas. Most of the broadleaved evergreens used in landscapes come from climates where moisture is available year-round, and to grow popular shrubs such as hollies, ligustrums, India-hawthorns, and pittosporums usually requires supplemental watering periodically during the year.

For plants from Mediterranean climates, whose growth cycles key to winter rainfall, the trick is to avoid moisture, especially in the summer. If these drought-loving plants are allowed to remain wet during periods of warm temperature, various soil fungi and bacteria may attack and damage or kill them as they lie dormant. Santolina, English lavender, Texas madrone (*Arbutus xalapensis*), Algerian ivy, and many spring-flowering bulbs fall into this group that prefers summer drought. Raised beds of chalky soil to help wick moisture away, or fast-draining sand or grit can help to keep these plants dry when summer thundershowers provide unwanted precipitation.

Moisture preferences affect winter-hardiness as well, and influence garden decisions about how best to prepare for severe cold. Broadleaved evergreens usually need a plentiful supply of soil moisture to endure long periods below freezing and should receive deep soakings before the arrival of an advancing norther. Yet, the same treatment to a drought-loving oleander or a trailing rosemary could be lethal, as it might stimulate a burst of turgid cool-season growth. For this reason gardeners need an intimate familiarity with their garden plants and the environments from which they originate so that they may distinguish those that prefer more or less water, and manipulate garden beds accordingly.

Many popular garden plants, including favorite lawn grasses and groundcovers, originate in humid subtropical countries and require continuous supplies of moisture to remain attractive. Gardeners understandably wish to have lush summertime landscapes, and by adding water it is possible to transform seasonally a semiarid parcel of limy prairie into a tropical paradise. This is one of the easiest and most appealing ways to garden in hot-summer regions and has the romantic attraction of converting the backyard into a lavish oasis.

However attractive, the difficulty with this style is that the opulent use of water on gardens consumes an inordinate amount of the fresh water available for our cities. As growth continues, ever stronger demands will be placed on already limited fresh water supplies, and gardeners will increasingly vie with agricultural and industrial users over this limited resource. Should a lush suburban display of flowers and green lawn win out over a farmer's field of cotton or an industrialist's new factory? While in our hearts we may long to answer yes, our heads stoically remind us that the answer must be no. Our future gardens will have to make use of less and less supplemental watering, and what we do use will come with an ever increasing price tag.

Water-efficient gardening techniques such as "xeriscaping" offer common-sense approaches to gardening with limited water and recommend practical methods for gardeners to employ in designing and maintaining their grounds. Perhaps the easiest way to conserve water in gardens is through limiting the size of irrigated lawns and planting beds, and this implies the use of low-water demand or drought-tolerant plant varieties in the remainder of the garden. Watering at night and utilizing efficient drip irrigation systems for vegetable beds and permanent tree and shrub plantings are ways to make the most of what water we do use, and by mowing our grasses at a relatively tall height we allow the living sod to create its own mulch and encourage deeper rooting.

There is some scientific debate over the moisture-conserving value of mulches, as tests indicate that they can encourage moisture to wick away from the soil. In practice, however, a mulch seems to offer other valuable properties that offset any increased moisture losses: by cooling the soil and keeping moisture in the upper layers of the earth, mulches help maintain soil organic matter and crumb structure and keep water more available for plants, and by preventing a crust from forming on the soil surface they encourage rainfall and irrigation waters to percolate into the soil instead of running off.

Organic mulches such as shredded bark are most popular as these make an attractive setting for the plants and slowly rot down to improve the soil. But for plants from naturally dry, rocky environments, or for plantings that require a more permanent solution, gravel or crushed rock makes a better choice. Beds of crushed stone provide the necessary reflected light and extra warmth to help rosemaries, cenizas, or Texas mountain laurels through cold winters that might have resulted in freeze damage had the same plants been surrounded by soggy, dark-colored bark. The problem with these inorganic mulches comes in the summer when their added heat can create an inferno around the plants, and careful gardeners avoid light-reflecting white stones or heat-absorbing black ones and instead seek neutral colors lest the pebbles cause the air above or the soil below to bake to lethal levels. Under shade trees gravel mulches avoid these heat problems and provide a good low-maintenance groundcover.

The World Garden

Even with growing limitations on irrigation waters and the challenges presented by soil and climate, a nearly endless variety of plants from around the world is available to populate our gardens, and an amazing number of them put up with the worst conditions we have to offer. The trick is to recognize those areas where climate and soils most nearly resemble our own and thereby take full advantage of the potential garden inhabitants these regions offer. The task of identifying these countries is made easier by tracking down the homelands of introduced plants that have proven themselves on the limestone heartland. When one does so a pattern begins to emerge that helps to characterize this climate and the regions that yield our most successful garden plants.

Argentina

Perhaps the closest match to the hot-summer regions can be found on the Argentine pampas of South America. As in much of the limestone area of Texas, the climate of Argentina reflects the transition between humid subtropical country (southern Brazil) and cold windswept plains (Patagonia). Gauchos ride amid mesquite trees much as Texas cowboys do on the opposite side of the equator and many plants closely related to Texas flora reside here. High heat and summer rainfall characterize the warm season, and brutal Antarctic cold fronts approach from the south during winter to bring hard freezes as far north as Buenos Aires. One of the rare characteristics of climate over many of the calcareous soils of North America is the severe cold received at relatively low latitudes, and Argentina comes close to duplicating this condition. It thus shares Texas' unusual seasonal combination of strong sunlight and heat with truly frigid winter chills.

Some of the many lime-loving garden plants from this region are the pampas grass (*Cortaderia selloana*), bird of paradise shrub (*Caesalpinia gilliesii*), pink wood-sorrel (*Oxalis crassipes*), and oxblood lily (*Rhodophiala bifida*). Just like the wildlings on the drought-prone limy soils north of the equator, these South American plants have developed strategies to deal with seasonally limited rainfall, and while the summer-growing pampas grass and bird of paradise shrub depend on deep root systems to survive drought, the wood-sorrel and the oxblood lily evade the dry season by adopting a winter cycle of growth.

China

The great treasure house of the world's garden plants is the Orient, and gardens on lime take their share of beauties from this realm. Unlike gardens in eastern America, which find good climate and soil matches in countries like Japan and Korea, most of the oriental natives adapted to limestone regions come from the Chinese mainland, particularly from provinces such as Zhejiang, Sichuan, and Shaanxi. Plants from these areas accept hot summers and limy soils better than those from Japan because of the higher heat and occasional drought received on the mainland in summer, and because underlying limestones in these Chinese provinces develop soils more closely akin to the calcareous soils of the North American heartland. In contrast, most Japanese natives are intolerant of lime and have little drought resistance.

Knowledgeable gardeners may be puzzled by these last statements, for many favorite lime-loving garden plants include the epithet "*japonica*" somewhere in their botanical name. There are two reasons for this. Many of the plants native to mainland China occur in Japan as well, and because early plant collectors found Japan easier to explore and visit, many oriental plants bear names indicating this origin. More importantly, long before western plant collectors reached Japan, the Japanese themselves had scoured the Chinese mainland for beautiful plants and introduced them to Japanese gardens and nurseries. With a few exceptions, most of the "Japanese" plants which do well on lime have a Chinese origin and occur in Japan only through the labor of forgotten horticulturalists of this ancient civilization.

The list of Chinese plants in gardens is a long one, including most of our popular woody shrubs and evergreens, as well as trees, roses, bamboos, ornamental grasses, perennials, annuals, and even a few bulbs. Such *sine qua nons* of modern landscapes as crape myrtle, nandina, photinia, India-hawthorn, shrub-althaea, abelia, Chinese holly, ligustrum, juniper, arborvitae, Lady Banks' rose, windmill palm, Asian jasmine, daylily, aspidistra, chrysanthemum, and lycoris originate from this plant-rich country.

The late nineteenth and early twentieth century provided a golden age for plant introductions from China, and many popular oriental garden plants came into cultivation at this time. Ernest H. "Chinese" Wilson, who collected plants for the Arnold Arboretum in Boston and Veitch's nursery in London, was one of the most famous of these plant collectors. His 1903 discovery of the regal lily (*Lilium regale*) growing on limestone in a remote Sichuan gorge profited gardeners on calcareous soils, for both this lily and its hybrid offspring thrive on limy grounds in gardens today. With moderating political conditions, recent years have seen a renewal of interest in the ornamental plants of China and many new and beautiful things promise to enter gardens in the future.

The Mediterranean

The region that stretches from Spain and North Africa east along the Mediterranean to Turkey, Iran, and the arid mountains of Afghanistan and Kashmir comprises a third great contributor of plants to calcareous-soil gardens and includes the homes of many of the plants brought by early European immigrants. Nurserymen have operated here for centuries and many garden hybrids selected for performance in this region thrive in areas of North America with similar soil and climate. Famous nineteenth-century plant breeders of central and southern France—such as Lemoine at Nancy; Chate, Crozy and Sisley at Lyon; Noisette, Verdier, Desprez, Barbier, and many others—have particularly enriched gardens on lime with suitable varieties of fruit trees, roses, mock oranges, cannas, dianthuses, irises, and a multitude of other worthy garden plants.

This "Euro-Middle-Eastern" realm represents the environmental transition between the temperate climate of Europe, the continental climate of central Asia, and the dry-summer climate that surrounds the Mediterranean and extends into the Middle East. Truly hardy plants such as pear, pyracantha, mock orange, boxwood, English ivy, St.

John's wort, irises, and daffodils, as well as more tender Italian cypress, rosemary, pomegranate, fig, Mediterranean fan palm, Afghan pine, deodar cedar, oleander, and cluster-flowered narcissus mingle in the microclimates created by the hills and mountains of this vast area.

Many of these plants are sensitive to excess summer rainfall and quickly succumb to attacks from soil fungi or bacteria in warm humid conditions. This can present a problem in gardens where easily waterlogged clay soils prevail. Yet, these same plants offer some of the best prospects for dry rocky bluffs and chalky soils, and are ideal for water-conserving landscapes. In many cases the construction of raised beds and restraint in adding organic matter and applying the water hose are all that is needed to accommodate plants from this region, and gardens on the heavy Blackland Prairie soils can greatly increase the diversity of plants they contain by including some of these Mediterranean plants in a small, well-drained raised bed.

Africa

Subtropical Africa has contributed several plants to gardens on lime, most importantly the Bermuda grasses of lawns (and most insidiously the pernicious weed Johnson grass). Other hardy lime-tolerant African plants are mostly annuals, or bulbs such as *Gloriosa* lilies or *Crinum* that survive unseasonable cold spells with little more damage than they receive from the dry seasons that affect their homelands. Only in the Drakensberg of Lesotho and Natal and the adjacent veld of the Transvaal does the African climate seem to produce a wider range of hardy plants and here one finds such curiosities as red hot poker plant (*Kniphofia*), hardy iceplants such as *Delosperma cooperi* and *D. nubigenum*, and weeping lovegrass (*Eragrostis curvula*), as well as popular subtropical perennials such as Transvaal daisy (*Gerbera jamesonii*), and Cape plumbago (*Plumbago capensis*).

North America

The limestone regions of North America are perhaps the most important source of garden plants for the heartland and nearly all of our first-class shade and ornamental trees are natives. Shrubs such as yaupon holly and ceniza provide some of the most beautiful and trouble-free of garden subjects, and the vast array of native perennials and wildflowers give an unsurpassed source of seasonal flower color. Those natives of the acid soil areas of America that will accept lime provide another source of plants, and beauties like Southern magnolia and Carolina jessamine have made themselves indispensable in many gardens on calcareous soils. Nearby Mexico, too, offers a rich array of beautiful lime-loving plants and plays a special part in gardens in hot-summer areas.

In contrast to these regions, many other warm climates of the world contribute few lime-tolerant plants of value. Gardeners on the limestone heartlands frequently look to California with its apparently similar regime of dry summers and alkaline soils and search hopefully for suitable subjects to include in plantings. The true winter-rainfall climate of the West Coast, however, affords an environment for a different suite of garden plants that, although hardy to light frosts, perishes in any really severe freeze, and requires mild dry periods of summer dormancy instead of high heat and thunderstorms. Those varieties that endure winters on the limestone heartland often perish with the first rains of summer, for warm, humid weather and calcareous soils encourage a wide range of microorganisms antagonistic to true Mediterranean-climate plants. For the same reasons the temperate climates of Australia, Chile, New Zealand, and South Africa, with their multitudes of gorgeous plant varieties, yield few plants for gardens in this region.

Climates that contribute plants adaptable to the limestone heartlands experience significant winter cold and regularly receive a long summer baking. Rainfall comes to these countries in seasonally short supply, creating drought most summers and occasionally at other times of the year. The unique aspects that these territories share and that distinguish them from the other warm-climate regions of the world are: long hot summers, brief cold winters, predominantly summer precipitation with some rainfall distributed throughout the remainder of the year, and occasional summer drought. Taken together these conditions combine to produce the unique routine of a climate in transition.

Horticultural Machismo

The plants that have evolved to endure these regimes comprise an unusually tolerant lot. Varieties that choose to grow through the torrid subtropical summers must be able to halt growth for drought, resume growth in response to summer rains, and yet not respond to precipitation that stimulates tender growth during the winter. Plants that opt for a cool-season growth schedule must endure the worst of winter's cold blasts, and have to resist the attacks of pathogenic soil organisms when summer rains waterlog the ground during their period of dormancy.

This is asking a lot, and with a variable climate from year to year, many varieties periodically suffer damage. Often it is a plant's inherent vigor and ability to recover from disaster that makes the difference between success and failure, and gardens on lime rely on truly strong-growing plants to overcome a difficult and unpredictable climate. Many of our most important garden plants are hybrids, either natural or manmade, which due to their parentage inherit an extra measure of strength known as heterosis, or hybrid vigor. Just as the pioneers depended on the extra power of mules to plow the tight prairie earths, our gardens rely on the added vigor of horticultural "mules" to survive and perform with the harsh climate and soils.

When designing plantings it is simple prudence to use the most vigorous and tolerant varieties for the garden framework. Gardens built with plants well adapted to local soil and climate will long outlast and outperform plantings of delicate outlanders, and perfectly beautiful gardens can be constructed using the many strong-growing hardy plants available. Yet, just as a sinner, after reform, may begin to falter in strict determinations, a gardener on the limestone heartland is likely eventually to desire a measure of the less thrifty, less hardy, less heat- and drought-tolerant, and less lime-tolerant plant varieties. Common sense dictates that these plants should be limited to modest proportions. This assures that the beauty of the garden will not be entirely placed at risk in a severe year, and that the efforts of the gardener will not be wholly consumed by the coddling and attention required by an undue quotient of finicky flora.

CHAPTER THREE

A Mixed Border for Long Season Performance

Gardeners want the most enjoyment possible from their plantings, and for lovers of flowering shrubs and perennials the more varieties that can be accommodated, the better and more continuous the show. Postwar planting styles that rely on a limited range of massed evergreens and shrubberies miss out on a great deal of the beauty of the botanical world, and because of their low plant diversity, often pass into a season-long slumber after their few inhabitants have finished their blooming cycles. Modern gardens tend more and more toward a naturalistic combination of plants with as high a variety as can be planned for, as this greatly lengthens the effective seasons of bloom and interest. By using the widest possible array of plants together, gardeners marshall the forces needed to overcome the challenges presented by climate and soil to create interest in the garden throughout the year. The mixed border offers an appropriate way to include a diverse array of ornamental flowers and shrubs in almost any garden, and provides one of the best means to have colorful blooms over a long season.

A mixed border is a style of garden-making evolved from the popular perennial borders of the late nineteenth and early twentieth centuries, which themselves derive from the so-called "cottage gardens" of the Old World. These ancestral plantings of the common people of Europe, like those of poor people the world over, displayed simple collages of favorite herbs and flowers gathered together in haphazard mixed plantings. Nineteenth-century garden designers such as William Robinson and Gertrude Jekyll authored books and articles that championed these humble flowers and helped to elevate this charming folk art to grand style in formal herbaceous borders. The classic perennial borders used strong architectural features to compartmentalize and set off the combinations of herbaceous flowers in carefully chosen color schemes and skillfully orchestrated successions displayed against high stone walls or hedges. When later garden designers admitted shrubs, roses, trees, and bulbs into the borders, and utilized more naturalistic designs, mixed borders came into being.

Modern concepts of the mixed border rely on an ever-changing tapestry of perennials, roses, and bulbs, anchored by a few well-chosen trees and shrubs to create engaging garden pictures over the course of the year. As each plant comes into bloom and takes its place on stage, others wait in the wings and provide a contrasting background of foliage against which the flowers can show to advantage. Deciduous shrubs contribute autumn leaves and berries, and evergreens and structurally distinctive trees carry interest through the winter months when the perennials are dormant. Early bulbs and annuals work to create a show before the bulk of perennial flowers begin growth in spring. With shrubs and trees to help create a framework, such plantings are less dependent on walls or hedges to set them off than the strictly herbaceous border, and where space permits may be used as island beds in the lawn. A great attraction of mixed borders is that, since they admit plants from all classes, they allow for the widest possible mixture of plant varieties to develop seasonal interest.

In equable climates such as Europe or eastern North America border shrubs and perennials experience a considerable period of dormancy, followed by a generous growing season during which the plants can give their best displays. In contrast, a mixed border on the limestone regions of Texas must endure a brief, erratic winter succeeded by an intemperate and seemingly endless summer of heat and drought. Few plants are up to the rigors of this long season and many flowers that make lovely displays in April and May hang on with decrepit and scorched foliage into the heat of July and August. Any border that depends too heavily on spring-blooming plants is likely to be very poor after the long hot days of the summer have taken their toll. This is doubly tragic in regions such as Texas, for the summer constitutes the longest part of the growing season and is precisely when the border should be at its peak.

Designing successful borders to endure and perform in hot climates requires gardeners to make special efforts to avoid plants that have a long, unattractive "off-season." It is, in other words, preferable to have rather ordinary garden subjects that hold up well and look reasonably attractive through the duration of the year than to have a garden dominated by fleeting displays of spectacular flowers that later burden the border with months of unsightliness. Herbaceous peonies serve as an unfortunate example to illustrate this principle. In Midwestern gardens peonies are considered among the most desirable plants for mixed borders, valued both for their huge fragrant flowers and their attractive shrubby mounds of foliage. Since peonies enjoy limestone soils, they grow and flower well in north Texas and in those parts of the central Texas Hill Country where they receive sufficient winter chilling. But after flowering, instead of being an asset to the border, the heat-scorched foliage of the peony soon becomes a liability that is best hidden behind some tall-growing plant for the remainder of the season. Even gardens whose fortuitously shaded eastern exposures and rich, moist soils especially favor peonies receive little return in the brief flowering season for the large amount of space taken up by these spring-bloomers.

One way to assure an attractive border over the season is to include a fair measure of foliage plants and shrubs. These need not be without color, as all shades of green and grey, gold, and reddish-leaved plants can play parts in the design. It is, in fact, possible to create very beautiful gardens entirely from foliage and without bright flowers at all. The restful temple gardens of Japan are successful examples of this kind of planting, and, although limited in color, display rich associations of texture and form. The disappointing side of such designs is their failure to celebrate seasonal change; there is a frustrating sameness to a garden planted exclusively with trees and woody evergreens, even when these are skillfully combined or sheared and trained into strange, wonderful shapes. But most gardeners find it difficult to resist the allure of beautiful flowers, and therefore chart a median course, using attractive foliage plants with colorful blooms to the advantage of each.

Flowering perennials and shrubs usually have distinct seasons of bloom that last a few weeks each year, after which the plants go about making seed or fruit or foliage. Some plants, however, flower continuously on the new growth of the summer season (hibiscus, lantana, salvia, plumbago), or in spurts between periods of foliage growth throughout the summer (crape myrtles, roses). Prodigal bloomers such as cenizas, crinums, and rain lilies produce crops of flowers opportunistically in response to summer thunderstorms, returning to dormancy when rains break off. It is these "everblooming" flowers that take pride of place in hot-summer regions, for the long season requires such performers to extend interest through the summer and into the fall. Nevertheless, a great deal of the seasonal beauty of any garden ensues from the performances of plants whose shorter blooming seasons help to create a succession of changing scenes over the year. By including a wide variety of both long-season and short-season bloomers, in combination with attractive foliage plants, gardeners ensure a continuity of color and interest, yet also savor the beautiful garden pictures created by annual floral events.

Gardeners on calcareous soils are often so preoccupied with seeking out and acquiring suitable plants for their borders that questions about appropriate color combinations receive little consideration. (Who cares about the colors? The struggle is in finding and establishing plants strong enough to continue in bloom over the season!) Nevertheless, even casual gardeners will eventually face dilemmas over how best to arrange the shadings and hues of favorite floral acquisitions.

Unfortunately for gardeners on lime, many of the most reliable border flowers suited to calcareous soil come in the shades of mauve, pinkish-lavender, maroon, or magenta which create havoc when combined with yellow, orange, or other warm hues. Nothing could be more unsettling than lilac prairie phlox next to primrose-yellow Hinckley columbine, or more garish than rhodamine-purple crape myrtle combined with golden-foliaged arborvitae, yet the hazard of producing such scenes awaits the unwary gardener at every turn. To top things off, one of the toughest and best-loved lime-tolerant perennials, the purple coneflower (*Echinacea purpurea*) actually clashes with *itself* (pink ray-flowers surrounding an orange disk) and sabotages the gardener's color scheme just by its presence, unless the chalky white-flowered form, 'Alba,' is planted instead.

Some experienced gardeners have solved these problems by banishing the pink and lavender flowers, or, conversely, those blooms of warm scarlet and yellow, to separate corners of the garden. Either group looks well combined with white or blue, and some gardeners use these colors to create a common meeting ground to help mix the more disparate hues. Gray-leaved plants offer useful foils as well, and borders with large quotients of gray will have few color problems, for the light-colored foliage softens the harsh aspects of difficult colors.

Strangely enough, bold contrasts can be one of the most effective color-combining techniques, so long as the colors selected balance each other in intensity. Bright orange *Zinnia angustifolia* planted among mats of purple heart (*Setcreasea pallida*) creates a vibrant contrast, but serves as an electric focal point in the garden. Such combinations are best used with restraint, however, or plantings can become so energetic that they lose any chance to give the "happiness and repose of mind" Gertrude Jekyll maintained to be the first purpose of any garden.

Hues and shades perceived by the gardener often depend on the direction and intensity of the sun's rays, and border plans should take this into consideration as well. The strong light of the summer sun can bleach out the pastel shades of many flowers, but also brings out the harsher aspects of strong flower and foliage colors. If the border will be viewed primarily from the south, then light will be on the plants much of the time, bringing colors out to their fullest. White flowers and gray foliage show up well under such circumstances. Conversely, if the border is constructed to the south of a property so that it will be seen from the north, then the plants will be back-lit much of the day. In these situations flower colors become hazy and tall gray-leaved plants look muddy. Plants with colorful new growth such as Fraser's photinia (*Photinia* × *fraseri*) or dwarf golden arborvitae (*Platycladus orientalis* 'Aureus') are especially effective with back-lighting, as are translucent flowers such as red yucca (*Hesperaloe parviflora*).

Successfully planning color coordinations and successions of bloom demands familiarity with a vast range of garden plants. Yet, novice garden designers need not be overwhelmed by the many varieties to consider for new plantings. The best-designed gardens frequently rely less on a well thought-out initial plan than on an alert eye and a ready border fork to dig up and move or eliminate flowers, or even trees or shrubs, when combinations fail to please.

Ornamental plantings are always experiments, of a sort, and trail-blazing gardeners in Texas and other regions with limestone soil are likely to explore several possibilities before they are fully satisfied with their borders. Ultimately, it is the plants themselves that make the gardens, and a great deal of garden-making derives from happy accident. While good gardeners appreciate the beauty afforded by competent landscape design, they also stand ready to recognize serendipity when it comes their way. It is this readiness for participation in an ongoing adventure—("Should I pull up this weed seedling or wait to see what kind of plant it develops into?")—that separates true gardening from the exterior decorating represented by most "professional" landscapes, and it is often the unexpected reward of a volunteer flower or the unintentional mixture of colorful blooms that gives a garden uniqueness and provides the greatest satisfaction.

Old favorite tried-and-true shrubs and perennials that tolerate a wide range of conditions, from heavy waterlogged blackland clay to dry chalky banks, and that miraculously put up with the vagaries of erratic climate, provide the backbone of a well-designed border, and ensure a continuity of bloom around which less certain subjects may be tried. A sufficiently wide range of proven performers has accumulated in the chalky soils of gardens to fill borders with strong, hardy, enduring plants adaptable to these difficult soils and changeable climates. By utilizing these reliable flowering friends, even inexperienced gardeners will soon be on the way to developing border plantings that fascinate and satisfy throughout the seasons.

A few large clumps of ornamental grasses will help establish an informal framework for a mixed border and are especially appropriate for gardens in prairie states such as Texas, for these plants evoke images of wildflower meadows while their leaves sway gracefully in the breeze. Because their deep fibrous roots penetrate the heavy prairie soil to draw up moisture, grasses are very drought-tolerant and may actually help to improve soil structure and moisture availability for other nearby border flowers. The Chinese eulalia grass (*Miscanthus sinensis*) has several ornamental forms suitable for use as tall back-row specimens. 'Variegatus' is one of the showiest of these, with vertical stripes of cream along the leaf blades, while the zebra grass ('Zebrinus') has its foliage curiously interrupted with horizontal bars of variegation. The compact, light green-foliaged maiden grass (*Miscanthus sinensis* 'Gracillimus'), as well as these variegated forms, overtops its leaves each autumn with feathery seed heads that glisten in the sunlight. Shorter grasses suitable for foreground planting include the fountain grasses (*Pennisetum* spp.), valued for their foxtaillike plumes. Rose fountain grass (*P. alopecuroides*) is especially fine and hardy, and doesn't become as invasive as its commonly planted cousin, *P. setaceum*.

Lists of suitable lime-tolerant ornamental grasses are long, but gardeners accustomed to showy flowers are apt to wonder where all the ornament is being kept! The chief value of many of these plants is in the subtle grace and sense of movement they lend to plantings. Massed by themselves, grasses can be disappointing. Yet, when used in the mixed border as a foil for brighter flowers their structural value shines forth. It was the humble use of modest flowers which Robinson and Jekyll admired most in the plantings of the cottagers. Mixed borders, likewise, profit from the level of subtlety and humility that ornamental grasses provide.

After the grasses, the border may include some small specimen trees to help develop a vertical framework. Evergreens such as the Texas mountain laurel (*Sophora secundiflora*), with its early spring trusses of grape-scented purple blooms, or a female yaupon holly (*Ilex vomitoria*), which in winter will be laden with glossy red berries, can provide seasonal color as well as masses of green glittering foliage year-round. Both of these will benefit from well-considered pruning to expose and show off the rugged character inherent in these scrubby trees, and this will greatly enhance their value in the border.

Tree-form crape myrtles merit a special place in mixed borders on lime, for they not only provide colorful flowers over the long summer, but also develop fine ornamental bark and fall foliage. The vivid purple-flowered cultivar 'Catawba' is one of the best varieties for autumn color and its leaves turn a glowing red each fall. 'Natchez' displays white blooms and develops dramatic cinnamon-red peeling bark as it matures. Although introduced from eastern Asian gardens as long ago as 1870, the gracefully drooping 'Near East' retains popularity and with its shell-pink panicles of bloom is one of the most tirelessly blooming crape myrtles, reaching six to ten feet in height. These small to medium-sized trees can be grouped towards the back of the border and look well spilling out over and above the other shrubs and perennials.

Redbuds are favorites among early spring-blooming trees and their wispy branches disappear in masses of tiny lavender-pink pea blossoms each March. Selections such as the wine-colored 'Oklahoma,' the white-flowered cultivar, 'White Texas,' and the wavy-leafed Mexican redbud are especially desirable, as these varieties follow their spring displays with shiny, leathery foliage that remains beautiful throughout the summer. 'Forest Pansy' leafs out with boldly purple heart-shaped leaves which mature to green later in the summer. A wide range of lavender, mauve, and burgundy-colored perennial flowers bloom in the spring and mix successfully with redbuds, a classic combination being with pink creeping phlox or thrift (*Phlox subulata*).

The chaste tree (*Vitex agnus-castus*) is a seldom-used border specimen with soft-textured sage-green foliage and graceful spires of lavender flowers from May into early June. With maturity it can develop a rough, rugged branch structure reminiscent of the ancient olive trees of Mediterranean hillside groves. Another uncommon tree is the possumhaw or deciduous holly (*Ilex decidua*) whose silky-white bare branches hold dramatic crops of scarlet berries throughout the winter months. Perhaps the most refined small tree available for use in limy gardens is the rusty blackhaw (*Viburnum rufidulum*). This is an ideal plant for a mixed border, as its milky plates of tiny spring flowers are followed by shiny green summer foliage, and then by an unrivaled autumn display of steel-blue berries against a backdrop of purple-red leaves.

With a selection of grasses and specimens in place, perennials, roses, and accent shrubs can be selected to fill in the bays between the larger trees. Texas sages or cenizas (*Leucophyllum* spp.) make graceful groupings with their soft gray or light green foliage, helping to blend the various floral elements together, and showering the garden with crops of pink, lavender, or white blooms in the summer months. The soft texture and color of these native shrubs conveys the air of relaxed informality appropriate to a diverse, well-arranged border. In exposed gardens where low winter temperatures test the hardiness of these invaluable plants, the fragrant silverberry (*Elaeagnus* × *ebbengii*) can deputize for the cenizas, and may be had in an attractive gold variegation called 'Sunset,' as well as in the striking silver of the common form.

Such gray-leaved shrubs provide the necessary foils to set off bright border flowers, as well as the showy foliage of many evergreens. Unexpectedly tough, reliable heavenly bamboo (*Nandina domestica*) combines well with gray, and blazes with red foliage and scarlet berries through the winter months. Its colorful cousin, the crimson pygmy barberry (*Berberis thunbergii* 'Atropurpurea Nana') forms neat mounds of dull burgundy foliage which turn brilliant scarlet in late autumn. These practically cry out for a contrasting mound of gray *Cotoneaster glaucophylla* or *Santolina chamaecyparissus* to grow nearby. Late winter flowers of scarlet flowering quince (*Chaenomeles speciosa* 'Rubra') show to best effect when associated with gray-leaved plants, and are sufficiently brilliant to warrant inclusion in the mixed border despite the unattractive appearance of these shrubs during the long summer months.

Conifers provide a source of richly textured evergreen foliage to add to this medley of colorful shrubs and offer distinctive forms to give accent and weight to the border. *Juniperus* × *media* 'Sea Green' is one of the best, forming a neat mid-row shrub with bright green, softly textured sprays of foliage held at a jaunty 45 degree angle. Dwarfs such as *J. horizontalis* 'Blue Chip' or the soft green 'Prince of Wales' make valuable low mosslike shrublets for foreground plantings. Upright growers such as the enormously popular Hollywood juniper (*Juniperus chinensis* 'Kaizuka') with its informal twisting branches, and dwarf golden arborvitae (*Platycladus orientalis* 'Gold Cone') rise out of the mass of the border to help give perspective and scale to the plantings.

Equally useful to give a vertical evergreen accent is the beautiful hybrid holly 'Nellie R. Stevens.' Its broad-based pyramid of dark green waxy leaves holds generous crops of large red berries through the winter months, and makes a somber backdrop to contrast with sunny yellow daisy flowers such as coreopsis and rudbeckia. Where a graceful mounding evergreen is needed to produce a similar background, the red clusterberry (*Cotoneaster lacteus*) obliges, and bears abundant clusters of orange-red fruits each autumn.

The long-flowering semidouble shrub-althaea (*Hibiscus syriacus* 'Lady Stanley') stands out prominently from such evergreens and its large blush-white blooms centered by maroon eyes show to advantage. Tirelessly blooming abelias, with their minute trumpets of white and pink, and lavish St. John's wort (*Hypericum calycinum*), whose golden blooms explode in a feathery boss of red-tipped stamens, also combine well with dark-leaved evergreens.

Roses provide an abundance of color and grace among the other shrubs and perennials and may be used in the middle rows of the border or as tall arching backdrops to the planting. Hybrid Musks and China roses are valuable where a long-blooming shrubby effect is needed, while old-fashioned Teas and Noisettes mature into large plants which each autumn give sumptuous silky-petaled fragrant blooms of uncommon size and quality. The modern Floribunda roses, and their immediate ancestors, the Polyanthas, can create neat masses of color in the garden, and look well in small groupings of a single tone. Skillfully placed strong-growing varieties of the Hybrid Tea rose yield both beautiful garden color and welcome blooms for cutting. For naturalistic effects such unusual species as the chestnut rose (*Rosa roxburghii*) create as much of a sensation with their ferny foliage as with their curious burlike flowers.

Southwestern native plants such as yuccas offer dramatic accents of bold spiky foliage to mix with the other border plants, and crown their evergreen clumps of leaves with pristine masses of pendulous white waxy bell-shaped flowers each year. *Yucca pallida* is an especially desirable variety for its low rosettes of wide silvery blue leaves. One of the most rewarding of all border plants on lime is the red yucca, treasured for its translucent coral-red wands of bloom which wave gracefully over its coarse grasslike foliage nearly the entire summer. As valuable as these for textural contrast is the shrubby spineless prickly-pear (*Opuntia ellisiana*), whose rounded pads bear orange-yellow May flowers followed by purplish-maroon fruits or *tunas*.

The swordlike foliage of irises and Byzantine gladiolus, bulbs such as crinums and spider lilies (*Hymenocallis* spp.), as well as the grassier leaves of daylilies may be used to echo the bold foliage and subtropical aspect of the yuccas, while providing a continuous source of extravagant bloom. Rain lilies, sternbergia, lycoris, and oxblood lily (*Rhodophiala bifida*) may be tucked in amongst the other plants where their inconspicuous grassy leaves will be open to the sun and their flowers can be enjoyed in season. Spring-blooming *Narcissus tazetta* 'Grand Monarque' (*N.* 'Grand Primo'), campernelles (*Narcissus* × *odorus*), the fine jonquil hybrid 'Trevithian', and summer snowflakes (*Leucojum aestivum*) may be planted in large clumps in the foreground of the border to guarantee a joyous spring display.

Clumps of pink *Oxalis crassipes* alternated with mats of double-flowered soapwort (*Saponaria officinalis* 'Flore Plena'), prairie phlox, magenta-flowered mule pink, and "German red carnation" (*Dianthus* × 'Querteri') provide a welcome variation of texture and form across the front of the border. The dwarf plumbago (*Ceratostigma plumbaginoides*) is also fine for such positions and displays its cobalt-blue flowers against a spreading mat of russet autumn leaves. Succulent-leaved purple heart (*Setcreasea pallida*) with its loudly purple foliage, as well as other setcreaseas with more subdued leaves of gray or bronzy green make useful long-blooming foreground plants as well.

To these may be added a multitude of thrifty verbenas and lantanas to spill out and spread color and charm as they creep amongst edgings of boulders or limestone flags. Fluttermill or Missouri buttercup (*Oenothera missouriensis*) also looks at home near an edging of rock or brick, and lights up foreground plantings with large lemon-yellow blooms that appear freshly on summer evenings. Nearly any low plant will prove suitable for the foreground of the border, so long as one resists the temptation to edge plantings with rows of a single variety. Traditional edgings of mondo grass (*Ophiopogon* spp.) or monkey grass (*Liriope* spp.), although appropriate with formal masses of evergreen shrubs, contradict the informal spirit of the mixed border and are best avoided.

Carefree, long-blooming daisy flowers such as purple coneflower, coreopsis, shasta daisy, black-eyed Susan (*Rudbeckia fulgida* 'Goldsturm'), heliopsis, and others provide bulky masses of color to mix with the flowering shrubs and evergreens. These contrast effectively with the invaluable spikelike blooms of salvias and penstemons, larkspurs, and standing cypress (*Ipomopsis rubra*). Tough, shrubby perennials such as aromatic aster (*Aster oblongifolius*), Turk's cap (*Malvaviscus drummondii*), Mexican petunia (*Ruellia malacosperma*), and blue mistflower (*Eupatorium coelestinum*) fill in among the other border flowers and take over difficult dry corners. Spectacular annuals such as prairie bluebell (*Eustoma grandiflorum*), as well as the humbler corn poppies, cornflowers, gomphrena, and balsam may be encouraged to self-sow among the more permanent border residents.

All of these plants have such long records of success on calcareous soils that mixed borders that avail themselves of these hearty flowers can be assured of continuity of bloom and interest. Although many more varieties can be considered as well, these serve to give a taste of the diversity of plants and the exciting prospects that await gardeners on limestone, alkaline clay, and caliche soils. Over the course of the year such plants endure and beautify despite the torturing heat, drought, and erratic cold inflicted by difficult climates. Yet, to enjoy all the plants mentioned above, gardeners on lime need do little more for their beds than provide the customary additions of organic materials and the initial waterings necessary to get their plants off to a good start. Thereafter, periodic mulching and an annual trimming to set the planting in order should return a maximum measure of beauty for a minimum investment of time and effort.

CHAPTER FOUR

Fabulously Successful Herbaceous Plants

For a variety of reasons it is the herbaceous perennial more than the other classes of garden plants that brings real excitement and distinction to gardens on lime and limy clay. Unlike annual flowers that (if they come back to the garden at all) return via self-sown seed and therefore move about, perennials stay put and resprout from their roots each year with fresh shoots and blooms. They earn the gardener's admiration and special favor by literally persisting *per annuis*—"through the years."

Limitations imposed by climate on the culture of many woody plants are effectively dodged by perennials, whose shorter cycles of growth enable them to evade the worst periods of drought, cold, or excessive heat according to their individual predilections. Although many popular shrubs and trees dislike lime, most well-known perennials thrive on calcareous soils so long as they receive sufficient summer moisture. For gardeners familiar with the beautiful native wildflowers of limestone regions it should come as no surprise that many perennials grow in our limy gardens like weeds, for some of the most desirable varieties can be found growing in abandoned lots, cracks in pavement, or even volunteering in our borders.

Our garden perennials are the domesticated descendants of the wildflowers of the world, and they provide gardeners with virtually endless opportunities to flaunt the diversity of the plant kingdom. Herbaceous plants confer the requisite variety to celebrate the changing seasons of the garden year, and a full palette of colors, forms and textures lies at the gardener's disposal. Because they are much faster-growing than woody plants, yet more permanent than annuals, these herbaceous ornamentals are the most versatile plants in the garden. Successful border perennials can be readily dug up and divided, and moved as needed to fulfill the gardener's vision. Through their beauty, longevity, ease of culture and propagation, and their abundance of bloom, these plants make themselves indispensable.

Perennials can fulfill a variety of useful roles in the garden, and the addition of a few lively herbaceous flowers may be all that is needed to brighten a stark edifice or an uninteresting hedgerow. When used en masse many varieties make good colorful groundcovers. Yet, in the majority of gardens the beautiful flowers and foliage plants we know as perennials make their most telling contributions as residents of specialized herbaceous borders. Here they are mixed with others of their kind and indulged with a position and importance that derives less from any practical service to the landscape than from the gardener's simple love for flowers. For many these beautiful perennial blooms are what gardening is all about.

Whether a plant falls into the category of "herbaceous perennial" or not is often a question of context. Coral trees (*Erythrina* spp.), firebush (*Hamelia patens*), and yellow bells (*Tecoma stans*) become large woody plants in frost-free countries, but make serviceable perennials in freeze-prone gardens where they die to the ground each winter. Bananas are familiar to many gardeners as trees, but these, too, function as perennials in many areas and redevelop their arborescent proportions annually over the long warm growing season. Some of our most popular summer "perennials" (such as lantanas and plumbagos) behave as evergreen shrubs in the tropics, as herbaceous perennials in regions with brief, relatively mild winters, and as annuals in colder gardens.

Old favorites such as hollyhocks, foxgloves, and bearded irises are typical of gardens in frosty regions, but are planted and enjoyed in hot-summer climates as well. These flowers bloom in northern gardens during high summer and in such cool climates perform over a fairly long season. In hot regions such as Texas these same flowers complete their blooming cycles in April and May before the onset of intense summer heat. Others, such as summer phloxes (*Phlox paniculata*) or foxgloves (*Digitalis* cvs.), give their best warm-climate performances in the shade.

The enormous variety of perennial flowers taken from diverse natural environments tempts gardeners to combine plants from alpine screes, Mediterranean brushlands, and subtropical savannahs side by side. Even on difficult limy clays such juxtapositions are possible, although combinations along these lines are most often short-lived follies instead of established successes. Subtropical plants may have the necessary vigor to recover from freezing weather, but if they fail to come into bloom until late fall (a common failing of *Cuphea*, *Salvia*, and perennial marigolds, or *Tagetes*), they will flower only a short time before autumn frosts silence the display. On the other hand, hardy perennials selected and hybridized by gardeners for the temperate climates and generous soils of Europe and eastern North America are likely to give mediocre performances in hot-summer climates on lime. What many gardeners regard as first-class selections of daylilies, irises, summer phloxes, and others will probably give only second-class results when planted in chalky flowerbeds in the torrid climate of Texas, if they bloom at all.

For garden performance show quality is an inadequate recommendation; it is strength and endurance that count most. Yet, no gardener wants to cultivate "inferior" flowers. Gardeners on lime or with hot summer weather must sometimes rogue out fancy cultivars (the gardener's abbreviation for "cultivated varieties") that fail to perform up to their reputations, and instead content themselves with "ordinary" flowers that put up with the soil and climate. By focusing on flower varieties that one may reasonably hope to grow to perfection, gardeners in limestone regions concentrate their efforts on the subjects most likely to return the greatest rewards.

Early Flowers

Spring comes early to the limestone heartlands, and the trickle of February- and March-blooming bulbs and perennials soon are joined by hosts of flowering trees, shrubs, and annual and perennial flowers. Many of these early blooms come in bright shades of pink, yellow, lilac, and white. Except among masses of winter annuals or grasses, spring color schemes are likely to include strong notes of brown as well, taken from the dried leaves of deciduous trees, shrubs, and grasses. With brown grass and clear blue skies as a backdrop, the flowers of early spring project a stark and unreal beauty unique to the season.

Anemones and Kin

Anemones are some of the typical flowers of spring, and introduce a large family of lime-loving perennials, most of which flower early in the year. Native *Anemone heterophylla* may be found from February through March brightening fields and roadsides, as well as garden borders and as an escape in lawns. This easy-growing wildflower is most often white, but occurs in shades of lavender and near-pink as well. With its narrow-petaled daisylike flowers it mimics the regrettably weak-growing Grecian windflower (*A. blanda*), a favorite in Sir Frederick Stern's garden at Highdown and in other English gardens on lime. For best effect large handfuls of the anemone tubers should be collected and planted in groups with other low perennials or bulbs, for although easily grown from seed, *A. heterophylla* rarely offsets, and these small flowers look best en masse.

The brightly colored poppy-flowered anemones of the Middle East, *A. coronaria* and *A. hortensis*, are usually short-lived perennials in gardens, although colonies may sometimes establish in protected sites with well-drained loamy soil. They are well worth planting in any case, for the tubers are inexpensive, and their brightly colored red, purple, pink and lavender blooms and bright green parsleylike foliage are among the most exuberant displays of spring. The double-flowered strains such as the 'St. Brigid' hybrids as well as the single-flowered 'Monarch de Caen' hybrids descend from plants originally developed by the Turks, and are among our older domesticated flowers. For a sunny spot on a chalky bank the related Mediterranean native *A. fulgens* offers a fleeting crimson spectacle. These large-flowered anemones suffer in extreme cold and may succumb to rot in poorly drained clay soils with summer moisture. For best success they are generally planted in December or later, so that their tender foliage will not emerge too early, and they may be dug and stored dry when their foliage dies down in late spring.

First cousins of the anemones, and just as inclined to early bloom are the various species of *Ranunculus*. These "buttercups" or "marsh-marigolds" enjoy plenty of moisture during their spring blooming season, a characteristic alluded to by their Latin name, which means "little frogs." Native large-flowered buttercup (*Ranunculus macranthus*) begins producing its generous inch-wide double-petaled golden blooms in late February and often continues to the first of May. This long-lived perennial welcomely self-sows and naturalizes in grass. In the summer it retreats to the distinctive clawlike cluster of tubers that characterize the genus.

Like the large-flowered anemones, the popular cultivated strains of *Ranunculus asiaticus* are a legacy of ancient Turkish ingenuity and were enormously popular flowers long ago (an English list in 1792 included over eight hundred named cultivars!). These Middle Eastern natives suffer in severe winter cold spells, and usually fail to return as perennials except in favorably protected sites. The tubers of *Ranunculus* are nonetheless so inexpensive and easily grown that they make a rewarding show even if they must be renewed every few years. They may be saved from season to season if dug and stored over summer for planting in December or January.

More along the lines of traditional perennials are the aquilegias or columbines. These shrubby members of the anemone family arise from stout rootstalks and overtop their gracefully divided fernlike foliage with clouds of dainty, long-spurred blooms. The delicate construction and proportion of these plants belies a surprisingly tough constitution. Columbines are best known as denizens of wild woodlands and rugged mountain slopes and they bring an irrepressible air of fairies and enchanted forests to the garden during their springtime blooming season. After bloom is past the lacy foliage makes an attractive backdrop for other flowers until it discolors and dies down in late summer. Fall rains stimulate a fresh surge of lush foliage which persists through the winter.

Most of the large-flowered hybrid strains of *Aquilegia* are short-lived perennials and require some shade to look their best, but native Southwestern species are very tough and long-lived, and tolerate a great deal of sun. The long-spurred columbine (*Aquilegia longissima*) and the short-spurred Hinckley columbine (*A. hinckleyana*) are two especially beautiful natives of West Texas with large yellow blooms. These attract hovering hawk moths and hummingbirds that come to sip from the peculiar tubular "spurs" of the columbine flowers. Hummingbirds also favor *A. canadensis*, whose pendant blooms have small inconspicuous petals, but display quietly attractive coppery red spurs.

Columbines hybridize promiscuously in the garden and self-sow generously. Gardeners can readily develop their own hybrid strains by mixing various colors in a planting and waiting for the hummingbirds to do their work. In this way the beautiful blue and purple shades found in the flowers of many hybrid columbines can be incorporated with the toughness and reliability of native species.

Delphiniums are tall-growing allies of the columbines that are favorite perennials in colder climates. Although tolerant of limy soil, they generally fail to return in droughty hot-summer climates. Carolina larkspur (*Delphinium carolinianum*) may be planted in lieu of the popular hybrid varieties, and provides useful spires of azure-blue, lavender, or greenish-white blooms to combine with other tall spring flowers such as penstemons and Byzantine gladiolus. These native perennials bloom in mid- to late spring and reproduce generously by volunteer seedlings.

Carnations, Pinks, and the Dianthus Family

Another plant group with a number of spring-blooming perennials is the large dianthus family. Dianthus are one of the classic European groups of plants for chalky soils and the entire group, including our popular garden pinks and carnations, seems to enjoy lime. Their downfalls, however, are heat, humidity, and poor drainage. The heavy clays and torrid summers of central Texas rule out all but the hardiest, most coarsely rooted types for use in this area.

Even in the temperate climates of Europe and eastern America dianthus have a reputation as ephemeral perennials. Many of these mat-forming evergreens succumb to soil fungi which damp off the dense leafy foliage at ground level. A raised position with good drainage, gritty soil, and minimal exposure to afternoon sun and irrigation will help many dianthus through long hot summers. Once cool fall temperatures prevail they can be given as much moisture as is available and are some of the easiest-growing plants in the garden. Fresh fall cuttings strike root readily and can be stuck directly in prepared garden soil to establish and renew or replace old matted, unkempt plantings.

The most enduringly perennial of the dianthus tribe in warm areas are the old magenta-flowered "mule pinks." Almost alone among the members of this genus, these old garden hybrids between border carnations and sweet william (*Dianthus barbatus*) tolerate the boggy Blackland Prairie soils. They make a valuable early spring showing of clustered magenta blooms against lushly green foliage.

Similar, but slightly less enduring, are the everblooming mule pinks whose flowers appear atop short, lightly branched flower spikes over the entire growing season. In mild years these delightfully fragrant hardy flowers may bloom practically year-round, and appear in nearly single to fully double forms in shades of pink or dark crimson. Nurseries have recently marketed these as "German red carnations," but their true identity will likely remain obscure. Nineteenth-century American nurserymen offered similar plants under the name "*Dianthus querteri*." These were likely of French origin, as most of the breeding with this group was accomplished in France during the last century.

By far the most popular garden dianthus are the China or India pinks derived from the Chinese native *Dianthus chinensis*. These are usually planted as bedding annuals, but in good, well-drained soil will persist for several seasons. China pinks earn a place in the flower garden for their generous displays of variously marked red, pink, salmon, and maroon blooms on compact plants. These flower most notably in the spring, but provide sporadic bloom through the rest of the year as well.

The sweet william (*Dianthus barbatus*) is a favorite denizen of old-fashioned flower gardens, and is another spring-blooming member of this group often planted in the fall as a bedding annual. Like the China pinks, sweet william tends to persist more than one year and augments the illusion of a perennial habit by producing generous crops of volunteer seedlings.

More truly perennial than the dianthus themselves are their near relatives, the soapworts (*Saponaria officinalis*). These humble flowers have a long history in gardens on lime and were valued by early planters as much for their lather-yielding roots as their attractive lavender-pink blooms. The double-flowered form is the choice selection for flower beds as its blooms appear over a long season from late spring through summer.

Spring Phloxes

Although not closely related to the dianthus family, spring-blooming phloxes casually resemble many pinks, and a horticulturally minded police detective would certainly include them in a hypothetical lineup of mat-forming spring perennials. Creeping phlox or "thrift" (*Phlox subulata*) is a cliché in many gardens, especially in its common, and almost intolerably harsh, pink form. Other color variants in shades of lavender, white and magenta are weaker-growing, but worth attempting in those moist, well-drained soils and east- or north-facing positions that will accommodate them.

Much better for poorly drained limy clay is the native prairie phlox (*Phlox pilosa*). Its thriftily spreading clumps of sweetly fragrant lavender-pink blooms are one of the unsung joys of spring on limy ground. In the wild these beautiful flowers favor stream banks; in gardens they respond to abundant moisture with heavy crops of bloom over a long spring season, often with an autumn encore to boot.

This native phlox belongs to the same group as the wild sweet william (*P. divaricata*) and the Louisiana phlox (*P. divaricata* v. *louisianica*), but unlike these easterners it tolerates droughty alkaline soils. Unfortunately, few nurseries have recognized the superior vigor of *Phlox pilosa* and avid gardeners in search of it may need to contact a specialist in prairie wildflowers to obtain this fine variety.

Oxalis

Gazing out at plantings of the small rounded clumps of *Oxalis crassipes* on a frosty February morning, a hasty gardener might fail to observe the folded nodding buds that with the warmth of the noonday sun will open to display cheerful magenta-pink blossoms. This resolute bloomer not only graces gardens in early spring, but continues well into May or longer where it receives shade from the western sun, opening its flowers progressively earlier in the day and closing them in afternoon heat. A tough, thrifty South American, *O. crassipes* often returns to bloom in late fall as well, persisting in flower through the winter on sheltered sites. This is an invaluable plant for gardens on lime, and is a prime choice for edging beds or pathways. Where its wine-pink blooms clash with other flowers or a red brick wall, the lovely snow-white form may be used successfully instead.

Mustards

The four-petaled cruciform blooms of the mustard family grant a welcome relief from these little, five-petaled flowers, and afford the relief of colors other than pink. Evergreen candytuft (*Iberis sempervirens*) makes a useful foil for other spring flowers, both with its snow-white blooms and its dark green mats of rosemarylike foliage. Perennial alyssum or basket of gold (*Aurinia saxatilis*) needs hiding during the long months of summer when its grayish foliage scorches in the heat, but during its early spring blooming season it provides a useful cloud of tiny golden-yellow blooms to drape over a rock wall or mix among early bulbs.

Better for limy gardens in hot-summer regions than the oft-planted but short-lived wallflowers are the evening-scented stocks (*Mathiola longipetala* v. *bicornis*). These Mediterranean natives develop short shrubby mounds of slick green lance-shaped leaves topped with fragrant lavender blooms in early spring. The biennial to perennial evening stocks are frequent denizens of old gardens and occasionally waifs of vacant lots, thriving on well-drained chalky soils, where they reproduce themselves prolifically with self-sown seedlings.

Spiderworts

Lovers of African violets, whose tender blooms and delicate constitutions demand coddling and precise siting near cool, brightly lit interior windows, will recognize a remarkably similar range of colors in the velvet-textured blooms of the easy-growing spiderworts (*Tradescantia* spp.). These native perennials can become pests by self-sowing in rich moist soil, but redeem themselves by the charm and beauty of their crystalline springtime flowers in shades and blushes of blue, violet, wine, and snow-white. *T. gigantea* is a native variety that thrives on limy ground and produces large, beautiful blooms in a range of colors. Named selections offered by perennial dealers are no more lovely than these wildlings, but they may afford a welcome reduction in rampancy of growth.

Penstemons

Most of the penstemon varieties suited to limy gardens bloom in late spring or early summer, but two of the finest choose to bloom in early April. The wild foxglove

(*Penstemon cobaea*) raises its spires of blush-white to lavender inflated bells above neat rosettes of glossy foliage, and thrives on well-drained limy clay or chalk. Even when measured against the numerous beauties within the enormous genus *Penstemon*, this is an outstanding garden flower with enviably large blooms and a tough constitution that makes it one of the indispensable perennials for gardens on lime. The wine-red Hill Country penstemon (*P. triflorus*) is equally valuable, and its spikes of tubular bloom afford an early-season attraction for northward-migrating hummingbirds, as well as a fine choice to contrast with carpets of violet-blue Texas bluebonnets.

Irises

Of all springtime perennials, perhaps the favorites are the irises. These beautiful flowers, appropriately named for the Greek goddess of the rainbow, come in such wealth and variety as to invite devotion, and, although some semiaquatic types dislike lime, this tribe includes a host of the classic flowers known to thrive upon limy soil. Botanists include within the genus *Iris* a widely varied array of invaluable perennials whose differing lifestyles bridge the arbitrary gaps between plants with fibrous roots, those with rhizomes or tubers, and those with true bulbs. All of these sections contribute varieties suited to calcareous soils, and with their easy-growing, hardy natures offer some of the finest flowers gardeners may hope to cultivate.

First to bloom each year are the white flags (*Iris albicans*) and the blue flags of its variety, 'Madonna.' These dwarfish, gray-leaved bearded irises are frequently misidentified as the superficially similar and historically famous Florentine iris, the source of the orris root used as fixative in perfumes. Although not as renowned as the Florentine iris, *Iris albicans* has an interesting past of its own, as this native of Arabia was cultivated in the Middle Ages and spread by the Moors around the Mediterranean to Spain, whence it came to the New World. Throughout the warm parts of America this is the commonest and most long-lived bearded iris of gardens, as it inherits great resistance to the basal rot fungi that attack the rhizomes of many modern hybrids.

In warm-climate gardens basal rot limits the choice of bearded irises for use as perennials, and this scourge becomes progressively worse as one goes south, so that while many varieties thrive at Dallas and northward, relatively few endure the climate of San Antonio. Although new and beautiful hybrids are available from specialist nurseries, such novelties can be expensive and disappointing gambles if their constitutions fail to include inherent resistance to the rot organisms. The easiest way for gardeners to verify the natural resistance of a particular variety is to acquire it from another gardener or an abandoned lot. A multitude of treasured, lovely old varieties can be obtained in this way. In general, the older "intermediate" hybrids that descend from the deep purple Italian iris (*I. kochii*) offer greater resistance to disease than either the modern dwarf or tall bearded irises.

The Italian iris sometimes imparts another useful character to its hybrids: remontancy. This ability to bloom again in the fall is one of the most desirable traits an iris may possess in this region, for although erratic spring fronts may play havoc with these early flowers, autumn-blooming irises often experience mild weather encouraging long-lasting, near-perfect blooms. In addition to the remontant purple-flowered *I. kochii*, the old yellow variety 'Golden Cataract' graces many established gardens, and its warmly colored blooms often make a welcome appearance at Christmas. Remontant bearded irises are available from mail-order suppliers in a bewildering variety of colors, and though most older varieties display solid shades, many newer hybrids show the same bicolor effects and petal ruffling found in other modern bearded iris.

These repeat-flowering irises are more valuable on the limestone heartlands than the famous winter iris (*I. unguicularis*), beloved in English gardens for its late autumn flowers. This Mediterranean native requires a sheltered site and sandy soil to endure intemperate blasts of winter cold, and its frail, pale-colored fall and winter blooms have less garden effect on sunny prairies than in regions dominated by cloudy winter weather.

An unusual group of irises warranting the attention of gardeners on lime are the "aril-bred" irises that derive from crosses with the strange Oncocyclus and Regelia sections of the Middle East. These fascinating plants inherit unusual netted and stippled color patterns in subtle shades of lavender, slate, maroon, and gold. Like their drought-loving parents, the aril-bred irises prefer arid summers and lean soil. Although these innovative hybrids are unproven, this group seems to hold much promise for dry chalky upland sites.

In contrast to the mixed results warm-climate gardeners achieve with bearded irises, the members of the beardless Spuria section recommended themselves without reservation, seeming to perform with complete success, and tolerating soils that vary from water-logged alkaline clay to dust-dry chalk. The commonest in gardens are the old Turkish salt-marsh irises (*I. orientalis*), known to many as *I. ochroleucus*, whose vanilla-scented white blooms are splashed with yellow. Like all Spurias, this old variety makes a fine cut flower and has beautiful tall dark green swords of foliage. Modern hybrids now exceed this oldster in beauty, if not fragrance, and may be had in sophisticated blends of yellow, blue, and fawn. In cold-climate gardens the Siberia irises offer similar valuable perennials especially suited to damp soil.

Drought and alkalinity present challenges to the culture of the water-loving irises of the Louisiana group, but this can be overcome with specialized culture. These gloriously beautiful flowers descend from selections and crosses of the native irises of the Mississippi delta and have both water-loving and land-loving ancestry. The deep violet *I. brevipes* is the terrestrial species involved and is the variety most likely to be encountered in older gardens. This type tolerates shade and thrives in heavy blackland clay soils, although, like all irises of this group, it suffers on dry chalky soils or under highly alkaline conditions.

The other Louisiana hybrids have similar preferences, but are less tolerant of drought or lime. It is a simple matter to accommodate them, however, by planting in a soil-filled tub or child's swimming pool buried in the ground to hold in moisture. These water-loving irises will also thrive if planted aquatically in a half whiskey barrel full of water, and such techniques are equally suited to the salt-marsh irises (*I. virginica*) and lime-loving yellow water irises (*I. pseudacorus*).

Choice flowers for garden beds with partial shade and rich soil are provided by the stoloniferous members of the Evansia section, whose delicate blooms are accompanied by lush, attractive foliage. This group includes the Japanese roof iris (*I. tectorum*) and the beautiful, unusual, and slightly tender *I. japonica*. *I. tectorum* bears crested lavender or white blooms and derives its common name from the oriental tradition of planting this flower on the thatched roofs of cottages. *I. japonica* and its hybrid with the Burmese bamboo iris (*I. wattii* × 'Nada') bear graceful sprays of white lavender-marked blooms. All of these irises produce valuable fanlike clusters of leaves that form colonies and spread by grasslike runners. These irises are natives of woodland margins and lack the customary rhizomes or bulbs of other sections of the genus.

Among the most rewarding iris for gardens on lime are the hybrid Dutch irises that derive from the Spanish *I. xiphium* and the Moroccan *I. tingitiana*. These develop true bulbs and grow naturally in seasonally wet areas in the granite and limestone hills and mountains of their homelands. They enjoy mucky black clay soils while in growth during the spring and prefer a long, dry summer baking afterwards. Strong-growing Dutch iris varieties such as the dark purple 'Prof. Blau' and the pale blue 'Wedgewood' naturalize readily. The older, now seldom offered strains of "Spanish iris" are similarly adapted, but bloom slightly later than the Dutch irises with more delicate blooms.

One other large-flowered member of the iris family commonly blooms in gardens on lime: the old-fashioned corn lily or Byzantine gladiolus (*Gladiolus byzantinus*). The magenta spires of this hardy member of the gladiolus tribe appear at the same time as bearded irises, reaching above its deep green clumps of swordlike leaves (*gladiolus* means "little sword" in Latin). These tough lime-loving flowers thrive on heavy clay soils and grow from corms that rapidly multiply with tiny seedlike cormels. They should be planted in the fall, as the frost-hardy foliage grows through the winter. For planting designs in which magenta might spoil a springtime color scheme, a diligent search of sources may yield a worthy reward in the white-flowered form of this old-time flower.

Less common in gardens, but hardy wherever the ground does not freeze deeply is the South African parrot gladiolus, *G. natalensis* (*G. psittacinus*). Its orange and yellow hooded blooms appear in late spring. In addition to these denizens of old gardens, a variety of modern dwarf "hardy glads" are available from bulb dealers and also grow well on lime, although they are less vigorous naturalizers and sometimes bloom too late in the season to be of much value.

Naturalizing Bulbs

Naturalizing bulbs are favorites in all gardens, and provide some of the best early perennial flowers of the year. Bulbs entice gardeners with a romantic appeal derived as much from the anticipation of their annual spring return as from their briefly glorious early display of flowers. Of the multitudes planted annually in gardens on lime and limy clay, relatively few types of spring-flowering bulbs establish and perennate, although several return for a few years after planting and are wishfully spoken of as "naturalizers." If more gardeners were familiar with the truly successful bulb varieties—those select few that not only return, but increase—our gardens would soon overflow with beautiful flowers, for even on the most waterlogged alkaline clays and the driest chalk banks there are adapted bulbs that one may confidently expect to outlive the planter, increasing in bloom and loveliness through untold springs to come.

The most eagerly awaited among these bulbous spring flowers are the luminous white and yellow blooms of the narcissi, known variously as daffodils or jonquils. Undisputed king of the narcissi on alkaline clay soils is *Narcissus tazetta* 'Grand Monarque,' whose strappy dark green foliage makes a perfect foil for its rounded clusters of creamy, yellow-cupped flowers. This sturdy antique has been in cultivation for nearly four hundred years and, like many of our best garden bulbs, originated as a natural hybrid. In this case the parents appear to have been the paperwhite (*Narcissus tazetta* v. *papyraceus*) and the Chinese sacred lily (*N. tazetta* v. *orientalis*), and they imparted to their offspring great vigor and unusual tolerance to poor soils.

Narcissus fanciers debate the true identity of this ancient clone and it is called 'Grand Primo' by some. Before wholeheartedly entering a discussion of this subject it is well to recall the tradition among students of these flowers that the English botanist, Sweet, went mad and died in Bedlam hospital after trying to unravel the classifications of the old garden narcissi! Let it suffice to declare that, by whatever name, these are the most reliable of our garden daffodils and provide the most beautiful and telling displays of spring in our gardens. Near relations, known by such names as 'Avalanche,' 'Pearl,' and 'Minor Monarque,' as well as the double-flowered form of this old-fashioned narcissus, are equally welcome in our plantings.

Of the yellow-flowered daffodils the most valuable on lime are the early-blooming old-fashioned campernelles (*Narcissus* × *odorus*). These honey-scented golden blooms belong to an ancient hybrid of the southern European native jonquil (*N. jonquilla*), and they inherit the jonquil's attractive rushlike foliage and habit of flowering in small clusters. With charm and grace these blooms bring early splashes of fragrant golden color to spring gardens and develop thrifty clumps on heavy clay soil.

The modern jonquil hybrid 'Trevithian' may be thought of as a twentieth-century successor to these antiques, and offers similar vigor and adaptability with a more refined, later-blooming light yellow flower. In comparison with other jonquil hybrids (Division VII in the modern narcissus classification) 'Trevithian' is a relatively early bloomer. Although most hybrids from this section will grow on calcareous soil, only early varieties such as this and the older 'Sweetness' and 'Golden Sceptre' are of much garden value on the limestone heartlands. This is because late-season bulbs of all kinds must contend with the blast-furnace heat of this region's early-warming spring. Nevertheless, the jonquil hybrids, many of which were bred in Oregon by the pioneer American hybridizer, Grant Mitsch, offer some of the best opportunities for gardeners on lime to explore variety in daffodils, and may be had in all the novel pink, white, and bicolor combinations found in the other classes of narcissus.

This is fortunate, for the large-cupped daffodils seem to perform on heavy alkaline clays only in the commoner yellow and yellow-orange color phases, with whites and pinks as consistent failures. Though most of the older, stronger-growing daffodils will flower for a season or two, only early-bloomers such as 'Fortune' or 'Carlton' grow with any vigor, and even these will require periodic division and replanting on well-drained prepared soil if they are to continue to bloom and increase.

Among the most reliable of spring bulbs on limy grounds is an unlikely-looking relative of narcissus, the summer snowflake (*Leucojum aestivum*), whose charming white bell-shaped flowers mark dooryards of many older gardens. The tiny white, green-spotted blooms suggest lily-of-the-valley to some, and in regions where the true lily-of-the-valley is absent these flowers are often so deputized. They should be planted in large clumps so that the lush green foliage can set off the tiny sprays of bloom. 'Gravetye Giant' is a select large-flowered form worth seeking out not only for its improved form, but as an assurance that the bulbs purchased are nursery-grown and not collected from the wild. It is a tragic irony of the modern bulb trade that this plant, which is so common in many older gardens, has been endangered by ruthless collection to the brink of extermination in its native Mediterranean homeland.

A choice bulb to combine with *Leucojum* and *Narcissus* 'Trevithian' for a simultaneous spring display is the lady tulip (*Tulipa clusiana*). These red and white flowers provide a treasured source of joyful color and lively entertainment in spring borders on limy soil. The graceful blooms constantly change in appearance as they track the sun across the sky, opening to wide stars at noon and then clasping closed and erect for the evening. *T. clusiana*'s small brown-coated bulbs, with their characteristic tufts of hair at the top, may be a source of dismay to gardeners accustomed to the large bulbs of Dutch hybrid tulips. But, whereas the latter are of value in warm areas only as highly contrived bedding annuals requiring artificial chilling, the modest lady tulip rewards gardeners perennially if merely provided with a well-drained spot in the border. A pale sulfur variety, 'Cynthia,' and the closely related bright yellow and red *T. chrysantha* also succeed on chalky soil, but achieve a smaller stature than the common red and white lady tulip.

Minor Bulbs of Spring

Sweetly fragrant white French-Roman hyacinths (*Hyacinthus orientalis*) are some of the earliest of all spring bulbs, often beginning bloom in late January. These "wild" ancestors of the popular Dutch hyacinths show none of the stiffness of their hybrid offspring, and bear their flowers in gracefully modest racemes. Less common and later-blooming than the white Roman hyacinths are the blue forms of this fragrant flower. Like the white Roman hyacinths, these naturalize well, forming mats of foliage and fragrant bloom.

These are joined in March by grassy clumps of the old-fashioned starch, or grape, hyacinth (*Muscari racemosum*) that abounds around many old homesites. The violet-blue clusters of blooms are beloved by children, who often mistake these fragrant early flowers for bluebonnets.

The large family of ornamental onions, or *Allium,* provides several valuable spring bulbs for gardens on calcareous soil. From central Texas southward the early-blooming Naples onion (*Allium neapolitanum*) is one of the most reliable of these, lighting up plantings beneath deciduous shade trees with pristinely white blooms. Because this variety makes foliage and blooms early in the year, it welcomes the protection of a south-facing wall or overhanging tree to ward off unusually severe cold.

Better for open, exposed areas is *Allium drummondii,* whose low clustered flowers vary from chalky white to pink or wine-red in color. In most Texas gardens these early flowers self-sow, creating a colorful mass display to combine with other blooms. The related A. *hyacinthoides* and A. *ecristatum* offer similar ranges in color, but have distinctive soil preferences, thriving best on chalky banks and wet muck respectively.

As spring progresses these early onions are followed by milk-white globular clusters of bloom sported by A. *canadense* v. *fraseri.* This native allium may have grassy green foliage, or, in the larger forms from the Texas Hill Country ("*Allium texanum*"), broad gray straplike leaves. These robust sorts make good subjects for the perennial border, as the tall spikes of bloom rise above shorter foreground plants, and the bulbs readily increase.

Near kin of the alliums are several lesser members of the lily family such as star of Bethlehem (*Ornithogalum umbellatum*) and its tall relation, *O. narbonense,* both natives of sunny Mediterranean lands. *O. narbonense* is sometimes listed as O. *pyramidale,* apparently in reference to its graceful upright wands of white blooms. The brittle long-necked bulbs of this variety thrive even on heavy clay soils and may be found about older gardens in north Texas. Perhaps a legacy of early French colonists in the Dallas area, this flower is a favorite in its homeland where the French have given it the lovely name of "virgin's spray."

Rather similar to these Old World bulbs are the American camas lilies or wild hyacinths (*Camassia scilloides*) of prairies and hillsides. These native bulbs vary in color from lead-white to violet, but most often appear in light lavender. Such pale colorings require skill to be properly shown off in the garden, yet when provided with appropriate foils of bright spring foliage and colorful blooms these graceful wildlings make a telling incident.

More easily shown to good effect are the closely related death camas (*Zigadenus nuttallii*) and the peculiar green lily (*Schoenocaulon texanum*). Death camas derives its nickname from its poisonous bulbs, which are a hazard to livestock throughout the American West. Bright green grassy leaves in three ranks accompany its creamy white spires. The green lily throws feathery pinkish-green wands up above its evergreen grassy clumps of foliage, providing a miniature fireworks display in the spring border or rockery.

Spring-blooming varieties of crocus are great favorites among bulbs for their cheerful miniature blooms nestled in grass or among rocks. Although these are tolerant to lime, most fail to naturalize and return in warm areas or on heavy alkaline clay soils, unless kept dry in summer. A variety that adapts to summer rainfall and hot climates is the purple-flowered *Crocus tomasinianus*, a native of limestone soils in the Balkans. This vigorous type will often settle in and spread if offered well-drained limy clay.

A crocuslike native of limy prairie soils worthy of a favored place in any garden is the celestial *Nemastylis geminiflora*. Like crocuses, these diminutive iris relations rise from true bulbs. Their pleated grassy foliage appears during the winter, and their ephemeral sky-blue flowers arrive in April and May. Celestials look best when planted in large groups, and grow well in partial shade as well as sun. Although seldom offered for sale, their bulbs may be collected from fields and roadsides, and grow quickly from seed if offered rich calcareous clay ground.

Valuable relations of celestials include the irislike pine woods lilies (*Alophia* spp.), the prairie nymphs (*Herbertia lahue*), and the clumping perennial blue-eyed grasses (*Sisyrinchium* spp.). These last are especially good dwarf perennials, dotted in late spring and early summer with showy clouds of tiny blue blossoms. Like all of these American iris relations, these tiny herbs open their blooms freshly each morning, and close up promptly each afternoon.

CHAPTER FIVE

Mid-season Flowers

F rom late April to early summer the rush of perennial bloom continues, and
reaches a climax just prior to the arrival of unforgiving heat. Flowers that appear at this season capitalize on warm temperatures and ample rainfall to achieve more
robust proportions than the cool-season blooms that precede them. Summer borders assume well-furnished appearances as the taller, background subjects fill in. This is the period for many a perennial's peak performance, and gardeners may plan for masses of
flowers.

Daisies

Daisies are apt to become ubiquitous features of mid-season gardens, because a great
variety come into bloom at this time. They are valuable for both cutting and garden ornament, and well deserve their popularity. Daisy blooms can be mixed with clumps of
platelike or spikelike flowers to avoid any sense of monotony.

The white, yellow-centered shasta daisies (*Chrysanthemum × superbum*) are lime-
loving perennials from the Pyrenees that enjoy heavy soils and abundant moisture
through their flowering season. 'Alaska' is a reliable tall-flowered strain; dwarf border
varieties and doubles are also available.

The lance-leaved coreopsis (*Coreopsis lanceolata*) reigns supreme among golden-
flowered daisies, and yields an impressive abundance of sunny blooms. Flowers continue
into summer if the spent blooms are trimmed off to discourage seed formation. 'Sunray'
is a compact, semidouble strain that readily propagates from division, and often repro-
duces by self-sown seed. These are easy growers on limy soils.

Other perennial *Coreopsis*, such as the feather-leaved *C. verticillata*, the low, creeping *C. auriculata*, and the pink-flowered *C. rosea*, accept lime, but need plenty of moisture
when grown in warm-summer regions. In colder areas these are often considered drought
resistant.

Purple coneflower (*Echinacea purpurea*) rates as the easiest-growing of the daisies,
and has the widest tolerance to heat, drought, and poor soil. Its pinkish-purple, orange-
centered blooms appear on cue about the first of May, continue into summer, and often

resume in fall. "White"-flowered strains of this perennial have chalky, leaded appearances in the garden, but are excellent for cutting.

Rudbeckias are close allies of purple coneflowers with black-centered, golden blooms and a liking for heavy, moist soils. They are known popularly in America as "black-eyed Susans." *Rudbeckia fulgida* generally waits until midsummer before making its show of massed, yellow, black-centered daisies. 'Goldsturm' is a popular, good-looking, midsized cultivar of this prairie native.

R. laciniata is a grandly tall, back row perennial that flowers from midsummer to fall. It needs deep soil and copious water to give its best performance, and may reach five to six feet in height and breadth. 'Golden Glow' is a handsome, double-flowered selection.

Native prairie daisies such as Mexican hat (*Ratbida columnaris*), cut-leaf daisy (*Engelmannia pinnatifida*), and yellow rosinweed (*Sylphium simpsonii*) are useful naturalizers that may be allowed to self-sow and fill in around early summer borders. The old-fashioned double, perennial sunflower (*Helianthus decapetalus* 'Multiflorus') is a cherished back-row plant. Its golden blooms stand out boldly against tall, dark green leafy stems.

The golden-flowered *Heliopsis helianthoides* v. *scabra* cultivars are bushy yellow daisies that accept both drought and excess moisture, and flower in sun as well as part shade. Their dark green, oval leaves remain attractive all season. 'Gold Greenheart' is a showy double variety.

Gaillardias are popular perennials in temperate regions, but generally perform in hot-summer climates only as annuals. One that might be tried for greater permanence, however, is the pincushion daisy (*Gaillardia suavis*). This variety frequently lacks ray-flowers altogether, but the best forms have orange rays surrounding a reddish disk. Unlike their rank-scented *Gaillardia* relations, pincushion daisies have a sweet honey/gardenia fragrance.

Few of the perennial cornflowers prosper in warm regions, but the Stoke's aster (*Stokesia laevis*) of the Southeast accepts heat and makes a welcome substitute. Its large, light blue flowers appear atop leafy, compact plants ideal for foreground plantings. *Stokesia* accepts lime, but prefers well-drained soil, and resents prolonged drought. As blue flowers are always at a premium, this cornflower-daisy warrants the minor attention required to accommodate it.

The Salvias

Other good sources of blue for the mid-season border come from perennial salvias such as the violet-flowered *Salvia* × *superba* and the dark blue *S. farinacea* 'Catima.' Both of these are compact and well suited to fore- and middle-ground plantings. Somewhat taller and inclined to spread invasively is the azure-flowered bog sage (*S. uliginosa*). A dwarf salvia species allied to the bog sage, *S. sinaloensis*, often shows a reddish tinge to its foliage that helps to set off tiny, deep blue, white-throated blooms.

The flowers of these salvias appear pleasantly along spikes, and often have interesting tubular or orchidlike shapes. Some salvias, such as silver sage (*S. argentea*), lyre-leaf sage (*S. lyrata*), cedar sage (*S. roemeriana*), and big red sage (*S. penstemonoides*), have ornamental foliage to complement their blooms. Nearly all of this group tolerate poor, limy ground. Although salvias flower throughout the growing season, several are at their best in late spring and early summer.

The cedar sage (*S. roemeriana*) is one of the premier performers of late spring, and offers dark crimson blooms atop its rosetted foliage. Lyre-leaf sage (*S. lyrata*) produces off-white blooms above its purple-veined, jagged-edged leaves. Autumn sages (*S. greggii*) also flower well at this time and make important contributions to early summer borders.

Subtropical sages such as the sapphire blue *S. guaranitica* and the deep violet *S.* × 'Costa Rica Blue' begin flowering in early summer and often continue till frost. These leafy types make two- to three-foot bushes before initiating bloom. The slender-spiked *S.* × 'Indigo Spires' also becomes rather tall, and bears its tiny violet blooms continuously if watered through summer heat. Although frosts cut these varieties to the ground, they return with great vigor in spring if their roots are protected by a layer of mulch.

The finest of the hardy perennial sages for summer gardens is the big red sage (*S. penstemonoides*). This native of the limestone Texas Hill Country forms glossy-leaved basal rosettes from which rise three- to four-foot stems bearing long-tubed, burgundy blooms. From early summer till fall its vinous flowers nourish hummingbirds and offer strong notes of color through heat and drought. Big red sage can be difficult to propagate by division, but often self-sows on limy ground to form large colonies.

Relatives of the salvias such as the useful wild bergamots (*Monarda fistulosa* cvs.) flower in early summer with clouds of frothy tubular blooms. These come in shades of purple, lavender, pink, or red, and are more reliable in hot climates than the related bee-balms (*M. didyma*). Their aromatic foliage and spreading, suckering habits give these plants an herbal character. Wild bergamots benefit from support, and a few twiggy branches may be lain over the mounds of foliage in early spring to help hold up the branchlets as they grow through.

Daylilies

Daylilies (*Hemerocallis* cvs.) rate as favorite perennials of early summer, and many gardeners fall under the enchanting spell of their opulent, ephemeral blooms. These fibrous-rooted relatives of the true, bulbous lilies share a measure of nobility with their aristocratic relations, but flower on easy-growing, grasslike plants. The individual blooms of daylilies last only a day or two, so their performance in the garden depends on daily renewal of bloom from freshly opened buds. For several weeks in late spring and early summer these perennials offer a showy succession of flowers and are the queens of the border.

In hot-summer regions few daylily cultivars continue in flower after the torrid weather of July arrives, so gardens are best served by those selections that make generous shows early in summer. Although fanciers of this highly bred group often specialize in delicate pastels and grayed colors, these are best left for cool climates. In hot weather the strongest, warmest tones give the best value, and better withstand the bleaching of strong sun. Although tough and durable, daylilies resent prolonged drought. Most perform best with steady supplies of moisture.

The old-fashioned, double orange *Hemerocallis fulva* 'Kwanso' is as valuable for garden show as any modern clone, yet harbors an ancient Japanese heritage of nearly one thousand years. Other species of daylilies such as the lemon yellow *H. lilioasphodelus* (*H. flava*) and the old cultivar, 'Hyperion,' are worth growing for their charming fragrance, which is absent from many modern hybrids. The orange-yellow *H. aurantiaca* imparts evergreen foliage to its offspring and has sired a useful race of sturdy "landscape" daylilies. 'Aztec Gold' is a popular clone of this type.

The favorites of many daylily fanciers are the tetraploid hybrids, twentieth-century superplants created by artificially boosting chromosomes through treatments of the hormone cholchicine. Tetraploid daylilies take on extra size, fullness, substance and lasting power, as well as improved vigor when compared to many older varieties. Hybridists have used this group to develop fully the daylily's potential colors, and have sought interesting picotees, throat markings, and rufflings so that these formerly common blooms are now highly bred indeed. Perhaps in rebellion, recent hybridizers have turned to breeding more natural-looking, open-petaled "spider" flowers in strong, clear colors.

Mallows

Mallows include some of the most useful perennials for warm-climate gardens. This is due in part to a facility for continuous bloom widely shared among members of this family. Like the daylilies, mallows open fresh flowers each morning to replace the faded blooms of the preceding day. Although mallows occasionally suffer from summer root rots on alkaline land, they are generally tolerant of limy soils, and a number are tremendously drought resistant.

Good mallow varieties for late spring and early summer bloom include the romantically named winecups (*Callirhoe* spp.). These are poppy-flowered, bright purple herbs of prairies and roadsides. *C. involucrata* is the common prostrate or trailing winecup. It looks well spreading along the front of the border. *C. digitata* is an upright, or "standing" variety that reaches two to three feet in height. Both of these rise from fleshy, carrotlike taproots that give them excellent resistance to drought.

For a really tall early summer explosion of bloom few lime-tolerant perennials compete with old-fashioned hollyhocks (*Alcea rosea*). These biennial mallows form winter rosettes of large, rounded leaves that throw up six-foot stems of four-inch-wide blooms. The flowers gradually open from the bottom to the top of the spikes. Colors range from white and pink to deep wine red, and hollyhocks may be had in both double and single strains. Although plagued by spider mites and leaf miners at times, these robust bloomers seem to perform with little loss of vigor.

From early summer onward everblooming mallows such as the Texas star (*Hibiscus coccineus*) and Southern rose-mallow (*H. moscheutus* cvs.) provide continuous displays of bloom. On rich, damp ground the rosy silk flower (*Abelmochus moschatus*) will self-sow to form colonies that return annually from swollen taproots. On dry banks or in partial shade the pink-flowered rock-rose (*Pavonia lasiopetala*); the yellow, brown-eyed Pondoland hibiscus (*Hibiscus calyphyllus*); and the orange sleeping mallow, or Turk's cap (*Malvaviscus arboreus* v. *drummondii*); afford perennial bushes suited to rugged, limy ground.

Distinctive Summer Flowers

Few members of the bluebell family (*Campanulacea*) are long-lived perennials in warm climates, and they are sorely missed by gardeners accustomed to their charms. One relative of the *Campanulas* that accepts hot weather and calcareous soil is the Chinese balloon flower (*Platycodon grandiflorus*). This big blue campanulalike flower produces swollen, inflated buds that look like miniature lavender-blue balloons. These open to star-shaped flowers and appear sporadically throughout the summer on foot-high plants furnished with waxy, gray-green leaves.

Balloon flowers take several years to mature their deep, carrotlike tubers before blooming heavily. They enjoy well-prepared, moist soils. 'Mariesii' is a popular dwarf strain in both white and violet. Doubles are available as well. All are charming, endearing flowers to mix with other hardy perennials.

The speedwells (*Veronica* spp.) are another group of blue-flowered herbs mostly denied to gardeners in warm regions. Although tolerant of lime, many members of this genus prefer cool, moist conditions. Exceptions may be found among useful mat-forming types such as *Veronica incana*. This attractive perennial effectively contrasts its pale blue spikelike flowers with rounded silvery foliage. It succeeds on well-drained limy clays.

One of the truest blue-flowered perennials suited to limy garden soils is the herbaceous *Clematis integrifolia*. This unusual variety hails from the calcareous hills of the Balkan peninsula, and breaks with usual viney clematis traditions by growing as a foot-high shrublet. *C. integrifolia* flowers over a long season from early summer through fall. Its nodding, cornflower-blue blossoms have an elfin charm and ripen to feathery heads of seed.

Another curious perennial of early summer is red hot poker or torch lily (*Kniphophia uvaria*). These South African mountain dwellers have clumps of grassy foliage out of which rise tall wands of drooping, tubular blooms. The exotic, aloelike flowers come in warm shades of orange, coral, or primrose. Although tolerant of heat, cold, drought, and lime, *Kniphophias* dislike poorly drained soils and need ample moisture while in flower.

Yarrows (*Achillea* cvs.) are tremendously valuable summer perennials with carrotlike leaves and flat platelike flower clusters. *A. millefolium* accepts poor prairie soils, and spreads quickly into an attractive clump. Red-flowered selections such as 'Fire King' and the 'Debutante' hybrids in shades of yellow, salmon, and pastel orange are less rampant than the naturalized white-flowered yarrows. Outstandingly beautiful silver-leaved *A. taygetea* selections such as the sulfury 'Moonshine' need well-drained soils, but are otherwise easy and long-flowering.

An architectural perennial useful for its broad, scalloped gray leaves is the plume poppy (*Macleya cordifolia*). Tiny flowers are born by this suckering plant on tall stems in early summer, but it's the attractive foliage that wins the hearts of gardeners, for these bold leaves provide an uncommon-looking foil for other bright blooms.

The boldly spiny sea holly, or eryngo (*Eryngium yuccifolium*), offers another foliage plant of uncommom demeanor. Its thistlelike blooms and leaves look and feel as though they were stamped out of metal. This drought-resistant, spiky evergreen herb has a deep taproot that makes division difficult. New plants are best started from seed or pot-grown transplants.

The perennial or biennial mulleins (*Verbascum* spp.) are tough, leafy herbs, well suited to poor, limy ground. In addition to the common waif of limy roadsides and waste places, *Verbascum thapsus*, a bewildering range of garden hybrids is offered by seed houses. All types make bold rosettes of enormous, often hairy, leaves that bolt to produce tall spikes of purple, white, or yellow bloom.

The morning-flowering moth mullein (*V. blattaria*) has quaint, orchidlike, yellow flowers with feathered purple stamens. The Cotswold hybrids of *V. phoeniceum* produce perennial plants with white, pink, or purple blooms. *V. chaixii*, *V. dumulosum*, *V. olympicum*, and their hybrids are mostly yellow-flowered perennials. *V. bombyciferum* 'Arctic Summer' is a biennial valued especially for its bold, felted rosettes of silvery leaves and its furry, white bloom stems.

Summer-flowering Bulbs

A June-blooming bulbous flower that does well on lime is the southern European drumstick onion (*Allium sphaerocephalum*). Its wine-purple, oblong heads of bloom are good for cutting. In the garden they last best in partial shade.

Although not a true onion, the tuberous-rooted society garlic (*Tulbaghia violacea*) looks and smells like one. It begins producing attractive lavender blooms at this time as well, and makes a useful border plant for milder areas. A variegated form ('Silver Lace') has a delicate creamy stripe down the center of each leaf.

Other summer bulbs include the moisture-loving *Crinums*, rain lilies (*Zephyranthes* spp.), cannas, and gingers. True lilies such as *Lilium formosanum* and *L. regale*, and the robust, lime-tolerant aurelian hybrids also flower over the summer season. 'Thunderbolt' is an especially strong grower, with a beautiful, warm saffron-orange flower. The Chinese martagon lily (*L. henryi*) carries clusters of down-facing blooms, whose papillae-covered petals recurve nearly to full circles. All of these lilies enjoy well-prepared calcareous soils. They last best when planted in partial shade.

The Acanthus Family

As summer temperatures climb the acanthus family contributes more and more heavily to the showiness of perennial gardens. These long-flowering plants have rugged tolerance for poor soil, and often endure great drought. Their flowering season spans the long period from early summer till frost.

Shrimp plants (*Justicia brandegeana*) and Mexican honeysuckle (*Justicia spicigera*) are well-known subshrubby flowers of this group with bracted blooms of beige or orange. Hummingbird bush (*Anisacanthus wrightii*) bears never-ending crops of tiny orange-red flowers on a twiggy shrub covered in glossy green foliage. Mexican petunias (*Ruellia malacosperma* and *R. brittoniana*) are suckering spreaders with dark purple or white blossoms. 'Katy' is a valuable, tufted miniature *Ruellia*, useful as an edging plant in sun or shade. Persian shield (*Strobilanthes dyerianus*) earns a place in borders for its iridescent purple foliage.

Lantanas and Verbenas

Like the acanthus family, verbenas and their allies function as everblooming subjects to carry interest through the hot days of summer. With adequate moisture these spreaders offer an endless display of colorful bloom. Tall perennial verbenas such as *Verbena bonariensis* provide good middle-row subjects with wands of tiny, electric lavender blooms. Most other types are low spreaders that display best in foreground plantings or as small-scale groundcovers. *V. erecta* is a leafy variety with royal purple blooms.

Hybrids of the South American *V. erinoides* inherit its deeply incised foliage and long-lived perennial habits. A bewildering number of such verbenas in several colors is available from perennial dealers. These flowers are often offered as cultivars of *V. peruviana*, *V. canadensis*, or with other equally dubious appellations. The true *V. peruviana* has dark crimson, white-eyed blooms and a low, prostrate habit of growth. It makes a good perennial in its own right for well-drained sites or rockeries.

Lantanas are slightly woody relations of verbenas with everblooming flowers in bright colors, and poisonous, berrylike fruits. Several *Lantana camara* cultivars exhibit changing colors as the tiny blooms open and fade. This affords a particularly festive, multicolored appearance to these plants. For performance in heat and drought they are unexcelled.

Dwarf lantana selections and hybrids are particularly valuable, and often avoid or mitigate production of the undesirable berries. 'New Gold' is a trailing type that never makes seed and constantly covers itself in golden yellow blooms. Other choice dwarfs include fiery 'Dallas red' and purple/yellow combinations such as 'Christine' and 'Mista.'

Taller, shrubbier lantanas of value include the orange-flowered 'Radiation' and the pink and yellow 'Confetti.' *L. horrida* is a hardy wild type with orange-red blooms. For trailing over a rocky embankment or along the front of a border the lush, lavender *L. montevidensis* is an old favorite.

Ornamental Grasses

With the arrival of summer the ornamental grasses reach full development, and have much to offer gardens on limy ground. Once enlightened to their subtle beauties, a gardener's devotion to these rewarding perennials is assured, and obsession often follows closely behind. An endless range of leaf textures, colors, and forms assures variety enough for many garden settings. Although seemingly puritanical and lacking in bloom, grasses touch even the most jaded flower-lover's heart with the reassuring fruitfulness of their ripening seed heads waving in the breeze.

Little bluestem (*Schizachyrium scoparium*) is a choice prairie native with narrow, upright growth two to three feet high or less. Its leaves take on a striking blue-gray color in summer. In autumn both the feathery seed heads and the entire clump of leaves turn bright cinnamon-brown. Little bluestem thrives on all types of calcareous soils, and intensifies its steely color with summer drought.

Another showy silver-leaved grass is blue Lyme grass (*Elymus arenarius*). Although an inhabitant of shifting coastal sands in its natural haunts along the English shore, it thrives equally well on heavy, calcareous clays. Its underground stems run slowly so that the clumps expand into masses of broad, jumbled, blue-gray foliage.

Blue fescues (*Festuca ovina* 'Glauca') are popular dwarf grasses in temperate regions. They are frequently attempted in hot-summer climates, but suffer unless provided with partial shade.

Seep muhly (*Muhlenbergia reverchonii*) lacks the blue color of the fescue, but affords a fair imitation of its tufted, wiry texture and useful dwarf habit. This rugged grass is a fine choice for low edgings, and naturalizes on thin rocky ground. It forms dense, slowly expanding clumps which may be used to soften the appearance of rugged limestone boulders.

One of the most graceful and airy grasses is feather needlegrass (*Stipa tenuissima*). A native of Southwestern uplands, feather needlegrass displays threadlike foliage and glistening, silvery heads of seed. It tolerates drought, lime, and partial shade.

Also graceful and particularly suited to draping over hills or embankments is weeping lovegrass (*Eragrostis curvula*). This South African native was introduced originally as an improved perennial pasture grass for limy soil. Its destiny seems likely to take it into many gardens, for it is one of the most appealing and useful grasses for massing on difficult slopes.

Inland sea oats (*Chasmanthium latifolium*) thrives best in bona fide shade. Its feature attractions are oatlike seed heads. Inland sea oats prefers moist soils and is indifferent to lime. It reaches about two feet in height and rapidly spreads into a leafy clump.

Canada wild rye (*Elymus canadensis*) looks much like wheat when in fruit. It tolerates shade and provides attractive material for dried floral arrangements. Like wheat, Canada wild rye is a cool-season grower that ripens its seed in late spring.

The fountain grasses (*Pennisetum* spp.) also develop wheatlike seed heads, but have summer-growing habits and denser, tufted leaves. Rose fountain grass (*Pennisetum alopecuriodes*) is a particularly choice, hardy perennial with soft pink plumes. Also good is silver fountain grass (*P. villosum*), whose mature plumes glisten in afternoon sun.

P. setaceum is the common self-sowing fountain grass often planted as an annual on dry, limy soils. Its popular red-leafed selection, 'Cupreum,' is frost-tender, and must be perpetuated from year to year by saving cuttings over winter.

Japanese blood grass (*Imperata cylindrica* 'Rubra') affords a more cold-hardy perennial with reddish leaves. This semidwarf grass relishes heavy, calcareous clay soils, but resents extended drought. The red color is most intense while in active, vigorous growth, and appears especially fine with back lighting. Partial shade is good for this grass in warm regions.

Among the larger grasses pampas grass (*Cortaderia selloana*) has a loyal following, and thrives on limy soils. Bold, stiff foliage and beautiful autumn plumes earn it a favored position in many gardens. Female selections such as 'Compacta' make the most attractive seed heads. The male cultivar, 'Gold Band,' has interesting variegated leaves, but produces inferior, sparse-looking plumes. The newer 'Sun Stripe' combines the best of bold variegation and handsome feathery spikes.

Ravenna grass (*Erianthus ravennae*) reaches nearly the same robust proportions as pampas grass, but has somewhat wider foliage and greater tolerance to cold. Its feathery seed heads have a purplish cast.

The eulalia grasses (*Miscanthus* spp.) are also particularly easy-growing and ornamental. Most fall into a middle-size range that suits them perfectly for mixed plantings. Maiden grass (*Miscanthus sinensis* 'Gracillimus') scores highly for its grace, fine texture, bronzy autumn color, and feathery heads of seed. 'Purpurascens' has even more pronounced reddish autumn coloring.

Of several variegated *Miscanthus* cultivars, the horizontally striped 'Zebrinus' and the vertically striped 'Variegatus' are best known. 'Morning Light' is a fine-leaved selection, like a striped version of 'Gracillimus.' 'Cosmopolitan' produces unusually bold, wide leaves with telling silver variegations. All of these thrive on limy ground.

Another useful group of medium-sized grasses are the muhly grasses (*Muhlenbergia* spp.). These include several natives of the limy soils of the Southwest.

Lindheimer's muhly (*Muhlenbergia lindheimeri*) earns popularity in central Texas gardens for its showy, upright grayish autumn plumes and tall, reedy clumps of dull, blue-green foliage. Purple muhly (*M. rigida*) appears similar to this variety, but has dark purplish seed heads. Gulf muhly (*M. capillaris*) forms a two-foot tuft of fine, wispy foliage topped with airy, many-branched heads of seed.

The most spectacular of the muhly grasses is a species from the Arizona desert whose leafy, creeping stems give it a resemblance to the exotic weeping bamboo (*Otatea* spp.) of Mexico. This outstanding grass, *M. dumosa*, forms lush clumps of pendulous green foliage and endures cold, drought, heat, and lime.

Late Flowers

Sometime after mid-August the garden begins almost imperceptibly to augment the cast of flowering subjects which have carried it through the heat of summer. New seasonal perennials join in floral display for the first time in several months, and the garden's bloom increases in abundance and size with the arrival of fall rains and cool evening weather. Although varied colors remain in the fall garden, many autumn performers assume rich tones of purple and gold, and a great number are white.

Cape plumbago, or leadwort (*Plumbago capensis*) softens and cools summer gardens with its pale blue or white blooms and bright green, mounded foliage. A semihardy subshrub, plumbago offers an almost phloxlike appearance and thrives on poor soils through heat and drought. As fall approaches, its performance improves, and the plants visibly perk up in response to cooler weather. Cape plumbago is often one of the last perennials in bloom before frost silences the autumn display.

Its creeping relation, *Ceratostigma plumbaginoides*, also endures in heat, drought, and poor soils. This cobalt-blue perennial withstands much more cold, however, and naturally sheds its leaves in fall. Before doing so, its leathery foliage turns to an attractive russet. Miss Willmott's plumbago (*C. willmottianum*) resembles the creeping plumbago in flower and foliage, but assumes a more shrubby habit. It is fairly hardy and grows well on prepared, calcareous soils.

The truly heat-loving firebush (*Hamelia patens*) often achieves five feet in height and spread before autumn frosts cut it to the ground. Orange-red tubular blooms cover its leafy mass, and attract hummingbirds as they migrate southward late in the year. Like the *Ceratostigmas* these lush perennials turn bronze as temperatures cool.

Esperanza, or yellow bells (*Tecoma stans*), is another massive late-season bloomer. Its golden trumpets top six-foot piles of shiny green from midsummer to frost. Cigar flower (*Cuphea micropetala*) gets modestly tall, but usually waits until October before flowering. Its tubular, yellow-orange flowers appear in earnest from then until frost.

Late-season salvias such as the lavender-on-white Mexican bush sage (*Salvia leucantha*) and the pale yellow *S. madrensis* are other October bloomers that profit from frost-sheltered positions near a south-facing wall. The azure-flowered prairie native, *S. pitcheri*, also joins these in autumn display. 'Grandiflora' is a more compact, earlier blooming variety of this showy, hardy perennial.

False dragon's heads, or obedient plants (*Physostegia virginica* cvs.) flower from mid-August through September, and make large colonies on damp soil. 'Vivid' and 'Summer Snow' are popular cultivars with lavender and white flowers, respectively.

Autumn Bulbs

Many gardeners are surprised by the variety of late-blooming bulbs that appear with summer and autumn rains. Any time from July onward thunderstorms may awaken the resting buds of the magic lily (*Lycoris squamigera*). This fabulous pink-flowered amaryllid produces broad gray leaves during daffodil season, but waits until midsummer to send up its leafless flower stalks. These are topped with sparkling pink blooms highlighted with touches of electric blue. Although thoroughly cold-hardy, *L. squamigera* often fails to bloom south of Dallas unless planted under cool, shady conditions.

Other *Lycoris* species are also shade-loving, and make excellent subjects for gardens under deciduous trees. The orange-red fall "Guernsey lily" or "red spider lily" (*L. radiata*) and the creamy white *L. albiflora* are easy-growing, hardy, and successful even in the heavy shade of live oaks. These generally flower in mid-September. Old-fashioned garden strains of *L. radiata* are more robust and perform better on heavy clay than modern Japanese imports.

The semitender, yellow-flowered *L. traubii* and *L. aurea* are among the most spectacular of garden bulb flowers. They produce their stunningly golden fall blooms only in gardens protected from harsh frost.

The most prolific, reliable and valuable of the fall-flowering bulbs is the oxblood lily (*Rhodophiala bifida*). Each fall these small amaryllids paint swaths of crimson across the yards of older homes in central Texas. The curious long-necked, black-skinned bulbs of this flower flourish and multiply on the heaviest clay soils. Like the *Lycoris*, these South American bulbs make foliage during winter and thrive under deciduous trees.

Several rain lilies flower late in the year, particularly the white *Zephyranthes candida*. Its hybrids, 'Grandjax' (pink), 'Aquarius' (creamy yellow), and the golden *Z. citrina* are other good late-season bloomers.

Another favorite late bulb is the autumn daffodil (*Sternbergia lutea*), known to many gardeners as "yellow fall crocus" and thought by some to be the Biblical "lily of the field." Although it resembles a golden rain lily or crocus when in flower, *Sternbergia* is in fact a Mediterranean relation of *Narcissus* and produces dark green, grassy winter foliage. Like oxblood lily and *Lycoris radiata*, these bulbs do well on heavy calcareous clay soils and tolerate partial shade. Thomas Jefferson grew *Sternbergias* beneath the oaks at Monticello, and is often credited with introducing this flower to American gardens.

Other valuable autumn bulbs include the lavender-pink prairie onion (*Allium stellatum*) of the Great Plains and a little-known native of south-central Texas, the coconut lily (*Schoenocaulon drummondii*). Like the spring-flowering green lily (*S. texanum*), this bulb produces a tall, feathery wand of bloom. The fall-flowering species is creamy white in color, instead of pinkish-green, and smells distinctly and deliciously of fresh coconut. Its leaves remain green throughout the winter.

Chrysanthemums and Asters

Chrysanthemums (*Chrysanthemum* × *hortorum* cvs.) vie with asters and other late daisies to be recognized as queens of the autumn garden. Certainly the color range of the perennial chrysanthemum, with its rich bronzes, yellows, and coppers, seems especially in tune with the fall season. These highly fancied blooms have been selected and cultivated in the Orient for over two thousand years, and presently offer an outlandish array of cultivars.

Our garden mums descend from obscure, ancient hybrids between *Chrysanthemum indicum* and *C. morifolium*, two modest-flowered daisies of China. Over centuries of cultivation all of the various incurved, spider, spoon, pompom, and anemone-flowered mums have entered into gardens. These popular flowers accept lime, but respond dramatically to good care. Mums desire unfailing moisture, generous feeding, and timely pruning and disbudding if they are to give their best. Gardeners often avoid such tasks by annually securing chrysanthemums in fresh bud for use as seasonal bedding.

As perennials the old Korean hybrid strains (*C. coreanum*) and modern dwarf bedding varieties are generally successful. One way to obtain chrysanthemums suited to poor limy ground is by taking cuttings from nearby garden plantings, and this is the best way to secure mums of obvious longevity. In the garden these older types assume more lax,

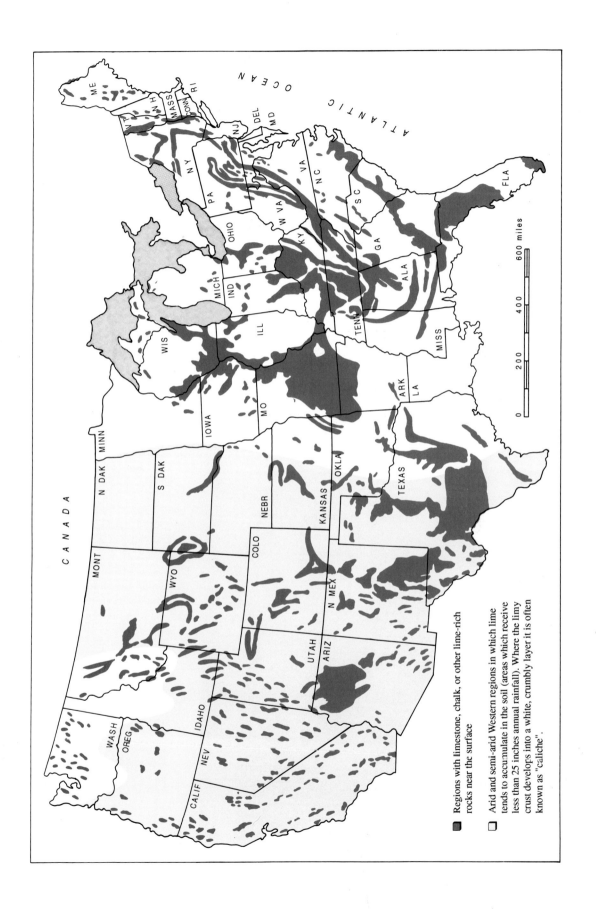

CANADA

ATLANTIC OCEAN

ME
N H
VT
MASS
CONN
RI
N Y
PA
NJ
DEL
MD
W VA
VA
N C
S C
OHIO
KY
TENN
GA
FLA
MICH
IND
ILL
ALA
MISS
ARK
LA
WIS
IOWA
MO
MINN
N DAK
S DAK
NEBR
KANSAS
OKLA
TEXAS
MONT
WYO
COLO
N MEX
IDAHO
UTAH
ARIZ
WASH
OREG
NEV
CALIF

600 miles
400
200
0

■ Regions with limestone, chalk, or other lime-rich rocks near the surface

□ Arid and semi-arid Western regions in which lime tends to accumulate in the soil (areas which receive less than 25 inches annual rainfall). Where the limy crust develops into a white, crumbly layer it is often known as "caliche".

Above. Yellow columbine (*Aquilegia hinckleyana*) and several other Southwestern species of *Aquilegia* have good tolerance to heat, drought, and lime.

Left. Large-flowered buttercup (*Ranunculus macranthus*) flowers early in the year and favors heavy, damp ground.

Above. Penstemon triflorus makes an early show of upright blooms that complement lime-loving annuals such as Texas bluebonnet (*Lupinus texensis*).

Right. Hybrid *spuria* irises offer delicate blends of color in their blooms and sport elegantly tapered swordlike evergreen foliage.

Above. The old-fashioned corn lily (*Gladiolus byzantinus*) thrives on heavy calcareous soils.

Left. *Narcissus tazetta* 'Grand Monarque' ('Grand Primo') offers a perennial spring show even in warm regions with heavy soils.

Above. Weeping Lovegrass (*Eragrostis curvula*) is especially suited to plantings on rugged banks or slopes. Its graceful, flowing lines belie a remarkably tough, drought-resistant constitution.

Right. Clockwise from top right: Verbena *hybrid,* Salvia penstemonoides, Dianthus × *"Querteri,"* Vernonia lindheimeri v. larsoni, Hibiscus syriacus *'Lady Stanley'*

Left. Double-flowered tawny daylily (*Hemerocallis fulva* 'Kwanso') was cherished in Japanese gardens nearly one thousand years ago. This robust perennial continues to merit cultivation today.

Below. Trailing lantana (*Lantana montevidensis*) offers an especially long-blooming perennial for warm regions.

Opposite. Salvia cv. 'Costa Rica Blue' mixes effectively with pink Tea roses 'Mamon Cochet' and 'Monsieur Tillier' (*far background*). Bronzy-leaved *Setcreasea* rambles underfoot.

Opposite. Late-blooming cigar flower (*Cuphea micropetala*) shows its curious tubular blooms to advantage against a backdrop of gray-leaved ceniza (*Leucophyllum frutescens* 'Compacta').

Above. Aromatic Aster (*Aster oblongifolius*) offers one of the best shows of the autumn-blooming "daisies" adapted to poor, dry soils.

Right. Fall spiderlily (*Lycoris radiata*) enjoys moist leafy soil and part shade. On heavy clays the old-fashioned Southern strains known popularly as "Guernsey Lilies" show greater vigor than more modern commercial imports.

Above. Purple coneflower (*Echinacea purpurea*) tirelessly yields large glowing pink and orange blossoms from late spring until frost. It relishes heavy, calcareous soil.

Left. Leatherleaf holly-grape (*Mahonia bealii*) enhances the winter scene with large trusses of blue berries and bronze-red foliage.

Above. Fine-textured dwarf yaupons (*Ilex vomitoria* 'Stokes') mass effectively in front of leafy, green Sandankwa viburnums (*Viburnum suspensum*) and tall, pink-flowered India-hawthorns (*Raphiolepis indica* 'Majestic Beauty'). .

Right. Possumhaw, or deciduous holly, (*Ilex decidua*) thrives even on dry, barren chalk and heavy alkaline clays.

Above. Cinnamon-scented late autumn blooms crown loquat, or Japanese plum, (*Eriobotrya japonica*), and later ripen to form tart, orange-yellow fruits following favorably mild winters.

Left. The brilliantly colored flowering quince (*Chaenomeles speciosa* 'Rubra') provides an unequaled display of bloom during its early spring season.

Above. Mature specimens of crape myrtle (*Lagerstroemia indica*) are spectacular in flower, and assume attractive bark and branching habits that are of value year round.

Right. Winter jasmine (*Jasminum nudiflorum*) dots its graceful, arching stems with small yellow blooms in late winter and early spring.

This outstanding single white mock-orange (*Philadelphus* × 'Natchez') is a U.S. National Arboretum introduction. Its late spring blooms nicely foil the golden flowers of creeping buttercup (*Ranunculus repens*).

Right. Cultivars of Chinese arborvitae (*Platycladus oroentalis*) thrive on limy ground. 'Green Cone' is a slow-growing selection that may reach ten feet in as many years.

Below. Compact Pfitzer juniper (*Juniperus × media* 'Pfitzeriana Compacta') offers a particularly pleasing dwarf habit of growth and soft green foliage that belie an extraordinarily rugged constitution.

Above. American smoketree (*Cotinus obovatus*) reveals its familial relation to the sumacs in its glowing display of organge-yellow fall foliage.

Left. Rusty blackhaw (*Viburnum rufidulum*) offers a first class display of purplish-red autumn foliage. Photo courtesy of San Antonio Botanical Center.

natural shapes than the artificially compact florist's varieties. A little extra care and feeding will be rewarded with larger, more lavish blooms.

Asters, or Michaelmas daisies, are American counterparts of the chrysanthemum, which compensate for their lack of breeding with added vigor and generosity of bloom. Like mums, the mostly violet-lavender asters have a tender and romantic association with autumn for many gardeners. Although several standard *Aster* cultivars dislike dry, limy soils and resent prolonged summer heat, a few species thrive.

Aromatic aster (*Aster oblongifolius*) rates highly among autumn perennials suited to limy ground. This bushy variety maintains a compact shape in the garden and slowly suckers to form two-foot-high clumps of gray-green, aromatic foliage. In September and October its mounds of rough-textured leaves disappear in splendid masses of lavender, yellow-centered daisies. Even with the most casual care, this aster performs mightily and accepts both heavy clays and shallow, chalky soils. Aromatic aster is a prairie native, and is the most commonly seen aster in limy-soil gardens. It is often confused with other garden varieties such as A. × *frikartii* by the nursery trade.

Meadow aster (*A. pratensis*) is a native prairie daisy with great vigor and wide soil tolerance. Its erect stems reach three to four feet in height and bear gracefully tapered, silky-textured leaves. Its autumn blooms approach pale azure in color, and are followed by glistening heads of seed. This aster spreads quickly to form large clumps.

Heath aster (*A. ericoides*) responds to extra moisture and a midsummer shearing by producing lush clouds of tiny white blooms. Texas aster (*A. texensis*) is a small-flowered, spray type daisy that performs admirably with a little extra shade and moisture. Its frothy masses of tender, blush lavender blooms reach three to four feet in height.

The moisture-loving sneezeweed (*Helenium autumnale*) is a lesser known fall daisy with small, cheerful flowers in tones or bicolors of yellow, orange, and coppery red. For dry sites golden-yellow autumn daisies include the aromatic Copper Canyon daisy (*Tagetes lemmonii*) and the shrubby, rock-loving golden-eye daisy (*Viguera dentata*). Both grow well even on thin, chalky soils.

Dry, limy ground also favors several of the modest, purple-flowered ironweeds (*Vernonia* spp.) and the showy gayfeathers (*Liatris* spp.), which offer their lavender blooms late in the year.

Blue mist flowers and bone sets (*Eupatorium* spp.) and goldenrods (*Solidago* spp.) are other choice, late-season perennials for calcareous ground.

Perennials for Showy Fruit

Barbados cherries (*Malphigia glabra*) offer an autumn show not only from their tiny, pink, orchidlike blooms, but also from crops of shining red berries. These perennial subshrubs resprout from their roots following freezes. The berries they produce are an important commercial source of vitamin C.

The perennial chili pequin pepper (*Capsicum annuum*) is even showier in fruit, and covers its mounded green shrublet with spicy berries that turn by stages from green to bright orange-red. In concert with the many berrying shrubs of autumn, these fruiting herbs help give the garden a sense of completeness as the year draws to a close. By taking advantage of a wide array of lime-tolerant perennials, gardens will be well on the way to achieving a measure of interest throughout the year and can continue to grow in beauty for seasons to come.

CHAPTER SIX

Hosts of Lime-tolerant Shrubs

As November frosts silence the last of the summer's perennial and annual blooms and signal the onset of winter, lime-loving woody plants assume center stage. Border plantings revel in the brilliant foliage of deciduous shrubs and trees, whose leaves confer color by the yard. Fruits and berries deepen in hue as they mature in the crisp weather of the season, and many shrubs provide colorful displays precisely at a time blessed with fine sunny days for exploration and enjoyment.

English gardeners on lime contend that autumn berries and foliage colors ripen better on limy grounds than upon acid lands. This may be so, for the gardens of limestone regions are endowed with a wide variety of colorful foliage and fruiting shrubs. Although popular flowering evergreens such as gardenias, azaleas and camellias generally fail on limy clay and chalky caliche soils, gardens need not suffer unduly by their absence. Many types of lime-tolerant shrubs remain to contribute bright flowers, colorful autumn fruits and foliage, lush evergreen leaves, or silhouettes of bare branches and strikingly textured bark.

Whatever their attributes and attractions, shrubs help to provide an essential framework to show off more temporary garden performers, and well-grown woody plants project a welcome sense of maturity to plantings. In particular, handsome shrub plantings contribute to the winter scene, on which they bestow much needed greenery and structure. It is during autumn and winter that the beauty of shrubs tells most, and varieties which perform at this time should be sought avidly.

Barberries and Their Allies

Especially reliable for limy grounds in difficult climates, and among the best shrubs for fall and winter interest are the barberries and their kin, the mahonias and nandinas. This family of hardy shrubs combines remarkably tough constitutions with attractive, often graceful foliage, lavish crops of edible berries, and colorful winter or early spring blooms. Evergreen types include choice plants for difficult, exposed northwest aspects and poorly drained soils, while both deciduous and evergreen varieties provide vibrant fall and winter foliage colors.

True barberries, as well as native Southwestern mahonias or *agaritas*, are generously endowed with prickles and thorns, and should be positioned safely away from traffic. They make formidable barrier hedges where such are needed. Red-leaved forms of the Japanese barberry (*Berberis thunbergii* 'Atropurpurea') are popular for this purpose, especially in the dwarf forms 'Crimson Pygmy' and 'Rose Glow.' These colorful shrubs maintain a beautiful burgundy color to their leaves that intensifies to crimson and scarlet in late autumn. They are briefly bare during the coldest part of the winter, leafing out promptly in early spring with an attractive crop of honey-scented yellow blooms.

Small, fragrant yellow flowers may be found on all barberries and mahonias, and their appearance in winter and early spring is especially welcome. Barberry blooms have a distinctive cup and saucer shape formed by the variously ranked petals, and their pleasant aroma carries far on the frosty winter air. The tiny sweet-scented blooms of the jonquil (*Narcissus jonquilla*), so common in older gardens of the South, display a similar form and breathe a nearly identical fragrance. One supposes they must attract the same winter-active pollinators.

Evergreen barberries such as *Berberis* × *mentorensis* and *B.* × *gladwynensis* 'William Penn' clothe themselves in hollylike leaves that take on bronze or crimson hues during the winter. These sturdy shrubs tolerate the worst extremes of drought, cold, and poor soil.

Even tougher are the native mahonias of Texas and the Southwest, which nurseries usually list among the barberries as *Berberis trifoliolata* and *B. swayseyi*. The gray-hued thorny leaves of these agaritas resist all the heat, drought, and cold that Texas weather-casters send upon them. These sturdy evergreens faithfully yield an abundance of golden spring blooms upon which follow orange-red berries, tartly flavored and suited for preserves or homemade wine.

Extreme thorniness, slow growth, and a reluctance to transplant from the wild discourage the cultivation of these shrubs. Yet, where browsing deer limit the selection of evergreens, these native mahonias offer prime choices. Leaves of agarita (*B. trifoliolata*) vary from a modest hollylike olive green in central Texas to wickedly spiny needles of silver-blue in many western forms, while the "Texas barberry" (*B. swayseyi*) may bear foliage with as few as five leaflets per leaf or cloak its stems in bristling feathery ferns of a dozen leaflets or more. *B. haematocarpa* and *B. fremontii* are Southwestern allies of Texas barberry with similar, but distinctively bluish leaves.

Differing in aspect from these red-fruited mahonias are the large group of "hollygrapes," so-called for their clusters of blue-black berries and hollylike leaflets. The Oregon grape (*Mahonia aquifolium*) and the closely-related creeping mahonia (*M. repens*) seem a bit out of their element in the hot gardens of Texas and the Southwest, as they derive from the cooler climates of the Rocky Mountains and Pacific Coast. Nevertheless, even in hot-summer regions they can make serviceable shrubs or groundcovers where given some shade and modestly well drained, well-prepared soil. In truly cold areas they provide some of the most dependable and tolerant of all evergreens.

More at home in warm climates is the Chinese leatherleaf mahonia (*M. bealii*). This gaunt, structural shrub can be disappointingly spindly in youth or if grown with too much sun. Its slowly suckering stems bear crowns of long compound leaves suggestive of holly ferns atop broomsticks! Yet with age and a generously shady position *M. bealii* matures into one of the most elegant shrubs in the garden, and its habit of flowering in December and ripening huge clusters of berries early in the new year wins admiration.

Leatherleaf mahonia puts up with waterlogged limy clays and exposed northern positions that would kill lesser plants. Sadly, its near relations, although even more beautiful, are mostly too tender (M. *lomarifolia*) or too acid-loving (M. *fortunei*) to perform well on lime. A popular European hybrid, 'Charity,' would be worth trying if it were made more available by American nurseries.

The thornless leaves and graceful habits of nandina, or "heavenly bamboo," obscure its close relationship to mahonia, although both share a similar suckering habit of growth. Instead of the holly-grape's yellow flowers and blue fruit, nandina bears panicles of small creamy white blooms which ripen to large clusters of shiny red berries.

As with its barberry cousins, the evergreen foliage of nandina assumes shades of bronze and scarlet when exposed to the winter sun. In this wonderful habit nandina far exceeds its relations, however, and it endows gardens on lime with an indispensable source of winter color. Moreover, these endearing shrubs possess the remarkable hardy constitutions common to the barberry family, and provide some of the toughest and most persistent evergreens in our gardens.

Old-fashioned seedlings of *Nandina domestica* set large clusters of colorful berries, and their wintertime leaves often turn a bronzy red as well. These ruggedly graceful plants are the easiest-growing of the nandinas and the most reliable on very chalky limestone soils, reaching three to five feet when allowed to grow to their natural height. As nandinas age they sometimes become leggy or top-heavy, requiring careful pick-pruning. By removing old stems down to the ground gardeners can encourage bushy growth to rise from the base, thus renewing even the most grizzled ancient specimens.

Alternatively, nandinas may be thinned to reveal a graceful silhouette, a common technique in oriental gardening. Special varieties of nandina are favored for bonsai and have been selected for their see-through qualities or strange narrow foliage. 'Royal Princess,' 'Filamentosa,' and 'San Gabriel' are some available types appropriate for large pots or special nooks on the rockery.

'Gulfstream' is a semidwarf nandina seldom in need of pruning, and it consistently develops striking reddish winter foliage color. Although it lacks the scarlet berries of the old-fashioned seedling nandinas, the compact leafy habit of 'Gulfstream' is attractive year-round and makes this shrub a fine choice for low, informal borders. 'Compacta' and 'Moonbay' are two other semidwarf nandinas useful where seedling *Nandina domestica* might become inappropriately large. They provide winter foliage with a yellowish tinge.

The peculiar dwarf nandinas, 'Nana Purpurea' and 'Firepower,' become even more brilliantly red than the larger forms, but do so on rounded shrublets whose spinachlike leaves form a colorfully jumbled garden salad. Summertime appearances of these dwarfs are less appealing than the more "natural" varieties of nandina, and, like many dwarf cultivars, they are more subject to leaf-yellowing and sunburn than their larger relations. Yet, if given shade from the afternoon sun and generous mulching, these varieties are remarkably easy to grow, and their brilliant winter coloring is unmatched. 'Harbor Dwarf' is quite distinct from these and resembles common *Nandina domestica* in leaf. It remains less than ten inches tall, spreading slowly as a groundcover.

Elaeagnus

The silverberry (*Elaeagnus* × *ebbengii*) provides a useful gray foil for the reddish nandinas and barberries, and bears small, sweetly fragrant blooms in the autumn months. Its broad leathery leaves are covered with tiny silvery dots that give the whole shrub a gray look. *E. pungens* 'Fruitlandii' is similar, but more rank-growing and slightly thorny.

Both types make especially tough, rugged evergreen shrubs, eventually reaching six feet or more in height. Variegated forms such as 'Sunset,' 'Gilt Edge,' and 'Maculata' are less vigorous and need well-prepared soil and shade from hot western sun to do their best.

Hollies

Hollies are often thought of as acid-loving shrubs unsuited to limy soils, and this is certainly true of varieties such as the American holly (*Ilex opaca*). Yet, gardens on calcareous soil nearly overflow with a wide variety of lime-tolerant *Ilex* cultivars, and this versatile group offers suitable plants for nearly any garden purpose. With their attractive glossy leaves and famous wintertime crops of berries, hollies provide an extraordinary range of ornamental shrubs and small trees.

Surprisingly, the bewildering variety of *Ilex* selections in modern gardens derives from only a few wild species. Through the diligence of plant breeders and horticulturists these have been selected to yield a wide array of lime-tolerant varieties. Thus, although it is probably true that most hollies dislike lime, gardeners enjoy a generous complement of what lime-tolerant hollies have to offer.

The Chinese horned holly (*Ilex cornuta*) is an evergreen that grows on limy hillsides lying along the Yangtse River as far west as the Chinese province of Hupeh. This species has had a long successful history in gardens on lime, and its spiny, glossy green leaves and large, dull red berries provide a familiar winter attraction.

Chinese holly leaves are roughly quadrangular in shape and somewhat suggestive of flying bats in outline, but they provide a passably similar appearance to the familiar English holly (*I. aquifolium*) popular for Christmas greenery. Introduced to European gardens by Robert Fortune in 1846, *I. cornuta* was offered by American nurserymen prior to the Civil War and still is planted today where its very thorny leaves and large size (ten to fifteen feet) present no objection.

Accepted gardening wisdom proclaims that berry-producing female hollies require a pollinator and set fruit most abundantly when provided with a nearby male. Yet, if one judges by the many berries born on isolated female specimens, most Chinese hollies are self-fruitful. These prolific shrubs provide a respectable show of berries even as virgins!

About 1895, a discovery from the Westview Cemetery in Atlanta, Georgia was introduced as 'Burford' in honor of the cemetery's superintendent, T. W. Burford. This nearly thornless type quickly became a garden favorite on calcareous soils. With its dense growth, attractive clusters of berries, and hardy constitution, 'Burford' remains a fine variety, and retains popularity as a hedge or specimen evergreen, wherever its natural height of six to ten feet may be indulged.

More popular today are lower growing selections such as 'Dwarf Burford,' whose one-pointed leaves resemble those of its larger namesake. 'Dwarf Burford' usually serves as a hedging shrub, where its glossy green foliage and three- to five-foot boxy growth can show to advantage. Better than this and nearly as dwarf is 'Needlepoint' (also known as 'Delcambre'). The self-branching habit of this variety helps it stay well-furnished to the ground, and its large crops of red berries stand out boldly from rich green, erect branches covered with willowy one-spined leaves.

A Chinese holly with the typical thorny leaves of the species is the viciously spiny 'Rotunda.' This globe-shaped dwarf reaches two or three feet and is a popular choice for industrial plantings. Curiously, although described as sterile when introduced in 1944, recent propagations offered in nurseries under this name often bear fruit. Perhaps this old cultivar, originally a barren child, has finally matured. 'Dazzler' is a similar thorny fruit-bearer that grows to three or five feet. It has a more open growth habit better suited to displaying its colorful berries.

Less strong-growing selections of *I. cornuta* often show chlorosis on alkaline soils and this seems to be aggravated by hot, sunny exposures. Varieties such as 'Berries Jubilee' and the fruitless dwarf 'Carissa' give their best performances when provided with some shade from a building or overhanging tree. Without such shelter, these otherwise choice evergreens may degenerate into scorched masses of unattractive yellow leaves.

I. cornuta has been crossed with several other hollies, and a number of these hybrids tolerate lime. 'Nellie R. Stevens' is a strong-growing female selection that derives from such a union with the English holly (*I. aquifolium*). Although gloriously beautiful and tolerant to a variety of soils in its temperate European homeland, English holly perishes quickly in hot-climate gardens on lime. This also is the usual fate of Wilson holly (*Ilex × altaclarensis* 'Wilsoni'), a hybrid between English holly and a holly from the Canary Islands, *I. perado* v. *platyphylla*.

In contrast, 'Nellie R. Stevens' endures in torrid summer heat and inherits great beauty from both its parents. This selection ranks among the finest of evergreens for gardens on lime. Its dark green leafy branches and substantial clusters of crimson berries recommend it for traditional Christmas greenery, as well as a for use as a stunning garden focal point. 'Nellie R. Stevens' grows slowly into an upright bush of ten feet or more and makes a fine choice for a tall background hedge, or a beautiful subject to shear as a formal pyramid. It succeeds in both sun and shade.

Recent hybrid introductions such as 'China Boy,' 'China Girl,' and the so-called "blue hollies" (*I. × meserveae*) have received much praise for their outstanding cold-hardiness and beauty and deserve consideration in many colder regions. It remains questionable if these hollies will prove well suited to warm-climate gardens, however, although they may win a place as north wall shrubs. Other novel hollies such as the hybrids of the oriental *I. latifolia* are unlikely to have much tolerance for lime.

The shade-loving American holly (*I. opaca*) is a notorious lime-hater and generally fails on chalk or caliche soils. Yet, a few of its more vigorous crosses will succeed on calcareous clay, if the site chosen isn't brutally sunny or drought-prone. 'Savannah' is an old selection originally discovered and propagated by W. H. Robertson, Commissioner of Parks in Savannah, Georgia. Although this variety was thought for many years to be an *I. opaca* cultivar, nurseries have recently determined otherwise and now list 'Savannah' as a form of *I. × attenuata*, a natural hybrid between American holly and Dahoon holly (*I. cassine*).

This extra measure of hybrid vigor inherited by 'Savannah' helps it to grow faster and tolerate limy soil conditions better than pure *I. opaca* cultivars. 'Savannah' makes a good choice for a small evergreen tree, which may mature to fifteen to twenty feet. It has the fine red berries, beautiful white bark, and light green spiny leaves typical of American hollies.

Another selection of *I. × attenuata* adaptable to limy clay is 'Foster' holly, which makes a slow-growing dark green spiny pyramid. Although attractive, hardy, and long-lived, this variety sulks in high summer heat, hardly growing at all during the long, hot part of the year. Nevertheless, 'Foster' holly may be grown in warmer regions if planted against cool north foundations or in the shade of trees. Female selections are especially colorful berry producers.

Yaupon (*Ilex vomitoria*) presents such a contrast to these spiny-leaved hollies that many fail to recognize the relationship. With its small, crenate leaves and rugged gnarled trunks this native evergreen suggests ancient oak or oriental bonsai rather than Christmas greenery. But holly it is, and a fantastically beautiful shrub by any measure. The female yaupon bears the glossiest and showiest of all holly berries, festooning itself each winter with hundreds of crimson pearls.

Although naturally a companion of pines and magnolias that grow on sandy acidic soils of the Southeast, yaupons also range westward into the central Texas Hill Country, where they miraculously ascend the limestone hills to grow amongst oaks and junipers. Thanks to this remarkable adaptability, gardeners on lime enjoy this fine shrub as a common and dependable friend, well-suited for service as a basic component of the landscape—from Florida to California.

Nurseries offer yaupons in a variety of selections fitting for various garden positions, and these versatile shrubs provide a favorite choice for shearing and training into formal shapes. Both male and female trees are worth having, the former for their dense evergreen foliage, and the latter for their beautiful berries, which, like the Chinese holly, seem to arrive with or without a nearby pollinator.

For crimson winter berries and rustic architectural form the female yaupon provides a classic choice. Large, ruggedly-branched trees may be identified and purchased while in fruit, providing a favored means to bring the grace of old age into a new garden. Smaller plants may be had in several named red-fruited selections such as 'Pride of Houston' or 'Jewel,' and these also develop great character after a few years growth. Of particular merit is the yellow-fruited 'Saratoga Gold,' whose translucent golden berries place it high on any list of yellow-fruited evergreens.

Novel and desirable, too, is the weeping yaupon, which sports downswept branches cloaked with tiny leaves. These tall, sparse evergreens are popular in nurseries and are offered in both male and female selections. A backdrop of sunny limestone or stucco wall serves admirably to help set off their delicate traceries of twigs and berries.

An unusual yaupon with an upright habit is 'Will Fleming,' a selection from the Houston nurseryman of the same name. This variety grows as a dark green vertical column, much like Italian cypress, and seems a fine choice for formal plantings. Older specimens begin to "fall out," however, so as the trees grow they should be firmly staked and tied to preserve their neatly fastigate appearance.

Gardens on lime make frequent use of several dwarf varieties of yaupon for neat low hedges and shrubberies or for massed cover over large areas. The enormous popularity of these shrubs derives from their formal, boxwoodlike appearance and their remarkable tolerance to neglect, heat, and drought. Proven varieties of dwarf yaupon provide refined, formal evergreens for use in garden beds where tight, compacted soils would support little else.

Over the years several different dwarf yaupons have been named and selected whose similar appearances confuse even experienced gardeners. 'Nana' (three to four feet high) is one of the oldest of these, and has large, bright green leaves and bears occasional crops of berries. Although popular for many years, it has been mostly replaced in nurseries with even smaller selections. The dwarf yaupon most likely to be encountered today is 'Stokes,' a female variety with dark green foliage and a dense rounded form two or three feet tall at maturity. 'Shillings' is similar, but more fine-textured and less common in the trade. All of these varieties have long records of success on limestone soils, and all make excellent choices for low-maintenance, semiformal plantings, where the natural globe shape of these evergreens can show to advantage.

In recent years nurseries have offered several new dwarf yaupons (among them 'Straughan's' and 'Gulftide') with especially refined, attractive foliage, and with leaves soft and feathery to the touch. As beautiful as these selections may be, they apparently lack the hardy constitutions of older varieties and frequently perish on the difficult soils that develop over limestone and chalk. Any added measure of beauty in these new selections hardly seems like fair recompense for their loss in vigor.

Even less hollylike than these yaupons, yet a true holly lovely in its own right, is the deciduous yaupon or possumhaw (*Ilex decidua*). This native shrub may be seen growing wild in rocky pastures and along fencerows during the winter months. In such situations it attracts the attention of passing motorists with hundreds of scarlet and crimson berries displayed along bare white branches. In this case the deciduous habits of the possumhaw confer an advantage over its evergreen brethren, making the brilliant berries even more conspicuous. Moreover, this thrifty holly is able to thrive on dry rocky sites with thin soils that would spell death to many of its evergreen cousins.

Although nurseries offer berry-producing selections of *I. decidua* in small sizes, few gardeners purchase such unpromising-looking plants. Like many fruit-bearers, the female possumhaw only begins to produce berries in earnest when it reaches six feet or more in height. *Ilex decidua* remains shamefully uncommon in gardens, and large fruit-bearing specimens are treasured by those lucky enough to have them.

Firethorns and Cotoneasters

Many gardens on limy ground are brightened by the abundant colorful berries of the firethorns (*Pyracantha* cvs.). These members of the rose family come from limestone hillsides in southern Europe, Asia Minor, and parts of China. Like roses, *Pyracanthas* have scrambling habits of growth and plenty of thorns. Clouds of tiny white spring blooms annually transform into enormous clusters of crimson autumn fruits and entice gardeners to plant these vigorous evergreens.

Pyracanthas are popular for plantings on dry rocky sites, for use as barrier hedges along fencelines, or, classically, as espaliers along sunny walls. To espalier a *Pyracantha*, gardeners fasten the flexible young stems of the shrub to a wall or support and prune them into a flattened pattern or design, either geometrical or naturalistic. This training not only develops a dramatic form for the garden, but helps the *Pyracantha* come into flower and fruit more profusely and effectively.

Pyracantha fortuneana 'Graberi' and *P. koidzumii* 'Victory' are popular large-growing selections with lavish clusters of red to orange-red fruit. 'Mohave' is a U.S. National Arboretum hybrid that is also good and reportedly disease resistant. All three types make excellent choices for espaliers.

Orange-berried pyracantha (*P. coccinea* 'Lalandei'), the upright-growing 'Teton,' and many dwarf cultivars are at their best in cool regions and may set little fruit in warm climates. Prostrate firethorns such as 'Walderi' and *P. koidzumii* 'Santa Cruz' perform well in hot-summer areas, however, and mature to colorful bushes three or four feet tall and up to ten feet across.

In many areas *Pyracanthas* suffer attacks of lace bug and this pest can quickly discolor the attractive dark green foliage a sickly yellow. Where close-up appearance is important these sucking insects may be controlled by spraying the undersides of the leaves with systemic insecticides or insecticidal soaps. A better plan for gardeners with little time to spend combating insects, however, is to enjoy these shrubs in more distant cor-

ners of the garden. Minor leaf spotting will not threaten the beauty of the overall plantings in such positions, and the *Pyracantha*'s brilliant red berries can continue to add to
the garden scene.

Very similar to the pyracanthas in flower, fruit, and leaf, but lacking the characteristic thorns are the *Cotoneasters* (pronounced ko-toh-nee-*ass*-ter, not "cotton-
Easter"). These are especially valuable shrubs for dryland gardens over limestone or
chalk, and many make useful bank covers on rugged slopes. An enormous array of
cotoneaster varieties is utilized in cold-climate gardens, and several adapt to warm
regions as well. In fruit and foliage they impart a graceful, refined quality to garden
plantings.

A cotoneaster that especially thrives on limestone and limy clay is the red clusterberry or Parney cotoneaster (*Cotoneaster lacteus*), a native of rugged, chalky mountains
in western China. This tough, adaptable, and uniquely beautiful shrub reaches four to
five feet in height and width. Its graceful arching branches hang with clusters of scarlet
fruit and heavily veined dark green leaves, felted white on their undersides.

The silver-leaved *C. buxifolius*, known popularly as the gray cotoneaster, also succeeds on calcareous soils. Its tiny gray-felted leaves make a lovely foil for its red berries,
and this can be especially striking in autumn when this partially deciduous variety adds
a measure of orange-red foliage to the color display. Nurseries offer desirable compact selections of gray cotoneaster under various trade names.

Another partially to wholly deciduous type, the rock cotoneaster (*C. horizontalis*),
provides even more reliable scarlet fall foliage, and has large red berries to contrast with
its shiny green, rounded leaves. Both rock and gray cotoneasters have feathery spreading
branches that associate well with informal or naturalistic plantings around boulders or
rustic stone walls.

Photinias, Cherry Laurels, and Loquats

The toyon or Chinese photinia (*Photinia serrulata*) is a berry-producing evergreen
from the dry mountainsides of western China that, like these other members of the rose
family, thrives on limestone soils. With four- to six-inch long leathery jagged-edged
leaves and big flat clusters of orange-red fruits, Chinese photinias present an impressive
winter appearance. This can be especially apparent with mature specimens, for old toyon
trees often achieve fifteen to twenty feet in height and spread. Large plates of white
spring bloom and handsomely burnished new growth make the toyon a memorable specimen evergreen or noble background hedge.

Although commonly offered by nurseries at the turn of the century, Chinese photinia has since been supplanted in horticultural trade by its more compact, faster-growing
offspring, *P. × fraseri*. This is unfortunate for gardeners on lime, for although the toyon
is slower growing and less easily envisioned in its mature form in the landscape, it is much
better adapted to drought-prone limestone soil than its relatives.

Gardeners frustrated by the absence of Chinese photinias at their local nursery may
profit by a winter stroll through neighborhood woodlands. This evergreen often naturalizes in the vicinity of older gardens and young bird-planted seedlings may be carefully
collected and transplanted to the garden.

Fraser photinia is, of course, a first-class shrub in its own right, and has become tremendously popular. This hybrid between the toyon and the Japanese *Photinia glabra*
seems to be constantly putting out a fresh flush of reddish new leaves, a trait that has

earned it the nickname "red-tip." Fraser photinia rarely flowers and sets little fruit, but it tirelessly dresses itself in red leaves, especially during fall and early spring.

This colorful habit and the photinia's dense, leafy growth make it a favorite choice for tall hedges and screens, in which position hundreds of thousands of these shrubs are planted annually. In fact, so ubiquitous are Fraser photinias that gardeners may long for the relief of plain green leaves instead of the monotonous bronzy red of these six- to ten-foot evergreens. This is especially true when garden color schemes are being planned, for the harsh purple-red of photinia leaves can be difficult to blend with bright flower colors.

Nevertheless, on deeper calcareous clay soils Fraser photinia thrives and makes itself indispensible by its hardiness and vigor. On chalkier, hotter soils over lime rock or caliche, these evergreens may develop chlorosis, presenting a horrible contrast of sickly yellowing foliage with reddish new growth. Gardeners on such sites can apply epsom salts or chelated iron supplements and provide cooling acidic mulches of pine bark to help reduce this leaf yellowing. Still better in most cases would be the substitution of a toyon or other lime-tolerant evergreen instead of the overused *Photinia × fraseri*.

Very similar to photinias, but lacking their bronzy new leaves are the cherry laurels (*Prunus caroliniana*). These fast-growing evergreens are natives of deep sandy soils in the Southern states and make very desirable lush green bushes or small trees. Although somewhat tolerant to alkalinity, cherry laurels often develop chlorosis on heavy calcareous clays. In this case it seems that tight, compacted soil and seasonal drought challenge the shrub's survival, rather than simple chemistry alone.

Hopeful gardeners on limestone and alkaline clay continue to plant these beautiful evergreens in spite of the mixed performances they usually give in these regions. Although individual plants succeed in certain fortunate positions, cherry laurels are generally unreliable for use as hedges or screens over chalk or limy clay. Borers, fireblight, and cotton root rot are frequent instruments of demise, and such plagues are difficult or impossible to combat. Extra care in preparing well-drained beds with generous mulches may be tried to help encourage survival. The European cherry laurels or skeps (*Prunus laurocerasus*), although occasionally planted on lime, also seem rather poorly adapted. They persist in favorably shady positions as curious large-leaved evergreen bushes.

Like the toyon, the Japanese plum or loquat (*Eriobotrya japonica*) is a lime-loving oriental evergreen of the rose family. With its ten- to twelve-inch-long leaves this specimen shrub or small tree presents a decidedly tropical appearance. Its cinnamon-scented December blooms and tart, edible, guava-shaped fruits convey a convincing statement of subtropical abundance.

Loquats provide adaptable, fast-growing tall screens or hedges, and their exotic demeanor makes them favorite subjects near swimming pools. North of central Texas, however, winter cold frequently intervenes to destroy the gardener's attempted illusion of tropical serenity, and usually decimates fruit production. Although selected fruiting types are available from some nurseries they are of questionable value. In most areas these big shrubs require sheltered positions simply to survive periodic hard freezes, let alone bear fruit.

Even in protected sites loquats are likely to suffer occasional freeze injury, as well as damage from drought, fireblight, boring insects, and sap-sucking birds. All these stresses combine to shorten the life span of these evergreens. Veteran trees often experience partial die-back and may need hard pruning to stimulate vigorous new growth. In spite of these difficulties, loquats are rewarding large evergreens for gardens on lime, and their enchanting fragrance wafting on the winter air cannot easily be re-placed.

India-hawthorns and Kin

The Chinese bronze loquat (*Eriobotrya deflexa*) is even less hardy than *E. japonica*, but its unique hybrid 'Coppertone' is fairly cold-tolerant and makes an interesting sub-ject for gardens with reasonable shelter from winter blasts. The lush evergreen foliage of this variety emerges with attractive coppery tints more easily blended in the garden than the harsh red of Fraser photinia leaves. 'Coppertone' presents an unusual bold tex-ture in plantings and its habit of growing twice as wide as it is tall is remarkable for such a large-leaved evergreen.

There is much uncertainty as to the exact parentage of this cultivar, and both the Japanese loquat and Fraser photinia have been suggested as possible progenitors. But with 'Coppertone's' spreading growth and small, pale pink spring flowers it seems more likely that an India-hawthorn was involved, and in form and general adaptability this shrub closely resembles the largest-leaved India-hawthorns.

In most gardens on lime 'Coppertone' grows slowly, performing best in well-prepared, thoroughly mulched beds with an exposure sheltered from extreme heat or cold north winds. In exchange for this coddling 'Coppertone' offers a nearly ideal dwarf stat-ure, eventually reaching three or four feet tall and four to six feet wide. Due to lack of vigor, however, in poorly drained or droughty soils these shrubs may develop severe chlo-rosis.

Sometimes this deficiency comes through no fault of the gardener, but results from poor production techniques at the nursery. Weak-growing shrubs such as 'Coppertone' are frequently affected by root girdling, a malady that ensues when young cuttings remain too long in small pots. Root systems of such plants eventually encircle and choke them-selves. In gardens root-girdled plants develop persistent chlorosis and fail to respond to attempts at treatment. Careful inspections of root systems before buying at the nursery provide the only practical defense against this problem, for there is no cure other than to discard and replace affected plants.

Other common victims of root-girdling are the India-hawthorns (*Raphiolepis indica* cvs.). These favorites are among the most impressively beautiful shrubs for gardens on calcareous soil. *Raphiolepis* are hardy and tolerant of extremes of climate; they maintain compact, often dwarf habits of growth with minimum pruning and attention; and they annually smother themselves in clouds of small pink or white springtime flowers.

If mulches of leaves, bark or gravel are maintained to help cool their root zones, India-hawthorns grow easily in prepared limestone or clay soils. These evergreens are bothered by few insects or diseases and need little care once established. They do, how-ever, require protection from browsing deer, who are fond of these and many other shrubs of the rose family.

Unfortunately, brutal winter freezes and erratic spring weather often play havoc on the flowering of *Raphiolepis*, freezing off flowerbuds before they can open, and abbrevi-ating the blooming season with unseasonable warm weather. After spring bloom, India-hawthorns spend the remainder of the year as quiet mounds of glossy evergreen leaves, modestly dressed in autumn with a few dark blue berries.

Sometimes an unusually long cool spring will serendipitously follow a moderate winter. Then old shrubs whose evergreen branches have flowered only sparsely through several seasons will burst into glorious bloom and remain in spring dress for six weeks or more. Such performances are no meager reward to receive from plants that otherwise ask very little. For these occasional springtime glories, and for tireless service as compact evergreens for hedges, India-hawthorns merit their status as favorite shrubs.

Many of the most popular *Raphiolepis* cultivars are dwarf varieties, and gardeners understandably desire these selections for use in front of low windows along foundations or in contrast to taller shrubbery. In practice, however, dwarfness may also mean weaker growth more susceptible to leaf-spotting fungi and chlorosis. In many garden situations standard varieties of India-hawthorn can be kept adequately small (three to four feet) and will prove more vigorous and easy to grow.

Choosing among the legion of *Raphiolepis* cultivars can be difficult, for varieties are often sold under duplicate names by nurseries attempting to avoid conflicts over trademark rights. Of the smaller types 'Ballerina' is especially fine, with dark pink double blooms and glossy bronze-tinted leaves. It matures to two feet in height and is among the healthier dwarfs. The pale-flowered semidwarf 'Elizabeth' is resistant to leaf spot and a good choice under overhead irrigation. 'Clara' ('Snow White') develops an outstanding dome shape to three feet and has single white blooms.

Of the large to medium growers 'Jack Evans' offers a fine dark pink with complementary bronzy foliage. It resembles a slightly larger version of 'Ballerina.' 'Pink Lady' and the upright-growing 'Delacouri' provide abundant medium-pink flowers on vigorous shrubs. The unusual white-flowered R. *umbellata* 'Minor' displays deep glossy green foliage and a compact upright habit. 'Majestic Beauty' is an especially robust, large-leaved type that grows six to ten feet tall and may be trained as a small tree. It blooms and performs reliably even on difficult sites.

Spirea, Quince, and Flowering Almond

Besides these valuable evergreens a number of spring-blooming deciduous shrubs of the rose family adapt to calcareous soils. Preeminent among these is the bridal wreath (*Spirea prunifolia*), commonly grown in its double form, 'Plena.' This is an ancient oriental garden plant unique among spireas in its tolerance to heat and humidity. Although gardeners in cold climates cultivate many plants in this group, only this Chinese cultivar regularly performs well enough in warm regions to warrant common planting.

Early residents on the bleak prairies learned to treasure bridal wreath for its lavish spring blooms, which romantic tradition holds were used as decoration at pioneer weddings. Older gardeners sentimentally recall bygone springs when the graceful swirling branches of these three- to four-foot shrubs enveloped themselves in pristine whiteness, painting drifts of floral snow over the landscape.

Spireas provide more garden interest over the year than most spring-flowering shrubs. After blooming, bridal wreaths cloak themselves in healthy gray-green, plumlike leaves for the summer. These turn deep shades of orange and russet before dropping in late fall.

Another ancient double-flowered shrub of the orient is the flowering almond (*Prunus triloba* 'Multiplex'), and this hardy native of Korea and north China has proven a dependable performer in many gardens on lime. Its light pink blooms line gracefully branched three- or four-foot stems in late winter or early spring, and appear sporadically over the growing season as well. In colder regions it sometimes is caught in bloom by a late fall of snow or ice, offering an enchanting winter scene.

Flowering almonds may develop chlorosis on light chalky soils or in too-sunny positions, especially during the hottest parts of the summer. Yet, if provided with shade from the west and a modest depth of earth, they show little objection to limestone or limy clay. As with many of the garden plants of China, the double-flowering almond was introduced to the West by Robert Fortune during the mid-nineteenth century.

Flowering quince (*Chaenomeles speciosa*) brings in the new year with a display of floral fireworks equaled by few shrubs. As soon as the first mild spells of weather in January or February permit, these three- to four-foot twiggy bushes begin their show of luminous red blooms along bare thorny branches. The quince's warmly colorful early season performance and its capacity to survive neglect have earned the affection of several generations of gardeners on lime, many of whom know these oriental shrubs as "japonicas."

Such spectacular displays of early flowers tempt many to plant flowering quinces, despite a long unattractive season after bloom. Like the double-flowered almond, *Chaenomeles* cultivars are likely to show chlorosis in the heat of summer. This seems to be a constitutional response to extreme temperature rather than an objection to alkaline soil, and careful siting in positions sheltered from the west sun can help forestall or minimize such problems.

Of the many varieties of flowering quince in cultivation only a few seem to have been tried on lime, and there is room to experiment with these hardy, easily grown shrubs. 'Rubra' is the large scarlet-flowered cultivar often seen in older plantings, and commonly preferred over the dwarf 'Texas Scarlet' for its stronger growth and more generous bloom. White, pink, and varicolored types are also available, although seldom planted. A cultivar with strange twisted branches, 'Contorta' merits consideration for its curious habit of growth, as this can add interest to the garden year-round.

Forsythia and Jasmine

In cool, temperate regions *Forsythia* cultivars provide favored companions for the quinces, offering brilliant yellow, early spring blooms along graceful sprawling branches. In warmer areas as well, these shrubs often are planted and may be modestly successful when well sited. Yet, even with generous care these rangy bushes can become scorched eyesores during the hot summer months and prove impractically large to hide behind other plantings. Cotton root rot often mercifully intervenes to end a forsythia's career, if a disappointed gardener has not already removed it.

This is, perhaps, just as well, for several of the forsythia's relatives can provide useful substitutes. Many older plantings include veteran bushes of the winter jasmine (*Jasminum nudiflorum*). This gracefully arching shrub lines its bare branches with small, unscented yellow blooms that appear over a long winter season. These provide a favorite source of cut branches to bring into the house, where their cheerful yellow blossoms can brighten sagging winter spirits. Like nearly all true jasmines, *J. nudiflorum* thrives on chalky limestone soils and has great resistance to drought. Its cascading growth habit makes it a prime choice for planting on steep rocky hillsides or embankments.

From Austin southward the leafy evergreen primrose jasmine (*J. mesneyi*) offers an even larger alternative and dresses itself with lemon yellow semidouble blooms over the same late winter season. Although subject to periodic damage from hard freezes, these rank-growing shrubs are remarkably tough and hardy. They are especially effective for difficult rocky sites where their long branches can be allowed to droop and sprawl.

More practical for most gardens, however, is the Italian jasmine (*J. humile*). This evergreen variety reaches four to five feet in height and spread. It has a similar form and texture to the winter jasmine, but bears its clusters of yellow blooms during the summer. Because it is less aggressive and more cold-hardy than *J. mesneyi* this variety fits more readily into most garden designs. It is an easily grown, colorful evergreen with a graceful, refined appearance year-round.

Spring Herald and Privet

Like *Forsythia* and *Jasminum*, spring herald (*Forestiera pubescens*) belongs to the lime-loving olive family and covers its downswept branches with yellow, early spring blooms. These are modest in comparison to those of its showy relations, but are a pleasant feature of spring in limestone regions. *Forestiera* varieties occur separately as male and female shrubs, and the latter bear black olivelike fruits in autumn. The males sport the showier blooms, which consist of tiny bundles of red-tipped golden stamens.

After flowering, these shrubs transform into cascading mounds of small, rounded gray-green leaves that turn clear yellow in autumn. They are well-suited for plantings at the top of chalky banks where their distinctive weeping growth can show to advantage. The desert olive (*Forestiera neomexicana*) is an upright-growing type popular as a hedge or specimen in colder areas.

Privets (*Ligustrum* spp.) are oriental counterparts of *Forestiera*, and include many of the workhorses of gardens on lime. Although most produce creamy white blooms attractive to butterflies, these late spring flowers are rather ill-scented, and gardens usually include *Ligustrum* cultivars strictly for utilitarian purposes as hedges or screens. The old-fashioned hedging privets (*Ligustrum sinense*, *L. amurense*, *L. ovalifolium* and *L. vulgare*) are uncommonly planted today, although they were important in early gardens and often persist or naturalize around older plantings. Frighteningly fast growth and an inclination to proliferate by self-sown seed make these varieties too aggressive for general use unless one can muster the opulent labor needed to shear and maintain them.

The variegated form of the Chinese privet (*L. sinense* 'Variegata') deserves a place in modern plantings, however, for its cream-colored leaves and soft-textured, billowing form. It makes a lovely, easily grown accent, eventually reaching four to five feet or more. Variegated privet is an especially appropriate choice for plantings in front of red brick walls, and ranks among the hardier and more sun-tolerant variegated shrubs.

Also valuable is the golden-foliaged Vicary privet (*L.* × *vicaryi*). This tardily deciduous shrub makes a dense, leafy hedge or specimen and is one of the best of all golden-leaved plants for hot, sunny exposures on alkaline land. Admittedly, plants variegated in yellow shades can be difficult to incorporate into planting designs. If poorly placed, gold-leaved plants may even suggest to the viewer that they have developed chlorosis and are desperately in need of care. Yet, when contrasted effectively with rich green or gray foliage, plants such as Vicary privet can provide bright, glowing focal points in the garden.

Another fairly sun-tolerant variegation belongs to the golden wax-leaf (*L. japonicum* 'Aureum'). The gold-margined leaves of this variety are not as showy as those of the wholly yellow-tinted Vicary privet, but the shrub is more evergreen and makes a stronger, hardier plant than the silver-leaved forms of *L. japonicum*.

Wax-leaf ligustrums (*L. japonicum* 'Texanum') have been greatly maligned by some gardeners for a supposed coarseness and lack of character. In actuality this probably reflects a general disgust at the tremendous overuse of these plants as suburban hedge material rather than any real deficiency. The virtues of *L. japonicum* are numerous, and for gardens on calcareous soils they provide thrifty, easy-growing evergreens with exceptionally glossy foliage and attractive rounded forms.

These six- to ten-foot shrubs are often more interesting when trained as small trees so that their light-colored, bony branches are revealed and can contrast against their dark green foliage. Where wax-leaf ligustrum is needed especially for use as hedge material the graceful variety 'Recurvifolium' is superior, as its undulate leaves and self-branching habit allow it to fill in more densely. It is slightly less cold-hardy than the common form, however.

Japanese ligustrums (*L. lucidum*) are especially well adapted to lime and succeed even on dry chalk and caliche. These large-leaved evergreens are so valuable as tall, fast-growing screens on these soils that gardeners happily forgive their many failings. Japanese ligustrums set modestly attractive clusters of blue-black olivelike fruits, which later fall to the ground and sprout into young plants. This facility for self-propagation makes these shrubs an inexpensive choice for tall hedges, but can create a nuisance on wooded properties where the young seedlings take over. Japanese ligustrums will also make attractive, single-trunked evergreen trees, although plants trained in this fashion will need frequent pruning.

Lilacs

Lilacs (*Syringa* spp.) look much like lavender-flowered ligustrums and, in fact, are close relations. Although these deciduous shrubs are typical favorites in cold climates, they are grown in hot-summer areas as well. Like most spring-flowering shrubs, they offer little to generate garden interest after bloom-time. Nevertheless, the romantic scent of lilacs has been indelibly imprinted on the senses of generations of gardeners. Once whiffed, this narcotic sweetness is something many are unwilling to do without!

Where winter temperatures regularly fall to 15° F or lower the old-fashioned common lilac (*Syringa vulgaris*) gives an acceptable performance, if one is willing to overlook its propensity for mildew during the summer months. The Descanso hybrids (such as 'Lavender Lady') are just as susceptible to this disease, but have larger flower trusses and bloom more reliably in mild-winter areas.

Cutleaf lilac (*S. persica laciniata*) resists disease in areas of high summer temperature and sports attractive, divided foliage. Its panicles of lavender bloom are rather small, however. Another healthy type with tiny, fragrant flowers is the dwarf Korean lilac (*S. patula*). This variety has dark green, heart-shaped leaves and a dense, bushy habit. Perhaps the most desirable combination of disease resistance, bloom size, and fragrance comes from certain forms of the thick-leaved lilac (*S. oblata*), a native of China and Korea. Like all lilacs, these varieties thrive on well-drained limy soils and will adapt to barren chalk or caliche if not unduly subjected to drought.

Philadelphus

There is a persistent confusion among gardeners over the botanical name of the lilacs (*Syringa*) and the common name for the syringas, or mock oranges (*Philadelphus* spp.). This is not hard to understand, for both produce endearingly fragrant blooms. Like the lilacs, *Philadelphus* varieties are particularly well adapted to limy soils and are old-fashioned favorites. Their snow-white late spring blooms are the probable origin of the custom of June matrimony services, for these were the "orange blossoms" in the bridal bouquets of a former era.

Most *Philadelphus* appreciate some shade in hot summer areas, and make appropriate choices for plantings in front of cold north-facing walls. The old, double-flowered, French hybrid, 'Virginal,' is still good and among the most fragrant. Gardeners looking for this type must be wary, however, of the many inferior, nearly scentless strains sold under this name. 'Natchez,' a single-flowered introduction from the U.S. National Arboretum, is also elegant, but needs a couple of years to establish before blooming heavily.

Small-flowered native mock oranges such as *Philadelphus texenis* and *P. ernestii* cover their wiry stems in attractive semievergreen foliage, as well as fragrant blooms. In the wild these types nestle in crevices in limestone rock, and they look at home in similar situations in the garden. The related *Fendlera* of the Southwestern mountains also enjoys such rocky nooks, and when so placed will show off its semipendant habit of growth.

Deutzias resemble *Philadelphus* in foliage and general aspect, but flower in compact clusters at the ends of their branches instead of scattering blooms along the stems. They seem to accept lime if given some shade from the hot western sun. *Deutzia gracilis* is an upright-growing Chinese species that comes in both white and pink-tinged selections. Because casual observers misconstrue it as a *Philadelphus*, this fine lime-tolerant shrub seldom receives the credit due for its good performances.

Crape Myrtles

Most gardeners recognize crape myrtles (*Lagerstroemia indica*), however, and these summer-blooming shrubs and small trees are among the most popular flowering plants for limy ground. They earn this favored position by their unbelievably long flowering season, which may begin in late spring and often continues into September. Many summer gardens depend on the brilliant torches of crape myrtle blooms to carry interest through to the fall, and these thrifty plants provide color through periods of intense heat that few flowers can endure.

This is all the more amazing, because the bloom clusters of crape myrtles come in arresting tones of watermelon, magenta, fuchsia, tyrian purple, and glistening white—just the colors to electrify the summer garden. What is more, these shrubs adapt especially to limy clays and often require only modest supplemental irrigations on soils of good depth. As autumn brings cooling temperatures many crape myrtle cultivars assume attractive russet-orange tones to their foliage. Throughout the year these shrubs display elegant habits of growth and attractive exfoliating (peeling) bark.

The larger-growing varieties of *L. indica* have been popular garden plants since the first settlings of the limestone regions. Early gardens included mostly pink or lavender types, and many fine specimens may be seen gracing older plantings. The value of such successful plants, many of which have endured over a century with minimal attention from their owners, speaks for itself, and these old tree-form crape myrtles, sold simply by color, still have much to offer.

Nurseries now provide many fine named selections as well, and this makes it much easier for gardeners to choose appropriate varieties. Fine dark red cultivars include 'Country Red' (12' to 14') and 'Cherokee' (6' to 12'), both with good resistance to mildew. A choice dark purple is 'Catawba' (6' to 12'), and this is one of the favorite crape myrtles for fall foliage color. Lavish clusters of clear pink flowers are generously born by

'Seminole' (6' to 12') and 'Potomac' (12' to 14'). Where its drooping panicles of shell pink flowers will show off, 'Near East' (6' to 12') is also good and long-blooming. Among the whites 'Glendora White' (6' to 12') is especially fine and has lustrous dark green foliage to set off its big clusters of pristine bloom, lending a cooling appearance to summer plantings. 'Peppermint Lace' (6' to 12') is a novel variety with watermelon flowers marked with a white picotee.

Of the shorter crape myrtles, the Petite series is good and includes white, orchid, pink, and rose-red selections that remain less than three feet tall. Like most dwarf varieties, these are more prone to mildew than the larger strains, and should be sited where they will have plenty of sun and good air circulation. Especially desirable for vibrant garnet-red blooms are low-growing selections such as 'Victor' (2' to 3') and 'Centennial Spirit' (3' to 6'). 'Royalty' is a vivid dark purple less than three feet tall.

Even smaller are strains offered as "crape myrtle-ettes" and miniature weeping forms such as the Pixie series. These diminutive types can be rather susceptible to cold damage and powdery mildew. Nevertheless, such miniatures make interesting landscape plants that may be massed for summer bedding. When used in this way, miniatures need other plants as foils during the winter, and these tiny crape myrtles may be interplanted with perennial flowers or small-scale groundcovers.

Recent years have seen a surge of interest in hybrid crape myrtles developed from the Japanese *L. faurei*. This species has long, pointed leaves and rather small, white flowers, but develops beautiful cinnamon-red bark as it matures. Its hybrids often inherit this feature, and are extraordinarily vigorous and disease-resistant. Nurseries have been quick to introduce these fast-growing types and they have been widely promoted for their superior characteristics.

'Natchez' (15' to 20') is a white selection with attractive cinnamon bark, and this is a feature of its amethyst-flowered sibling, 'Muskogee,' as well. 'Basham's Party Pink' (15' to 20') is a pale mauve variety with impressively fast growth, but otherwise too similar to 'Muskogee' to justify planting in the same garden. 'Tuskegee' and 'Tuscarora' (12' to 15') are back-crosses to the *indica* cultivar, 'Cherokee,' and more closely resemble traditional crape myrtle varieties. Their blooms are dark watermelon and coral-red, respectively, and are borne in large upright clusters.

The U.S. National Arboretum has an ongoing breeding project with crape myrtles and continues to introduce new types, named for tribes of Native Americans. Some of these will probably prove to be desirable garden plants, but many seem confusingly similar to one another. Although vigorous and resistant to mildew, these hybrids often lack the strong colors and large clusters of bloom of older *indica* types, and are more likely to freeze in sudden snaps of cold. Gardeners on lime may look forward to improved hybrid crape myrtles in the future, but should not forget or neglect the many beautiful *indica* cultivars currently at their disposal.

Rose of Sharon

Another summer-flowering shrub that enjoys lime is the rose of Sharon, or shrub-althaea (*Hibiscus syriacus*). Although a native of China, the rose of Sharon first entered European gardens from the Middle East, hence its botanical name commemorating Syria. These hardy deciduous shrubs have a long history in cultivation and many of the varieties in gardens today are selections of eighteenth- and nineteenth-century French breeders. Often these were selected for their good performances on calcareous soils.

The old white maroon-centered single, 'Redheart,' is a sentimental favorite and still worth planting. Other worthy singles include rose-red 'Woodbridge,' lilac 'Blue Bird,' and white-flowered 'Diana.' Double varieties sometimes open poorly in hot-summer areas, but the vigorous rose-red 'Amplissimus' and the pale pink 'Lady Stanley' are usually good performers. Hard pruning and generous manuring will reward gardeners with larger, more widely expanded blooms on most varieties of shrub-althaea.

Coniferous Evergreens

Such deciduous shrubs call for evergreen plantings nearby to carry interest through the year. The versatile junipers can provide this in many gardens on lime. These conifers come in an enormous array of forms and habits and include many dependable shrubs for poor, calcareous soil. The natural affinity towards lime possessed by junipers is apparent in the native groves or "cedar brakes" typical of limestone regions.

The Pfitzer group (*Juniperus* × *media* cvs.) includes many of the best varieties for hot-summer areas, although some types may become impractically large. 'Compact Pfitzer' makes a useful spreading gray-green shrub two feet tall and three to four feet wide. 'Silver Spreader' is similar, but with bluish foliage. 'Sea Green' matures to a three- or four-foot bush with rich green semierect sprays of foliage. 'Blue Vase' makes a blocky silver-gray tousled mass four to five feet tall, and bears attractive blue berries when mature.

All of these are ideal soft-textured evergreens to contrast with colorful foliage and flowers in informal mixed plantings. These cultivars will also succeed on dry, rocky ground where deer browse and few other evergreens may be grown. On wooded lots with native "cedars" (*Juniperus ashei* or *J. virginiana*) these cultivars may be used to create an appropriate transition between the garden and its natural surroundings.

Spreading junipers are desirable for their low, mossy growth and tough constitutions. Although best adapted to cooler regions, if provided with good drainage and mulches of neutral-colored gravel (or, better still, decomposed granite), these types will accept warm-summer areas as well.

The blue-gray *J. horizontalis* 'Blue Chip' and soft green 'Prince of Wales' are prostrate cultivars with dense, lush habits of growth, more beautiful than the older 'Bar Harbor' and 'Wilton.' Moss-green *J. procumbens* is similarly dwarf, but has stiff, prickly foliage that spreads neatly and may be draped around rocks. Its creeping variety, 'Green Mound,' is popular for use in Japanese-style gardens. Unless provided with partial shade, however, 'Green Mound' may develop chlorosis in hot-summer regions, and this variety particularly dislikes heavy clay soils. Gardeners on lime will find the slightly larger *J. procumbens* v. *procumbens* easier to grow and very nearly as beautiful.

Blue shore juniper (*J. conferta* 'Blue Pacific') is an oft-planted trailing selection with needlelike foliage marked silvery blue on the underside. It originates from the sandy shorelines and moderate climate of Japan. Not surprisingly, this cultivar develops chlorosis when planted in poorly drained limy clay in hot-summer regions. Raised beds with pockets of sandy soil and positions shaded from west sun will accommodate this juniper nicely.

Slightly taller are the spreading members of the *J. sabina* group, all of which do well on lime. The Mediterranean native, v. *tamariscifolia*—known familiarly as the "tam" juniper—is especially popular and a useful dark green. Unfortunately, it often suffers twig blight (phomopsis) in humid areas. 'Broadmoor,' 'Buffalo,' and 'Calgary Carpet' are disease-resistant cultivars derived from wild types collected in the Ural Mountains of central Asia. They resemble *tamariscifolia* in growth, but have foliage colored a somewhat lighter camouflage-green.

"Andorra" (*J. horizontalis* 'Plumosa') also resembles "tam" juniper and is popular for its plum-colored winter foliage. This cultivar succeeds on heavy alkaline clays if watered through the year, but generally is short-lived on droughty chalk or caliche soils. Spider mites are a common pest, and these troublesome creatures also limit the usefulness of low-growing cultivars such as 'San Jose' and 'Variegated Prostrata.'

Upright junipers serve as bold accents or focal points in plantings, and are favored for use as tall screens or windbreaks. Vertical-growing cultivars of *Juniperus chinensis* are widely adaptable and include favorites such as rich green, columnar 'Spartan' (15' to 20'), pyramidal 'Blue Point' (6' to 8'), and sculptured, many-branched "Hollywood juniper" (*J. chinensis* 'Torulosa'). Large-growing *J. virginiana* cultivars such as 'Canaertii' (15' to 20') and the *J. chinensis* selection, 'Keteleeri,' are easily grown as well, and bear attractive crops of powdery blue berries to contrast with their dark green foliage.

Many of the varieties of Rocky Mountain juniper (*J. scopulorum*) have striking gray foliage, and selections such as 'Blue Haven' and the even more silvery 'Wichita Blue' form invaluable fine-textured blue-gray pyramids six to ten feet tall. These types will stand any amount of cold or drought, but may suffer twig blight in humid regions. A position near a sunny west-facing wall, and a mulch of reflective gravel will provide a suitably arid microclimate in many gardens.

The oriental arborvitas (*Platycladus orientalis* cvs.) comprise another family of conifers useful on lime and chalk, and this group performs well on dry, rocky ground. These flame-shaped evergreens hold their tiny leaves in dense, vertical sprays. Arborvitas were important plants in many nineteenth-century gardens, and old, ragged specimens may be seen marking former homesites or estates. The smaller, gold-foliaged types are familiar, often overused, features of suburban gardens.

Large-growing arborvitas are impractical for most modern properties, although tall varieties such as 'Bluespire' or 'Baker' make useful screens or windbreaks. More valuable, and suitable for mixed borders of drought-tolerant shrubs and flowers, are dwarfs such as the miniature pyramid, 'Gold Cone' (3' to 4'), rounded, green-leaved 'Bonita' (4' to 6'), and golden 'Berkman' (6' to 10').

'Rosedale' is an unusual cultivar with prickly blue-green foliage, interesting to include in a mixed border while young. In time, however, this type grows to an unmanageable fifteen feet, and overly generous growing conditions shorten its period of usefulness. Where summers are long and hot arborvitae of all types will remain more compact and attractive when grown in lean, dry soil with plenty of sunshine.

Sumacs and Their Relations

Evergreen junipers and arborvitae mix well with the beautiful autumn colors and lush, fernlike foliage displayed by members of the sumac family. Sumacs and their kin are tough, fast-growing shrubs, valuable for large-scale, naturalistic plantings, and the entire family enjoys limy soils. In warm climates the deciduous members of this group provide unequaled fall foliage colors, and many produce attractive clusters of berries or seed. Evergreen types are among the most drought-tolerant of shrubs.

Prairie flame-leaf sumac (*Rhus copallina* v. *lanceolata*) is a common native over limestone and makes an attractive specimen less prone to suckering than most types of sumac.

Its feathery foliage turns brilliant orange-red in early autumn. Fragrant sumac (*Rhus aromatica*) also colors in the fall, but forms a wiry bush with small three-parted leaves. This species produces modestly attractive spring blooms as well, and has interesting winter branches with fat buds that resemble pine cones. Its leaves and bark emit a pungent balsamlike aroma when crushed or bruised.

The smoke tree (*Cotinus obovatus*) is a sumac relation native to the limestone regions of North America. It earns its common name from curious feathery flower clusters, which in early summer resemble clouds of smoke rising above its leaves. A more impressive show comes in autumn, however, when the rounded leaves of these large shrubs assume tones of orange and scarlet. The related European smoke tree (*C. coggygria*) is a favorite in English gardens on lime, especially in purple-leaved variants such as 'Royal Purple.' These benefit from afternoon shade in hot-summer American gardens.

Evergreen sumac (*Rhus virens*) makes a glistening shiny-leaved shrub, and bears panicles of small, white September blooms. These ripen into fat clusters of orange-red berries in late fall. Upon exposure to cold weather the entire plant often takes on tints of bronze or purple, offering an effective display against light-colored limestone walls.

Evergreen sumac is especially valuable for dry, rocky sites and grows rapidly on well-drained chalk or caliche soils. In some unfortunate gardens, especially those in which poorly drained clay soils prevail, this shrub mysteriously perishes after summer rains, apparently a victim of some unseen blight or root rot. Extra attention in selecting a well-drained, sunny position may help avoid this difficulty.

Texas pistache (*Pistacia texana*) closely resembles evergreen sumac, but has more finely divided, feathery leaves. These display attractive reddish tints while in growth. In warm regions with calcareous soils Texas pistache makes a fast-growing hedge or screen and offers a graceful substitute for *Photinia* × *fraseri*. It becomes partially deciduous where temperatures regularly drop below 15° F.

Other rugged shrubs that may be used in semiwild plantings are rough-leaf dogwood (*Cornus drummondii*) and Carolina buckthorn (*Rhamnus caroliniana*). Like the members of the sumac family, both of these offer attractive fall foliage colors and bring to the garden the aspect of native woodland. They tolerate drought and rocky limestone soil, and survive brutal cold.

Pittosporum

Pittosporum cultivars have lost favor in recent years due to their susceptibilty to cold, and sudden winter blasts sometimes split the bark of these broadleaf shrubs, fatally injuring them. Their great beauty contributes to this situation, however, by tempting gardeners to plant pittosporums beyond their range of hardiness. Lush evergreen foliage, dense mounded habits of growth, and easy-growing, near maintenance-free natures make them hard to resist. When the intensely fragrant spring blooms and attractive dwarf and variegated varieties are placed in consideration, otherwise sensible horticulturists hasten to plant these shrubs in positions they know full well will place them at risk.

Although too tender for general use in some sections, pittosporums are, indeed, worthwhile gambles in many gardens on lime. In *P. tobira* 'Variegata' gardeners have one of the finest of all variegated shrubs. Its lush, cream-marbled leaves are worthy of cutting for floral decoration, and its full rounded form three to four feet tall makes it a good choice for informal borders to light up shady garden corners.

The dwarf *P. tobira* 'Wheeleri' develops an outstanding dome-shaped mound of leaves and maintains a lush, symmetrical form less than two feet tall. This variety is prone to chlorosis in extreme heat or cold and has brittle wood, but makes a fine specimen for a favored east-facing wall or nook. Its variegated form usually requires partial shade.

These types, as well as the valuable green form of *P. tobira*, are generally hardy in gardens where winter temperatures remain above 12° F. In colder regions gardeners may experiment in sheltered corners, but ought to be prepared to replace these shrubs every few years. 'Winter Pride' is a recent introduction with reputedly improved cold tolerance.

Euonymus

The spindles (*Euonymus* spp.) are all quite cold-hardy and lime-loving, and include many valuable garden shrubs. The deciduous varieties are particularly worthwhile, and combine showy autumn foliage with tough, hardy constitutions. Several also bear interesting four-sided fruit capsules that explode when ripe to reveal brightly colored berries. Evergreen euonymus species include valuable varieties for hedges and many favorite variegated cultivars.

The European spindle (*E. europaeus*) and the "pink lady" (*E. bungeanus*) make small, lightly branched trees or specimen shrubs and bear light gray-green foliage and pendant pink fruit capsules. It turns clear yellow to rose-pink in autumn. Wahoo (*E. atropurpureus*) is an American counterpart that remains slightly smaller (4′ to 6′) and turns reddish in fall. The dwarf Japanese burning bush (*E. alatus* 'Compacta') is favored for its brilliant autumn colors and rugged cold-hardiness. These deciduous euonymus varieties grow well on heavy alkaline clay soils and appreciate partial shade in hot-summer regions.

Of the evergreen types the Manhattan euonymus (*E. kiautshovica* 'Manhattan') is especially good and offers a rugged, medium-growing evergreen in areas too cold and dry for most broadleaf hedging shrubs. This type is seldom bothered by pests or disease.

Unfortunately, the same cannot be said of the many variegated cultivars of Japanese evergreen euonymus (*E. japonicus*). In warm-summer regions these often suffer attacks of scale insects, and may also be bothered by powdery mildew and anthracnose. Careful siting in positions sheltered from hot sun will help minimize these pests, which seem to affect the more heavily variegated types (i.e. 'Aurea-Marginata' and 'Silver Queen') with the greatest severity. In contrast, all-green cultivars, such as miniature box-leaf euonymus (*E. japonica* 'Pulchella'), grow with sufficient health to encourage liberal use and provide gardeners on lime with wonderfully formal, compact, upright evergreens.

Boxwoods

Boxwoods (*Buxus* spp.) are sometimes said to dislike alkaline soils, yet many types grow well on the chalkiest limestones. It seems that it is the internal compaction of heavy alkaline clays that creates difficulty, and on poorly drained sites these evergreens are frequent victims of twig blights and root-knot nematodes. If care is taken to provide prepared beds of well-drained soil these problems will be less severe and gardeners may succeed with several types of boxwood.

The common box (*Buxus sempervirens*) is most beautiful and desirable, and its shining green leaves make it among the richest of evergreens. Edging box ('Suffruticosa') is popular in many areas as a miniature hedge or low garden border. Larger types make a better choice in warm regions, however, for 'Suffruticosa' grows at a painfully slow pace in such climates. In these regions common box will welcome partial shade as well. Occasional syringing with the hose can help keep spider mites at bay during dry spells.

Much speedier in growth are the Japanese boxwoods (*B. microphylla* 'Japonica'), and these are popular for hedges in many gardens. Their rounded, light green leaves have a perpetually fresh appearance and arrive in flushes throughout the growing season. In colder regions these evergreens assume bronze colors during the winter, and may suffer twig damage after blasts of severe cold. More reliably green in winter and more cold-hardy are selections of Korean box (*B. microphylla* v. *koreana*). 'Wintergreen' is a strong-growing cultivar with attractive dark green foliage.

Viburnums

Although often featured in the plantings of acid soil regions, many viburnums happily accept lime. These aristocratic shrubs bring rare sophistication to gardens on calcareous grounds and offer showy flowers and fruit, as well as outstanding foliage, both deciduous and evergreen.

Of the deciduous types the rusty blackhaw (*Viburnum rufidulum*) is especially good and well adapted to difficult limy soils. Its white spring blooms attractively crown branches furnished with shining green foliage. In mid-autumn the leaves turn a glossy maroon to create a backdrop for berries that darken from yellow and pink to blue. The semievergreen *V. obovatum* offers similar attractions and bears its small rounded leaves along dense, oppositely branched twigs.

The infertile form of European cranberry or snowball bush (*Viburnum opulus* 'Sterile') produces handsome balls of single white blooms in early spring. Fertile cultivars such as 'Compactum' have smaller, less globular flower clusters that later mature to glossy red berries. Maplelike leaves are born by both types and turn russet tones in autumn. Shady positions near north-facing walls offer suitable homes for these hardy shrubs in warmer regions.

North exposures are also good for the white-flowered, semievergreen *V.* × *burkwoodi*. The fragrant early spring blooms of this popular variety expand from tightly clustered pink buds. It makes a slow-growing, lax, graceful shrub. *V.* × *pragense* is similar, but more evergreen and better suited to strong sun.

V. odoratissimum is a reliably evergreen type, most often cultivated in the hardy, compact-growing variety, *awabuki*, whose special attractions are long lustrous leaves. This dark green foliage combines with its pyramidal habit to suggest a magnolia in aspect. *V. odoratissimum* makes an excellent slow-growing six- to ten-foot hedge or screen, tolerant of shade and seldom molested by browsing deer. Although sometimes called "sweet viburnum" in reference to its fragrant white flowers, these appear in gardens with disappointing rarity, hardly justifying this appellation.

In contrast, the laurustinus (*V. tinus*) blooms abundantly, but requires a position sheltered from temperatures below 15° F. Its tiny pink flower buds over winter on the ends of its branches, opening white in spring and maturing to bluish-black berries in autumn. This Mediterranean native grows well on chalky limestone soils and caliche. The dwarf cultivar, 'Spring Bouquet,' is especially compact and floriferous.

Sandankwa viburnum (*V. suspensum*) is often planted in warm regions as a hedge, and grows well in dry shade. Its flowers are small and unpleasantly scented, however, and this Okinawan native has little tolerance to cold. More beautiful, but also rather tender is *V. davidii*, a low-growing variety from the Chinese province of Sichuan. It forms a gracefully spreading evergreen that needs partial shade to look its best and has unique parallel-veined leaves and blue autumn berries.

Abelias

The abelias are long-blooming cousins of viburnums, and have endeared themselves to generations of gardeners on lime. Toughness, hardiness, and abundance of bloom are characteristic of abelias, and their lax, graceful form belies unusual vigor. The white-flowered glossy abelia (*Abelia* × *grandiflora*) grows swiftly to four to six feet and is a popular choice for hedges. In addition to multitudinous tiny tubular blooms, it offers ornament from bronze calyces and fine-textured glossy foliage that reddens during cold weather.

Low-growing selections fit more easily in many gardens. 'Prostrata' is one of the smallest and resembles a two- to three-foot version of glossy abelia. 'Sherwoodii' makes a dense globular shrub three or four feet tall and has especially tiny leaves and flowers. 'Edward Goucher' also matures at three or four feet, but bears rather large, light pink blooms. 'Francis Mason' is a golden-variegated sport with pinkish flowers.

Shrub Honeysuckles

Although adaptable to lime, few of the shrubby honeysuckles (*Lonicera* spp.) are planted in warmer regions. Several types are popular in gardens of cold climates for their attractive spring blooms and autumn berries. Gardeners in hot-summer areas sometimes plant the rugged native *L. albiflora* for its unscented white flowers, grayish rounded leaves, and scarlet autumn berries.

More endearing is the sweetly fragrant winter honeysuckle (*L. fragrantissima*). This old-fashioned shrub makes a big arching plant up to ten feet across. Gardens that can accommodate this bulk will be rewarded with delicately transparent magnolia-scented blooms through the winter months. Although deciduous in severe cold, these shrubs often retain a portion of their rounded gray-green leaves through the winter. They are tough and undemanding, and adapt to the poorest calcareous soils.

Wintersweets and Strawberry Shrubs

Another lime-tolerant winter bloomer is the wintersweet (*Chimonanthus praecox*). Like the winter honeysuckle, these big shrubs bear parchmentlike flowers with a sweet, penetrating fragrance. In shape these blooms differ markedly, however, resembling tiny coppery waterlilies. In the cultivar 'Lutea' they are an even more telling translucent yellow, and in the evergreen *C. nitens* a glistening white. These shrubs convey the aspect of magnolia or rhododendron, and give to the gardener on lime a sense of the forbidden beauty of such acid-loving shrubs.

For this reason the wintersweet and its spring-flowering American relation, the strawberry shrub or Carolina allspice (*Calycanthus floridus*), are especially choice shrubs to include on limy grounds. The strawberry shrub displays its curious maroon blooms among its leaves, requiring something of an effort on the part of the gardener to hunt them down and inhale their spicy fragrance. The leaves of this suckering shrub are also aromatic. Both the wintersweet and the strawberry shrub are at their best in partial shade.

Along with these varied shrubs, the bushier roses and old-fashioned flowering shrubs such as *Kerria* and buffalo currant (*Ribes odoratum*) may be included in plantings on lime. Drought-loving oleanders, cenizas, and a variety of subshrubs may be mixed to extend seasonal interest and colonize rocky slopes. In warmer areas such tender subjects as pineapple guava (*Feijoa sellowiana*) and *Xylosma* may be tried. With this incredible range of shrubs adapted to lime, the garden on calcareous soil can be rich indeed.

CHAPTER SEVEN

A Special Breed: Lime-tolerant Trees

Ⅰn gardens on lime, as in other regions, trees provide the chief framework for plantings and establish the characteristic views of the territory. They extend the garden up and outward from its limits on the ground and connect it with the elements of the surrounding countryside. Through their size and maturity trees define the garden's age. By their longevity they transcend the limits of the lives of those who plant them, and carry the gardener's original vision to subsequent generations. More than any other plants trees attach the garden to its unique place in time and space.

Calcareous soils require a special breed of trees capable of colonizing these difficult grounds, for when lime soil is left to its own it often supports only grass or scrub. Many lime-tolerant trees are natural pioneers, which in habitat wage a continuing battle on the fringes of prairie and woodland. In order to win this fight, they have developed techniques to help overcome poor soil conditions and competitive grasses. Gardeners on lime can help their trees by respecting these natural strategies.

Young saplings growing on limy ground often branch heavily and cover their stems in short bushy twigs. This gives them a shaggy, unkempt appearance, but offers shade for tender bark, as well as for roots near the base of the tree. Shade from the lower branches not only helps keep moisture in the soil, but also suppresses competing grasses. The many short twigs help to strengthen and thicken the developing trunk, making it more resistant to wind. Leaves falling around the tree accumulate to form a natural mulch, providing nutriment and improving soil texture and aeration.

In utter disregard of these processes, hasty gardeners with visions of lofty forest giants prune away the lower branches of young trees. Nurseries are often equally guilty, and cater to the public demand for tall, slender-trunked specimens. As aesthetically appealing as these may be, unless the trees are already five to six inches in diameter such removal may greatly stunt growth. If grass is allowed to grow beneath the saplings competition will ensue and tender young bark may be inadvertently bruised or cut as the grass is trimmed ("lawn mower blight"). On heavy alkaline clays simply walking or sitting beneath the trees may result in damaging soil compaction.

Prudent gardeners avoid these threats by keeping a generous mulch around tree bases. Optimally, branches should be left to shade the developing trunks, and then shortened and removed in stages so that their beneficial effects may last as long as possible. This somewhat untidy technique is known appropriately as the "trashy trunk" method of training. For trees already "brought up" at the nursery all that may be done is to shorten the remaining branches and ensure that the soil beneath the young canopy is well mulched and free of grass. In only a few years, however, a properly tended seedling left untrimmed can readily surpass in growth much larger, more expensive saplings abused by premature pruning.

The condition of a young tree's root system also has a profound effect on its subsequent growth and success. Unfortunately, this is usually difficult for the gardener to assess, except when planting bare-root, a practice nowadays limited mostly to fruit and nut trees. Trees produce both large heavy taproots, in which food reserves are stored, and delicate fibrous roots that absorb water and food. Optimally, both types should be present and in good condition at planting. For practical reasons this is seldom possible, however, and gardeners must choose among the available types of nursery stock, each of which has special virtues and pitfalls.

An increasingly wide range of trees is made available rooted in containers, and this is a convenient way to handle smaller trees. For evergreens such as magnolia or live oak, and for summer planting, container trees are the gardener's first choice.

Well-grown container trees have actively growing root systems that can quickly establish in the ground and firmly anchor the new tree. Often, however, container-grown trees develop encircling or twisting roots. Unless these can be pruned off at planting such trees may fail to establish in their new homes, an unfortunate fact that can turn the purchase of a large container specimen into an unwise and expensive gamble.

For the majority of tree varieties, planting balled-and-burlapped during the dormant season is a more pragmatic alternative. Balled-and-burlapped trees lose a portion of their roots during the digging process at the nursery, but if properly handled will have most of their taproots and a fair measure of fibrous roots intact. Vigorous, healthy stock will have stored enough energy in the heavier roots and stems to regenerate quickly the missing parts when planted. These new roots will develop directly in the soil around the tree, immediately establishing it in its new home. For best results balled-and-burlapped trees should be set out in early spring before growth commences. January and February are ideal in Texas.

Although more cumbersome and less convenient than container-grown trees, balled-and-burlapped stock carries with it an inherent assurance that the plants are sufficiently strong-growing to succeed in the ground. The weaklings will have been left behind at the nursery. If the trees were raised on alkaline land gardeners can see this and ascertain the lime-tolerance of their purchases as well.

Some nurseries also offer trees grown in bags of synthetic cloth so that most of their roots remain intact at planting. These are not essentially different from balled-and-burlapped trees, but require that the gardener slash or remove the bag instead of leaving it to rot as may be done with burlap. This method is especially valuable for varieties that are otherwise difficult to transplant, but requires careful handling to keep the root ball intact as the cloth is removed.

The Elms

In regions of lime soil trees often occur as isolated specimens loosely spaced in savannahs or prairies, so that the outlines of their mature crowns become familiar features of the landscape. It is the elms that take pride of place in this, and they frequently punctuate skylines as abiding backdrops to the day-to-day activities of human life. Their characteristic arching and spreading silhouettes evoke the traditional romantic images of the countryside in many limestone regions.

For difficult calcareous soils in hot climates such as Texas, no finer elm (and no finer tree) could be wished for than the native cedar elm (*Ulmus crassifolia*). Its tiny twisting twigs and cork-winged branchlets combine to develop a soaring cloudlike canopy that broadens and weeps with age. In spring and summer this is filled with tiny sandpapery leaves of rich green. In autumn these turn haphazardly to golden yellow, and then fall neatly to the ground and disappear into grass or underplantings.

For general use as a shade tree the cedar elm excels. It is widely recognized and appreciated for its longevity, ease of transplanting, moderately rapid growth, and resistance to heat, drought, and alkalinity. Mature trees reach fifty feet in height, rarely require treatment for pests or disease, and usually need only minimal pruning and training.

This tree has its detractors, to be sure. Some complain about the cedar elm's propensity to mildew and rust in late summer, and others object to its irregular twisting growth and consequent weak branch angles. For those who love the cedar elm, however, these are simply more of its charms. The bronzy color of its mildewed late summer foliage is yet another note of seasonal interest, and its ruggedly gnarled branches speak eloquently of the tough, limestone country that this tree calls home.

For those who prefer a more "civilized" shade tree, the classically vase-shaped American elm (*Ulmus americana*) offers another lime-tolerant possibility. This elegant tree is capable of great size if planted on deep soil and provided with an unfailing source of moisture. On thin rocky sites or in regions beset with hot summer weather it performs best at the water's edge.

On heavy clays American elm is likely to develop aggressive surface roots. Under drought stress it shows its displeasure by dropping leaves and in summer heat may experience minor attacks of elm leaf beetle or stinging puss caterpillars. Despite these troubles, the majestic qualities of the American elm remain readily apparent and climax in a show of autumn gold, contrasted against black-barked trunk and branches.

When selecting an American elm to plant on lime soil it is important to choose only locally native stock that will be naturally tolerant to alkalinity and regional climate. Such trees are seldom available from nurseries. Because the American elm has fallen prey to the devastating Dutch elm disease in much of its former range, it now is rarely planted. Ironically, the Southwestern habitats of this tree in which calcareous soils prevail have been little affected by this plague. American elms have understandably lost favor over much of North America, but are still worth planting in the Southwest if local strains can be obtained.

More available and more practical for small properties is the Chinese lacebark elm (*Ulmus parvifolia*). This variety is sometimes known as "evergreen elm" because in mild areas such as the Gulf Coast its leaves hang on through winter. In Florida and California this tree is popular and several named varieties (including 'Drake' and 'Truegreen') have been selected and propagated. Lacebark elm makes a beautiful small tree with attractive reddish flaking bark. It has the graceful vase-shaped growth habit typical of the elm tribe.

From central Texas southward lacebark elm is less successful than in more northern sections. The warm subhumid climate and droughty calcareous soils of this area promote cotton root rot (*Phymatotrichum omnivorum*), a soil fungus to which this tree is particularly susceptible. Another notable weakness of lacebark elm is its extremely thin, tender bark. This makes young specimens especially prone to damage from weed trimmers or improper staking. Like the American elm, it is a thirsty, fast-growing tree likely to develop surface roots on heavy clay soils. These failings aside, if well-positioned and well cared for the lacebark elm is a good modest-sized tree to live under.

The Oaks

If the soaring spirit of the elms defines the skyline in regions of lime soil, then the ponderous spreading branches of the oaks convey the strength and soul of the rugged chalk bluffs and rocky limestone ledges. More than any other trees, the oaks project a sense of stability. Their sturdy branches spread widely over the landscape, and oak trees achieve legendary antiquity. Above all others, the oaks are the trees we inherit from our predecessors, and the ones we plant for the glory of generations to come.

Along with their famous longevity, these trees carry reputations for slow growth, but oaks can be impressively vigorous in youth. On droughty limestone soils they are often among the fastest growing trees, for their coarse, wide-spreading roots efficiently seek out and retrieve food and moisture on such difficult ground. For gardeners on calcareous soil the oaks are the first choices among shade trees, and include within their clan enormous variety.

The White Oaks

Botanists separate the oaks into two broad divisions, the more ancient and widespread of which is known as the white oak group. These are the classic oaks favored for use as lumber because of their massive trunks and branches, and their light-colored, close-grained wood. For gardens on lime the white oaks offer choice medium- to small-sized trees as well as majestic towering giants.

The most popular of the white oaks on limy ground is the bur oak (*Quercus macrocarpa*). This lofty native of the prairie states has been admired for its size and rugged beauty since the earliest pioneer days. Huge acorns held in burlike cups are the origin of its common name, and a perennial source of wonder and amazement. Its deeply lobed leaves reach six inches or more in length and give the bur oak a coarse appearance unusual for a tree adapted to dry prairie. Although its leaves turn only to dull yellow in the fall and its branches appear angular and graceless in youth, gardeners on lime hold a special reverence for this majestic tree, as it ranks among the largest which may be grown.

The heavy wide-spreading branches of an old bur oak may span one hundred feet, and will densely shade the ground below. These big trees truly transform the local environment, breathing cooling oxygen and humidity onto the hot, dry prairie. The planting of a bur oak initiates the natural processes whereby grassland converts to forest, and these trees eventually will shade the garden as if it were beneath the roof of a great mansion.

For bur oaks to achieve their customary heights of fifty to one hundred feet, they need soil of moderate depth, such as the alkaline prairie clays. On thin rocky limestone or chalk they will remain smaller, usually thirty-five to forty feet or less. Even at this reduced size bur oaks are welcome and trusted providers of shade, and generally have long lives little marred by attacks of pests or disease.

More at home on rocky ground and more graceful at all stages of its life is the chinquapin oak (*Q. muhlenbergii*). This tree gets its name from a Native American word for the chestnut, whose leaves closely resemble the serrated foliage of this oak. The chinquapin oak is a true lime-lover and prefers rocky limestone soils above all others. On such sites it is among the largest and fastest-growing of trees.

The dark green saw-edged leaves of chinquapin oaks hang down from the branches, giving a well-furnished look. As the wind blows they flutter and reveal attractive silvery undersides. Although most chinquapin oaks turn a modest yellow-brown in autumn, some trees display showy reddish tints to their foliage. Chinquapin oaks show diversity in their branching character as well, and some trees spread widely, while others develop upright habits and may reach sixty feet or more in height. The trunks of these trees are covered in light-colored bark that flakes attractively and gives an aged, shaggy look. No matter where their individual variations take them, chinquapin oaks offer reliable shade and ornament for gardens on calcareous grounds.

Nurseries that specialize in native plants occasionally offer the Lacey oak (*Q. glaucoides*), a small, shrubby tree possessed of unusual refinement and beauty. In its full, rounded form and medium-sized shallow-lobed leaves it resembles the English oak (*Q. robur*). In loveliness the Lacey oak exceeds its European cousin, however, for its foliage has an unusual smoky blue cast. In late autumn these blue leaves change to clear butter yellow, and on some trees may show tints of russet and orange.

Lacey oaks are natives of the Southwestern limestone uplands and are slow-growing scrubby trees. They may take several years to develop noticeable trunks and often grow as multiples or clumps. If trained to a single stem, however, Lacey oaks will grow twenty to thirty feet tall and make dome-shaped trees perfectly appropriate for the smaller garden.

More truly scrubby is white shin oak (*Q. sinuata* v. *breviloba*), and this is a common native on thin soil over chalk or limestone. Its leaves are much like those of the Lacey oak in form, but greener in color, and the trees generally have a rugged, flat-topped appearance. Shaggy bark is the hallmark of this tree, which most often occurs as a fifteen- to twenty-foot clump of several stems.

White shin oak brings into gardens a sense of age and wildness. Its rough stems and ragged appearance seldom offer much shade, but often convey considerable charm. Toughness, character, and an undemanding nature make white shin oak a good choice for informal or naturalistic gardens, and this is a recommendation that extends to many of the scrubbier oaks. (The evergreen Hinckley oak [*Q. hinckleyi*], a rare dwarf from West Texas, is superb for limy gardens and has beautiful grayish hollylike leaves. Unfortunately, it remains only a collector's curio, and is seldom offered in nurseries.)

Although coarse in appearance and uncommonly planted, post oaks (*Q. stellata*) often enter gardens as an inheritance from native woodland and make tough, slow-growing shade trees. Durand oak (*Q. durandii*) is an obscure type that occasionally appears in woods on calcareous soils as well. It resembles a larger, shinier-leafed version of white shin oak.

The many oaks of the Old World have been slow to enter American gardens, and a mere handful have established credentials for lime tolerance. Turkey oak (*Q. cerris*) is one with a reputation of doing well on the chalky soils of Europe. It has long serrated leaves and upright growth suggestive of the chinquapin oak. Its acorns are held in mossy cups like those of the bur oak.

The evergreen holly oaks (*Q. ilex*) and cork oaks (*Q. suber*) tolerate lime, but are rather tender. These Mediterranean natives perform best in the dry, near frost-free climates of California and mild parts of the Southwest. Lucombe oak (*Q.* × *hispanica*) is an evergreen hybrid of cork oak and Turkey oak that ought to prove hardier and more widely adapted.

Most of the oriental oaks seem to struggle on lime soil and often show chlorosis, especially if drought stressed. Japanese evergreen oak (*Q. acuta*) sometimes succeeds on deep limy clay soils, if well watered. This small variety benefits from the shade of other trees. Tougher and more likely to accept drought is the shrubby Chinese *Q. phillyreaoides*. This oak makes a multistemmed, windswept evergreen much like an olive in appearance. Unlike most oaks, it grows easily from cuttings as well as seed, an attribute that may encourage more nurseries to offer this species in the future.

The Red Oaks

As varied and wonderful as the white oaks may be, their ornamental qualities pale when compared to those of members of the red oak group. Where the white oaks are bulky and lumbering, the red oaks are sleek and symmetrical. Their leaves are crisply designed with pointed bristlelike tips on each lobe, and in autumn they assume shades of scarlet and bronze. Red oaks are exclusively New World trees, and their riotous autumn colors and deeply cut foliage are profoundly entrenched in the American psyche. For many gardeners the vision of a glittering crimson red oak against the blue sky of Indian summer touches a place in the heart that other trees simply fail to reach.

A cloud hangs over the red oaks, however, as well as their evergreen cousins, the live oaks. Like the dreaded Dutch elm disease that swept American elms out of favor earlier in this century, oak wilt (*Ceratocystis fagacearum*) threatens to drive red and live oaks out of gardens in many areas on lime soil. Large, venerable trees have succumbed to this fungal disease, which is spread by nitidulids, or sap beetles. Once a tree is infected its fate is sealed and the disease rapidly moves to neighboring trees through root grafts beneath the soil so that large wooded areas can quickly be devastated.

Antifungal treatments are available, but costly, and usually require extensive trenching around the tree's roots to restrict the spread of the disease. Prevention is easier than such cures, and careful, speedy removal of dead trees and prohibition and destruction of infected oak firewood can help discourage new infections and save other trees nearby. It is also wise to avoid major pruning on red or live oaks during winter and spring, as this is when the fungus-carrying sap beetles are most active and attracted to wounds.

Although oak wilt is a serious concern in localized areas, in many regions it poses little threat. Even where the disease is prevalent, after infected trees have been removed, new oaks may be planted to replace them and seem to run little risk of reinfection. A practical strategy for gardeners is to diversify their choices of shade trees, and include such nonsusceptible or resistant types as elms and white oaks in plantings along with the red and live oaks. This will mitigate any future disaster at the same time that it widens the range of trees to enjoy.

A more serious concern for gardeners on lime than oak wilt is the tremendous confusion that surrounds the red oaks. This manifests itself in an ongoing debate over the relative lime tolerance of various red oak varieties, many of which appear so similar as to confound the most experienced botanists and horticulturists.

Texas red oak or Spanish oak (*Q. texana*) is a true lime-lover that naturally grows on the rocky limestone ledges and hillsides of central Texas. Its tolerance to alkaline soil is beyond question, and this variety is without doubt among the finest and most ornamental trees for gardens on calcareous grounds. Texas red oak is smaller than many other red oaks, usually maturing at twenty-five to thirty-five feet, and it often grows naturally as a clump of several stems. Its leaves are variable, but usually are deeply lobed and slightly cupped. They turn shades of russet, maroon, or scarlet in late fall.

Where their ranges overlap near Dallas, both Texas red oak and its eastern relation, the Shumard oak (*Q. shumardii*), may be found growing on lime soil. Often the Texas red oaks will be found on the top of chalky uplands, while the Shumard oaks seem to seek the deeper bottomland soils. On the slopes between, all manner of intermediate types may be found, and these are customarily explained to be the results of natural hybridization.

In its more easterly range the Shumard oak occurs on rich bottomland soils with near neutral pH. On these deep, moist soils this oak may reach fifty to one hundred feet in height. Mature trees develop spreading, symmetrical crowns. The leaves of *Q. shumardii* are typically more shallow-lobed and flattened than those of Texas red oak, and the trees hold them horizontally, as is customary in forest vegetation. Like the Texas red oak, the Shumard oak turns brilliant reddish shades in the autumn.

Although Shumard oaks occurring naturally on the north Texas prairies have good lime tolerance, the same may not be true for Shumard oaks from farther east in its range. For gardeners on lime the provenance (place of origin) of these trees is all-important. Even relatively lime-tolerant forms of Shumard oak may struggle if planted on shallow rocky ground, and this variety often develops chlorosis when planted on the drier, limier soils of central and southwest Texas.

Nurseries attempting to meet the tremendous demand for these colorful red oaks have generally selected the most vigorous, straight-stemmed types from which to collect seed. Unfortunately, these are frequently the least lime-tolerant. Truly acid-loving varieties such as pin oak (*Q. palustris*), water oak (*Q. nigra*), and southern red oak (*Q. falcata*) are also commonly confused with Shumard oaks in the nursery trade. For gardeners contemplating the purchase of a red oak the principle of *caveat emptor* comes as sound advice.

The best course for many gardeners on limy ground is to choose the smaller Texas red oak instead of the Shumard oak. Texas red oak is commonly offered in nurseries as a balled-and-burlapped specimen, often multitrunked and wild-collected. In these cases gardeners can inspect and verify the black alkaline clay soil around its roots and be assured of lime-tolerance. In contrast, nursery-grown red oaks of unknown provenance, however attractive when purchased, may prove disappointingly lime-hating and turn sickly yellow when planted on calcareous ground.

Another excellent resolution to this red oak dilemma is to plant an acorn. Growing your own red oak from seed has several attractive aspects that gardeners ought to find compelling. First of all, it's easy and inexpensive. All one need do is gather acorns as they fall in autumn and pot them up or bury them shallowly in the ground. In ten years' time a young seed-grown oak might easily grow to equal or exceed expensive nursery-grown trees planted at the same time.

More importantly, by selecting acorns from a locally successful parent tree, gardeners can be reasonably assured of the adaptability of its offspring. Because red oaks vary a great deal in the brilliance of their fall coloring, this also offers an excellent opportunity to select for better autumn foliage. A properly chosen red oak tree will be a long-lived garden companion. Gardeners ought to select such a tree carefully and take advantage of all the beauty it might provide.

In addition to the well-known *Q. shumardii* and *Q. texana*, the Chisos red oak

(*Q. gravesii*) offers gardeners a distinctive tree tolerant of lime and drought and deserving of wide use. This variety makes an excellent small- to medium-sized garden tree, but remains uncommon in the nursery trade, except among native plant specialists. Its natural range extends over the mountains and canyons of far western Texas. Unlike *Q. texana* and *Q. shumardii*, the Chisos red oak often turns shades of yellow and gold, as well as scarlet and crimson, in the fall. This late autumn show is especially satisfying because the sleekly cut foliage of this oak hangs down from the branches, giving the tree a lush, full appearance. Attractive blackish bark helps complete this glorious scene.

Vasey oak (*Q. pungens* v. *vaseyana*) is another worthwhile red oak that does well on calcareous ground, and it flaunts especially lustrous semievergreen foliage. This small scrubby tree has shiny, dark green hollylike leaves. It makes a rugged multitrunk specimen and thrives on dry rocky limestone or caliche soils.

The Live Oaks

Although botanists place the live oaks (*Q. virginiana* and *Q. fusiformis*) within the red oak group, gardeners are generally skeptical of such broad views. Their practical natures lead them to dispense with such taxonomic nonsense and recognize these evergreen trees as unique! Scarcely any other tree develops the distinctive, spreading habit of the live oaks. Their weighty, massive branches, covered in shining dark green foliage, lean outward and then bend down toward the ground as if to stroke the earth. This peculiar blend of strength and grace lends romance and enchantment to the scenery of limestone regions and provides the background and structure of many gardens.

On droughty calcareous soils live oaks are the largest and most massive of evergreens, and such oaks are the only evergreen trees gardeners customarily plant for shade. Except for the brief weeks of early spring during which live oaks shed and renew their small, oval leaves, the evergreen boughs of these trees convey to the garden a continuous sense of substance and wealth. When provided with deep soil and a century of growth live oaks often achieve fifty to one hundred feet in height and spread. Even on thin, rocky ground these trees somehow find a sufficient foothold to grow to twenty to thirty-five feet.

The two varieties of live oak commonly included in gardens are so similar that only botanists usually bother to separate them. The most common native type on lime soils is the Texas live oak (*Q. fusiformis*). This variety is especially suited to dry, rocky limestone soils, and its moderately large acorns sprout to produce seedlings with thick carrotlike taproots. *Q. fusiformis* is probably the commonest live oak in gardens on lime and it has the greatest tolerance to cold and drought. Some trees assume attractive purplish tones during the winter.

The other evergreen oak of gardens is the coast live oak (*Q. virginiana*), a native of the coastal plains of the Southeast. Its acorns are smaller and its seedlings are less robust than those of the Texas live oak, but *Q. virginiana* may grow somewhat faster and larger if provided with good, moist soil. Both types accept lime and are usually offered by nurseries as *Q. virginiana* or simply as "live oaks."

The Emory oak (*Q. emoryi*) of the Southwest is another attractive evergreen adapted to lime soil and worth growing in more arid regions. Its small dark green leaves resemble those of *Q. virginiana* and *Q. fusiformis*, but often have hollylike points. Its branches have a distinctively layered horizontal appearance.

The Maples

In the gardens of acid-soil regions the maples (*Acer* spp.) reign supreme and are widely loved as the most colorful trees of autumn. Their lush, graceful columns line the shady avenues of New England and this image resides in the minds of American gardeners as a sort of collective race memory. As a group these trees are mostly denizens of forests, and the majority of them prefer acid soils. A few types venture out and accept the limy prairies, however, to the great joy of gardeners on calcareous ground. Although the number of lime-tolerant maple varieties is small when compared to the vast range of acid-loving types, this group includes choice trees for gardens on calcareous soil.

The toughest and fastest-growing maple adapted to lime is the box-elder (*Acer negundo*), a tree that hardly resembles a maple at all. Instead of the typical lobed foliage and layered canopy of other maples, the box-elder bears a moplike head of ragged compound leaves. These are a bright shade of grass green, as are many of its stems and twigs. Box-elders seem to be growing so fast that they haven't time to bother developing mature, brown bark.

The box-elder is a typical prairie tree: aggressive and hardy, but lacking the sophistication of its relations. Its value in gardens is mostly as a rugged shade provider for country places, or a tree to plant on dry, rocky ground. Under such difficult conditions the box-elder rapidly develops a bright green, rounded crown and will turn a showy clear yellow in autumn. In city or suburban gardens it seems a graceless tree, however, and hosts plagues of green "box-elder bugs" that match its leaves and stems in color.

For most gardeners the "hard" or "sugar" maples are the stately trees that come to mind when they think of the maple tribe. The trees of this group generally tolerate lime, but usually prefer deep, moist soils. Sugar maples from more southern and western areas such as Florida maple (*Acer barbatum*) and Caddo maple (*A. sacharrum* 'Caddo') will accept limy clay soils more readily than trees from eastern sections. They make slow-growing, symmetrical trees that turn yellow or orange in the fall. The chalk maple (*A. leucoderme*) is a similar type that remains slightly smaller.

For truly rocky limestone grounds the canyon or bigtooth maple (*A. grandidentatum*) is a better choice than these, and has the added attraction of fall foliage that generally turns orange-red or scarlet instead of yellow. This variety is a native of limestone canyons and rocky mountainsides and occurs in scattered groves throughout the western states. Although often a crooked-trunked understory tree in the wild, if given a place in the sun *A. grandidentatum* will develop a rounded symmetrical crown much like the sugar maples of New England. Bigtooth maples are slow growing and may struggle on poorly drained soils, but mature into graceful, drought-tolerant shade trees twenty to thirty-five feet tall. In good years they rival any in the brilliance of their fall foliage.

The Old World allies of the American hard maples also tolerate lime, but are uncommon in American gardens. European hedge maples (*A. campestre*) make sturdy round-headed trees well adapted to cold, dry prairie and turn clear yellow in the fall. The Israeli maples (*A. obovatum* v. *syriacum*) are unusual for their evergreen tendencies, and in mild areas may retain their leathery leaves through the winter. They resemble bigtooth maples in size and general appearance.

Other maples occasionally attempted on lime include the aggressive, coarse-leaved silver maple (*Acer saccharinum*), Southern red maple (*Acer rubrum* v. *drummondii*), trident maple (*A. buergeranum*) and the Chinese variety, *A. truncatum*. These are modestly tolerant of alkalinity if not stressed by drought or extreme heat. A generous mulch over their shallow roots and shade from the west sun will help discourage chlorosis. The lobed green leaves of these maples often unfold with a purplish tinge, and color bright orange or yellow in the autumn.

Ashes and Fringe Trees

Although the winged seeds of the ashes (*Fraxinus* spp.) suggest an alliance to the maples, these trees are actually cousins of the ligustrums and lilacs and belong to the lime-loving olive family (*Oleacae*). A wide variety of ashes adapt to lime soil, and this group includes both soaring shade trees and shrubby types grown for their flowers. The ashes are dependable and thrifty trees that often have considerable beauty as well as great practical value.

Gardeners in search of a quick source of shade often select the Arizona ash (*Fraxinus velutina*). This is an easy-growing tree well adapted to dryish limy soils, and it speedily develops a spreading, rounded crown. Its shining green, narrowly compound leaves emerge fresh and early in the spring and turn clear yellow in the fall.

Although fairly compact and long-lived in arid sections, Arizona ash often develops lanky growth in humid areas, and this makes its limbs weak and subject to breakage. In these regions it often suffers from borers and tent caterpillars ("webworms") as well. On heavy clay soils its aggressive roots spread shallowly across the surface.

For many gardens a better choice is the 'Fan-Tex' ash, a seedless selection of the Mexican ash (*F. berlandieri*) that grows along streams in the hot, humid lowlands of South Texas. 'Fan-Tex' ash has broader, glossier green leaves than Arizona ash and develops a dense, symmetrical crown. Although this tree is likely to have shallow roots on difficult clay soils, its compact, attractive crown and seedless nature make it a good, clean shade provider. It is impressively fast-growing in youth.

On truly dry, rocky grounds, however, these fast-growing types soon exhaust the soil's supply of moisture. In such situations the deep-rooted Texas ash (*F. texensis*) is a more appropriate choice and will exceed other ashes in growth. This is a diminutive South-western ally of the white ash (*F. americana*), which it resembles in leaf and in its custom of turning purple or maroon shades in the fall. Texas ash is especially adapted to rocky limestone soils and grows at a moderate pace into a shapely, round-headed tree twenty-five to thirty-five feet tall.

The green ash (*Fraxinus pennsylvanica* v. *lanceolata*) also accepts lime, and on deep, moist soil may achieve forty to fifty feet or more. It resents drought and extreme heat, however, and grows slowly in hot climates. 'Summit' and 'Marshall' are seedless selections often used as street trees. Their symmetrical, upright habits of growth suit them especially for formal avenues and parkways. Good yellow fall color is another attractive feature of these ashes.

Most of the European species of *Fraxinus* enjoy lime soil, although they generally dislike high summer heat. The claret ash (*F. oxycarpa* 'Raywood') is a particularly orna-mental type with showy wine-colored fall foliage. The curious Hessian ash (*F. exelsior* 'Diversifolia') has simple leaves comprised of only one leaflet instead of the customary compound foliage of most ashes.

The southern European flowering or manna ash (*F. ornus*) is especially beautiful and desirable for limy gardens, as is its cousin from the American Southwest, the fragrant ash (*F. cuspidata*). These trees differ markedly from other ashes and show their relation to the lilacs and fringe trees by bearing panicles of narrow-petaled white blooms in mid-spring. The flowers of these small trees smell deliciously of vanilla, and show up well against their dark green, pointed, compound leaves. Both the manna ash and the fragrant ash mature to bushy, round-headed trees that turn butter yellow in fall. They are especially fine choices for rocky slopes over limestone or chalk.

For gardens with a modest depth of soil the Chinese fringe tree (*Chionanthus retusus*) provides a gracious ornamental with white, spidery-petaled blooms much like those of the flowering ashes. Its leaves differ considerably, however, and consist of glossy dark green ovals reminiscent of Japanese privet. Female trees bear ligustrumlike black berries. Another beautiful and distinctive feature of the fringe tree is the attractively mottled bark of its oily textured trunk and branches. Chinese fringe tree performs well on limy clay, unlike its American relative, the "grand-daddy gray-beard" (*C. virginicus*), which is a favorite in the gardens of acid-soil regions.

Walnuts

Although not outstandingly ornamental, fast-growing, or easily transplanted, the walnuts (*Juglans* spp.) deserve the interest and affection of gardeners on lime. The flavorful nuts of these trees, the generous shade provided by their leafy branches, and the beautiful and valuable hardwood lumber that forms beneath the dark, furrowed bark of their trunks are attractions that can slowly weave a spell of enchantment over gardeners' hearts.

As with the oaks, the walnuts are substantial trees that people plant not simply for their own enjoyment, but for generations to come as well. A walnut tree is an investment destined to accrue in value over the years, both intangibly as a beautiful provider of shade, and quite literally as the best and most valuable of hardwoods for furniture and veneer.

On deep clay soils the black walnut (*Juglans nigra*) performs well and makes a long-lived, drought-tolerant shade tree. Farm folk often plant it in dooryards, and many may be found shading the modest frame houses that dot the limy prairies. Although capable of great height when grown on rich bottomlands, walnuts planted in the open on heavy alkaline clays develop rounded spreading heads and mature at forty to fifty feet or less.

The nuts of the black walnut are tasty, but require considerable effort to extract from the hard case and messy black husk. These husks, the litter of falling walnut leaves, and the roots of the black walnut all exude juglone, a mild poison that inhibits the growth of neighboring plants. In nature this helps keep competing trees away from the black walnut; in gardens it generally makes anything other than rough grass or groundcover difficult to grow near this tree. The kingly walnut is a tree determined to rule its immediate domain, and gardeners had best place it safely away from any pretenders to the throne!

On rocky limestone ground the Texas or Arizona walnut (*J. major*) deputizes for the black walnut and resembles it closely, save in size. Texas walnut and the related river walnut (*J. microcarpa*) are western trees native along rocky streambanks that grow to twenty to thirty feet in height. Although the nuts of these varieties are small, they make excellent medium-sized shade trees, and their yellow fall color is showy. The river walnut often grows as a rugged, multistemmed specimen.

For high quality nuts these American trees must yield the stage to the English walnut (*J. regia*), although the black walnut usually remains to serve as the understock for this

European variety. The lime tolerance of the English walnut often depends on which root-stock is selected, and in alkaline western areas the Arizona walnut and river walnut make good choices for this purpose. The English walnut makes a sturdy-looking, compact tree. Its canopy is formed of stiff, upright branches, cloaked in large, coarse-textured foliage.

Most nut-producing varieties of English walnut perform best in temperate climates and few have been selected to bear in the harsh weather typical over the limestone regions of America. 'Carpathian' yields modestly well in cooler areas. Although English walnuts are unlikely to produce commercial quantities in home gardens, the nuts they provide will be among the most delicious and valuable. Locally adapted varieties may be available from state agricultural research stations, and extension personnel can instruct gardeners on appropriate rootstocks and budding techniques.

Pecans and Hickories

The pecan (*Carya illinoiensis*) is a more practical nut-bearing tree for most gardeners on lime, and in the quality of its nuts and the ornament it provides it is the equal of any walnut. Pecans are by nature graceful, soaring trees of river bottoms, and perform best on deep, well-drained soils. They are tougher than most trees, however, and will put up with difficult limy clays and searing summer drought so long as their deep taproots can penetrate sufficiently into the ground. On thin rocky soils they may grow, but will be greatly stunted in size and productivity.

The long taproots of young pecans make them troublesome to transplant, and require gardeners to dig holes at least three feet deep when setting out bare-root saplings. Although readily transplanted container trees are available, these seldom redevelop taproots properly, and can be slow to establish and grow off. Budded trees of all varieties, although faster-growing and more productive than seedlings, have greater susceptibility to insects and diseases than plants on their own roots.

The most practical way to obtain a vigorous, productive, disease-resistant pecan for the garden is to plant a nut. In five years or less a seed-planted pecan is likely to surpass nursery stock of any kind, and its longevity and resistance to drought and disease will be superior. This is due to the deeper, more natural development of its root system, and its less "forced" top growth. If the seed is carefully selected from a strain of pecan that produces well locally, then its offspring will likely do well also and should yield bountiful quantities of tasty nuts. A healthy, productive type such as 'Desirable' is an excellent seed parent for gardeners in many areas and is readily available commercially.

As garden trees pecans can be messy to live with, especially if drought stressed. Although they are generous providers of shade, their wood rots easily and their graceful canopies of spreading branches seem to be in constant danger of collapse. Twigs, leaves, husks from the nuts, and branches big enough to stoke the fire fall like a steady rain from above. Although troublesome to clean up, this abundance of vegetable refuse can be a boon to the gardener on lime, who must constantly search for organic material to return to the soil. A large pecan is a productive factory of potential humus, just waiting to be harnessed for use on the compost pile.

Although relatively tolerant to lime, pecans require large amounts of zinc, and on calcareous soils profit from supplemental foliar sprays of this element. Naturally available zinc in lime soils commonly derives from the droppings of visiting birds, and organic gardeners sometimes intersperse fruiting mulberry trees among pecans to attract birds and thereby improve the soil's content of this mineral.

The hickories comprise a vast group of pecan relations that reside mostly among the other forest trees of the eastern American silva. Only the modest nutmeg hickories (*Carya myristicaeformis*) show much affinity for lime, and, although beautiful and long-lived, they receive little attention from gardeners. Like the pecan, the hickories have deep taproots that make them difficult and unprofitable for nurseries to handle. Nutmeg hickories make stiffly upright trees with attractive shaggy bark and compound leaves. Their nutmeglike fruit may be collected in the fall and planted directly in the ground.

Chinese Pistache

Although by no means related to the pecans and hickories, the Chinese pistache (*Pistacia chinensis*) might easily pass as such to the uninitiated, for it has similar pinnate leaves and furrowed bark. Any question of identity would be resolved in the fall, however, when the pistache revealed its brilliant autumn foliage. This singular tree provides some of the most outstanding shades of scarlet and crimson offered by any tree on alkaline land.

The Chinese pistache is a large-growing ally of the sumacs, and shares their tolerance of poor dry soils, as well as their colorful habits in autumn. Although gawky and poorly branched in youth, pistache eventually matures into a remarkably symmetrical, well-branched tree up to fifty feet tall. Female trees bear sumaclike orange-red berries that are attractive, but can pose a cleanup problem near pavement. In spite of this fault, pistache rates highly as a drought-tolerant, colorful provider of shade. It grows at a moderate pace and is relatively long-lived.

The Planetrees

It seems that wherever one travels the favorite trees of city streets and urban parkways are the planetrees (*Platanus* spp.), known popularly in America as sycamores. This is certainly not because of any practical features, for the huge scalloped leaves of these trees collect in great masses on the ground each fall and are difficult to sweep up. Their patchy, flaking bark, as well as their well-known seed clusters or "sycamore balls" continuously rain down on sidewalks and streets. While professionals in grounds maintenance regularly curse the sycamores, gardeners continue to plant them, for they are loveable, lush in foliage, alive and interesting in winter, and big and filled with all the luxuriance a tree can muster.

In youth most sycamores display striking pyramidal growth, which is all the more arresting because of their enormous maplelike leaves. In age they assume picturesque spreading or windswept shapes, and the light-colored peeling bark of their ever-widening trunks shows freshly at all times. On deep soil with abundant moisture sycamores are among the fastest-growing trees and are likely to be among the largest as well. Fifty to one hundred feet is common.

In gardens on lime it is best to plant sycamore seedlings propagated from locally native trees. Trees brought from acid regions will not only suffer chlorosis on alkaline land, but also experience greater susceptibility to other maladies such as anthracnose. Sycamores infected by this disease seem to "burn up" in late summer; their leaves turn brown and crisp, and entire limbs die and fall to the ground. So many of the lime-hating eastern sycamores have been thoughtlessly planted on shallow, droughty lime soil that anthracnose-infected trees are a common sight, and sycamores in general have earned reputations as short-lived, disease-prone trees.

On appropriately deep soils with adequate moisture sycamores can be beautiful and successful, and lime-tolerance can be assured by selecting native Southwestern varieties. Texas sycamore (*Platanus occidentalis* v. *glabrata*) is a vigorous inhabitant of limestone regions that has exceptionally ornamental white peeling bark. Its leaves are thicker and more heat-resistant than those of the common American variety (*P. occidentalis*) and often have fewer serrations along their edges. Mexican sycamore (*P. mexicanus*) also has leaves that tend toward simple five-pointed stars in shape, and this foliage is often felted white on the underside. Mexican sycamores make big, lanky trees that flash glimpses of silver as the wind blows through their huge leaves.

The planetrees of the Old World also tolerate lime, and both the Turkish plane (*P. orientalis*) and its hybrid with the American sycamore, the London plane (*P.* × *hispanica*), may be planted on calcareous ground. These are generally sturdy, long-lived trees with good resistance to disease and to air pollution, but lack the showy white bark of American sycamore species. Their patchy trunks display various shades of green, buff, and brown. In hot regions they are slow growing, and remain smaller than their American relatives.

Sweetgums and Witch Hazels

The spiky ball-shaped fruits of the sweetgums (*Liquidambar* spp.), their star-shaped leaves, and their pyramidal growth all point to a relationship with the sycamores, which are their distant cousins. Aromatic, resinous sap flows in the branches of sweetgum trees and is the source of both their common and scientific names. Since the Middle Ages this "liquid amber" has been harvested for incense, medicine, or as a breath-freshening chewing gum. The glossy foliage and rubbery cork-winged twigs of these trees have a succulent quality that seems to derive from impregnation with this fragrant sap. In autumn their maplelike leaves provide a great show and turn shades of crimson, yellow, purple, and scarlet.

The American sweetgum (*Liquidambar styraciflua*) tolerates limy clay, but requires a copious and unfailing supply of water. Drought is the enemy of these swamp-loving trees, and on thin dry soils over limestone, chalk, or caliche they are likely to develop chlorosis. Although liable to perish during any extended periods of drought, the formal, upright habit of the sweetgum and its tremendous autumn show have encouraged its culture in some areas of blackland prairie.

Californians have selected several types for fall foliage such as 'Palo Alto' and 'Burgundy.' Gardeners may also choose the usefully sterile 'Rotundifolia,' which has round-lobed leaves and lacks the troublesome spiny fruits typical of sweetgums. Chinese sweetgum (*L. formosana*) seems to enjoy the same conditions as the American type, and may be tried on well-watered limy clay. It has three-lobed leaves that emerge with a purplish tinge.

Of greater interest for gardens on calcareous grounds is the Asiatic sweetgum (*L. orientalis*), which in nature occurs on the arid, rocky limestones of southern Turkey. On chalk or caliche this is the sweetgum to plant, if it can be obtained. Its lacy, five-lobed leaves are smaller than those of *L. styraciflua* and more deeply divided. They turn shades of gold, red, or russet-purple in autumn.

Another member of this family that naturally grows on lime is the Persian ironwood

(*Parrottia persica*). Although differing from sweetgum in its wide-spreading horizontal branches and oval leaves, the parrottia equals it in brilliance and succulence of foliage. Like many Asian trees, it seems to dislike the intense heat of American summers and performs best with partial shade and deep, moist soil. It grows slowly to twenty or thirty feet and bears tiny crimson flowers along its branches in early spring.

This last character shows the parrottia's relation to the witch hazels (*Hamamelis* spp.), whose similar flowers appear in the autumn and winter. The pliant stems of these small, crooked trees were favored for "water-witching" or "dousing" by early American colonists. Their fragrant flowers consist of spidery twisted petals. Over a year's time these develop into woody seed capsules that open explosively along with the flowers of the following season.

The showy witch hazel cultivars favored in gardens derive mostly from the lime-hating Chinese *Hamamelis mollis*, and perform poorly on calcareous soils unless provided with special beds of acid compost. This is generally true for the American *H. virginiana* and *H. vernalis* as well. However, small populations of common witch hazel (*H. virginiana*) occur naturally on the limy soils of central Texas, and propagations from these trees readily accept calcareous soil. They have pale yellow flowers that open in concert with their yellowing autumn leaves, and make quietly attractive subjects for gardens with partial shade. *H. virginiana* grows slowly to ten or fifteen feet.

Cottonwoods and Poplars

Like sweetgums and parrotias, the cottonwoods and poplars (*Populus* spp.) feature waxy, shining foliage and exude aromatic balsam-scented sap. They are frequently the fastest-growing and largest trees in their immediate neighborhoods, and achieve towering heights. Although limited to yellow tones, the spectacle of their glittering fall foliage is among the best witnessed on alkaline land.

Nevertheless, gardeners generally dismiss these trees in the same breath with box-elders, for cottonwoods and poplars exhibit all the liabilities that customarily accompany excessively fast growth. Although appropriate for plantings in the country, they are too aggressive, shallow-rooted, and short-lived to recommend for most city or suburban gardens. Cotton root rot is a frequent problem on heavy alkaline clays, and these trees continuously shed leaves when stressed by summer heat.

Nevertheless, the vision of a cottonwood in full autumn gold will stop the heart of any Westerner, and the astonishingly fast growth of these trees tempts many to plant them for shade. The widely-spreading eastern cottonwood (*Populus deltoides*) can reach enormous size and is a popular, generous shade-provider. Its large heart-shaped leaves are glossy green in summer and turn shining yellow in the fall. 'Robusta' is a favorite "cottonless" selection of this species. Like all male cottonwoods, it lacks the messy cottony seed of the female trees. The Texas cottonwood (*P. wislizenii*) and Fremont cottonwood (*P. fremontii*) are similar species useful in the arid Southwest.

Ineffectual for shade, but good as a dramatic, upright landscape tree is the "balm of Gilead" (*P. × candicans*), a hybrid between the eastern cottonwood and the balsam poplar of the American northwest (*P. balsamifera*). Even more vertical is the lombardy poplar (*P. nigra* 'Italica'), whose erect silhouettes line country roads and edge farmers' fields throughout Europe. The picturesque outlines of these trees and the elysian scenery they create appear with frequency on the canvasses of the French impressionists.

Although tolerant of lime, both the Lombardy poplar and the balm of Gilead readily succumb to cotton root rot on heavy clay, and are likely to develop stem canker in warm humid regions. They perform best on well-drained rocky soils or near streams or ponds.

The aptly-named white, or silver, poplar (*P. alba*) has dark green leaves felted white on the underside, which flutter attractively in the breeze and almost (but not quite) make up for its unfortunate habit of suckering from the roots. Its bark is a showy white, accented by corky, black, transverse markings. An upright selection of silver poplar ('Bolleana'), and a hybrid with the quaking aspen (the gray poplar, *P. × canescens*), have similar virtues and vices.

The Willows

The graceful willows (*Salix* spp.) share many of the habits of the poplars, which are their close cousins. Although tolerant of lime, in warm, humid climates willows are short-lived and suffer stem-cankers and die-back. Cotton root rot is a serious problem on limy clay.

Still, no other tree offers the lithe, flowing outline of the weeping willow (*Salix babylonica*), and few are as telling to associate with water. Weeping willows are tremendously fast-growing, and empower gardeners to create romantic landscape scenes in a very short time. Such stage sets have short runs, however. At first small twigs, then large branches, and eventually the entire tree will turn brown and die off, usually in ten to fifteen years or less. The Wisconsin strain of weeping willow (*S. × blanda*) and the curly-leafed *S. babylonica* 'Annularis' are reportedly somewhat stronger and longer-lived, but even these die young unless planted with their roots at the water's edge.

For dry chalky ground the globe willows (*S. matsudana* 'Navaho' and *S. matsudana* 'Umbraculifera') are much better trees. In contrast to the familiar weeping willows, globe willows hold their branches upright and develop rounded, symmetrical crowns, in outline suggesting gigantic lollipops. In autumn they give memorable displays of golden yellow. These trees are healthier and more drought-tolerant than other willows, and make serviceable fast-growing screens or windbreaks on rocky limestone soils. Although closely related, the strange corkscrew willow (*S. matsudana* 'Tortuosa') suffers badly from die-back and stem-canker.

Mulberries and Bois d'Arcs

Although tough and fast-growing, mulberries (*Morus* spp.) generally have coarse, artless appearances, that are only slightly redeemed by interesting buttressed trunks and flaking bark. These wide-spreading trees project low profiles, and their large leaves efficiently overlap one another to shut out the sun. This makes mulberries practical, if uncultured, shade trees. In China the leaves of these trees are the favored food for silkworms.

Although moderately long-lived, drought-tolerant, and easy to transplant, mulberries are notoriously difficult to garden under. Their shallow spreading roots and dense shady canopies compete with and eliminate grass, and all but the toughest ivy or jasmine.

Male selections of the white mulberry (*Morus alba*) such as 'Fruitless' or 'Mapleleaf' are the most popular for shade purposes, and lack the messy fruits. Unusual weeping forms of this tree such as the sterile 'Chapparal' and the fruit-bearing 'Tea's Weeping' are sometimes planted as garden curiosities and seldom exceed ten to fifteen feet in height. White mulberries are especially valued in arid regions for their dark shining green foliage; in areas beset with humid summers they suffer from bacterial leaf spots and may shed much of their foliage prematurely.

For fruiting purposes the black mulberry (M. *nigra*) is the type to plant. Its tart blackberrylike fruits turn deep wine red when ripe. Although rather tasty, these berries are impractically soft and difficult to harvest, and much of the crop invariably falls to the ground as a sticky, red-staining mass. Fortunately, this crop partially departs in the beaks of excited local birds.

Native red mulberry (M. *rubra*) is rarely planted, but succeeds on limy clay soils and produces large, lightly felted leaves. Hairier, but otherwise rather similar is the paper mulberry (*Brousonettia papyrifera*). This is a common tree of old farmsteads and waste places, and often seeds itself into large groves. Its soft gray leaves exhibit heart-shaped, mitten-shaped and three-lobed variations, often all on the same tree. Although usefully tough and drought-tolerant, paper mulberry is too aggressive for any but the roughest types of plantings.

On rocky limestone or caliche soils the Texas mulberry (M. *microphylla*) makes a small, shrubby tree that appears refreshingly fine-textured for a mulberry. Its two-inch-long leaves are delicately lobed and serrated, and remain a luxuriant shining green through grueling summer heat and drought. Another novel type is the contorted mulberry (M. *bombycis* 'Unruyu'). This ancient Chinese cultivar has bizarre twisted branches and makes a weird, squat tree or large shrub.

The bois d'arc or Osage orange (*Maclura pomifera*) is a mulberry relative and a familiar component of native vegetation on limy blackland prairie. In the late nineteenth century this uniquely American tree was widely planted in hedgerows along the farm fields of the prairies states, and its glittering green leaves and huge grapefruitlike fruits have become familiar sights throughout mid-America. These "hedge-" or "horse-apples" have entertained generations of children on the prairies.

Although as coarse as any mulberry, and just as difficult to garden under, the bois d'arc has value as a shade provider and is exceptionally long-lived and drought-tolerant. Gardens often inherit these trees as parts of old hedgerows, and it is far better to accept and utilize such trees in the garden than to ruin saws and other pruning equipment on their outrageously strong, hard wood. The resilient, durable lumber of these trees was favored by Native Americans for their bows and served pioneers as fenceposts, wagons, gates, and railroad ties. This "ironwood" will quickly dull any chainsaw, and it smolders cantankerously and explodes when placed in the fireplace.

Such a courageous and historic tree inspires admiration, and the clear shining yellow of the bois d'arc's autumn leaves creates a winning scene for gardens on limy ground. Although its popularity as a hedge tree faded decades ago with the introduction of barbed wire, the bois d'arc's tough, hardy nature recommends it for planting in gardens today, especially in difficult situations on the prairies. 'Fan d'arc' and 'Wichita' are two good male selections that lack the enormous, impractical "horse-apples." A curious Chinese relation of the bois d'arc, *Cudrania*, is also worth trying on difficult limy soils. It has similar glossy foliage and small, reddish, rounded edible fruits.

Chinaberry

Although short-lived, and laden with messy grapelike yellow berries in the autumn, the "Texas umbrella tree" or chinaberry (*Melia azederach* 'Umbraculiformis') has a loyal following among gardeners. Its exotically fragrant lavender spring flowers and fernlike compound leaves are unusual for a hardy tree. This member of the mahogany family develops a lush, umbrella-shaped canopy, densely furnished by dark, glossy green foliage. Scarcely any tree grows as fast on rocky limestone soils, and chinaberries persevere through torturous heat and drought. These trees have unusually good yellow fall foliage as well.

Soapberry, Golden-rain Trees, and Mexican Buckeye

The western soapberry (*Sapindus drummondii*) is another unusual tree useful for limy gardens. Like the chinaberry, it ripens clusters of large amber berries in the fall and displays them attractively through most of the winter. These berries were crushed by early settlers to produce a cleansing lather, hence the common name of "soapberry."

Soapberries grow at a modest pace and are long-lived and tolerant of drought, lime, and salt. They make small, upright trees, often forming groves or clumps along fence-lines. Their slender trunks develop shaggy gray, flaking bark. Narrowly compound pale green leaves cling to their angular branches, and turn a showy clear yellow in the fall.

This beautiful yellow autumn foliage is a family trait shared by allies of the soapberry such as the oriental golden-rain trees (*Koelreuteria* spp.). Golden-rain trees derive their fanciful common name from the clouds of tiny yellow flowers that they hold above their foliage in early summer. Like chinaberries, these exotic-looking trees produce large, bipinnate leaves and have umbrella-shaped, spreading crowns.

The panicled golden-rain tree (*K. paniculata*) is the hardiest and most popular variety, and makes a drought-tolerant tree twenty to thirty feet tall and wide. Its dark green foliage makes a good foil for its tiny golden blooms. These ripen in late summer to papery brown capsules shaped like tiny Japanese lanterns.

An occasional difficulty with this tree is a reluctance of certain seedlings to flower. For this reason, when shopping it is best to select golden-rain trees while in bloom, or to look for last year's seed pods as evidence of good flowering capacity.

Although subject to freeze damage where temperatures dip below 15° F, the southern golden-rain tree or Chinese flame tree (*K. bipinnata*) is even more beautiful than *K. paniculata*. Pinkish-red seed capsules (instead of brown) make its ripening fruit seem like a second spectacular season of flower! Its large leaves are twice-pinnately compound, but vary from strain to strain, and may or may not have terminal leaflets. It is worth a gardener's time to take notice of this obscure leaf morphology, for strains with truncated leaves are generally the most desirable and hardy to cold.

Although relatively easy to live with in a lawn area, pesky volunteer seedlings are likely to proliferate if the Chinese flame tree is planted near garden beds. Its tiny, shotlike seeds can be troublesome to sweep up from pavement as well.

By enlarging these shiny, black seeds to the size of marbles, and hardening the papery capsules that hold them into three-sided woody contraptions, the Mexican buckeye (*Ungnadia speciosa*) has come up with its own unique variation on the soapberry family theme. Like its allies it has excellent yellow fall color and does especially well on drought-prone, limy soils. This curious native Southwestern tree makes a small, multi-trunked specimen and has lush green pecanlike foliage. Its shiny rounded seeds often serve as entertaining "marbles" for children. Although mildly toxic to some, these nuts are flavorful and edible in moderation.

Mexican buckeye lines its branches with fascinating orchidlike flowers to create a show in early spring. These pink blooms appear as the new leaves of the season are emerging, and later ripen to form the dark brown seed capsules. Although inclined to suckering, and often more shrub than tree, Mexican buckeye is always interesting and ornamental and rates among the best trees for lime soil.

A Chinese ally of *Ungnadia*, equally original and garden-worthy is the "yellowhorn" or "popcorn tree" (*Xanthoceras sorbifolia*). Like Mexican buckeye it makes a small multi-stemmed specimen, has compound leaves, and does well on lime. Instead of bearing tiny pink orchids, however, it smothers its branches in clusters of inch-wide white flowers, each with a deep carmine throat, so as to resemble hundreds of blooms of the old-fashioned rose of Sharon in miniature. Its fruit look like a green version of the Mexican buckeye's and include several dark brown chestnutlike seeds. Yellowhorn is more cold-hardy than Mexican buckeye, but less tolerant of heat. In Texas it performs best with partial shade and deep, moist soil.

The Buckeyes

In spite of having similar, hard, shiny nuts, true buckeyes (*Aesculus* spp.) are only distant relatives of *Ungnadia* and *Xanthoceras*, and produce their mildly toxic "conkers" in rounded leathery husks, usually one or two together, instead of in three-sided woody capsules. They have distinctive palmately compound leaves and hold their spring blooms in big pyramidal clusters at the ends of their branches. Buckeye trees often look like gigantic red or white bluebonnets (*Lupinus texensis*) when in flower! Like pecans, buckeyes have heavy taproots that make them difficult to transplant. They are easy to grow from the large, round seeds, however, and often will begin to flower in only two or three years.

Red buckeye (*Aesculus pavia*) is one of the most attractive varieties suited to lime soil, and makes it a nice small garden tree with brilliant scarlet flowers. The enormously fat buds of this tree are among the first to burst open in spring. Its luxuriant green leaves unfold and expand before almost any other woody plant, and can be nearly as satisfying as the floral fireworks that grow along with them in March and April. Although red or scarlet in most of its range, *Aesculus pavia* varies to chartreuse yellow (*v. flava*) on the limestone hills of central Texas. Intergrades are often lovely shades of peach-pink.

Unfortunately, the lush spring appearance of red buckeyes begins to visibly tarnish in short order. On dry rocky ground these trees may become completely bare as early as June or July, and this habit of early leaf drop is also shared by the cream-flowered California buckeye (*A. californica*). Woodland settings offer appropriate textural contrasts for the buckeye's bold foliage, provide shade to help retain the leaves in summer, and make useful places to hide these thick-stemmed shrubby trees during the long "off-season."

Ohio buckeye (*A. glabra*) and its Southwestern cousin, the Texas buckeye (*A. arguta*), are more upright and treelike, and usually retain their foliage long enough to offer an attractive display of russet autumn leaves. Except for the smaller size of the Texas variety, these buckeyes are difficult to separate, and botanists often regard them as regional forms of a single species. The creamy yellow spring blooms of these dense, symmetrical trees look well dressed against their erect, oval forms and sharply divided leaves. Texas buckeye may be only a shrub on thin rocky ground, but reaches fifteen to twenty feet on good bottomland soil. Ohio buckeye becomes a large tree in its native Midwestern woodlands, but on dry limy soils is unlikely to exceed twenty-five or thirty feet.

Although the Eurasian horse-chestnuts (*A. hippocastanum* and *A. × carnea*) tolerate lime, these huge trees need cool climates to be at their best and suffer from foliar blights and disease in the warm, humid summer weather of North America. American species such as bottlebrush buckeye (A. *parviflora*) and sweet buckeye (A. *octandra*) prefer cool, forested conditions.

Crabapples, Pears, and Hawthorns

In temperate regions of North America, flowering crabapples (*Malus* cvs.) head many gardeners' lists of ornamental trees. They are little-used in warm climates, however, for the spring displays of these trees are fleeting, and their summer foliage is often marred by rusts and leaf spots. Cotton root rot is a serious threat on alkaline clay soils. In garden regions where the warmth-loving evergreen relatives of the crabapples (i. e. the photinias, cherry laurels, loquats, and India-hawthorns) succeed, only the toughest and most disease-resistant crabapple cultivars are likely to prosper.

Nevertheless, crabapples are pleasant trees to have in any garden that can accommodate them. The exuberance of their delicately colored, fragrant spring flowers is part of the annual excitement of the season, and never fails to touch the heart. Many "crabs" follow this spring show with an autumnal display of colorful fruit. They frequently develop attractive patchy bark and pleasant, rustic habits of growth as well.

Although not particularly disease resistant, the old rose-red cultivar, 'Eleyi,' is vigorous and adaptable, and accepts limy blackland prairie better than most types. The native prairie crab (*Malus ioensis*) also succeeds on lime and is popular in Northern regions in its double-flowered form, 'Plena,' known popularly as the "Bechtel" crab. 'Brandywine' is a red-leaved, rosy-flowered hybrid that descends from this double prairie crab.

In hotter gardens the related "Texas" or "Blanco" crab (M. *ioensis* v. *texana*) and the Southern crabapple (M. *angustifolia*) would be appropriate types to try. These are scrubby, suckering trees with delicate, pale pink blooms in spring. Their inch-wide green crabs are deliciously aromatic and may be used to make tart preserves. In a good autumn their leaves turn bronzy-red.

The callery pears (*Pyrus calleryana*) feature attractive fall colors as well, and are remarkably tough and fast-growing. These ornamental trees eventually become large enough to compete in the shade tree category, but are most often planted for their white spring blooms and bronze autumn foliage.

'Bradford' is the most popular type, and retains a dense pyramidal growth habit in youth. This makes it a favorite choice for parkway and avenue plantings. 'Bradford' pears adapt well to limy clay soils, so long as they are not overly stressed by drought. Like all callery pears, they bear fruits that are pea-sized and inedible, and not at all bothersome.

Other varieties such as 'Aristocrat' and 'Capital' offer more loose, open branching, and more narrow, vertical silhouettes, respectively. Seedling callery pears are good as well, and make spreading, informal garden trees that often bloom more readily than these named selections. They are difficult to obtain in nurseries, however, and usually develop threateningly large thorns along their branches.

Although several types of pears besides P. *calleryana* will accept lime soil, few are used in America due to their susceptibility to fireblight. The lovely silver-leaved pears—the weeping P. *salicifolia* 'Pendula' and the Mediteranean native, P. *nivalis*—seem likely to succeed on lime, but remain unproven in American gardens.

Gardeners might well consider blight-resistant varieties of the common fruiting pear (P. *communis*) such as 'Keiffer' and 'Orient.' These are certainly attractive enough to be planted as ornamentals, and actually have larger, more voluptuous spring flowers than the callery pears. Their fall colors can be striking orange-reds.

Like the flowering crabs, the hawthorns, or mayhaws (*Crataegus* spp.), are mostly plants of cold climate gardens and regularly suffer from diseases in areas with warm, humid summers. Fire-blight often shows up as lesions or cankers on stems and branches. The autumn fruits of hawthorns are abundant and showy, but usually remain on the trees only a short time.

Although these deficiencies are common to the hawthorn race, a few types make useful spring-flowering trees and perform modestly well on heavy clay soils. Hawthorns often have great character, and their gnarled trunks are frequently covered in flaking chestnut-brown bark. The heavy-scented white flowers of the mayhaws are customary and sentimental contributors to a generous spring season.

Mountain hawthorn (*Crataegus tracyi*) grows naturally on rough limestone hills in central Texas, and is one of the healthier types. It has showy red fruit and bronze-red autumn foliage. Other native lime-loving hawthorns include *C. reverchonii* and *C. mollis*.

Mayhaw (*C. opaca*) is a common Southeastern native, sometimes available in improved selections such as 'Superberry' and 'Superspur.' Parsley-leaf hawthorn (*C. marshalli*), Cockspur hawthorn (*C. crus-gallii*), Washington hawthorn (*C. phaenopyrum*), and the unusual blue-fruited Blueberry hawthorn (*C. brachyacantha*) are other attractive types suited to wet soils but inclined to chlorosis on dry, chalky ground.

Peaches, Plums, and Cherries

In sheer floral glory the flowering peaches (*Prunus persica* cvs.) easily outdo the crabapples, pears, and hawthorns. In their frivolously brief moments each spring the double-flowered peach cultivars smother gardens in lavish clouds of pink, white, or—most popularly—vibrant rose-red. Although these trees hold little interest after bloomtime, and may be rather short-lived, they are easy, fast-growing, and tolerate considerable abuse. For gardeners on drought-prone lime ground this is as close an approach to the sumptuousness of spring-flowering cherries as they may expect to achieve.

A particularly novel and worthwhile cultivar is the 'Peppermint' peach. This riotously colorful type has won a niche in the hearts and gardens of country folk. On prairie farmsteads it often loudly reigns over hodge-podges of colorful spring blooms. The flowers of 'Peppermint' peach are mostly white with pink streaks and variegations. However, whole branches of the tree may take off towards the rose-red spectrum, while others sport to pristine white. The overall effect can be raucously charming.

Several flowering plums are popular garden trees and do well on lime soils. The most commonly planted are the purple-leafed cultivars of the Asian cherry-plum (*P. cerasifera*). 'Krauter Vesuvius' is the darkest-leaved type, with 'Newport' and 'Thundercloud' following in decreasing intensities of purple-red pigmentation.

These trees descend from types selected by a M. Pissard, French gardener to the Shah of Iran in the 1800s. Purple plums generally thrive in cool, arid regions similar to Persia. In areas where summers are warm and humid they suffer attacks of foliar diseases and are rather short-lived. "Shot-gun" leaf spot is common on purple plums in hot climates like Texas. This fungal disease gives these trees a tattered appearance, for the leaves slough off the infected spots, leaving hundreds of tiny holes.

Gardeners insistent on including such dark-foliaged trees in their designs may substitute one of the red-leaved flowering peach cultivars or the much healthier American plum hybrid, 'Allred.' In addition to reddish summer foliage 'Allred' produces sparse crops of edible red plums, and makes a nice show of pink spring flowers. Although vibrant red while in active growth, the mature leaves of these trees fade to bronzy-green in late summer. Nurseries usually offer 'Allred' as grafts with a single trunk. Like most American plums, when grown on its own roots, 'Allred' can be allowed to sucker and naturalize. The garden effect often resembles a grove of red bamboo!

One of the best spring-flowering trees for limestone regions is the "big-tree" or Mexican plum (*Prunus mexicana*). Unlike most native plums this type seldom spreads from root suckers and usually grows into a single-trunked tree fifteen to twenty feet tall. Its white early spring flowers are cloyingly fragrant and light up the dark, shady positions in which this tree prefers to grow.

If planted in the open sun, Mexican plum may show some scorching and wilting of its leaves in late summer, especially on dry rocky ground. Nevertheless, it can offer a grand show of orange-red leaves in autumn. Mexican plum is long-lived and develops attractive cherrylike peeling bark. Its pinkish-orange fruits have the look and smell of persimmons and usually ripen late in the fall.

It is a sad truth that the delicately-hued flowering cherries that are so popular in the maritime climates of Europe and eastern America perish quickly on droughty, lime ground. However, the electric-rose Taiwan cherry (*Prunus campanulata*) sometimes succeeds, and is worth trying on well-watered limy clay.

On the limestone hills of central Texas the escarpment black cherry (*Prunus serotina* v. *exima*) makes an attractive, upright tree with glossy, peeling bark and good yellow fall color. Although tolerant of drought and lime, this variety struggles on heavy clay soils. On well-drained chalky uplands, however, it may soar up to thirty or forty feet. It bears crops of small bittersweet cherries that turn from red to black as they ripen.

Redbuds

Of all the spring-flowering trees grown on calcareous soils the redbuds (*Cercis* spp.) are the most cherished. Although neither as brilliantly colorful as flowering peaches, nor so striking in form as flowering pears, redbuds manage a measure of charm that few other trees approach. Their deceptively lifeless gray bark annually disappears in a froth of tiny pink pea-blossoms, and this heartwarming scene is a sentimental rite of spring passage on the limestone heartlands.

Redbuds are small, fast-growing trees whose spreading forms and heart-shaped leaves give them an impish character. All types of redbud seem to enjoy calcareous soils, but vary according to strain in their tolerance of heat and drought. Properly selected redbud varieties, carefully positioned and chosen to meet local soil and moisture regimes, can be long-lived and fairly pest free. On poorly drained sites, however, cotton root rot and borers are frequent enemies.

Eastern redbuds (*Cercis canadensis*) thrive on deeper clay soils and are the most popular redbuds of American gardens. They are more treelike and easily trained to single trunks than other types, and they grow quickly to fifteen or twenty feet. The leaves of the variety, 'Forest Pansy,' are uniquely attractive and emerge with an impressive dark purple tone before slowly maturing to dull green. The flowers of this selection are deep wine as well.

Eastern redbuds grow naturally in shady understories along woodland margins and prefer partial shade in hot regions such as Texas. Without it they often scorch in summer, and this added stress encourages leaf-spotting diseases, making them unsightly. This is true also for the Chinese redbuds (C. *chinensis*), which flower at their best only in regions with fairly cold winters.

More tolerant of sun and heat and adaptable to shallow, lime soils are the Texas redbuds (C. *canadensis* v. *texana*) and Mexican redbuds (C. *canadensis* v. *mexicana*), which in horticulture are sometimes known as "C. reniformis." These varieties have thick, leathery leaves that are kidney-shaped instead of heart-shaped. They often sucker to form many-stemmed small trees. Attractive crops of purplish legumes (bean-pods) hang from their branches during the summer months.

The rounded, wavy foliage of the Mexican redbuds imparts a pert, lively appearance that makes these trees especially choice. Their fuzzy-stemmed leaves vary from the size of quarters to over six inches across. Some strains have especially intricate, shrubby branching habits.

The best forms of these native Southwestern varieties exhibit lustrous, glossy foliage and dark-colored flowers. Gardeners can be sure of getting this wine-red, shiny-leaved type by planting 'Oklahoma.' This outstanding cultivar comes from the Arbuckle mountains and is one of the most beautiful of all lime-loving flowering trees. Equally desirable is 'White Texas,' a selection from near Ft. Worth. It has white spring blooms and tremendously glossy, heat-tolerant leaves. These redbuds look good all season long and their lustrous foliage turns clear yellow in the fall.

Because nurseries propagate 'Oklahoma' and other redbud cultivars by budding onto Eastern redbud rootstocks, the roots of these trees (the Eastern part) need fairly deep soils to be happy, and have less drought tolerance than seedling Texas or Mexican redbuds. Gardeners on thin rocky ground will do better with true Texas or Mexican redbuds grown on their own roots.

Deciduous Magnolias

Few spring-flowering trees can compete with the opulent displays of the deciduous magnolias. The ends of their twigs may hold hundreds of fuzzy buds that burst precociously to reveal huge white or pink lilylike blooms. The whole scale of this performance has a lavish tropical character unique among hardy trees. In their oversize proportions these ancient flowers hark back to the age of dinosaurs, from whence the earliest fossil traces of the magnolias are known.

Unfortunately, few magnolias have any liking for lime, and their fragile, early blooms are easily spoilt by late spring freezes. In hot-summer regions their big, lush leaves may be shredded or scorched by parching winds. Nevertheless, if preference is given to selecting strong-growing types, magnolias are not difficult to accommodate on limy ground.

These shrubby trees have fleshy roots that remain near the soil surface. This makes them especially sensitive to drought and soil compaction, but allows gardeners to easily adjust garden beds to meet their needs. Slightly raised plantings with generous organic mulches maintained over the root areas will enable magnolias to grow even over shallow rocky ground.

Partial shade and shelter from wind are also enjoyed by magnolias. In most gardens north-facing walls offer the best placement for these early-blooming trees. The added shade and moisture in such positions helps them through the heat of summer, and the colder exposure in winter discourages dangerously early bloom.

Our magnificent garden magnolias owe their existence to the labors of a defeated French calvary officer, Etienne Soulange-Bodin, who, after Napoleon's surrender at Waterloo, chose to devote his remaining life to the cultivation of beautiful plants. Soulange-Bodin founded the Royal Institute of Horticulture, Fromant at Ris near Paris.

He introduced the hybrid saucer magnolia (*Magnolia* × *soulangiana*) early in the nineteenth century, and this type quickly surpassed its Chinese parents, the white-flowered Yu-lan (M. *denudata*) and the purple-flowered Mu-lan (M. *liliflora*), in popularity. These vigorous hybrids are among the best of the spring-blooming magnolias for limy ground, and produce large tulip-shaped blooms blushed with pink or purple on the outsides of the petals. Later-blooming types such as 'Alexandrina,' 'Lennei,' and 'Verbanica' are the safest to try in regions with erratic spring weather.

Another magnolia that accepts lime is M. × *loebneri* 'Merril.' It produces starry white blooms at the ends of its twiggy branches. This vigorous, hardy type was bred from a cross of the lime-hating star magnolia (M. *stellata*) and the cold-tolerant Kobushi (M. *kobus*) of northern Japan. It was introduced by the Arnold Arboretum at Boston in 1939.

Although rarely grown in American gardens, the summer-blooming M. × *highdownensis*, which Sir Frederick Stern developed at his estate in Sussex, England is yet another magnolia hybrid that tolerates lime. Its pendant white blooms have an attractive boss of reddish stamens.

Southern Magnolia

The frail beauty of the shrubby deciduous magnolias hardly prepares one for the lustrous fifty-foot tower of burnished evergreen leaves sported by the Southern magnolia (M. *grandiflora*). This grand tree of the Old South doesn't cower in the shade like its cousins, but proudly gleams in the sun. In warm-climate regions it is *the* magnolia. Its waxy white blooms scent the sultry air of summer evenings wherever it is grown. Although reputed to dislike limy soils, Southern magnolia grows with complete success on calcareous ground if care is taken to avoid drought and tight, compacted soil.

Like its deciduous cousins, the Southern magnolia keeps its roots near the soil surface. Whether on heavy calcareous clay, or over drought-prone rocky limestone, these trees demand a large well-mulched grass-free region about their roots. In most cases it is best to let the magnolia keep its branches low to the ground, as it naturally prefers. This shades the earth and helps retain moisture, and it discourages careless soil-compacting foot traffic. A shade-loving groundcover such as English ivy or mondo grass (*Ophiopogon*) may be planted to cover the area beneath the tree, if desired.

Because this fragile-rooted tree is evergreen, it suffers considerably if its roots are disturbed during transplanting. Nurseries usually accommodate the finicky magnolias by growing them in containers. Unfortunately, this exacerbates the notorious susceptibility of these trees to root-girdling, and gardeners should check carefully when purchasing magnolias to avoid any with self-strangling roots.

Several fine cultivars of Southern magnolia are available, and bloom more quickly and reliably than common seedlings. 'St. Mary's,' 'Samuel Sommer,' and 'Majestic Beauty' are large-flowered, bold-foliaged types. 'Russet' and 'Little Gem' are choice small-leaved selections with brown fuzz ("indumentum") on the undersides of their leaves. 'Little Gem' in particular is a good dwarf tree easily kept at six to ten feet or less.

Unfortunately, these grafted selections are so often root-bound when offered at the nursery, that one suspects well-chosen seedlings would make better investments.

Above. Winter honeysuckle (*Lonicera fragrantissimma*) makes a big, lax, ordinary-looking shrub, but scents the winter air with the sweet fragrances of hundreds of tiny transparent blooms.

Right. Cultivars of shrub-althaea (*Hibiscus syriacus*) are surprisingly tough summer-bloomers. Their papery flowers open best during periods of high humidity.

Opposite. Bur Oak (*Quercus macrocarpa*) makes up for its lack of grace by affording one of the best and largest shade canopies of trees adapted to limy soils.

Right. Texas Red Oak (*Quercus texana*) thrives on shallow limy soils and provides outstanding displays of reddish fall foliage.

Below. Bigtooth or Canyon maples (*Acer grandidentatum*) grow naturally on rocky limestone or granite soils, and make fine garden trees in alkaline soil regions.

Above. Most ashes (*Fraxinus* spp.) enjoy lime. Fragrant ash (*Fraxinus cuspidata*) makes a small drought-tolerant tree, especially garden-worthy for its vanilla-scented spring blooms.

Left. Beautiful yellow fall color is a feature common to Mexican buckeye (*Ungnadia speciosa*) and many other members of the soapberry family (*Sapindacea*).

Above. The true buckeyes (*Aesculus* spp.) are novelly constructed plants with spectacular early-season flowers and foliage. Red buckeye (*Aesculus pavia*) makes a shade-loving understory tree that seldom exceeds fifteen feet in height.

Right. Peppermint flowering peach (*Prunus persica* 'Peppermint Stick') explodes in a charming, chaotic burst of early spring color.

Above. Mexican plum (*Prunus mexicana*) grows well in hot-summer regions, but performs and displays best when used as an understory tree.

Left. Remote, or "papershell," pinon pine (*Pinus remota*) accepts both limy soil and a hot-summer climate. It slowly matures to an impressive height.

Opposite. The Texas hill country river cypress (*Taxodium distichum*) has a greater natural tolerance to lime than seemingly identical bald-cypresses from Louisiana and the Southeastern U.S., but all *Taxodium* varieties thrive when planted near water.

Above. Redberry juniper (*Juniperus pinchotiti*), and other native treelike junipers, or "cedars," acquire rugged grace as they age.

Left. Crinum cv. 'Bradley' and hybrid coral tree *Erythrina × bidwillii* give a subtropical flair to the summer garden and perform well on heavy clay.

Above. American buttonbush (*Cephalanthus occidentalis*) makes an intriguing garden subject for damp ground. The Chinese *Adena rubella* is similar, but smaller. Both shrubs have attractive glossy green summer foliage. Photo courtesy of San Antonio Botanical Center.

Right. Hybrid rose-mallow (*Hibiscus coccineus* × *mutabilis*) makes a showy, moisture-loving perennial well-suited to heavy ground.

Opposite. The Bermuda palmetto (*Sabal bermudana*) rates among the most hardy and lime-tolerant of its clan, but grows at a painfully slow pace.

Above. Night-blooming rain lilies (*Zephyranthes drummondii*) waft musky primrose fragrances over the early summer air. Their blooms appear en masse following summer downpours.

Right. Brazil rattlebox, or "scarlet wisteria" (*Sesbania punicea*), makes a fast, easy-growing deciduous shrub for damp soil.

Above. Rudbeckias are late-blooming daisies that enjoy heavy, moist ground. *Rudbeckia fulgida* 'Goldsturm' is an especially popular compact-growing selection of the native American "black-eyed Susan."

Left. Hybrid rainlily cultivars occur in a charming range of warm pastel shades. *Zephyranthes* 'Sara Margaret' is a free-flowering flesh pink selection, choice for the warm-season flower border.

Right. Bluebonnets (*Lupinus texensis*) especially favor well-drained calcareous soils.

Above. The oxblood lily (*Rhodophiala bifida*) is a fall-flowering garden treasure that grows thriftily both on sand and heavy clay. Clover fern (*Marselia macropoda*) makes a good groundcover companion for its leafless crimson blooms.

Above. *Huacos* or snakeplants (*Manfreda* spp.) are fascinating native American perennials that afford lush, succulent, spotted foliage for plantings on dry banks.

Right. This nearly everblooming, chalk-loving ally of verbena (*Bouchea linifolia*) is a Southwestern native with an uncanny resemblance to similarly-colored wild petunias (*Ruellia* spp.).

Opposite bottom. Versatile and graceful red-flowering yucca (*Hesperaloe parviflora*) blooms from early summer till frost, and thrives on both dry rocky sites and on heavy clay soils.

Opposite top. This festive array of warm-season subjects includes vari-colored annual Joseph's coat (*Amaranthus tricolor*), orange narrowleaf zinnia (*Zinnia angustifolia* 'Classic'), golden swamp daisy (*Melampodium paludosum*), and a curious perennial cigar flower (*Cuphea* × 'David Verity'). All thrive on limy ground.

Starry white flowers of the Mediterranean asphodel (*Asphodelus fistulosus*) open
freshly on early summer mornings, but close during the heat of afternoon.

'Semmes Select' is a large-leaved type that propagates successfully from cuttings, and thus may avoid the root-girdling often associated with these grafted magnolias.

Hybrids between Southern magnolia and the swamp-loving sweet bay (M. *virginiana*) of the Southeast tend to take after the Southern magnolia parents. This is due to the greater chromosome number contributed by M. *grandiflora*, which geneticists have determined to be a natural "hexaploid," with six sets of genes instead of the customary two.

M. × *freemanii* 'Timeless Beauty' derives from this curious parentage and passes as a fairly ordinary Southern magnolia in appearance. Only slightly longish foliage and a distinctive spicy "iced tea" fragrance belie its sweet bay ancestry. This wonderful scent is reason enough for planting 'Timeless Beauty,' as it can be more readily grown and enjoyed on limy ground than the sweet bay itself.

The Pines

In contrast to the brassy, bold-textured magnolias, the needle-leaved pines (*Pinus* sp.) seem to construct their tall pyramids out of silk and gossamer. Although famously sturdy and robust, these fine-textured evergreens manage an air of grace, even as they grow upwards in geometrically precise Christmas-tree fashion. Their reptilian-looking cones are among the most fascinating and ornamental of fruits produced by hardy trees. Pines are well-loved in cooler regions, and many types do well on acid lands. Those few, tough varieties that accept lime and tolerate heat and drought uniquely enrich gardens on lime soil.

Like the magnolias, the fibrous-rooted pines resent heavy compacted soils and often perform better on dry, rocky limestone or chalk than on soggy prairie clays. Gardens with heavy, poorly drained soils can accommodate pines by planting them on slightly raised mounds of soil.

Afghan pine (*Pinus eldarica*) is the variety most often planted on the dry, limy soils of the Southwest, and has the traditional pyramidal habit many gardeners associate with pines. Its dark green needles give it a lush appearance greatly welcomed in arid regions. This pine was among the first ornamental trees ever grown in gardens, for the ancient Persians used its formal, upright spires to line plantings along the canals that irrigated their geometrically arranged desert gardens.

The Afghan pine's debut in twentieth-century America has been accompanied with much Madison Avenue hooplah and grandiose claims for its hardiness, drought tolerance, and rapid growth. Although certainly a beautiful tree with laudable toughness and vigor, the Afghan pine grows rather slowly if planted on poorly drained clay soils. Pine tip moth and cotton root rot are occasional problems in humid regions.

Before the introduction of Afghan pines many limy American gardens relied on Aleppo pine (P. *halepensis*) to fill the heat-tolerant conifer niche. P. *halepensis* is a near relation of Afghan pine with a more open, windswept branch habit and lighter green needles. Because it grows naturally at lower elevations than P. *eldarica*, Aleppo pine is less hardy to cold and suffers freeze damage when temperatures drop below 10° F. Aleppo pines develop picturesque, spreading silhouettes in maturity and make tough, drought-tolerant evergreens for milder regions.

The Calabrian pine (P. *brutia*) features a useful combination of the attributes of both the Aleppo and Afghan pines, which are its near relations. This tree develops a broad-based pyramid intermediate in form between P. *haleppensis* and P. *eldarica*. Its dark green needles are five to six inches long or more, and give the tree a bushy appearance. Calabrian pines seem to suffer less from tip moth and cotton root rot than Afghan pines, and are more attractive and cold-hardy than Aleppo pines. Maritime pine (*P. pinaster*) is another unusual southern European pine of this general type.

Italian stone pines (*P. pinea*) are close allies of these lime-loving Mediterranean natives, but mature into tall dome-shaped trees whose appearances are thoroughly original and unpinelike. Dark green needles cover the mushroom-shaped canopies of these curious-looking trees. They are the classic pines of the Roman countryside, famed for the long plantings that line the *Via Appia*. Their seeds are the edible *pignioli* nuts of Italian cooking. Mature Italian stone pines may rise fifty feet atop tall, straight stems covered in lively-looking reddish, flaking bark.

Because Italian stone pine is considerably slower-growing than its near relations, it is less commonly planted in gardens. A protracted shrubby youth makes it difficult to place in landscapes, and its juvenile foliage is short and bluish and quite unlike the long, dark green needles of the adult trees. If nurtured on a well-drained limy knoll, however, this pine eventually matures into one of the most beautiful varieties adapted to calcareous soils. It is rather hardy to cold as well.

The American relations of these Mediterranean pines are the *piñons* of the Southwest, most of which perform well only at higher altitudes. A pinion that accepts low elevations, summer heat and humidity is *P. remota*. This type naturally grows on the limestone hills of central Texas, where it makes a bushy, bright green, irregularly-shaped tree up to thirty feet tall. It is available sometimes from specialists in native plants, but can be slow growing. The more symmetrical Mexican pinion (*P. cembroides*) is another member of this group that seems to accept lime and summer heat, so long as it is planted on well-drained soil.

Japanese black pine (*P. thunbergii*) is a strong grower with great endurance. Although tolerant of lime, like all pines, it resents heavy clay soils. In hot-summer regions this pine is apt to become rather rank and irregular, and it often sheds yellowed needles when stressed by heat. Nevertheless, its easy, rapid growth has made it a great favorite.

Japanese black pine is at its best only when carefully maintained. Annual pinching of the candles which form at the end of the branches encourages denser, bushier growth. Japanese black pine also responds well to shearing and training to globular or picturesque shapes.

In many of the prairie states the lime-tolerant pine of choice is the Austrian pine (*P. nigra*). Although tough, bushy, and cold-hardy, this popular wind-break evergreen sulks in high summer heat and resents heavy clay soils. Corsican pine (*P. nigra* v. *maritima*) is a southerly strain of this rugged species that might offer better heat tolerance.

Junipers and Cypresses

The scaly, appressed leaves of junipers and cypresses give these trees an artificial look not shared by other plants. They also impart great drought resistance to these hardy conifers. The cones of these prickly, fine-textured evergreens are small and woody in the case of the cypresses, but mature to fleshy berries on the junipers.

Arizona cypress (*Cupressus glabra*) is a beautiful, silvery tree, well-suited to dry calcareous soils. It hails from arid Southwestern uplands. Bluish wax secreted by glands along its turpentine-scented leaves gives this cypress its gray sheen, and increases its ability to withstand drying winds. Pyramidal in youth, Arizona cypress often broadens in age and develops attractive peeling red bark. It is fast-growing up to thirty feet or more, and often lives to considerable age.

Selected cutting-grown varieties of Arizona cypress guarantee more uniform appearances to grove plantings or windbreaks. 'Silver Smoke' is a good cultivar for a tall screen. 'Blue Ice' is a telling cold steely blue unmatched by any conifer adapted to warm climates. It is more compact, pyramidal, and slow growing than most selections, and makes an ideal medium-sized specimen tree.

Italian cypresses (C. *sempervirens*) are known for their tall, pencil-thin silhouettes and dark green foliage. They tolerate extremes of drought, heat, and limy soil. 'Glauca' is the cultivar that soars up from the palatial homes of southern California movie stars, and is the variety commonly offered in the nursery trade.

Seedling Italian cypresses may sometimes be seen in older plantings around cemeteries or Victorian dwellings. These impressive trees often have more open forms than the selected cutting-grown types and can reach heights of fifty feet. Their dark-colored, upswept branches and pyramidal form give them silhouettes reminiscent of spruce or fir.

Of the many tree-form junipers suited to calcareous ground, some of the most valuable are the native Eastern red cedar (*Juniperus virginia*) and the chalk-loving mountain cedar (*J. ashei*). These share rich green foliage and shreddy bark, but the berries and foliage of *J. virginiana* have more refined, small-scale appearances than those of the mountain cedar. Eastern red cedar also retains a more formal, pyramidal shape than the rounded *J. ashei*. Both are valuable for windbreaks or screens, but shallow roots make these trees difficult to garden under.

The scrubby-looking red-berry juniper (*J. pinchotii*) appears rather similar to these "cedars," but generally has more ragged, twisting branches and yellow-green foliage. Its winter fruits are an attractive dull reddish shade that contrast well with its greenery. Old specimens may assume rustic, contorted shapes of great beauty.

The alligator juniper (*J. deppeana*) is a refreshing original with dense grayish needles as silvery as the Arizona cypress. Mature trees develop open habits and checkered bark resembling alligator hide. Alligator juniper has a dense, pyramidal form in youth, however. It tolerates heat, drought, and lime. 'McFadden' is a cultivar with good, silvery foliage.

True Cedars

The true cedars (*Cedrus* spp.) are conifers of graceful, majestic appearance and enormous proportion. All tolerate lime, and most endure considerable drought once established. Like pines, however, these trees fare poorly on heavy clays and should be planted on raised berms in areas with tight, poorly drained soil. Whorled needles and up-facing cones unite cedars with the deciduous larches, but their evergreen nature and frequently blue-gray foliage more often reminds gardeners of spruce or fir.

Deodar cedars (*Cedrus deodara*) are the popular sprucelike conifers of warm-climate gardens, the so-called "California Christmas trees." These fast-growing, robust cedars are also the most tender and sometimes freeze when temperatures fall below 10° F. Deodar cedars are at their best in regions such as the Texas Hill Country, where warm day temperatures can be moderated by pleasantly cool, dry evenings through the summer. In more humid regions they frequently abort leading branches, and assume widely spreading shapes.

More cold hardy and tolerant of humidity than these, but much less vigorous are the cedar of Lebanon (C. *libani*) and the blue Atlas cedar (C. *atlantica* 'Glauca'). These trees require cool moist root runs if they are to endure long, hot summers, and they grow slowly in warm climates. Cedar of Lebanon is a famous tree in English gardens, where its dark green, spreading silhouette graces many manor houses. The Atlas cedar is another choice, silvery conifer whose appearance imparts refinement and sophistication to any garden that includes it.

River Cypresses

The most valuable of all coniferous trees for limy garden soils breaks with the traditions of its relatives by dropping its leaves in autumn. This comes as a shock to some gardeners, who expect needle-leaved trees to be evergreen. But, never was such a shedding of foliage offered for a more worthy cause. The bald, or river, cypress (*Taxodium distichum*) turns by stages from its soft summer gray-green to a glowing fawn, and thence to rich cinnamon, and in the process provides one of the true spectacles of autumn.

These conifers belong to the same ancient family as the redwoods and giant sequoias, and like them, achieve great age and huge size. Although symmetrical and pyramidal in youth, river cypresses broaden into picturesque, wispy shapes at maturity. They are among the fastest-growing trees suited to lime, yet possess strong wood and branches, and seldom suffer attacks of insects or disease.

Taxodiums have adapted themselves especially to wet soils and enjoy the warm climates that their relations abhor. River cypresses often line streambanks in habitat and keep their roots constantly immersed in fresh water. Special woody projections ("knees") rise around the base of the trees and are thought to assist these plants in growing in waterlogged ground. However, in cultivation cypress knees seldom develop unless the trees are planted by water or on poorly drained soil.

Although river cypresses are indifferent to lime when growing by a stream or pond, when cultivated under drier conditions the provenance of these trees may be critical to success. Trees from the limy streambanks of central Texas have much greater tolerance to alkalinity than those from the swamps of Louisiana and the Gulf coast. For plantings on calcareous soils central Texas river cypresses are thriftier and more attractive than their Eastern relations, and often show a distinctive bluish cast to their summer foliage. Eastern cypresses often develop chlorosis when planted on limy ground.

Another lime-tolerant cypress of special value in warmer regions is the Mexican or Montezuma cypress (*T. mucronatum*). Of more open and spreading habit than *T. distichum*, Montezuma cypress also differs in having foliage that remains evergreen in mild areas. Where winter lows fall much below 25° F, however, its leaves promptly shed. This cypress is somewhat easier to grow than the river cypress on dry, chalky sites. At the latitude of San Antonio it offers one of the finest and most graceful of lime-tolerant trees.

CHAPTER EIGHT

Mbuga!

Plants for Heavy, Wet Clay Soils

In sub-Saharan Africa the natives have a special name for the heavy black clay soils on which they raise their cotton and corn. The Swahili term for these earths has a somewhat onomatopoeic ring—one can readily imagine the sound of shovels gooily sliding through the ground as the disgusted local farmers mutter, "*Mbuga!*"

Where underlying rocks are soft chalks or marls, and the climate above is warm and humid, fast weathering results in soils that can be outrageously heavy, sticky alkaline clays. This intractable stuff makes gardening uniquely difficult and calls for special strategies, and special plants.

These expansive clays are sodden in the spring months. The pore spaces between the tiny soil particles become drenched, leaving little air for plant roots. In late summer, however, high heat extracts this moisture and these prairie earths dry and shrivel, forming deep cracks, unless provided with supplemental irrigation.

This presents a tough cycle for growing plants, but it is one that occurs frequently in nature. The seasonal "buffalo wallows" of the American prairies and the temporary pans or *vleis* of the African savannahs are examples of such environments. These habitats offer distinctively adapted plants geared to grow in concert with alternating surfeits and deficits of moisture.

Many spring-blooming bulbs come from soggy abodes and have the capacity to grow in waterlogged soils during the cool spring months, while later estivating during the dry heat of summer. Contrary to the common wisdom that bulbs require good drainage, such flowers as summer snowflake (*Leucojum aestivum*), Dutch iris (*Iris × hollandica*), Naples onion (*Allium neapolitanum*), large-flowered buttercup (*Ranunculus macranthus*), and jonquil hybrids such as *Narcissus* 'Trevithian' will bloom happily even in standing water. The strong-growing, old-fashioned campernelle narcissus, the tazetta variety 'Grand Monarque,' white French-Roman hyacinths, Byzantine gladiolus, and virgin's spray (*Ornithogalum narbonense*) are also good on heavy ground.

An unusual California flower with a special tolerance for heavy adobe soils is the dark blue-violet Ithuriel's spear (*Triteleia laxa*). These alliumlike plants rise from underground corms and flower in nature among ripening stands of grass in late spring. In the garden they withstand any amount of winter moisture, and enjoy a long summer baking. 'Queen Fabiola' is a popular hybrid strain of this type, that is often sold as "*Brodaiea*."

Several spring perennials tolerate seasonally wet conditions, the spiderworts (*Tradescantia* spp.) and the shasta daisies (*Chrysanthemum* × *superbum*) being especially valuable. Iris of the spuria group and the dark blue *Iris brevipes* accept any amount of irrigation while in spring growth and endure summer drought with ease.

The mint family contributes several perennials that do well on wet ground and bloom over a long season. The bog sage (*Salvia uliginosa*) is an easy-growing, hardy type with azure blooms and aggressive, spreading roots. The European meadow sage (*S.* × *superba*) enjoys wet feet and produces violet-colored flower spikes.

False dragon-heads or "obedient plants" (*Physostegia* spp.) are mints with clustered spikes of rose-pink blooms, most often appearing in late summer or fall. Their "obedient" tubular flowers may be repositioned on the bloom stems, and remain pointing in whatever position the gardener directs them. *Physostegia virginiana* is the common garden variety, usually grown in named selections such as rose-colored 'Vivid' or white 'Summer Snow.' *P. pulchella* is an attractive rose-purple spring-bloomer. Like the bog sage, *Physostegias* spread by runners along the ground and may be invasive on heavy, damp clay.

Other hardy perennials adapted to seasonally wet conditions include Gulf Coast penstemon (*Penstemon tenuis*), summer phlox (*Phlox paniculata*), violets (*Viola* spp.), showy sedum (*Sedum spectabile*), and pink milkweed (*Asclepias incarnata*). The daisy family contributes such bog-tolerant types as the black-eyed Susans (*Rudbeckia* spp.), goldenrods (*Solidago canadensis*), sneezeweeds (*Helenium*), swamp gayfeather (*Liatris spicata*), golden glow (*Heliopsis* spp.), perennial sunflowers (*Helianthus* spp.), meadow asters (*Aster pratensis*), and blue mist flowers (*Eupatorium coelestinum*).

Many grasses tolerate soggy ground, and native prairie varieties such as Lindheimer's muhly (*Muhlenbergia lindheimeri*) and inland sea oats (*Chasmanthium latifolium*) are especially adapted to seasonally moist conditions. Pampas grass (*Cortaderia selloana*), Japanese blood grass (*Imperata cylindrica* 'Rubra') and maiden grasses (*Miscanthus* cvs.) are also notably good on wet, heavy soils.

Poke-weeds (*Phytolacca americana*) make interesting perennials for damp ground and produce lush, green leaves in spring followed by attractive wine-colored berries in late summer. Their mildly toxic spring foliage makes a flavorful, edible green (poke-salet) if boiled and rinsed to remove the poisons.

The spectacular cardinal flowers (*Lobelia cardinalis*) are well-known for their moisture-loving habits. These beautiful flowers have a special fondness for limy ground, and their spires of blood red late summer blooms arise prolifically when planted on wet, calcareous soil. The Mexican cardinal flower (*L. splendens*) features blood red foliage that makes it even more striking. Both species of cardinal flower attract hummingbirds in swarms.

Unlike many other bog flowers, however, these lobelias have little tolerance to seasonal drought and must be kept constantly moist through the summer. Along with Louisiana irises and other true water flowers, they may be cultivated in tubs of water or planted along the margins of a garden pond. If these flowers are to be grown in borders, a special plastic-lined bed should be excavated and filled with good soil. This artificial swamp may then be irrigated in times of drought to provide the continuously wet feet these plants require.

In addition to these heroic perennials, annuals such as golden wave (*Coreopsis tinctoria*) and coneflower (*Rudbeckia amplexicaulis*) provide easy, colorful border flowers for heavy, saturated clays. After finishing bloom in early summer, the seeds of these wild-flowers lie dormant through drought and heat, awaiting drenching fall rains to stimulate germination. The spectacular biennial bluebell-gentians (*Eustoma grandiflorum*) enjoy similar conditions, and readily self-sow on waterlogged calcareous clay.

A few evergreen shrubs are noted for their tolerance to boggy soils. Yaupon (*Ilex vomitoria*) is one of the most worthwhile, as it has many cultivars suited to different garden needs. Wax myrtle (*Myrica cerifera*) is useful on soggy clays as well. Its flexuous branches hold narrow, bright green, aromatic foliage and bear small bluish berries. Although generally trained as a six-foot multistemmed specimen, its dwarf cousin, M. *pusilla*, may be kept at three to four feet and makes a dense shrub. As with the sweet gales of the Old World (*Myrica gale*) and the bayberries of the Northeast (M. *pennsylvanica*), the fragrant wax produced by these evergreens may be made into candles. These native shrubs were favored for this use by early settlers.

A deciduous cousin of the yaupon, the possumhaw (*Ilex decidua*), grows well on wet soils and bears clustered red berries along its bare winter branches. Flowering shrubs especially tolerant to seasonally drenched ground include the deciduous blackhaw viburnums (*Viburnum rufidulum* and V. *prunifolium*) and the semievergreen Southeastern native, V. *obovatum*. Where partial shade is available the burning bushes (*Euonymus alatus* and E. *atropurpureus*) provide shows of red autumn foliage, and the strawberry shrub (*Calycanthus floridus*) offers fragrant rust-colored blooms through spring and early summer.

The native American buttonbush (*Cephalanthus occidentalis*) and its Chinese ally, *Adina rubella*, are interesting shrubs for sunny exposures on damp, alkaline clays. They tolerate alternating hydrologic feasts and famines, and put forth whorls of glossy green leaves and globular clusters of white tubular blooms all summer. Where the suckering habits of buffalo currants (*Ribes odoratum*), elderberries (*Sambucus* spp.) and coralberries or Indian currants (*Symphoricarpos* spp.) present no objection, these old-fashioned deciduous shrubs may be allowed to colonize wet, heavy ground.

There is a tropical flavor to many of the plants adapted to seasonally moist soils, for heavy, calcareous clays often form in warm, humid countries. In the course of plant evolution several erstwhile tropical plant families have followed these moist habitats northward into the temperate zones, wherever summers are long and hot enough to allow it. People accelerate this natural process by bringing tropical plants into their gardens to try as perennials. Often, subtropical plants can be coaxed into substituting the cold weather of winter for their naturally arid dormant seasons. Where winters are too cold to permit use as perennials, these heat- and swamp-loving varieties earn spots as annuals for summer bedding.

One of the most typical of tropical flowers is the hibiscus, and this group includes several hardy forms especially adapted to wet, heavy ground. Texas star (*Hibiscus coccineus*) makes an exotic-looking four- to six-foot perennial with narrow-petaled six-inch crimson blooms and glossy, palmately divided foliage. (This last character gives the Texas star an uncanny resemblance to marijuana when out of bloom, so it is wise to locate this plant safely out of sight of overly curious passersby!) Despite its common name, the Texas star is a native wildflower of the coastal swamps of Georgia and northern Florida.

The enormous papery flowers of the rose-mallows (*Hibiscus moscheutos*) come in holly-hock shades of rose-red, pink, and white. 'Southern Belle' and 'Frisbee' are two popular seed strains with flowers ten inches across or more. These huge five-petaled blooms have cartoonish personalities, and one almost expects them to leap from the garden in a dance or break out in some cheerful song. Although long-flowering and easy-growing on damp clay, rose-mallows need shelter from wind, and their foliage can be ragged looking, especially in hot sun. Like the Texas star mallow, these varieties die down to carrotlike roots in winter.

Hybrids between the rose-mallows, the Texas star, and other native hibiscuses such as the halberd-leaf hibiscus (*H. militaris*) offer desirable compromises of bloom size, beauty of foliage, and resistance to heat and wind. 'Lord Baltimore' is an intense blood red cultivar; 'Lady Baltimore' and 'Ann Arundel' are lovely pinks with contrasting rose-red centers. Even better is a cross between *H. coccineus* and the confederate rose (*H. mutabilis*), as it inherits more tolerance to alkalinity than many of these hybrid mallows.

The horrible-sounding botanical name, *Kosteletzkya virginica*, belongs to an attractive ally of these hibiscuses, known more readily and pronounceably as salt marsh mallow. Its small, lavender-pink blooms appear freshly each morning on plants three to four feet tall. It thrives on heavy, alkaline clay.

Although not related to these hibiscuses, the shrub morning glory (*Ipomoea fistulosa*) rather resembles a ragged, pink-flowered rose mallow when in flower. Its lilac-pink, floppy blooms have contrasting dark purple centers. These flowers open freshly each morning, much like the rose-mallows. Although a tender tropical shrub, this morning glory makes a semihardy perennial in frost-prone regions and flourishes on wet, heavy clay or alongside ponds.

Crape myrtles (*Lagerstroemia* spp.) are special favorites on damp, heavy ground and typify a large tropical family that includes teakwood, as well as familiar garden perennials such as loosestrife (*Lythrum* spp.) and cigar flower (*Cuphea* spp.). The whole bunch seems to thrive on wet clay soils, so gardeners on boggy earth may have their pick of whatever varieties are locally winter-hardy.

Lythrums are the most cold-tolerant of this group and make long-blooming shows of garnet-red and rose-pink on wet ground. 'Morden Pink' and 'Morden Gleam' are two sterile selections that reproduce vigorously by runners instead of seed. Although these types purportedly lack the dreaded ability to self-sow, in several states their cultivation is prohibited by law, for similar lythrums have disastrously invaded hundreds of acres of native wetlands.

In regions with gentle, frost-free fall weather, late-blooming lythrum allies such as *Cuphea micropetala* make valuable shows on wet, heavy ground. The dwarf Mexican heather (*C. hyssopifolia*) is generally too tender to return as a perennial, but makes a wonderful warm season bedding plant with clouds of tiny lavender blooms. One of the better cupheas for regions with brief, frosty autumn weather is the hybrid, 'David Verity.' This type combines the red-tipped "cigar flowers" of *C. ignea* with the tough constitution of *C. micropetala*, and blooms in summer as well as fall.

Some other subtropical perennials suited to heavy ground include firespike (*Odontonema strictum*), Cashmere bouquet (*Clerodendrum bungei*), Mexican hydrangea (*C. fragrans* 'Pleniflorum'), firebush (*Hamelia patens*), night jessamine (*Cestrum nocturnum*), and Mexican petunia (*Ruellia malacosperma*).

Mexican petunia is a dark, metallic purple in its most common form and can be rather difficult to display in the garden unless shown off against a pale pink backdrop. However, an attractive white selection is in cultivation and worth seeking out. Both of these types, as well as the willow-leafed Mexican petunia (*R. brittoniana*) have aggressive spreading roots that make them difficult to restrain in the garden. A tiny miniature form of these ruellias ('Katy') seems to lack these invasive tendencies, and makes cute rosettes topped with crowded purple blooms.

The pea family has many tropical members, several of which make good perennials for soggy ground. Scarlet wisteria or Brazil rattlebox (*Sesbania tripetii*) is fast-growing and particularly worthwhile. It bears attractive orange clusters of pea blossoms followed by decorative, winged bean pods, and it makes a deciduous shrub hardy to 20° F. In colder gardens it freezes back as a perennial or may be started each year as an annual.

Indigofera kirilowii is a hardy water-loving shrub of the Orient with much the same aspect as *Sesbania*. Rosy pink pealike flowers appear along its stems in May and June.

The flowering sennas (*Cassia* spp.) include several types good for heavy, damp soil such as the gold-flowered perennial *Cassia hebecarpa* and the semievergreen *C. corymbosa*. The yellow-blooming annual partridge-peas (*C. fasciculata*) are especially well adapted to wet ground as well, and reseed freely. Candlestick senna (*Cassia alata*) reaches enormous proportions in a single season if grown on heavy, moist ground. These leafy tropical shrubs may be used like the sesbanias as annuals. Their fall show of upright golden bloom clusters atop ten-foot stems can be truly tremendous.

The exotic-looking coral trees (*Erythrina* spp.) adapt to dry sandy soils as well as heavy clays and make particularly appropriate companions for these moisture-loving subtropical flowers. The everblooming hybrid, *Erythrina* × *bidwillii*, produces two-foot spikes of siren-red blooms generously throughout the summer. It derives from a cross of the spring-blooming perennial coral-bean (*E. herbacea*) and the treelike South American fireman's cap (*E. crista-galli*). All three types may be grown as perennials, and withstand frost down to 0° F. Their scarlet beans are attractive in winter arrangements, but are poisonous and hallucinogenic if consumed.

Hardy trees of the pea family that tolerate heavy, waterlogged soils include honeylocust (*Gleditsia triacanthos*), black locust (*Robinia pseudoacacia*), silk tree or "mimosa" (*Albizzia julibrissen*), and Eve's necklace (*Sophora affinis*). The ferny, divided foliage of all of these trees gives a subtropical feeling to garden plantings. The black locust and Eve's necklace bear pale-colored springtime pea blossoms in pendant clusters, while the silk tree provides generous crops of pink powder-puff blooms in late spring and early summer. Although these trees will endure dry, thin rocky ground, they perform much better and suffer fewer diseases on well-watered clay soils.

Castor beans (*Ricinus communis*) are old-fashioned summer annuals valued for quick tropical effects, which they achieve by producing towering stems covered in lush palmate leaves. The dark red-foliaged 'Atropurpurea' is especially striking. Both the green and red-leaved forms are outstanding performers on damp ground. In late summer castor beans top their stems with burlike capsules filled with attractively mottled, poisonous nutlike seeds. These seeds are the source for well-known medicinal oils.

The three-sided seed capsules of the castor bean mark this plant as a member of the spurge family, whose tropical members include the florist poinsettia, as well as numerous cactuslike African shrubs. The tropical crotons (*Codiaeum variegatum* cvs.) and copper leafs (*Acalypha wilkesiana*) are relatives of castor beans popular for their colorful foliage. Both make useful annuals for summer bedding on moist ground. Copper leaf and its close relation, the chenille plant (*A. hispida*), are especially good for hot, sunny exposures.

Chinese tallow (*Sapium sebiferum*) is an oriental representative of the spurge family that makes a small, semihardy tree. Tallow trees are true swamp-lovers and will even thrive in shallow standing water. This makes them good choices for heavy clay soils, where these modest-sized plants make easy, fast-growing shade trees. Gnarled and buttressed trunks create a sense of age and afford an impish quality to these small trees. In autumn dress the Chinese tallow is often one of the prettiest subjects in warm-climate gardens, its brilliant orange-red poplarlike leaves providing a colorful backdrop to its ripening white seeds.

Although tolerant of lime when planted on well-watered ground, Chinese tallows grown on thin, dry, caliche soils are liable to chlorosis, and these trees are a poor choice for gardens over chalk or limestone. Freeze damage is another common problem; tallow trees often suffer or perish when temperatures fall below 10° F. In spite of these failings, the colorful fall foliage and easy-growing nature of the Chinese tallow makes it a popular tree for gardens on calcareous clay.

Other trees of subtropical appearance and good tolerance to waterlogged soils include Chinese parasol tree (*Firmiana simplex*), western catalpa (*Catalpa speciosa*), and trifoliate orange (*Poncirus trifoliata*). With adequate moisture these varieties tolerate alkalinity, but, like the Chinese tallow, are inclined to chlorosis when subjected to prolonged drought.

Although frequently confused with Chinese parasol tree, the varnish tree, or tung oil tree (*Aleurites fordii*), has less enormous heart-shaped leaves and makes a smaller, less hardy tree. Instead of the tiny flowers and pinkish-green winged seed clusters of *Firmiana*, it produces showy white flowers, followed by big golf-ball-sized fruits. Tung oil trees tolerate alkaline soils, but suffer on compacted, soggy clays.

For warm climates with occasional mild frosts the subtropical trees of the forget-me-not family offer tough, attractive choices for heavy alkaline soils. Anaqua (*Ehretia anacua*) is a scrubby tree with dark green rough-textured foliage and small white flowers in spring and summer. These blooms ripen to showy clusters of orange berries.

Anaqua withstands frosts as severe as 10° F, but its spectacular cousin, the wild olive or "anacahuita" (*Cordia boissieri*) may be severely damaged at 25° F. Wild olive bears big clusters of white petunialike blooms and has long, lush velvety leaves. Its common name derives from the large, olive-shaped yellowish berries that follow its blooms. Anaqua and wild olive tolerate wet soils, as well as fairly arid situations, and are indifferent to lime.

The amaryllis family includes several bulbous perennials that enjoy heavy clay ground, and many *Crinum* "lilies" are particularly well suited to perform with erratic rainfall. In nature these bulbs are found in seasonally flooded depressions, and their growth cycles respond to the irregular supplies of water they receive. Leaves and flowers arise following each summer downpour. After blooming and making seed, these tough bulbs rest, and await the next shower.

For perennial borders in warm climates, few subjects could be easier and more rewarding than the *Crinums*. These huge, glamorous flowers flourish on heavy clay soils, and are indifferent to drought. *Crinums* are long-lived and improve with age if planted deeply (twelve to eighteen inches) and fed generously. When summer thundershowers moisten the ground, awakening their enormous bulbs, *Crinums* respond by erupting in lush fountains of straplike foliage. In a week or two these leaves are joined by big stalks of lilylike blooms that open at dusk and permeate the garden with sweet, exotic fragrance.

In colder regions the gray-leaved Orange River lily (*Crinum bulbispermum*) and its hybrids, such as the white or pink-flowered C. × *powelli* or the pink-striped "milk and wine lilies" (C. × *herbertii*), are the best types to plant, for they have the greatest resistance to cold. From central Texas southward more tender types may be enjoyed, and a tremendous variety of wondrous crinum hybrids may be found in the gardens of specialists and collectors. The practically immortal character of many older crinum hybrids has made these bulbs popular heirloom flowers, and old clumps of crinum may often be found marking abandoned gardens in warm climates.

In addition to *C. bulbispermum*, other species of garden value include the white-flowered *C. moorei* v. *schmidtii*, *C. erubescens*, and *C. asiaticum*. *C. macowanii* deserves special mention for its unusual tolerance to drought and heat and its enormous umbels of bell-shaped pink-striped flowers. The semitender *C. scabrum* is fantastically colorful and fragrant, with deep wine-striped blooms in early June.

Especially favored by crinum fanciers are the darker wine-hued hybrids such as 'Ellen Bosanquet,' 'Elizabeth Traub,' 'Carnival,' and 'Bradley.' Good pinks include 'Cecil Houdyshel' and 'Emma Jones.' The *Crinum* × *worsleyi* group sports pink blooms with contrasting wine stripes. 'Walter Flory' is a hardy selection of this type. Of the multitudes of white-flowered hybrids 'White Queen' and 'Ollene' are outstandingly good.

For gardeners whose attraction to crinums revolves around heady, delicious fragrances, the delicately blushed turn-of-the-century hybrid, 'Mrs. James Hendry,' makes a fine choice. Exquisite floral form, lush, compact green foliage, and an everblooming habit are additional assets of this fine variety. Other notably fragrant crinums include 'Peachblow,' 'Royal White,' 'Alamo Village,' and *C.* × *amabile*. 'Summer Nocturne' produces small fragrant blooms in late summer atop especially lush, bright green clumps of foliage; it makes an outstanding variety for use as an edging plant in semishade.

American relations of the largely African crinum lilies such as the night-blooming spider lilies (*Hymenocallis* sp.) and the diminutive rain lilies or fairy lilies (*Zephyranthes* sp.) also perform well on wet clay ground. The rain lilies in particular imitate the habits of crinums by reblooming in response to erratic summer rainfall. Their tiny, colorful blooms are charming to include in summer borders and offer fragrance as well as warm, brilliant colors.

The *Cooperia* section is the group of rain lilies to explore for scented blooms. The giant prairie lily (*Zephyranthes drummondii*) produces large, white primrose-scented flowers in early summer to complement its broad gray foliage. The Mexican *Z. morrisclintii* resembles this fine variety, but has blooms tinted a delicate, icy pink. *Z. smallii* flowers from April till frost, following rains, and bears its sulfur-colored star-shaped blooms prolifically atop clumps of grassy foliage.

Less fragrant, but more brightly colored are the light yellow *Zephyranthes regina* 'Valles' and the golden, goblet-shaped *Z. citrina*. The rich rose-pink stars of *Z. grandiflora* are especially lovely in borders, and withstand considerable cold if thoroughly mulched with leaves each autumn.

The ivory-flowered *Z. candida* is well suited to heavy clay soils, and is cold-hardy for a rain lily. Unlike most varieties, this South American native produces its foliage during the winter months, remaining dormant through summer heat, and returning to flower with autumn rains. Sheets of silvery blooms along the shores of the Rio de la Plata ("River of Silver") so impressed early explorers that they named the new country they discovered the "Land of Silver" (Argentina) for these snowy, water-loving flowers.

In addition to these species, several lovely hybrid rain lilies are popular with specialists and collectors of the amaryllids. 'Libra' is a robust, coarse-leaved, dark rose variety, well suited to borders on heavy clay ground. 'Grand-Jax' and 'Aquarius' are two prolific hybrids of *Z. candida* with pale pink and light cream flowers respectively. 'Capricorn' is deep burnt orange, 'Prairie Sunset' blooms with a lovely pastel blend, and 'Ruth Page' flowers a vivid rose. All of these types benefit from generous additions of organic matter to the soil.

Organic matter is also of great benefit for the *Habranthus* group of rain lilies, whose blooms nod in one direction like miniature amaryllis. The large-flowered, light pink *Habranthus robustus* and maroon-centered, lilac-pink *H. brachyandrus* make valuable mats of color in warm-climate borders. The bronzy yellow Texas copper lily (*H. tubispathus* v. *texanus*) provides dainty, warm-colored blooms to naturalize among other plantings.

Easier and more effective in the garden than these rain lilies, however, is their South American ally, the oxblood lily (*Rhodophiala bifida*). This small amaryllid produces clusters of three or more blood red blooms atop its stems each autumn and follows its late-season displays with dark green, straplike foliage through the winter months. This is one of the best of all bulbs for heavy clay soils, and performs outstandingly well through drought, flood, heat, and cold.

Because its foliage emerges during the winter, the oxblood lily makes an ideal subject for plantings under deciduous trees. The old-fashioned orange-red fall-blooming spider lily (*Lycoris radiata*), the yellow-flowered *Sternbergia lutea*, and the pink, globular *Allium stellatum* make fine companions for this bulb and flower at the same season.

The most successful of the true amaryllis (*Hippeastrum* sp.) adaptable to heavy garden soils are *Hippeastrum* × *johnsonii* and hybrids of its type. Fortunately, this antique English clone is one of the most beautiful and prolific of all amaryllis. Its bold scarlet-red trumpets are striped white down the keels of the petals and rise in clusters of four to six atop two-foot stems in early April. *H.* × *johnsonii* is one of the most cold-hardy *Hippeastrum* cultivars as well, and succeeds wherever the ground does not freeze deeply. It follows its spring blooms with attractive bronzy strap-shaped foliage. Partial shade suits *H.* × *johnsonii* best, but it will accept full sun if watered through the summer.

Pineapple lilies (*Eucomis* spp.) are curious subtropical bulbs with long-lasting, clustered summer blooms that resemble the fruits of a pineapple. They are easy-growing on heavy, well-watered ground, and remarkably hardy if mulched for the winter. Another useful bulb from the same region of South Africa is the monarch-of-the-veld (*Ornithogalum saundersii*). It bears tall stems topped with clustered white flowers in midsummer.

The orchidlike blackberry lilies (*Belamcanda chinensis*) are easy-growing iris relatives with spotted blooms in shades of orange and red. Hybrids come in spectacular mixtures of yellow, purple, and lavender as well. In late summer the seed capsules burst to reveal showy, berrylike fruit. Other subtropical iris relations of value on damp ground include the American walking irises (*Neomarica* and *Trimeza*) and the African fortnight-lilies (*Dietes* spp.). These evergreen types resent hard freezes, but endure and recover from occasional cold if mulched heavily to protect their roots.

The gingers are another useful group of subtropical bulbs that thrive on heavy soils and don't mind waterlogging. The white, yellow, or apricot-colored butterfly gingers (*Hedychium* spp.), and the pinkish-orange hidden gingers (*Curcuma* spp.), are the most cold-hardy and adaptable. Although tolerant of calcareous clay soils, these perennials resent drought and excessively limy caliche soils. They are at their best in partial shade, where their lush, graceful leaves can contribute elegance to plantings. Like all subtropical bulbs, gingers benefit greatly from additions of manure and other organic matter.

Easier and more adaptable to sunny positions are the Indian shots (*Canna* cvs.), and these popular tuberous flowers offer a wide range of brilliantly warm colors, as well as delicate blushes and pastels. Many cannas have attractively striped or purple-tinted foliage, and most of the tall-growing nineteenth-century hybrids were developed specifically for their striking leaf characters.

Canna edulis 'Purpurea' and *C. warscewiczii* are two old-fashioned types with six-foot stems, purplish leaves, and small scarlet blooms. Just as tall, but with green leaves and pendant clusters of large crimson flowers, is the iris-flowered canna (*C. iridiflora*) of Peru. Its famous hybrid, *C. iridiflora* 'Rubra' ('Ehemannii'), is an especially robust type, well adapted to heavy clay soils, and less bothered by leaf-rolling caterpillars than most cannas. This variety differs from *C. iridiflora* proper by holding its large, crimson flowers in erect clusters between its heavy, rich green leaves.

Other fine garden cannas include the orchid-flowered *C. flaccida* hybrids, whose graceful blooms come mostly in pastel shades. The pin-striped foliage of the *C. limbata* (*aureo-vittata*) hybrids makes them especially good to combine with the dark-foliaged types. 'Pretoria' is a medium-tall orange-flowered canna of this group; 'Striped Beauty' ('Nirvana') is a low-growing yellow-flowered selection. Yellow blooms brilliantly speckled with glowing red spots and freckles characterize 'Cleopatra,' a spectacular derivative of the tiger canna (*C. childsii*).

In addition to these unusual cultivars, the general run of hybrid cannas in the popular dwarf 'Pfitzer' strains, and old favorites such as red-flowered 'President' and rosy-pink 'City of Portland,' provide a wealth of material for gardens on heavy clay ground. All of these bloom over exceptionally long seasons if provided with adequate moisture, and generous feeding.

The bananas are close allies of the cannas, well adapted to warm regions, and well suited to damp clay soils. The common banana (*Musa paradisiaca* v. *sapientum*) is the toughest and most cold-hardy, but is only likely to bear fruit following a succession of unusually mild winters. Gardeners cultivate it instead for its prodigious, exotic foliage. In most years its enormous green leaves and ten- to fifteen-foot pulpy stems freeze to the ground, and must be cut back in the spring. New plants usually sucker up from the roots as temperatures warm.

The ornamental blood bananas (*M. zebrina*) make useful garden perennials as well. This variety has leaves mottled attractively with splashes of reddish purple, and makes a small clump up to six feet tall. The short, squat-looking Abyssinian banana (*Ensete vetricosum*) and its bronze-leaved variant, 'Maurelii,' are semihardy, popular foliage perennials in milder regions. These large-leaved plants need shelter from wind, and partial shade to look their best.

The moisture-loving aroids exult in waterlogged, limy clays, but suffer if allowed to dry out in late summer. Like the Lousiana irises, the elephant ears (*Colocasia esculenta*) may be planted in artificial swamps to help satisfy their lusty water requirements. The closely related *Xanthosmas* and *Alocasias* also respond to "bog culture," and all of these plants enjoy generous feeding. Their huge heart-shaped leaves can be spectacular additions to the summer garden when well grown. Elephant ears stand considerable cold if mulched in winter.

Several palms make excellent evergreen plants for poorly drained positions. The slow-growing palmettos (*Sabal* spp.) are particularly well-known denizens of swamps. Young palms begin their lives as grassy seedlings, most often growing in the moist shade beneath trees or shrubs along watercourses. All but a few thrive when grown with wet feet. Palms generally withstand severe drought once established.

Sensitivity to cold presents the greatest limitation to palm culture, and even the hardiest palms are uniquely susceptible to freeze damage. Because these plants often depend on a single growing point (the "heart") from which to develop their new leaves and blooms, any damage to this tender growth may critically disable these trees. For this reason gardeners in colder sections do best with the shrubbier, more easily protected palms.

One of the most cold-hardy and beautiful varieties is the slow-growing needle palm (*Rhapidophyllum hystrix*) of the Southeast. This six-foot species grows in dense swampy hammocks, and particularly favors calcareous clay soils. Its densely furry beehive-shaped stems produce long black spines and lush dark green fan-shaped leaves. In age it suckers into attractive clumps.

Were it more widely available and faster-growing, the needle palm would be among the first choices for garden use, for it withstands temperatures down to 0° F with little damage. Unfortunately, slow growth and difficult propagation make needle palms expensive and hard to find. For gardens on limy clay this is a true collector's treasure.

The commonest, fastest-growing, and most manageable of the hardier palms is the oriental windmill or Chusan palm (*Trachycarpus fortunei*). This ally of needle palm sports a trunk equally endowed with brownish fur. Windmill palms rarely sucker, however, and usually produce slender ten- to fifteen-foot stems, top-heavy with crowns of green, fan-shaped leaves. By planting several windmill palms of differing heights together in groves gardeners can achieve unusually lush, exotic-looking effects with these small trees.

Windmill palms are wonderful subjects for waterlogged clay soils and adapt to sun or shade. They are reliably hardy from central Texas southward and are seldom damaged where temperatures remain above 15° F. In colder regions these palms may be grown in protected courtyards or against south-facing walls. Some dedicated palm fanciers wrap the crowns of these trees in winter to assure their survival in marginal areas.

Mediterranean fan or "dwarf windmill palm" (*Chamaerops humilis*) comes from the dry brushlands of southern Europe and North Africa. This relative of *Trachycarpus* produces similar, but smaller, thornier leaves and develops a shrubby, suckering habit. Although tolerant of heavy clay soils, Mediterranean fan palm withstands greater cold when planted on dry, rocky sites. If grown "hard" in this way, *Chamaerops* survives temperatures down to 10° F with little damage. Planted on well-watered clay, this tree might fail to harden to winter cold and could be fatally injured at such temperatures.

A palm with a unique solution to the threat of freeze damage is the dwarf palmetto (*Sabal minor*), a common native of coastal Southeastern swamps. Dwarf palmetto also grows along streamsides and seeps on the limestone hills of central Texas, and on alluvial bottomlands northward to Dallas. In most of its range it remains less than six feet tall and keeps its heart tucked safely beneath the ground along with its deep taproot. Dwarf palmettos are extremely hardy and remain evergreen to 0° F. If frozen to the ground by colder temperatures, they will usually recover from their underground stems.

Because of their taproots, dwarf palmettos (and many other *Sabal* species as well) can be difficult to transplant. Their slow growth makes them unattractive and unprofitable crops for nurseries, and small container-grown specimens are difficult to find. Patient gardeners can easily start palmettos from seed, but will have to wait four or five years before the young palms grow out of the "grass" stage and begin to produce their attractively bold, fanlike fronds.

From central Texas southward the dwarf palmetto's larger cousins may be tried. These palms constitute the hardiest of the big, tree-sized palms suited to formal avenue plantings. Many turn of the century gardens have thriving specimens of the massive Bermuda palmetto (*Sabal bermudana*), formerly known as *S. blackburniana.* The interlocking leaf bases of this variety split where they join the trunk to reveal tufts of fawn-colored fiber. In age these leaf bases shed to expose fairly smooth, rounded bark decorated with horizontal rings or ridges.

Bermuda palmetto thrives on calcareous clay soils, and grows slowly to fifty feet or more. On its native island home old specimens bear scars that show that the sap of their crowns was tapped to make an alcoholic brew ("bibby"). The governor of Bermuda outlawed this practice early in the 1600s, yet many of these trees have grown only a few feet since that time. They bear witness to the great longevity and excruciatingly slow growth of these hardy palms.

Very similar, but coarser in appearance and minus the furry leaf bases, is the Texan or Mexican palmetto (*Sabal mexicana*). This type holds its cross-hatched leaf bases late into life, and these often remain green long after the fan-shaped leaves have been removed. Mexican palmetto grows wild along rivers and bayous in South Texas and throughout the Gulf basin of Mexico. It is a common feature of subtropical gardens in central Texas, and bears large clusters of edible olivelike dates in autumn. In Mexico the leaves of this palm are a popular source of thatch for roofs, and this tree has been cultivated since pre-Columbian times for this valuable material.

The deep taproot of the Mexican palmetto makes it drought resistant when established, but presents a considerable challenge when transplanting larger specimens. When setting out young palmettos it is wise to keep their leaves tied up to protect the heart from dessication. When the trees have safely resumed growth the bundles of leaves will begin to bulge of their own accord and may be opened at that time. An insecticidal drench poured over the heart at planting will discourage the palm-eating grubs that sometimes attack these trees when they are placed under stress.

Florida palmetto (*S. palmetto*) withstands severe cold when grown on the moist, acid soils of its native range in the Southeast, but often performs poorly on alkaline clay. This palm has less resistance to drought than other *Sabal* species, and sometimes develops chlorosis. These added stresses may fatally aggravate freeze injuries during spells of cold weather.

More practical than the slow-growing palmettos for avenue plantings are desert fan palms (*Washingtonia filifera*). These unique Southwestern trees occur in oases along mountain foothills in California, Arizona, and western Mexico. They are noble palm trees whose botanical name thus fittingly honors George Washington. The resort of Palm Springs gets its name and fame from the desert fan palm.

Washingtonia filifera is sometimes known as "petticoat" palm because of its habit of retaining dead leaves in a dense brown thatch around its trunk. Unpruned trees resemble giant haystacks topped by tufts of big gray-green fans. If the thatched leaves are removed they reveal a thick, smooth trunk that reaches thirty to fifty feet with age.

The massive trunks of this palm make it heavy and impractical to move at large sizes. However, young specimens grow quickly and may reach ten to fifteen feet in as many years. In spite of its desert origins, the petticoat palm enjoys moisture and endures heavy, compacted clay soils as well as light, sandy ones. It withstands temperatures as low as 12° F with little damage.

This palm is often confused in the nursery trade with its slenderer, faster-growing cousin, the Mexican fan palm (*W. robusta*). The ridiculously tall thin trunks of the Mexican fan palm bulge comically near their bases. These trees provide the exotic "Dr.

Suess" silhouettes that characterize landscapes in the truly mild climates of California, Arizona, and the warmest parts of Texas and Florida.

Mexican fan palm lacks the cold-hardiness of the desert fan palm and usually perishes where winter lows regularly fall below 20° F. Hybrids between these two species have better hardiness, and often survive nearly as well as *W. filifera* itself. These "filibusta" palms are desirably tall, slender, fast-growing, and graceful. Other semihardy palms include the dwarf gray feather-leaved pindo palm (*Butia capitata*) and the silver-leaved Mexican fan palm (*Brahea armata*). Although both enjoy moisture and tolerate lime, they prefer soils with good internal drainage.

The sago palm (*Cycas revoluta*) is a cone-bearing relation of pines, rather than a palm. Its dark green, feathery leaves unfurl from fernlike fiddleheads and develop into a lush crown. These relics from the age of dinosaurs are treasured, slow-growing specimens for protected nooks in warm-climate gardens and accept both drought and excess moisture. Although tolerant of light frost, temperatures below 25° F may damage cycad leaves, and below 20° F, they may lose their fleshy stems.

Where winter temperatures rule out such subtropical evergreens the oversized woody members of the grass family (the bamboos) may be used to provide similarly exotic notes in the landscape. Bamboos are truly at home on moist clay soils, and revel in waterlogged ground. When the plants are well grown their rampancy lives up to its legendary reputation.

Few of the clumping bamboos endure limy soils, so gardeners on alkaline land must choose among the hardier running types. In rough plantings among grass and trees these bamboos may be allowed to naturalize, and may be successfully controlled by a sharp mower and a ready pair of pruning shears. Near treasured perennials or shrubbery these aggressive plants present a distinct hazard, and should be permanently restrained by edgings of concrete or metal. A border not less than eighteen inches deep will be required to prevent bamboos from sending their runners beneath the soil.

Of the innumerable varieties available for gardens, the golden bamboo (*Phyllostachys aurea*) is the strongest-growing and most popular. Its fifteen- to twenty-foot canes have curious patterns of crowded nodes near the base of the stems. Lush evergreen foliage densely furnishes its yellow-barked "trunks" and gives a grove of this giant grass the feeling of dense, overgrown forest. This bamboo provides a ready source of stakes to cut as support for favorite flowers and may be used to construct attractive, weather-resistant garden fencing.

Black bamboo (*P. nigra*) is slightly smaller and slower growing. Its young stems turn slowly from yellowish-fawn to deep ebony as they mature in their second year. Although tolerant of lime, black bamboo inclines to chlorosis in hot climates and benefits from partial shade. It makes an easy-growing evergreen of great distinction and uncommon beauty.

The grassy *Arundinaria* cultivars benefit from extra shade and moisture as well. Although less woody than the *Phyllostachys* species, these hardy bamboos are even more aggressive spreaders. Simon bamboo (*Arundinaria simonii*) and arrow bamboo (*A. japonica* [= *Pseudosasa japonica*]) reach about ten feet in height and are popular and hardy. Dwarf bamboo (*A. pygmaea* [= *Sasa pygmaea*]) makes a dense groundcover six to twelve inches high that may be mown periodically to keep it dense and uniform.

Along with these true bamboos the herbaceous giant reeds (*Arundo donax*) may be included in plantings on boggy ground to give an authentic jungle flavor to the garden. The variegated form of this fifteen-foot grass (*A. donax* 'Versicolor') emerges with corn-like leaves boldly striped with ivory. This show is much improved if these aggressive clumping plants are cut back hard each spring.

Moisture-loving subtropical sedges such as umbrella grass (*Cyperus alternifolius*) make good substitutes for these rangy grasses on smaller properties. This lovely perennial thrives on heavy soils and enjoys a warm position. Its reedlike stems bear glossy tufts of green leaflets at their tips like hundreds of miniature umbrellas. Along with the many heroically tolerant plants mentioned above, umbrella grass makes gardening on tight, alkaline clays a joyful experience filled with numerous delightful possibilities.

CHAPTER NINE

Dry Banks and Chalk Gardens

J ust as one group of plants prefers heavy waterlogged ground, another suite of flowers seeks out the high, dry places. Chalky limestone soils favor a rich variety, and many beautiful plants thrive in such habitats. The fast drainage and high capillarity afforded by limy rubble suits a diverse array of shrubs, perennials, and bulbs. These often succeed more readily on lean, arid soils than on rich ground. A patch of well-drained chalk or caliche offers the opportunity to cultivate choice flowers unsuited to other garden conditions.

Plants adapted to chalky soils rarely suffer from drought and generally require less care, feeding, and attention than those grown on deeper, more generous earths. The chalk garden is a boon both to a flower-lover's craving for diversity and to a practical, environmentally minded quest for low-maintenance, self-sustaining landscapes. Lush, attractive plantings not only are possible on stingy calcareous soils, but may actually prove more successful than on traditional deep-soil gardens, if appropriate plant varieties are chosen.

If broken up so that roots may penetrate deeply, caliche soils serve as reservoirs of moisture and mete out necessary water to plants throughout the year without the dramatic seasonal surfeits and deficits characteristic of expansive clay soils. Although inclined to droughtiness during the heat of summer, well-drained chalky soils give plants a relatively cool root-run. These earths retain high porosity and make plenty of air available to plant roots. This ability to breathe makes chalky soils easier to garden than many heavy calcareous clays.

Maquis Gardens

Plants that come from southern Europe and Asia Minor are particularly well suited to chalk and often occur naturally on limy ground. The brushy shrubs and herbs (*maquis*) that grow along the Mediterranean's shores accomplish most of their growth during the winter months when moisture is readily available, but receive little rainfall during their long summer dormancy. These plants frequently succumb to soil fungi if kept moist and growing through summer heat. A raised bed of caliche simulates the dry summer habitat of these winter-rainfall plants and affords them congenial homes in gardens where they might otherwise perish.

Where heavy clay soils prevail, it is a simple matter to construct beds of raised limy rubble to accommodate these drought-loving varieties. This enterprise is easier and more rewarding than the construction of special beds for difficult acid-loving subjects. The value of maquis beds holds up indefinitely, even under the prolonged influence of alkaline irrigation waters. Once built and planted, these chalky plantings require only minimum maintenance. They greatly extend the variety of beautiful plants that can be cultivated.

In areas underlain by calcareous rocks, limy construction rubble can often be obtained at little cost and offers suitable material from which to build a chalk bed. In colder regions rocky fragments of marl and chalk can be gathered into piles and allowed to weather and fragment naturally over the winter. Where these materials are unavailable, commercially prepared road base may be used to construct raised beds of artificial caliche.

A bed eighteen to twenty-four inches tall is sufficient to accommodate a wide range of shrubs, perennials, and bulbs. Attractive edgings of limestone flags or boulders can help consolidate the mounded plantings and will offer valuable niches and crevices in which to nestle dwarf creeping and trailing plants. A thin mulch of composted bark, dried leaves, or stony gravel should be spread over the chalk to dress up the bed and get the plantings off to a good start.

Drought-loving Trees

Several small trees are particularly fond of chalk and make good structural elements around which other maquis or chapparal type plants may be grouped. Texas mountain laurel (*Sophora secundiflora*) is one that offers grape-scented purple flowers resembling those of wisteria and glistening evergreen foliage. Old specimens reach six to fifteen feet or more in height. These ruggedly beautiful small trees convey a sense of age and strength and are often planted for their rustic appeal. Large mountain laurels can be expensive and difficult to transplant, but trees may be grown to flowering in three to four years by inserting their red-shelled, poisonous beans directly into chalky garden soils.

Anacacho orchid tree (*Bauhinia congesta*) makes a bushy, many-stemmed specimen, graced spring and fall with crowded clusters of white orchid-shaped blooms. These have a delightful wild rose fragrance, unexpected from a plant that favors arid limestone slopes for its home. The cloven, hooflike leaves of this rare West Texas native resemble flocks of tiny green butterflies and provide an interesting texture when the tree is out of bloom. Anacacho orchid tree is unusually cold-hardy for a *Bauhinia*; it withstands temperatures as low as 10° F with little damage.

The Argentine bird of paradise shrub (*Caesalpinia gilliesii*) is even hardier than this. Its exotic, flamboyant blooms are yellow, with long, protruding red stamens. Tremendous heads of showy flowers appear freely throughout the heat of summer atop its short, sparse stems. These are furnished with feathery compound foliage. *C. mexicana* makes a similar shrubby tree with clusters of yellow blooms, hardy to 20° F.

Barbados pride or "flower-fence poinciana" (*C. pulcherrima*) becomes a prickly stemmed six-foot perennial and bears brilliant orange flowers in hot weather. Its exotic look belies a surprising tolerance to drought and cold, and this subtropical shrub returns faithfully even after exposure to 0° F. *Hoffmansegias* are dwarf allies of these plants with yellow-orange clustered blooms. They enjoy caliche soils and make good low perennials for foreground plantings.

Ornamental sennas (*Cassia* spp.) produce quantities of golden blooms in the summer months that resemble those of the *Caesalpinias* and *Hoffmansegias*, but lack their long feathery stamens. Most of the drought-loving sennas are subshrubby perennials, but *C. wislizenii* makes a wiry deciduous bush and blooms over a long season. Valuable perennial types for caliche soils include *C. lindheimeri* and *C. roemeriana*.

Jerusalem thorn (*Parkinsonia aculeata*) bears clustered golden flowers along the same lines as the *Cassias*, but makes a small, gracefully spreading tree. Its peculiar foliage is thoroughly original, resembling long, thin strips of greenish leather. Under threat of drought or cold these "leaves" shed, while the green bark of this tree continues photosynthesis.

Jerusalem thorn and its desert-loving relation, *Cercidium macrum*, are sometimes known as "palo verdes" for their green bark. Both tolerate temperatures down to 15° F with little damage and thrive on dry chalky ground. They are cruelly thorny, however, and the Jerusalem thorn often makes a pest of itself with unwanted volunteer seedlings.

The deep-rooted honey mesquite (*Prosopis glandulosa*) is better behaved. Its exotically lush, bright green foliage and spreading canopy offer ideal filtered shade under which to grow many favorite perennials. Creamy yellow, oblong, clustered blooms scent the air around it with the aroma of honey. After a long flowering season, these ripen to sweet, edible pods.

The ubiquitous, oft-reviled mesquite is a weed tree of overgrazed ranchland. Yet when well cared for and nurtured in gardens, it responds with vigorous, attractive growth duplicated by few others. Its unfortunate habit of shedding branches in later life is well compensated for by the value of its twigs on the barbecue pit. A funereal pyre of mesquite branches yields fragrant culinary incense capable of converting ordinary fare into cuisine fit for a celebratory wake.

Like the drought-tolerant mesquites, the *Acacias* do well on dry, calcareous soils and lend a subtropical feel to plantings. Few, however, have much cold hardiness. One of the most hardy and ornamental types is Texas catclaw acacia (*Acacia roemeriana*). This small, scrubby tree follows its creamy, powder-puff spring blooms with lush compound summer foliage. Both the new shoots and ripening seed pods assume attractive vinous tints. Like most acacias, *A. roemeriana* defends itself from unwary gardeners and browsing deer with wickedly hooked spines.

Even thornier are the pink-flowered shrubby "catclaws," *Mimosa biuncifera* and *M. borealis*. These shrubs have attractive blooms in midspring and grow well on rugged, heavily browsed terrain. The perennial sensitive briars (*Schrankia uncinata*), the fern-leafed prairie acacia (*Acacia angustissima*), and the trailing yellow-puff (*Neptunia lutea*) are less thorny than these woody *Mimosas*, and have pink, white, and yellow powder-puff blooms, respectively. They are fine herbaceous perennials for dry, chalky ground.

Most yellow-flowering acacias are woefully tender for areas regularly visited by frost. Huisache (*A. smallii*), however, survives even where cold weather decimates its early spring blooms. More useful in frosty regions are the mescat acacias (*A. constricta*) and the huisachillos (*A. tortuosa*). These shrubby types bloom reliably even after temperatures as low as 10° F. Fragrant, golden, ball-shaped flowers cluster along their slender stems in early spring.

Golden ball lead-tree (*Leucaena retusa*) is an attractive, hardy relation of these trees with yellow flowers and similar but more coarsely divided foliage. Lemon-scented globular blooms appear at the ends of its branches through most of the summer. Happily, it forgoes the painful thorns of these other woody legumes.

Desert willow (*Chilopsis linearis*) gets its common name from its narrow leaves that resemble those of the willows. Its lavender-tinged tubular blooms belie a relation to the catalpas and trumpetvines, however, and show attractively against its grassy foliage. These graceful, spreading trees are among the toughest and hardiest available for dry, limy soils. Selected forms may be had with white blooms or with dark purple-stained flowers.

A hybrid between desert willow and catalpa developed by researchers in Soviet Central Asia is a uniquely beautiful tree. It inherits the spreading habit and lavender-colored blooms of the desert willow, but has big trusses of flowers and broader leaves more like the catalpa. This "chitalpa" is a good shade provider and remains constantly in bloom. It grows at a frightful pace.

Another member of this family that thrives on dry, limy ground is the yellow bells or esperanza (*Tecoma stans*). This half-woody perennial grows along arroyos in the Southwestern mountains and makes a tall, shiny-leaved bush topped with big yellow trumpets through summer and fall. Although a small tree in tropical countries, *Tecoma stans* functions as a perennial in frosty regions. It is important for less than frost-free gardens to secure the hardy form, *angusta*, which flowers longer and better withstands winter cold.

A particularly elegant small tree for chalky ground is the Texas persimmon (*Diospyros texana*). Its feature attraction is bony white exfoliating bark, which contrasts effectively with dark green, rounded leaves. A sense of great age is conveyed by the persimmon's rugged branching habit. Although desirable and attractive year-round, female individuals of this species bear messy crops of black fruit that readily stain pavement or masonry.

Mexican and Texas redbuds, junipers, cypresses, and sumacs are other small trees that do well on chalky soils. Texas pistache, fragrant ash, and the scrubby Vasey and shin oaks are additional choices excellent for caliche beds.

More cherished and desired than any of these, however, are the peculiar madrones or "lady legs trees" (*Arbutus xalapensis*), so-called for their beautiful pinkish, exfoliating bark. These unusual evergreens belong to the acid-loving heath family (*Ericacae*), but defy the common preferences of their relations by succeeding on chalky lime soils. A big madrone is one of the most impressive trees adapted to calcareous ground, with lusciously tinted bark, dainty white blooms in spring, and big clusters of orange, strawberrylike fruits in autumn. Its bony, ascending branches and lush, leathery foliage give it a romantic blend of strength, grace, and exoticism.

Madrones have well-earned reputations as difficult garden subjects, and they are among the first trees to perish on heavy, waterlogged ground. Raised knolls of chalky soil offer the well-drained substrate these trees require. Partial shade during youth may also be helpful, and madrone seedlings can be planted between fast-growing butterfly bushes (*Buddleia davidii* cvs.) to provide shelter from hot western sun. These nurse trees may be removed as the madrones mature.

Like all members of the heath family, madrones rely on associations with helpful soil fungi (mycorrhizae) to retrieve food and moisture efficiently with their wiry roots. By introducing soil collected from the base of established trees, gardeners can inoculate ground for freshly planted seedlings. While not absolutely critical to success, this procedure may help madrones establish and grow more quickly; these delicate trees need—and warrant—all the coddling and attention they can get!

The European strawberry trees (*Arbutus unedo*) are easy-growing relations of madrones, but lack their cold-hardiness and their outstanding pinkish bark. However, the eastern Mediterranean A. *andrachne* looks remarkably like A. *xalapensis*, with nearly identical, reddish stems and branches. Its hybrid with the strawberry tree, A. × *andrachnoides*, might provide a useful blend of beauty and vigor, more easily accommodated in gardens than the madrone itself.

Sycamore-leafed snowbells (*Styrax platanifolia*) share the madrone's lush, exotic appeal and are likewise remarkable for their tolerance of chalk. Their pendant April blooms resemble tiny white bells and look as though they belong among fairy forests of rhododendron instead of growing on gruelingly arid, rocky slopes. Like madrones, the lime-tolerant snowbells are enticing rarities to include in gardens on chalk. In addition to the green-leaved S. *platanifolia*, the less common S. *texana* and S. *youngiae* are worthwhile plants for caliche soils. Their foliage is whitened on the undersides with silvery powder and silky white hairs, respectively. Although rarely tried in American gardens, the Chinese S. *wilsonii* is reported to tolerate lime as well. This variety has a reputation for fast growth and prolific bloom.

Invaluable Subshrubs and Shrubby Perennials

A richly varied array of scrubby, soft-wooded plants provides the characteristic vegetation of the heathlike Mediterranean maquis. Such subshrubby plants are equally typical of the chapparals of the American Southwest, whose flora has developed in parallel fashion. For low-maintenance plantings on dry, limy ground these semiwoody perennials are invaluable, and they have great appeal year-round.

Among the most beautiful and useful of these brushy plants are the cenizas or "Texas sages" (*Leucophyllum* spp.). Like many subshrubs from arid lands, the cenizas offer telling, soft-textured, gray foliage. This provides a wonderful foil for their summer flowers and makes them valuable to associate with other brightly colored border plants.

The common form of ceniza (*Leucophyllum fructescens*) reaches four to six feet in height and sprawls gracefully in age. Crops of lilac-pink snapdragon blooms appear in the summer months and litter the ground beneath these scraggly bushes as they fade. Although somewhat less dramatic in flower, L. *fructescens* 'Compacta' provides a lush mass of gray, frothy foliage. For hedges or formal plantings this dwarf, bushy cultivar is the type to choose. It shears well and may be kept at three to four feet in height.

Rosy-flowered 'Green Cloud' produces especially vigorous upright growth and has pale sage-green, semievergreen leaves. 'White Cloud' has snowy white flowers and soft gray foliage. Most spectacular of all is 'Convent,' a loose-growing bush with silvered leaves and incandescent magenta blooms. All of these are hardy to 10° F or less.

The compact, small-leaved Monterrey sage (L. *langmaniae*) offers its long-tubed lilac flowers late in the season. It makes a useful green-foliaged bush to mix with the silvery 'Compacta.' Chihuahuan sage (L. *laevigatum*) also possesses these fine-textured green leaves, but has a more open habit. This helps to show off its crops of blue-lavender flowers during the summer.

'Rain Cloud' is a ceniza with loose, upright growth. Its foliage is small and silvery, and its tiny flowers are pink. 'Rain Cloud' is a hybrid of the cold-hardy L. *minus* and is especially valuable where winter lows regularly fall below 10° F. Other attractive cenizas include the cold-sensitive, blue-flowered L. *zygophyllum* and the finicky, dwarf, violet L. *candidum* 'Silver Cloud.'

Another large group of chalk-loving subshrubs belongs to the mint family (*Labiatae*), which includes many popular ornamental and culinary herbs. Although the flowers of these soft-wooded perennials are small, they are often brightly colored, with charming appearances that invite close inspection. These modest yet complex blooms combine into striking spikes or whorls and are exceptionally freely borne.

English gardeners favor the gray-foliaged lavenders (*Lavandula* spp.) in their dry borders, and several different cultivars are popular in Europe. In warm climate American gardens only the common blue-flowered forms of English lavender (*L. latifolia*) seem to have much staying power. These should be carefully positioned atop well-drained mounds of chalk, lest they melt away during a humid summer. Spanish lavender (*L. stoechas*), with its chubby violet spikes of bloom, succeeds on similar sites if offered some shade. The frost-tender *L. dentata*, *L. heterophylla*, and *L. multifida* may be annually bedded onto chalky banks, where their fragrant, serrated foliage will make lush summer displays.

More valuable, hardy, and amenable to culture than these lavenders is the Jerusalem sage (*Phlomis fruticosa*), a bushy native of the Mediterranean basin. This evergreen subshrub makes a three- to four-foot mound with sagelike foliage. In April and May robust whorls of yellow flowers rise above its gray-green leaves. Jerusalem sages are tough, easy-growing plants with considerable hardiness. Other *Phlomis* species are worth trying on chalk as well, and some herbaceous types offer pink and cream-colored flowers.

The huge group of *Salvias*, or ornamental sages, includes a nearly unending array of valuable chalk-loving plants from both the Old World and the New. Even the Mediterranean culinary sage (*Salvia officinalis*) makes an attractive shrubby evergreen for dry caliche soils. It has blue-violet flowers in April and provides flavorful leaves for use as seasoning. Although short-lived on heavy clay soils, this sage thrives on well-drained chalk.

Spanish sage (*Salvia lavandulifolia*) has a taller, lankier habit and bears squat spikes of lavender-blue flowers continuously through the summer and fall. Although tender to frost, this vigorous woody perennial recovers rapidly from winter cold damage. It speedily matures to an attractive four-foot bush on even the driest chalk banks.

Other Old World sages good on dry, limy ground include the biennial clary sage (*S. sclarea*) and its silvery relation, *S. argentea*. These varieties are valued as much for their bold rosettes of felted leaves as for their tall spikes of lavender flowers. They appreciate deep root-runs and benefit from extra attention to breaking up chalky ground.

Autumn sage (*Salvia greggii*) and its allies are among the most popular and useful of the many New World sages. Their flowers appear throughout the growing season following rains, but achieve particularly large size and bright color in the cool weather of fall. *Salvia greggii*'s dwarf, shrubby habit and its everblooming red, magenta, pink, white, yellow, or salmon flowers give it great appeal. Related types such as *S. lycioides* and *S. chamaedryoides* have violet-blue flowers, the latter with attractive silvery leaves for contrast. Hummingbirds sometimes effect hybrids between these various sages with attractive raspberry or plum purple blooms.

Other shrubby *Salvias* especially good on caliche soils include the blue-flowered mejorana (*S. ballotaeflora*) and the scarlet royal sage (*S. regla*). Both of these are deciduous in cold weather, but flower over a long summer season. *S. ballotaeflora* has daintily crimped pale green foliage and tiny blooms that give it a smoky cast when in bloom. The royal sage's large, showy flowers make it attractive to hummingbirds. It requires at least partial shade for best performance.

Perennial *Salvias* good on dry, rocky ground include the fall-blooming pitcher sage

(*Salvia pitcheri*) and the everblooming mealy blue sage (*S. farinacea*). Both make excellent cut flowers and require little care, other than staking for the tall stems of the azure-flowered *S. pitcheri*. Attractive selections of *S. farinacea* such as the violet, dwarf 'Victoria' and the lead-white 'Porcelain' are popular for bedding. 'Grandiflora' is a compact strain of *S. pitcheri* with sky-blue flowers over a long season. Where adequate room is available the tall *S. farinacea* hybrid, 'Indigo Spires,' is a good choice, and quickly rises to three or four feet. Its dark violet-blue flowers appear over a long season and, like all of these blue sages, are excellent for cutting.

Exquisite crimson blooms rise from the rounded leafy rosettes of the cedar sage (*S. roemeriana*) in April and May. This type freely self-sows on rubbly lime ground and makes a fine choice to naturalize among limestone boulders. Its flowering ceases with the advent of hot weather, but may resume again with cooling fall rains.

The leafy betonies (*Stachys* spp.) resemble these perennial sages and make equally good foreground plants for chalky borders. Lamb's ears (*Stachys byzantina*) is especially popular for this purpose. Its silvery, felted leaves are velvety to the touch and make wonderful gray mats in the landscape. Although inclined to rot out on heavy clay, these perennials thrive on well-drained chalk or lime rubble.

Scarlet-flowered Texas betony (*S. coccinea*) provides a low-growing, leafy carpet that makes it a good small-scale groundcover. Its colorful blooms appear over a long season from spring until late fall.

Especially useful for chalk are the dwarf, shrubby Texas sage (*Salvia texana*) and Engelman sage (*S. engelmanii*). These rise in April to produce dense eight- to ten-inch clumps with violet-purple and sky-blue flowers, respectively. Their West Texas relation, *S. dolichantha*, blooms through the summer, following rains. Its long-tubed lilac flowers appear at the end of branchlets of gray, lavender-like foliage.

These dwarf *Salvias* and the superficially similar dwarf skullcaps (*Scutellaria* spp.) work well in formal bedding schemes, as well as with the naturalistic treatments of the rockery. The deep violet *Scutellaria wrightii* and the pink-flowered shrubby skullcap (*S. suffrutescens*) are especially long-blooming, neat, and compact.

Another useful subshrub belonging to the mint family is the deciduous "Russian sage" (*Perovskia atriplicifolia*). A tough, cold-hardy bush, it complements hazy blue flowers with gray-green ferny foliage and blooms throughout the summer.

"Mexican oregano" (*Poliomintha longiflora*) makes an evergreen shrub covered all season with lavender-pink tubular blooms. Although not a true oregano, this shiny-leaved perennial has a similarly pungent fragrance and may be used as a culinary herb. The oreganos properly belong to the Mediterranean *Origanum* genus, which includes several ornamentals that favor chalk. These dainty rockery plants were named by the ancient Greeks for their rubbly hillside habitats. "*Oreos ganeos*" translates as "beauty of the mountain."

Hybrid oregano (*Origanum* × *hybridinum*) is one of the best, with rounded mats of evergreen foliage, topped in summer by airy sprays of pink blooms. *O. libanoticum* has similar bracted flowers and neat, green hypericumlike leaves. The wooly foliage of *O. calcaratum* gives this perennial a white, frosted appearance. *O.* × *majoricum* is a glistening silver.

Germanders (*Teucrium*) are widely distributed perennials named for Teucer, the ancient king of Troy. Wall germander (*Teucrium chamaedrys*) is a dwarf evergreen shrublet from southern Europe, popular for miniature hedges and edgings. Its trailing form, 'Prostrata,' makes a tough groundcover. Shrubby germander (*T. fruticans*) comes from the

Mediterranean coast of Spain and forms a dense gray-foliaged bush, accented in summer with bluish flowers. Although liable to freeze back at 15° F, this germander readily resprouts as a perennial. The narrow, needlelike leaves of silver germander (*T. cossonii*) give it a texture and appearance similar to rosemary, but with a distinctive gray color. In summer it bears wine-pink flowers on the ends of its creeping branchlets. With its evergreen leaves, dense, trailing habit, and below-zero hardiness, this variety is especially valuable.

Rosemaries (*Rosmarinus officinalis*) are choice ornamentals for gardens where frost is not too severe, but are likely to suffer when temperatures drop below 15° F. 'Arp' is an upright type with better than average cold-hardiness; 'Tuscan Blue' is also fairly hardy and has beautiful deep blue spring flowers. Another upright cultivar, 'Aureum,' sports an attractive golden variegation.

Prostrate rosemaries such as 'Huntington Carpet' only seem hardy in mild areas, but are great to drape over limy embankments. Extra care to avoid watering and fertilizing in the fall will help harden these types to winter cold, and they should be sited on lean, chalky soils with south or west exposures. 'Lockwood de Forest' is a beautiful, vigorous hybrid between prostrate and upright rosemaries. It seems to be constantly in flower and withstands cold to 15° F or less.

The daisy family (*Compositae*) contributes almost as many subshrubs to the chalk garden as the mint family. Often, these varieties share gray foliage and the common appellation of "dusty miller." Although the flowers of these daisies are modestly attractive in their season, many gardeners prefer to keep them sheared off so as to avoid marring or detracting from the display of showy gray leaves.

Some of the faster-growing dusty millers are popular for annual bedding, especially *Senecio cineraria*. This type is fairly cold-hardy and remains evergreen down to 10° F or less. The larger, shrubbier *S. vira-vira* and *Centaurea cineraria* are additional gray-leaved daisies well suited to dry, limy ground. They should be protected from frost below 20° F, however, or started annually from cuttings or seed.

Hardier and more reliable than these dusty millers are the "cotton-lavenders" (*Santolina chamaecyparissus*). These provide ever-gray mounds of frothy, aromatic foliage, dotted in May with small, golden, button-shaped flowers. *Santolinus* may sometimes prematurely expire if planted on heavy soils or if neglected after bloom. They perform well, however, when sited on lean, chalky ground and trimmed to remove their flowers promptly following (or just prior to) bloom.

Santolinas are valuable creepers for foreground plantings; they also shear well, and their fine texture suits them to small scale hedging. The green-foliaged *S. virens* is as desirable as the gray-leafed *S. chamaecyparissus* and even more attractive when in flower. Its rounded, creamy yellow blooms show up especially well against its forest green leaves.

Curry plant (*Helichrysum angustifolium*) is another useful evergreen subshrub of the daisy family. This native of Italy and southern France resembles a gray-leafed rosemary and emits a pleasant currylike aroma when rubbed or bruised.

The rabbit-brushes of western North America are drought-loving composites with wispy greenish foliage and frothy, yellow late-season blooms. Rubber rabbit-brushes (*Chrysothamnus* spp.) are popular types in colder regions. On the hot, dry limestone slopes of central and west Texas the tatalencho (*Gymnosperma glutinosum*) provides an autumn show of airy, greenish yellow flowers. All of these subshrubs have narrow, aromatic foliage resistant to browsing deer.

Wormwoods and sagebrushes (*Artemisia* spp.) comprise a big group of mostly gray-foliaged composites, famous in the gardens of colder regions. Many members of this group favor sandy, acidic soils, however, and perform poorly on lime. Only the strongest and most vigorous *Artemisias* seem to accept the combination of warm climate and calcareous ground.

Silver king (*Artemisia ludoviciana*) is a native prairie plant that spreads vigorously by runners. Although among the showiest of silver-leaved perennials, and well suited to dry, chalky ground, this variety can become a garden pest if its aggressive root system is not confined by appropriate barriers.

Artemisia 'Powis Castle' is better behaved and has beautiful silvery leaves and a shrubby, semievergreen habit. Because 'Powis Castle' is sterile and does not flower, it needs less pruning and attention than other *Artemisias*. It prefers a well-drained spot on a chalky bank, where it provides one of the best of all middle-row shrubs.

Other *artemisias* suited to warm climates include the rather dowdy perennial wormwood (*A. absinthum*) and the gracefully feather-leaved southernwood (*A. abrotanum*). The most glisteningly silver of all is *A. arborescens*, a large-growing native of southern Europe. Although tolerant of heat and alkalinity, this vigorous evergreen is liable to freeze severely at 20° F.

Rather like these *Artemisias* in form and color, but representative of the pungent citrus family, is the shrubby rue (*Ruta gravolens*). Its blue-gray, evergreen leaves and greenish-yellow April flowers provide an attractive foil for other nearby plants on dry, chalky borders. It is neat and easy-growing if kept dry in summer.

For attractive gray foliage, and color from both flowers and winged insects, the half-woody butterfly bushes (*Buddleia davidii* cvs.) can hardly be surpassed. They thrive especially well on limy rubble and are more long-lived in such situations than on "good" garden soil. As their common name suggests, these lively plants are surrounded all season with fluttering nectar-hungry butterflies.

Dark violet and white-flowered cultivars are the most effective for garden display. 'Nanhoensis' is an especially rich purple with orange-eyed blooms. This variety resists the unpleasant tendency shared by many *Buddleias* of beginning to brown out old flowers before the entire bloom spike has finished. Butterfly bushes may be trained as small specimen shrubs or cut back annually as perennials. They are fast, easy, and rewarding. Although tolerant of heat and drought, *Buddleias* are really at their best during the cooler autumn months, and this is when butterflies are most abundant as well.

In the heat of summer, drought-loving shrubs such as oleanders (*Nerium oleander*) command attention with their brilliant clustered blooms. These soft-wooded Mediterranean shrubs often freeze if given too generous care, but will endure cold down to 15° F or less if properly sited on dry, chalky ground. They are otherwise absurdly easy-growing and fast. Most varieties reach six to eight feet in height or more.

'Single Hardy Red' and 'Sugarland' are two popular types with vivid cerise-red blooms and good cold tolerance. Their flowering season is shorter, however, than that of the slightly more tender, pink-flowered 'Appleblossom' and 'Single Hardy Pink'. 'Isle of Capri' is a double, cream-colored oleander with a subtle, sweet fragrance. This yellowish selection and the tall-growing 'Single Hardy White' are both hardy to 20° F or less.

Of the dwarf oleanders only 'Little Red' can be rated as cold-hardy. Although it maintains a desirable three- to four-foot stature, its dark crimson blooms appear over a disappointingly brief season.

Where oleanders are poor risks to winter cold the electric orange-flowered pomegranates (*Punica granatum*) make good substitutes. These fast-growing, suckering shrubs are hardy to 0° F or less. Their carnationlike blooms appear over the entire summer and show especially well against their glossy green leaves. 'Wonderful' is a six- to ten-foot variety that produces sparse crops of edible fruit and makes a suitable screen or hedge. 'Spanish Ruby' (*P. granatum* 'Nana') is a miniature that reaches three to four feet in height and bears tiny decorative orange fruits. 'Chico' is compact-growing and fruitless. All of these cultivars thrive on dryish, limy ground and turn a beautiful clear yellow in autumn.

The true Mediterranean myrtle (*Myrtus communis*) is a compact evergreen that appreciates dry, lime soils. Although, like oleanders, prone to freeze damage when overwatered, it stands temperatures to 10° F when dry. Its aromatic, boxwoodlike leaves carry starry white blooms in spring and ripen blue-black berries in autumn. Old plants display attractive exfoliating bark.

Although the brooms of the genera *Cytisus* and *Genista* have little liking for chalk or warm climates, the Spanish broom (*Spartium junceum*) provides a similar-looking shrub adaptable to brutal heat, drought, and lime. Its nearly leafless green stems bear sweet-scented golden pea blossoms in early spring. Spanish broom makes a wiry shrub that reaches four to five feet in height and spread.

Even more airy in construction, yet equally adaptable to drought and lime, are the tamarisks or salt-cedars (*Tamarix* spp.). These big shrubs were especially popular in Victorian gardens and were treasured for their strange, wispy, gray-green foliage and rosy summer flowers. They are not as often planted today as they might be. Dark rosy-pink forms of *Tamarix chinensis* are among the most cold-hardy and popular.

Another tough flowering shrub for dry caliche beds is the chaste tree (*Vitex agnus-castus*). *Vitex* flower mostly in May and June, with spikes of misty, lavender blooms above gray-green, hemplike leaves. *V. negundo* has box-elderlike foliage and tolerates below-zero cold. Both may be trained as small, rugged trees. The sprawling, shrubby *V. rotundifolia* forms a gray-foliaged mound, dotted in summer with blue blooms.

Where these big shrubs are out of scale their diminutive cousins, the "blue spireas" (*Caryopteris* sp.), may be substituted. These are tireless bloomers and have great cold and drought tolerance. *C.* × *clandonensis* makes a particularly effective hazy blue froth to mix among other late-season flowers on a chalk bank.

These lavender-blue blooms look well, for instance, nestled among shrubs of the gold-flowered, chalk-loving *Hypericums*. The old-fashioned St. John's wort (*Hypericum calycinum*) is reliably tough, hardy, and showy. For truly arid positions the diminutive *H. balearicum* makes a curious-looking, resinous shrublet with oversized golden blooms all season. Although liable to freeze at 20° F, this Mediterranean undershrub may be grown as a perennial in frost-prone regions.

In European and Californian gardens some of the most popular and charming lime-loving shrubs are rock roses (*Cistus* spp.). These rugged, aromatic plants accept cold to 10° F or less if grown "hard" by positioning them atop a raised bed of lime rubble, but are prone to freeze damage if overfed. In late spring they bear fleeting crops of poppylike blooms. These come in shades of rose, pink, and white, and in some varieties are patterned with bold maroon spots. *Cistus* × *purpureus* and *C.* × *skanbergii* are two of the hardier types.

Although lovely in their season, these Mediterranean shrubs cease flowering when hot summer weather arrives and are less valuable in warm-climate interior gardens than in those near the sea. The pink Texas rock rose (*Pavonia lasiopetala*) blooms over a longer period in warm regions and makes a good substitute for cistuses in general size and appearance. The pavonia's inch-wide pink or rose blooms betray its relation to the hibiscus tribe, which, like the cistuses, open new flowers each morning.

Yuccas and Agaves

Some of the most valuable plants for dry, chalky gardens are the yuccas, *agaves*, and their allies. These fibrous-leaved perennials provide accents of bold, evergreen foliage, as well as stunning lilylike blooms in season. Their distinctive spiky or grasslike foliage lends an exotic Southwestern flair to mixed plantings of drought-loving shrubs. Where browsing deer limit garden choices, these tough evergreens are especially welcome.

Desirable dwarf yuccas include the gray-leaved *Yucca pallida* and its green-foliaged cousin, *Y. rupicola*. These make neat, low evergreen clumps of foliage, topped in May with three- to six-foot spikes of pendulous white blooms. Bold, sword-shaped evergreen leaves give the Indian date (*Y. baccata*) an exotic appearance, yet this stemless species withstands brutal, subzero cold. The several variegated selections of *Y. filamentosa* are also cold-hardy and desirably dwarf. However, this Southeastern variety can be short-lived when cultivated in warm-summer regions on alkaline soils.

Y. recurvifolia appears in both a green-leaved and a gray-foliaged phase ('Glauca') and has a lusher appearance than most yuccas. Its broad evergreen leaves droop at the tips, and their spines are less threatening than the stiff leaves of other varieties. Along with the shrubby, spike-leaved *Y. aloifolia*, these yuccas withstand occasional waterlogging and heavy soil, as well as dry, limy conditions.

Of the shrubby or treelike yuccas the best bloomers are the Spanish bayonet (*Y. treculeana*) and the shaggy-trunked, gray-leaved *Y. thompsoniana*. The cold-hardy, silver-foliaged *Y. rostrata* takes the prize for elegance and matures to a shimmering ten- to twelve-foot single-trunked tree. The enormously massive giant dagger (*Y. carnerosana*) is shy to bloom, but provides a noble, treelike specimen with grand symmetry and power.

For floral beauty red yucca (*Hesperaloe parviflora*) is unique and choice, and so long-blooming and easy to grow as to be indispensible. Its coral-colored blooms drape from graceful three- to six-foot wands throughout the summer, and its spineless clumps of grassy leaves remain evergreen throughout the year. A few nurseries offer selected forms with yellow blossoms, and some red yuccas have leaves edged with curling white fibers. All types thrive on chalky limestone ground.

Although their blooms are modest greenish-yellow panicles, the beargrasses (*Nolina* spp.) provide graceful, yet ruggedly evergreen foliage. Sacahuista (*Nolina texana*) is especially grasslike in appearance and makes a squat sprawling mound of green cordlike leaves. Devil's shoestring (*N. lindheimeriana*) forms long fountains of flat strappy leaves well suited for draping over a raised limestone wall. This deceptively tough evergreen blooms with tall wands in May. *N. erumpens* develops three- to four-foot bunches of stiff, razor-edged leaves that give it a bold appearance.

Even more robust are sotols or "desert spoons" (*Dasylirion* spp.). These beargrass relations hold their spiny-edged leaves in symmetrical whorls four or five feet across or more. When they flower, compact spikes of brownish-green or straw-colored blooms rise six to ten feet high above their evergreen foliage.

Sotols are unusually hardy and fast-growing and have exotic appearances shared by few other hardy plants. Texas sotol (*Dasylirion texanum*) is especially tough and easy-growing. Its shimmering green foliage reflects sunlight as it moves in the wind. Blue sotol

(*D. wheeleri*) lacks this iridescent quality, but compensates with robust whorls of blue-gray, spine-edged leaves.

The agaves share the toughness and rosette forms of the yuccas and sotols but differ by producing thick succulent leaves. Another peculiarity of agaves is their distinctive life cycle. After years of slow, steady growth, these big evergreen perennials end their lives in a burst of floral glory. This monocarpic habit is the source of the common name "century plant," for these curious succulents have earned a reputation for blooming only once every hundred years.

In fact, most agaves require only ten to twenty years to mature and bloom. Nevertheless, any who have witnessed the spectacular rise of their twenty-foot, asparaguslike bloomstalks, expanding to majestic, symmetrically tiered plates of flowers, can well imagine that this effort required a century of preparation. Although the flowering of a large agave provides unparalleled drama, it is an ephemeral event, and usually a sad one for the gardener, as it signals the end of the agave's life.

Agaves are generally propagated from small suckers that appear at the base of mature rosettes. These may be allowed to remain and replace the parent after it flowers and dies, or may be transplanted to begin a new clump. Although most large century plants are slow-growing and stingy with these offsets, some smaller types are aggressive spreaders and should only be planted in beds where they can be restrained. Most agaves are cruelly thorny and unpleasant to transplant or garden around. For dry gardens on rocky limestone ground, however, they are tough and carefree and are seldom bothered by pests or browsing animals.

The New Mexico century plant (*Agave neomexicana*) is one of the most cold-hardy types and makes a compact three- to four-foot rosette of gray, black-spined leaves resembling a large artichoke. *A. havardiana* and *A. parryi* v. *huachucensis* are similar and withstand cold to near 0° F.

Where temperatures seldom fall below 12° F the compact dwarf *A. victoria-reginae* is well worth nestling on a chalky bank. It forms a two-foot rounded ball of dark green, nearly spineless leaves, formally edged in white. This agave has especially pronounced leaf-imprinting and bears white streaks on its leaves to mark the former positions of leaves in the bud. This imprinting is a form of art characteristic of agaves and often has great ornamental value.

Of the large growing agaves the sinuous, rough-textured *A. scabra* and the cabbagey, dark green *A. salmiana* are easy-growing and withstand cold to 10° F or less. The stiff-leaved common century plant (*Agave americana*) and its attractive variegated forms are slightly less hardy. *A. americana* 'Medio-picta' is so compellingly beautiful with its ivory-striped rosettes, however, as to justify any extra coddling required. It makes an especially fine pot plant for a sunny patio.

Where the thorny leaves of agaves are too threatening, their diminutive herbaceous relations, the manfredas, may be enjoyed instead and will form attractive clumps on dry caliche soils. The leaves of these tuberous perennials are often curiously spotted and mottled with brown, and they have a unique flaccid succulence.

Manfreda tuberosa and *M. sileri* are evergreen types with spotted leaves and tall spikes of bloom in brown and chartreuse tones, respectively. These curious, spicily scented flowers have long protruding stamens and attract both hummingbirds and night-flying moths. *M. maculosa* produces small rosettes of spotted leaves and waxy white, fragrant blooms. All of these are hardy to 10° F or less. In colder regions the deciduous *M. virginica* may be planted to similar effect and comes in both spotted and unspotted strains. Its strange-looking flowers comprise a mass of chocolate-colored stamens atop tall, slender stems. Although adaptable to full sun, manfredas are lusher when grown with some shade. On dry, limy borders they have much the same appeal as hostas, aloes, and other lilylike foliage plants.

Hardy Cacti and Succulents

Several vigorous, cold-hardy cacti are worth considering for positions in the chalk garden, and, like the yuccas and agaves, offer interesting form, bold texture, and tough constitutions. The prickly pears (*Opuntia* spp.) are the most garden-worthy for colder regions, and many types display compellingly beautiful flowers. Their detachable barbed spines (glochids) are an unpleasant feature, however, and gardeners generally seek out more or less spineless types. All *Opuntias* propagate readily from cuttings, which may be simply laid on the ground to root where they are wanted.

O. ellisiana is a shrubby, spineless variety with yellow blooms, cold-hardy to near 0° F. Several prostrate forms of *O. compressa* are useful where winter lows regularly fall below zero. The bright green, nearly spineless, creeping pads of this variety make a lovely foil for its clear, golden-yellow blooms. Other hardy opuntias may be tried with orange, red, and pink flowers.

Where its vicious thorns will not threaten passersby, the treelike cholla (*Opuntia imbricata*) makes a nice-sized cactus for the cold-winter garden. This cylindrically stemmed type withstands 20 degrees below zero and crowns its stems with bright magenta blooms following summer rains.

Hedgehog cacti (*Echinocereus* spp.) are another hardy group worthy of a place on a chalky border. The claret cups (*Echinocereus coccineus* and *E. triglochidiatus*) are especially good and form large clumps in age. In early spring these are dotted with long-lasting bright red blooms.

Other *Echinocereus* such as the lace cactus (*E. reichenbachii*) are sufficiently hardy, vigorous, and attractive for the chalk garden, but are small. These types should be bedded out in quantity for garden effect. Like most small cacti, they enjoy a rich, humusy soil that dries out in summer. A thin mulch of compost or well-rotted manure over a raised bed of chalk or caliche suits them perfectly.

Other hardy succulents suitable for chalky ground include the stonecrops and iceplants. *Sedum potosinum, S. reflexum, S. forrestianum, Delosperma cooperi,* and *D. nubigenum* are thrifty spreaders with attractive blooms in early summer. In hot summer regions these perform best with some shade and extra watering during July and August. They may be nestled in crevices between limestone boulders for a charming, rustic effect.

The rosette-leaved *Sempervivums* are generally too heat-sensitive and tempting to snails for gardens in warm regions, and the related hen and chicks (*Echeveria* spp.) are mostly intolerant of extreme temperatures. However, *Echeveria runyonii* succeeds in gardens exposed to lows of 15° F, as well as in heat near 100° F. The ghost plant (*Graptopetalum paraguayense*) is equally tolerant and makes an easy-growing succulent to nestle in a dry, chalk crevice in half shade.

Perennials for Chalk

The number of perennials suited to chalky ground is amazingly diverse and includes many of the most beautiful garden plants adapted to warm regions. Mention has already been made of the numerous salvias and subshrubby daisies. More traditional perennials of the daisy type, as well as penstemons, dianthuses, evening primroses, and others thrive on dry caliche soils in abundance.

Several of the dwarf daisies make particularly charming subjects for limy borders. The white, yellow-centered blackfoot daisy (*Melampodium leucanthemum*) is one that blooms tirelessly. It makes neat six-inch mounds of creamy white and thrives especially on rocky caliche ground. The rather similar-looking lazy daisies (*Aphanostephus* spp.) also do well on chalk, but have more narrow-petaled blooms that nod and close up in the early morning hours. Both perennial and annual types are available.

The feathery-leaved Dahlberg daisy (*Dyssodia tenuisecta*) is one of several dwarf, yellow composites suited to chalky soils. It reliably self-sows on dry limy ground and will persist as a perennial under suitable conditions. Another attractive small daisy is *Hymenoxis scaposa*. Cheerful yellow blooms rise above its tufted mounds of green foliage from early spring through summer and fall.

The nearly endless roll call of chalk-loving composites includes the shrubby, aromatic damianita (*Chrysactinia mexicana*), narrow-leaved *Viguera stenoloba*, and late-flowering Copper Canyon daisy (*Tagetes lemmonii*). Other useful types are threadleaf coreopsis (*Thelesperma* spp.) and the ubiquitous Mexican hats (*Ratibida columnaris*).

Zexmenia hispida is a shrubby daisy with golden blooms all season long. Rosinweeds (*Sylphium* spp.) are tough sunflowerlike perennials with white or yellow blooms. Maximilian sunflower (*Helianthus maximiliani*) is a perennial variety that offers a spectacular blaze of golden yellow along its upright stems in autumn.

For late-season bloom and for interesting form and texture the gayfeathers or blazing-stars (*Liatris* spp.) are other worthy composites for the chalk garden. Their mostly lavender flowers provide an appropriate contrast to these yellow-flowered daisies. Prairie gayfeather (*Liatris mucronata*) and dotted gayfeather (*L. squarrossa*) are successful in warm climates, as they delay their flowering until cooling fall weather arrives. Their spires of purple, white, or lilac blooms look like exploding fireworks among the other late flowers.

Prairie gayfeather (*Liatris mucronata*) demands lean, arid ground, lest it become unnaturally tall and lanky. In what might be defined as the "gayfeather/Maximilian sunflower syndrome" avid gardeners often transplant these drought-adapted perennials to rich garden soil, only to discover that generous culture induces the formation of grotesque giants that require tedious staking and tying if they are not to collapse of their own weight. A raised bed of caliche provides a surer recipe for success with these composites.

Lindheimer's ironweed (*Vernonia lindheimeri*) is a close ally of the gayfeathers with similar purplish blooms and narrow, rosemarylike foliage. Its western subspecies, *var. larsonii*, has showy, silvery leaves to contrast with its clustered purple heads of bloom. Both types like rocky limestone ground. *Eupatoriums* such as *E. odoratum* and *E. wrightii* are other useful composites for dry, chalky soils.

Most of the numerous penstemon tribe enjoy limy ground and provide tall spikes of tubular bloom that signal nearby hummingbirds to visit for a drink of nectar. Although this group is entirely perennial, like many chalk plants, they tend to bloom themselves to death after a few years and should be renewed with young seedlings every other season or so.

One penstemon that defies this custom and behaves as a long-lived perennial is the subshrubby *Penstemon bacharrifolius*. If cut back hard after bloom this variety returns each season as a dense ten-inch-high shrublet crowned with white-throated, scarlet flowers. It likes nothing better than a dry crevice among limestone boulders.

More typical penstemons such as *P. cobaea*, *P. triflorus*, and the shrubby, scarlet *P. havardiana* usually bloom themselves out after a few years, but are reasonably perennial if not overfed. The exquisite cerise-flowered *P. wrightii* is a West Texas variety that unfortunately tends towards a short life span. However, the vivacious, siren-red *P. cardinalis* behaves well as a garden perennial.

Dianthuses in variety are good for chalky ground, and raised beds of limy soil are ideal for accommodating a collection of these charming mat-formers. The hybrid border carnations are particularly thrifty and rewarding. 'Flamingo' is a warm salmon-pink selection with good gray foliage for contrast.

A relative of *Dianthus* with similar matlike foliage, but with airy sprays of tiny yellow-green flowers is whitlow-wort (*Paronychia virginica*). This humble flower especially thrives on rocky lime soils and will slowly seed itself around a chalky bank.

Many verbenas and lantanas perform nearly as well on dry limy ground as on more generous earths. They are highly valued on chalk gardens for their long seasons of bloom. A curious ally of verbenas from the deserts of the Southwest, *Bouchea linifolia*, is a valuable perennial for rocky sites. It bears lavender flowers throughout the summer on a small, narrow-leaved shrublet.

Scarlet musk flower, or devil's bouquet (*Nyctaginea capitata*), is another drought-loving perennial good on dry soils. Its prostrate stems and clustered blooms give it a casual resemblance to verbena or lantana.

Flame flowers (*Talinum* spp.) earn their nickname for their brilliant cactuslike blooms in shades of orange, yellow, and pink. These perennial relatives of the annual portulacas rise from succulent underground tubers. *Talinum aurantiacum* makes a leafy dwarf bush covered in azalealike displays of yellow or orange blooms. These fleeting flowers open only in late afternoon, however, and stay tightly closed until after four o'clock. The tiny cherry sunbright (*Talinum calycinum*) bears luminous, cherry-rose blossoms in airy panicles above its tiny tufted leaves. It self-sows prolifically on gritty lime soil.

Evening primroses such as Missouri buttercup (*Oenothera missouriensis*) and *Calylophus hartwegii* offer large papery flowers in shades of yellow. The Missouri primrose sometimes may be had in a particularly choice silver-foliaged strain. These thrive on the barest rocky soils.

False-gaura (*Stenosiphon linifolius*) is a tall, white-flowered relative of evening primroses with wandlike stems. It makes a graceful background subject for a chalky bank.

The wiry-stemmed daleas bloom in small heads or clusters. These ripen to feathery seeds that give these perennials a fluffy, silvery look in autumn. Black dalea (*Dalea frutescens*) flowers late in the season with wine-purple blooms and makes a small suckering subshrub. *D. bicolor* v. *argyraea* is similar, save for its silvery white, fine-textured foliage. *D. greggii* retains the silver leaves and purple blooms of this variety, but displays them on trailing stems. It remains evergreen in mild regions.

Herbaceous legumes with similar flowers and seed include the golden-yellow *Dalea aurea*, the white-flowered prairie clover (*Petalostemum multiflorum*), and the pink prairie clover (*P. pulcherrimum*). These self-sow freely on chalky ground and bloom in early summer when few other perennials are peaking.

English gardeners are fond of the perennial spurges (*Euphorbia* spp.) of southern Europe and include a number of these in their chalk gardens. Only *Euphorbia myrsinites* has much staying power in warm-summer climates, however. It makes a strange, snaking mass of evergreen scaly-leaved, trailing stems. These are gray in tone and bear small, yellow-green blooms in early spring. American gardeners might well substitute the queen's delight (*Stillingia texana*) for some of the shrubbier European spurges. This lime-loving perennial has handsome, shiny green foliage and forms lush clumps on dry, rocky ground. Its leaves turn a showy bronze in autumn.

One of the most surprising groups of plants suited to chalk are several tough little ferns. Bulb cloak-fern (*Notholaena sinuata*) is an especially ornamental type with gray-toned, upright fronds. *N. aurea* is similar, but more olive-green. These, and a variety of other ferns in the genera *Notholaena*, *Cheilanthes*, and *Pellaea* make choice plants to nestle around limestone boulders. Unlike most ferns, they are quite tolerant of sun.

Because raised beds of chalk may be relied upon to dry out in summer, they afford homes for a number of winter-growing bulblike plants that fail on more generous soils. One of the most characteristic of the Mediterranean natives is the asphodel (*Asphodelus fistulosus*), whose graceful wands of small, white blooms open cheerfully on spring mornings. Asphodels develop spiky, succulent-leaved rosettes during the winter months. They often die back to fleshy roots during late summer. Self-sown seedlings welcomely increase colonies of these lime-loving herbs.

The fall blooming members of the genus *Crocus* are another group of winter-growers that find a haven on chalk. The lilac-pink *Crocus goulimyi* of the Peloponnese is one of the most robust and vigorous types. After a year or so it settles in and spreads to form a mat of autumn bloom. Saffron crocus (*C. sativus*) and the showy *C. speciosus* cultivars are less certain, but also worthy of trial. Where browsing rabbits nibble at their winter foliage, a few boughs from a prickly evergreen may be placed over these autumn crocuses for protection.

One of the most glamorous of the onion tribe also enjoys rubbly lime ground. The golden-flowered *Allium coryi* of West Texas is perfect for naturalizing on a scree of crushed limestone or caliche. Its brilliant yellow flowers appear in midspring atop its tufted clusters of tiny gray-leaved bulbs. It is the only yellow-flowered onion known to occur in North America.

A spectacular bulbous specialty of the chalk garden is *Scilla peruviana*. The sprawling leaves of this plant form a starfish rosette on the winter ground. Its intensely violet blooms open in an explosive bee-swarm cluster in midspring and look electrifying against honey-colored limestone rocks.

CHAPTER TEN

Annuals and Biennials: Beating the Heat

The harsh, dry conditions typical of limestone soils in summer are too brutal for many moisture-loving plants to endure. Oriental poppies, gentians, lupines, delphiniums, gaillardias, and other perennial flowers dearly loved by gardeners in temperate climes are short-lived in these warm-summer regions and often struggle to flower, if they bloom at all.

However, these hardy perennials have annual relations that adapt to hot summers by estivating as seeds. Such annuals reverse the seasons: they germinate in the fall, grow through the winter months, flower in spring, and go dormant in summer. Many beautiful lime-loving flowers follow such cycles and afford gardeners an opportunity to enjoy types of plants that otherwise abhor conditions offered by warm climates and calcareous soils.

A key to successful culture for most of these cool-season annuals is planting at the proper autumn season. To enjoy attractive spring displays of flowers like bluebonnets, corn poppies, larkspurs, or cornflowers, seed must be planted in the fall. Hard-shelled varieties like bluebonnets may also need treatments to soften seed coats ("scarification") and extra care to assure that seeds are raked into the ground where they can be readily moistened.

Difficult germinators like bluebonnets (*Lupinus texensis*) are sometimes happily available as transplants for bedding. A few of these young plants bedded onto a modest-sized chalky bank will give a fair measure of bloom and provide enough seed to assure generous crops for seasons to come. In addition to the traditional navy blue, these annual lupines are available in white and pinkish strains that may be mixed together for a colorfully fragrant jumble.

Other choice annuals adapted to fall planting include Drummond phlox (*Phlox drummondii*), scarlet flax (*Linum grandiflorum*), Indian blanket (*Gaillardia pulchella*), golden-wave (*Coreopsis tinctoria*), lemon horsemint (*Monarda citriodora*), honesty (*Lunaria annua*), butter and eggs (*Linaria vulgaris*), stocks (*Mathiola incana*), sweet alyssum (*Lobularia maritima*), and California poppy (*Escholzia californica*). Especially charming flowers for informal gardens on limestone soils are double opium poppy (*Papaver somniferum*), corn poppy (*P. rhoeas*), cornflower (*Centaurea cyanus*), larkspur (*Consolida* sp.), love-in-a-mist (*Nigella damascena*), and German chamomile (*Matricaria recutita*). Planted together with bearded irises and Byzantine gladiolus these flowers offer a romantically colorful vision that will faithfully reseed and return each year.

Less certain to repeat than these robust varieties, but also useful and endearing for gardens on calcareous ground, are bells-of-Ireland (*Molucella laevis*). These old-timers have long-lasting green calyces surrounding their tiny flowers and belong to the mint family. They are particularly favored for cutting.

Gentians are treasured in whatever gardens they are grown and are famous for richly colored blooms. Although virtually none of the perennial types endure warm climates and many are lime-hating, the annual prairie bluebells (*Eustoma grandiflorum*) and mountain pinks (*Erythium beyrichii*) belong to this family, yet thrive on heat and lime. They are among the finest and most rewarding of garden flowers.

These showy wildflowers have tiny seeds that require care in germinating. A bed of coarse, limy grit or a surface of limestone pavers with moist crevices between offer suitable starting places for these annual gentians. Bluebells are often available as transplants and may be encouraged to self-sow around such habitats. Although resistant to drought once established, bluebells and mountain pinks require unfailing moisture to start.

These annuals sometimes emerge with cool fall weather, but just as often seem to come up following summer thundershowers. Plants may live over several winters before blooming and exhausting themselves or may flower and perish promptly the first season, depending on cycles of weather and germination. Both are summer bloomers. Their opulent displays of blue and pink stand up to grueling heat.

Mountain pinks are uncommon in the nursery trade, but may be collected as seed from colonies growing on the limy uplands of central Texas. Bluebells are more widespread and may be found throughout the Great Plains region on moist sites. Selected strains in shades of pink, white, and violet and with handsome double blooms are available under the horticultural name, "Lisianthus."

Long summers provide for annuals whose life cycles gear to the intense heat and occasional droughts of this period. Unlike cool-season varieties whose allegiance is to temperate countries, true warm-climate annuals have distinctly tropical affinities. Many of these plants evade winter cold completely and germinate only after soils have safely warmed for the summer. A few, like petunias, are half-hardy and withstand light frosts as well as torrid heat.

Most summer annuals flower more generously when grown with steady supplies of moisture. Balsams (*Impatiens balsamina*) require it. However, the majority continue to bloom under treacherously dry conditions and a select few perform miraculously well without added water.

Several daisy-type flowers are especially drought-tolerant and valuable for dry, rocky ground. Tahoka daisy (*Macheranthera tanacetifolia*) reseeds itself on chalky soils and makes a hazy mass of lavender, asterlike flowers and fine-cut gray-green foliage. Dahlberg daisy (*Dyssodia tenuiloba*) and Arkansas lazy daisy (*Aphanostephus skirrhobasis*) are also tough, low-growing, and long-flowering. The Dahlberg daisy bears tiny yellow daisies atop ferny clumps of aromatic leaves, while the lazy daisy earns its nickname from white, yellow-centered blooms that nod and close in the heat of the afternoon.

The thrifty, golden-flowered *Melampodium paludosum* offers a rugged, leafy shrublet which flowers over the dog days of summer. *Zinnia angustifolia* 'Classic' is a choice, dwarf grower with small blooms of brilliant orange. Its glowing colors take on a special intensity when combined with purple-foliaged *Setcreasea*. Chippendale daisy (*Zinnia haageana*) is another tough, prostrate variety adapted to heat, drought, and calcareous soil. Its blooms are a mix of golden-yellow and coppery red and add a festive, Latin appearance to the border.

Taller daisies of value in the summer garden include the pink-shaded cosmos (*Cosmos bipinnatus*) and its shorter, orange-red or yellow cousin, the Klondike (*C. sulphureus*). These have been crossed together, and their hybrids are offered under a variety of names. Cosmos are showy in flower borders and provide a wealth of blooms for cutting.

Even more robust than these daisies are the bright orange Mexican sunflowers (*Tithonia rotundifolia*), popularly offered in the compact strain, 'Torch.' Common zinnias (*Zinnia elegans*), cut-and-come-again (*Helianthus debilis*), and gloriosa daisies (*Rudbeckia hirta*) are other large sunflowerlike annuals that thrive on heat and calcareous soil.

An original-looking annual with unusual tolerance to heat and drought is spider-flower (*Cleome hasslerana*). Its airy blooms are pale-colored, but appear fresh and soothing in the summer garden. Cleomes attract butterflies, hawk moths, and hummingbirds throughout the summer.

Amaranths such as love-lies-bleeding (*Amaranthus caudatus*) and Joseph's coat (*A. tricolor*) are reliable in heat. Their coarse appearances require careful placement for best garden effect, however. This is true as well for the brightly colored cockscombs (*Celosia argentea* cvs.). These warmth-loving South American annuals are frequently offered as flowering bedding plants with their curious spiked or crested heads in iridescent shades of yellow, orange, and red. Better garden performance may be secured from plants started by sowing seeds directly in place.

As with the celosias, the most successful garden marigolds are those planted directly from seed. 'Queen Sophia' is an especially robust hybrid between the dwarf French marigold strain and the taller African marigolds. It better resists the attacks of spider mites than weaker-growing marigold varieties. 'Queen Sophia' makes a dense, leafy shrublet covered in dark green foliage and golden-orange double blooms. Faded flowers should be removed continuously to prolong bloom.

Globe-amaranth or bachelor button (*Gomphrena globosa*) is a ubiquitous summer annual of country gardens. In addition to the very common dark purple variety, attractive mauve- and white-flowered forms are available and dependable in poor, dry soil. *G. haageana* produces bright orange-red blooms and may return as a perennial on well-drained sites.

Old-fashioned purple and white petunias (*Petunia purpurea*) and moss roses (*Portulaca grandiflora*) resist heat and drought once established, but enjoy well-watered, fast-draining soils and cool temperatures while getting started. Both should be planted as early in spring as possible. Petunias are also sometimes successful if fall-seeded, providing that winter weather is not too severe.

An exceptionally tough annual suited to dry soils is wild poinsettia (*Euphorbia heterophylla*). This rugged, bushy flower self-sows to make patches of miniature blooms similar to those of the poinsettia throughout the summer. Its lime-loving relation, the snow-on-the-mountain (*Euphorbia bicolor*), affords a refreshing late summer vision in white and green. It may be sown in spring for flowers from August to frost and succeeds on even the driest, rockiest sites.

Other robust, heat-loving annuals include summer cypress (*Kochia scoparia*), perilla, dark opal basil, and red-leaf hibiscus (*Hibiscus acetosella* 'Red Shield'). These are planted for their showy summer foliage instead of flowers. The aggressive, self-sowing fountain grass (*Pennisetum setaceum*) earns a place for its graceful pinkish-fawn seed heads and resistance to grueling heat and drought.

For quick shows bedding annuals offer an eminently practical solution and allow gardeners the luxury of selecting instant color. Like the hardier seed-grown flowers they fall into both a cool-season class suited to fall planting and warm-season group for bedding out after frost has safely passed.

Good bedding annuals for fall and winter planting on limy ground are pansies, violas, snapdragons, dianthus, calendulas, English daisies, and flowering kale and cabbage. For summer beds heat-loving periwinkles and copper plants are good in sun; impatiens, begonias, caladiums, coleus, torenia, and pentas are excellent in shade. Scarlet salvia, geranium, ageratum, and flowering tobacco enjoy half-day sun or filtered shade.

Biennials are not planted as often as they might be, due, perhaps, to impatience. The extra year these flowers exact before blooming goes to good cause, however, for they are able to store extra energy for their flowers in the following season. The rewards are often worth the wait!

Verbascums, clary sages, and foxgloves (*Digitalis* spp.) come to mind as typical lime-tolerant biennials. All are leafy the first season and rocket up with robust, spiky blooms in their second. The low-growing sweet williams (*Dianthus barbatus*) seldom exceed six inches in height, but are also particularly generous when in flower during their second year. The wooly leaved Maltese Cross (*Lychnis chalcedonica*) and mullein-pink (*L. coronaria*) are other useful lime-loving members of the pink family with colorful blooms born after a season of leafy growth.

For gardens on poor, lime soils, however, the essential biennial must surely be the standing cypress (*Ipomopsis rubra*). On even the driest chalk bank these tall, wandlike flowers explode heavenward into brilliant orange-red floral fireworks. The tiny green first year rosettes look rockery-perfect nestled among rubbly lime boulders and hardly hint at the towering stack of bloom they will become in the following summer. A colony of these easy-growing flowers may be begun by simply scattering the seeds on any well-drained patch of bare earth or chalk. These easy growers will thereafter return each summer for many seasons to come.

CHAPTER ELEVEN

A Moonlight Garden

As summer days dawn to cloudless blue, they auger the inevitable heat that will sear gardens on the limestone prairies in the afternoons to come. By mid-morning the sun's warmth will become uncomfortable, and the flowers of salvia, pavonia, hibiscus, and portulaca will fold and close for the day. Gardeners will scurry indoors to protective air conditioning, leaving only droning cicadas to register a note of liveliness.

When the torrid weather of high summer arrives in mid-June, many flowers enter a period of dormancy that lasts until fall. This siesta can leave gardens with little to entice visitors outside, and the grueling heat makes even a casual stroll around the backyard an unpleasant experience. The few valiant crape myrtles and lantanas that flower at this time warrant garden positions from which they can be safely viewed through a window, leaving the gardener on the air-conditioned interior.

In true Southwestern tradition, warm-climate gardeners shift their summer activities to the evening hours. Obliging flowers also follow such night schedules, and they and their pollinators offer some of the most rewarding experiences of gardening. For hot-summer regions the period from mid-June through August is a time for an extraordinary world of nocturnal activity.

Day-blooming flowers rely on bright colors and distinctive shapes to attract bees, butterflies, and birds to effect pollination. Night flowers must attract a different cast of creatures and often use fragrance to draw pollinators in from the darkness. Nocturnal blooms come mostly in shades of yellow or white. Many are sweetly or spicily scented.

The principal pollinators of night flowers are hawk moths or hummingbird moths (*Sphynx* spp.). These are the same large insects whose caterpillars are familiar as "hornworms" in vegetable gardens. On their nightly floral visits these hovering moths use long tongues to sip nectar from freshly opened blossoms. Many nocturnal flowers have deep tubes that protect this nectar from other creatures and thereby reserve it especially for the night-flying moths. These large, fast-moving insects are fun to watch as they make floral rounds on a summer evening.

A few nighttime flowers specialize in other curious pollinators. In subtropical Mexico and parts of the adjacent Southwest several cacti are pollinated by bats. Tiny nocturnal beetles are attracted to the huge, sweet-scented blooms of magnolias. The familiar yuccas of the desert Southwest depend on a close relationship with yucca moths. The yuccas sacrifice a portion of their developing seed to feed the moth's caterpillars, but are rewarded by assured cross-pollination.

An amazing diversity of night-blooming flowers await summer gardeners. Special gardens designed to showcase nocturnal blooms can be romantic and rewarding projects on limy soils, as many of the most desirable night flowers are lime-tolerant. Such plantings are not likely to be overly colorful, but they certainly can be fragrant. The sweet smells of honeysuckle, magnolia, and jasmine typify aromas of the nocturnal garden. Other peculiar scents suggestive of iced tea, chlorine, or ammonia show up in some flowers; a few of the best smell of vanilla!

Flowers of the Night

Because most nocturnal blooms are white or yellow, gardens devoted to these flowers become somewhat monochromatic and fall within the general realm of a "white" garden. Vita Sackville-West's famous all-white garden at Sissinghurst castle has been so successful and influential that her scheme of combining silver and gray-foliaged plants with pale-colored flowers has inspired many gardeners. Such silvery gray plantings have an ethereal quality when viewed in moonlight.

By combining ordinary gray-foliaged plants, common day-blooming white flowers, and those of truly nocturnal habit, the ghostly paleness of leaves and flowers and the mysterious whirring and hovering of hawk moths may be enjoyed together. Sweet, sensuous fragrances waft heavily on the night air of the moonlight garden, and the entire scheme can be directed to showcase the unique beauty of plants in cold, blue lunar light.

Good lime-tolerant, gray-leaved subjects include cenizas, elaeagnus, artemisias, Jerusalem sage, and junipers. Low edgings or borders of gray santolina, lamb's ears (*Stachys byzantina*), trailing spurge (*Euphorbia myrsinites*), or silver sage (*Salvia argentea*), and groundcovers of silver germander (*Teucrium cossonii*), silver dalea (*Dalea greggii*), or trailing *Stemodia* show up dramatically on moonlit evenings and perform well on dry, chalky soils. On heavier, damper clay ground gray-leafed *Setcreasea*, wooly velvet creeper (*Tradescantia sillamontana*) or *Liriope muscari* 'Silver Dragon' may be used instead.

Long-blooming summer flowers for such displays include white crape myrtles such as 'Natchez' and 'Glendora White,' and musk roses such as the ivory 'Nastarana' and pale saffron 'Penelope.' The sweet-scented creamy white butterfly bush, *Buddleia asiatica*, cream-colored lantanas, white Cape plumbago, and white-flowered *Salvia farinacea* 'Porcelain' are other suitable flowers.

Silver-foliaged conifers such as Arizona cypress give a hauntingly pale effect when planted as garden backdrops. Dark green Afghan pines provide telling contrasts to the gray and white within the lunar garden itself. A luxuriant hedge of a dwarf Southern magnolia such as 'Little Gem' not only defines the whiteness of such a garden, but adds its own creamy, globular blooms and heavy fragrance to the nocturnal melee.

Star performers in moonlight gardens are the true night-pollinated blooms of evening primroses, spider lilies, crinums, jimson weeds, and others. These active flowers open freshly each night, and gardeners can literally watch as the petals unfurl and the hawk moths begin their rounds.

Evening Primroses

The evening primrose family is especially at home on rugged, limy soils and includes a variety of flowers suited to harsh climates. Sulphur yellow, light pink, and creamy white blooms are frequent among the nocturnal members of this group.

Oenothera hookeri makes an easy growing three-foot-tall biennial. Although somewhat ragged-looking during the daylight hours, this leafy wildflower lights up with masses of inch-wide sulfur blooms each evening.

Neater and bushier is fluttermill, or Missouri primrose (*O. missouriensis*), whose sprawling stems bear long-tubed lemon yellow blooms four inches across. Silver-leaved selections of this plant from northwest Texas are especially showy in the garden. The light yellow blooms of *Calylophus hartwegii* are square in outline and smother these compact plants during the summer months.

Pale rose to white evening primroses include Baja primrose (*Oenothera stubbii*) and tufted evening primrose (*O. cespitosa*). The white wild honeysuckle (*Gaura lindheimeri*) is another member of this family deserving of a place in a collection of nocturnal blooms.

Spider Lilies

The spider lily clan (*Hymenocallis* spp.) is comprised of uniquely graceful evening flowers and offers some of the garden's most exquisite summer fragrances. The botanical name of these tropical American bulbs translates as "beautiful membrane," a reference to the gossamer cups of webbing that center inside their spidery white petals. These bizarre blooms have an exotic, mysterious quality that makes them especially choice.

The most commonly available *Hymenocallis* in horticulture are the deciduous South American "Ismenes" or Peruvian daffodils. They should be planted deeply and mulched heavily to discourage the bulbs from splitting up to less than flowering size. *H. narcissiflora* and 'Sulfur Queen' are two of the easiest and most popular strains and are pleasantly primrose-scented.

Also deciduous, but rarely grown, save by connoisseurs of exotic, tropical bulbs, are the diminutive spider lilies of the Mexican alliance. *H. harrisiana* is the most commonly seen. It has modest tongue-shaped leaves and spidery blooms crowned by tiny white cups. Larger-flowered and more showy is the gray-foliaged *H. glauca*. Its large-cupped snowy blooms smell of ammonia or chlorine.

Hymenocallis sp. 'Tropical Giant' is a favorite evergreen type with robust, glossy foliage and big, white, spicily fragrant flowers in July. The narrow grassy-leaved *H. maximiliani* and the wide-leaved *H. imperialis* and *H.* sp. 'New Lion' flower earlier. *H. latifolia* blooms from late summer into fall on long-tubed blooms with dangling petals. Its close ally, *H. pedalis*, has one of the finest of nocturnal fragrances: a warm, buttery scent suggestive of vanilla and almond. The last spider lily to flower, sometimes as late as November, is *H. acutifolia*. Its big, frilled, snowy cups look startling against the mass of its straplike, dark green foliage. All of these are easy on well-watered calcareous soil and are hardy where the ground does not freeze deeply.

The native spring-flowering *H. liriosme* is a true aquatic that thrives best in standing water. It is quite cold-hardy, and well worth accommodating in a tub or half-barrel of water. This culture also suits other American spider lilies such as the miniature *H. traubii* and is good for the white, night-blooming *Crinum americanum* and its allies.

More Night-blooming Bulbs

Crinum often have colorful flowers in shades of pink or wine-red, as well as white, but are nevertheless night-bloomers in the truest sense. All crinum open in the evening hours and have the characteristic long-tubed blooms of moth-pollinated flowers. For the moonlight garden, fragrant, everblooming types such as 'Alamo Village' or 'Mrs. James Hendry' are choice. 'Empress of India' is a Victorian hybrid with huge, wine-striped, powerfully scented blooms that rise on tall stems above prostrate foliage. Its flowers are seen at their best only on a moon-filled night, for they fold promptly and wither at first light.

Other fragrant, nocturnal bulb-flowers may be had from tuberoses (*Polianthes tuberosa*). Mexican single tuberoses are the easiest and most reliable in hot climates, but the double 'Pearl' is also satisfactory, if its blooming can be delayed till cool autumn weather arrives. Both are deliciously scented, half-hardy perennials. They should be reset in fresh soil every few years to avoid damage from nematodes.

Rain lilies of the *Cooperia* section may be used to create a fragrant border of grassy foliage and elfin nocturnal bloom. The giant prairie lily (*Zephyranthes drummondii*) and its smaller relations, *Z. chlorosolen* and *Z. traubii*, offer long-tubed white blooms with a heavy primrose scent. *Z. smallii* continuously produces myriad sulfur-yellow goblets, and *Z. morrisclintii* yields frosty pink flowers for several evenings following summer rains.

For gardens with partial shade, the tuberous-rooted butterfly ginger (*Hedychium coronarium*) is an easy growing, sweet-scented perennial with white evening blooms similar to those of orchids. Most other *Hedychium* species are nocturnal as well.

The section of true lilies, which includes the popular, fragrant Easter lily, has night-flowering predilections. *Lilium formosanum* and *L. regale* are good summer garden performers from this group with white, trumpet-shaped blooms. The madonna lily (*L. candidum*) has a nocturnally pollinated flower, but blooms in midspring. It enjoys lime soils, but is more finicky than other lilies and often sulks if overfed.

The more open, bowl-shaped blooms of the lime-tolerant aurelian hybrids derive from crosses between both day and night-flowering species. Strong-growing types such as 'Thunderbolt' and 'White Henryi' have warmly colored blossoms reminiscent of the moon itself. Such lilies are ideal for a lunar garden and last well in partial shade.

Nightshades

The nightshade family includes a variety of lime-tolerant evening bloomers. The most luxuriant are the thorn-apples or jimson weeds (*Datura* spp.), whose giant petunialike trumpets open on summer evenings. "Thorn-apple" is a reference to the spiny, globular, poisonous fruits of these heat-loving perennials.

Datura inoxia is the common white, hardy jimson weed of gardens. It makes luxuriant clumps of foliage even on poor, dry, lime soils and bears large, fragrant blooms. *D. metel* is familiar in its double, violet-tinged form, but occurs also in a single, creamy yellow strain. Both are delectably fragrant.

Night jessamine (*Cestrum nocturnum*) is another nightshade well-known for its nocturnal habits. A narcotic perfume wafts heavily from its tubular, greenish blooms at night, but vanishes mysteriously during daylight hours. Although tender to frost, this subtropical shrub may be grown as a perennial if mulched for winter protection to its roots.

Annual flowering tobaccos (*Nicotiana* spp.) also belong to this family and open their tubular blooms at night. The old-fashioned greenish-white *Nicotiana alata* has more fragrance and charm than the colorful, modern hybrid strains.

Periwinkles

Many members of the periwinkle family have nighttime flowers, and their five-parted, pinwheel-shaped blooms often have some of the best nighttime fragrances. Confederate jasmine (*Trachelospermun jasminoides*) is a favorite evergreen vine in warm regions. It may be trained against a wall or over a wire support for best effect. Although the common white form suffers badly from freezes below 15° F, the pale yellow 'Mandaianum' survives somewhat lower temperatures and may be preferred in areas where these vines are marginally hardy.

Amsonias are tough perennials with fragrant, tubular blooms in colors from lead-blue to ivory. The blue star (*Amsonia tabernaemontana*) is most generally planted. It spreads slowly by underground runners. *A. ciliata* and *A. salpignatha* are suited to dry chalky ground. The latter tops its feathery green foliage clumps with clusters of muddy white, long-tubed, jasmine-scented blooms in early summer.

Another chalk-loving perennial of this group is "flor-de-San-Juan" (*Macrosiphonia macrosiphon*). Like the amsonias, this rugged spreader colonizes thin rocky soils. Its large periwinklelike blooms are produced singly during the summer months and have a rich sweet-spicy aroma reminiscent of crinum or spider lilies. Its Mexican nickname is often applied to these other fragrant blooms as well.

More Night-bloomers

Perennial wildflowers such as blazing star (*Mentzelia decapetala*), Rattlesnake plant (*Manfreda* spp.), and angel's trumpet (*Acleisanthes longiflora*) are good night-bloomers for rocky, upland gardens and withstand considerable drought. An unusual sage, *Salvia dolichantha*, behaves as a nocturnal bloomer as well. It opens pale lavender, tubular flowers atop clumps of narrow, grayish foliage at dusk. The subshrubby jasmine-scented *Menodora longiflora* unfurls its long, primrose-yellow buds on summer evenings and thrives on dry, chalky ground.

In partial shade the old-fashioned yellow-flowered forms of four o'clock (*Mirabilis jalapa*) are useful for a moonlight display. Long-tubed yellow columbine (*Aquilegia longissima*) is another shade-loving perennial whose light yellow blooms attract night-flying hawk moths. On damp, shady positions cultivars of *Hosta plantaginea* such as 'Royal Standard' may provide evening blooms. Corms of the fragrant acidanthera (*Gladiolus callianthus*) may be bedded in moist ground for their scented, chocolate-stained, ivory blooms, but should be dug and stored dry over winter to ensure their return.

Evening-flowering vines such as Japanese honeysuckle and moonflower (*Calonyction aculeatum*) are easy and indispensable for nighttime gardens. The latter may be grown as an annual and will rapidly cover a summer trellis with its big white morning-glory blooms. Carolina jessamine (*Gelsemium sempervirens*) will cover itself in masses of sulfurous yellow in early spring and makes a lush evergreen vine throughout the year.

For added effect, tubbed tropical plants with nighttime flowers may be combined with these hardy garden subjects. Arabian jasmine (*Jasminum sambac*), frangipani (*Plumeria* sp.), and cape jasmine (*Gardenia jasminoides*) are excellent night-bloomers for large pots. Night-flowering tropical water lilies (*Nymphaea* cvs.) may be planted in tubs of water or a garden pond for their exotic summer blooms.

Night-blooming Cereus

The most romantic and exotic of nighttime flowers belong to the cacti known popularly as night-blooming cereus. A famous nineteenth-century painting from Robert Thornton's *Temple of Flora* fancifully depicts one of these spiny, vining cacti opening its huge flower and ascending an ivy-covered oak by an English manor house. In the background a clock atop a tower strikes midnight and the moon peers from behind the clouds. Few English manors actually afford such scenes, but these warmth-loving cacti can easily be grown in a hanging basket, and one variety is sufficiently hardy to train up live oaks in south-central Texas.

Night-blooming cereus are actually a mixed lot and include several different types of cacti. *Epiphyllum oxypetalum* has passed under this name among several generations of gardeners in the American Midwest. Its green, spineless stems bear several summer crops of swan-necked buds that open to white, spicily fragrant blooms of incredible beauty.

The night-blooming cereus in Thornton's painting is the "Queen of the Night" (*Selenicereus grandiflorus*), a tender vine of the Caribbean islands. Its name is well deserved, for in fragrance and beauty it has no equal. Huge furry buds hang from i ɔ spiny, snakelike stems in the summer. At dusk these expand to many-petaled goblets with amber sepals framing creamy inner petals. A heavenly aroma, something like buttered-pecan ice cream, signals passing hawk moths to come and dine. As with all night-blooming cerei, these enormous flowers expand most widely at midnight and have already folded by the time dawn breaks.

For gardens where temperatures seldom fall below 15° F, *Selenicereus spinulosus* offers a fanciful night-bloomer to train up a tree or along a fence. Its nocturnal blooms are white and starry, and its stems are snakelike and capable of climbing with aerial roots. This hardiest of night-blooming cerei comes from eastern Mexico and was collected once as a wildling in southern Texas at the turn of the century.

CHAPTER TWELVE

Attracting Wildlife

One of the great joys of a garden is its ability to enmesh and enjoin civilization with the living communities of nature. In addition to the sensual beauty of trees and flowers, a measure of any garden's appeal comes from its attraction to the beautiful birds and insects that reside everywhere in the environment, yet are rarely seen and appreciated outside the specific plant associations that attract them. By carefully selecting appropriate plants, a cast of entertaining garden creatures may be enticed to visit year-round.

Song birds are favorites that may be readily attracted to gardens. Around city and suburban neighborhoods the natural, brushy cover these birds enjoy has often been largely destroyed, and they welcomely flock to any manmade oasis provided for their refuge. Twiggy, berry-laden shrubs and trees attract song birds and should be planted in abundance around garden perimeters to provide cover and nesting sites. Native evergreens such as *Juniperus virginiana* and *J. ashei* are especially favored perches that grow readily on the poorest lime soils.

Berry-producing shrubs such as yaupon, possumhaw, American beauty-berry, and blackhaw viburnum do double duty as wildlife cover and forage providers. Fruiting trees such as sugarberries (*Celtis laevigata*), hawthorns, and Mexican plums are also excellent for food and habitat. Vigorous, suckering berry providers such as Indian currant, elderberry, and rough-leaf dogwood may be allowed to naturalize where space is available.

Seed-eating birds such as finches enjoy shrubs and perennials with dry fruit, rather than berries. Crape myrtles such as the hybrid 'Tuscarora' make a great deal of seed, which such birds enjoy removing from the husks during winter. Perennials of the daisy family such as frost weed, ironweed, and gayfeather are generous providers for seed-eaters as well.

For nesting purposes, many birds prefer the safety of tall trees. Cedar elms are particularly good, for their twiggy branches offer plenty of cover, and their upright habit of growth affords good height even while the trees are fairly young. Evergreens such as Afghan pine, deodar cedar, and Arizona cypress also provide attractive nesting sites.

Some of the most amazing creatures that American gardeners are privileged to witness are hummingbirds. These frenetic miniatures whir busily about flower-filled gardens, sipping nectar to replenish the stores of food for their supercharged metabolisms. In addition to providing iridescent glamour from their subtropical plumage and entertainment as these aerial gymnasts cavort, hummingbirds prey on mosquitoes and other small insects to the benefit of gardeners who attract them.

Hummingbirds are so popular with gardeners that many invest in artificial feeders to provide continuous sources of "nectar" for these birds. Although such feeders are certainly appreciated by the hummingbirds, gardeners must constantly refill them as the sugar water they contain disappears. In many cases it is easier, less time consuming, and more rewarding to cultivate nectar-bearing flowers.

Hummingbirds are tropical American creatures that migrate northward annually, following the rush of spring flowers as they pass up from Mexico. Many hummingbirds summer in the mountains of the western states, where flowers remain in abundance even through the dog days of August. For gardeners to attract and keep hummingbirds in their neighborhoods, a continuous diet of nectar-filled blooms must be offered from spring till frost.

This task is less daunting than it might seem, for many bird-pollinated blooms have lengthy flowering seasons. Long, pointed bills suit hummingbirds especially for feeding on tubular and trumpet-shaped flowers. The hummingbird's favorites are those in shades of orange and red, and many plants have evolved just such blooms to attract these winged pollinators.

A heroically long-flowering hummingbird attractor, and one which adapts well to lime soil, is coral honeysuckle (*Lonicera sempervirens*). This attractive evergreen vine may be trained up a post near a garden window so that the birds may be observed as they feed. Coral honeysuckle remains in continuous flower from March through November.

For shady gardens the crimson tropical sage (*Salvia coccinea*), scarlet royal sage (*S. regla*), orange shrimp plant (*Justicia tomentosa*), orange Turk's cap (*Malvaviscus drummondii*), and firespike (*Odontonema strictum*) are all good and long-flowering. For sunny positions, crimson *Canna* 'Iridiflora Rubra,' red yucca, coral tree (*Erythrina* × *bidwillii*), bird-of-paradise shrub (*Caesalpinia gilliesii*), Barbados pride (*C. pulcherrima*), autumn sage (*Salvia greggii*), big red sage (*S. penstemonoides*), hummingbird bush (*Anisacanthus wrightii*), Mexican honeysuckle (*Justicia spicigera*), silvery acanthus (*J. suberecta*), Texas betony (*Stachys coccinea*), and the biennial standing cypress (*Ipomopsis rubra*) are excellent. Penstemons, cypress vines, firebush (*Hamelia erecta*), trumpet creeper, wild bergamot (*Monarda fistulosa*), cupheas, crape myrtles, and *Manfreda* species are also favored by hummingbirds.

The other class of creatures gardeners often try to entice with flowers are butterflies, or *Lepidoptera*. These gay insects have wings covered in scales that overlap to reflect bright colors and patterns. They are graceful and colorful as adults and pass through fascinating transformations (metamorphoses) from their caterpillar larvae and cocoon-encased pupae. Butterflies have inherent appeal for children and, like all insects, afford invaluable learning opportunities for growing minds of any age.

Butterflies can be attracted to gardens both through appeal to the adult insect's thirst for nectar and by offering suitable foliage plants for the browsing caterpillars. Attention to the many stages of the butterfly life cycle will reward gardeners with opportunities to witness all the aspects of these insects' dramatic lives.

Red admirals, buckeyes, and painted ladies are attracted to early spring-flowering trees and shrubs with white, cloyingly fragrant blooms. Mexican plum, hawthorn, and privet attract clouds of these butterflies early in the year.

During the summer, perennials such as lantana and the aptly named butterfly bushes (*Buddleia davidii* cvs.) are centers of butterfly attention. The long-flowering milkweeds and butterfly weeds (*Asclepias* spp.) also attract their share, especially the orange-flowered *Asclepias currasavica* and *A. tuberosa*. Such milkweeds are host plants for monarch butterflies, whose yellow and black-striped caterpillars feed on their poisonous foliage. This renders the adult insects toxic to birds, which learn not to molest them.

Monarchs, queens, and various sulfur butterflies are migratory and fly south in the fall to Mexican sanctuaries. By planting a goodly selection of fall-flowering perennials it is not difficult to entice these insects to stop and rest on their way. Special favorites of the migratory butterflies are eupatoriums, frost weeds, and asters. They also enjoy lantanas and butterfly bushes, whose flowers peak in autumn. In warmer regions the Mexican orchid tree (*Bauhinia mexicana*) may be planted to attract these travelers as well. It exhibits white, feathery blooms typical of butterfly-pollinated flowers.

Swallowtails are among the showiest and most readily encouraged garden butterflies. Unlike other *Lepidoptera*, these insects constantly flap their wings while feeding. A garden full of swallowtails is eternally in colorful motion. Dill, fennel, and parsley are suitable hosts for caterpillars of the black swallowtail, while the giant swallowtail prefers rue or other members of the citrus clan, and pipevine swallowtail dines on *Aristolochia* species. If molested, the caterpillars of these attractive insects will defend themselves with an unpleasantly scented spray from just behind the head.

Although some gardeners shrink at the sight of stinging insects such as bees, others enjoy the busy work of these insects and take pleasure observing their assiduous floral visitations. Those who keep bees for honey, or who wish simply to marvel at the workings of these insects, can attract them with a variety of plants.

Honeybees are Old World natives, and many of the best bee-attracting plants come from Europe and Asia. Lime-loving Mediterranean herbs such as rosemary, borage, and hyssop are often cultivated to attract bees. Horehound is another perennial of this type with great appeal for honeybees, but is generally excluded from plantings because of the bitter flavor it imparts to honey.

Lime-loving shrubs such as Texas kidneywood (*Eysenhardtia lindheimeri*), whitebrush (*Aloysia gratissima*), guahillo (*Acacia berlandieri*), and honey mesquite (*Prosopis glandulosa*) are highly valued as honey plants. Cool season annuals such as bluebonnets and clovers are also good bee attractors.

The most obvious of native American bees are the bumblebees, which are rumored by aerodynamics engineers to be unsoundly designed for flight. Yet, fly they do, albeit clumsily. Their bumbling movements are often entertaining and accompanied by noisy buzzing. A good flowering shrub with a peculiar appeal for these insects is mejorana (*Salvia ballotaeflora*). Its tiny, pale blue flowers provide ridiculously small landing pads for the oversized bumblebees when they visit. Thistles make effective, bold-looking bumblebee attractors as well. They are tough, prickly-leaved winter annuals or biennials, well suited to poor, limy ground.

A childhood favorite of many youngsters on the limestone prairies is the ticklebee (*Andrena verecunda*). This churlish, stingless bee leads a solitary life and visits only one type of flower, the Texas dandelion (*Phyrhopappus geiseri*). This dandelion is a specialty of the limestone regions of mid-America, and both it and its devoted insect visitor occur nowhere else.

Texas dandelions open their luminous yellow flowers each morning and soon attract the small, black-bodied ticklebees. Children like to capture the insects and hold them up to their ears to listen to their whirring and buzzing. Although this generally tickles the palm of the captor, some bees manage an occasional nip with their mandibles, which assures their release and the perpetuation of the species.

By noon the dandelions close for the day and the bees disappear until the next day's flowering. Although Texas dandelion is more often regarded as a weed than a garden flower, it is actually rather showy and well-behaved, and, with its curious visitor, proves a decided asset to gardens on lime.

One of the most bizarre insect attractors adapted to limy soils is a pink-flowered orchid tree from northern Mexico, *Bauhinia macranthera*. Like a handful of true orchids native to southern Europe, this tree is pollinated by paper wasps. Fortunately, its blooms are born on up-facing limbs and branches, well away from the ground, so it presents a minimal risk to gardeners from its stinging visitors.

CHAPTER THIRTEEN

Garden Roses

Although many roses have reputations as finicky subjects requiring carefully developed soil and generous additions of fertilizer and chemical spray, the stronger-growing types hardly warrant such coddling. Unlike the delicate woodland plants from which modern hybrid azaleas, rhododendrons, and camellias descend, the forbears of our garden roses were hardy denizens of hedgerows and prairie margins. The ancient vigor and remarkably tough constitutions of these vining shrubs often can be found in hybrid roses today. Of the most loved and highly cultivated flowering shrubs, it is the rose alone that offers suitable subjects for plantings on rugged ground.

In large part it is the propagation techniques and priorities of modern rose growers that have created a finicky reputation for the rose. An endless stream of hybrid novelties budded onto easily propagated rootstocks churns out annually from rose nurseries, each pictured in catalogs with enticingly beautiful blooms opened to perfection. Although these modern roses certainly fulfill their promise of beauty when lavished with care, few endure or perform under the more casual treatment most gardeners are prepared to offer.

The principal culprit for this lack of longevity is the rootstock that many growers choose for their roses. Rose fanciers often debate which understock is best for a particular region; for most gardeners the answer might just as well be none. This is particularly true for regions with calcareous soils, for few common commercial rootstocks perform well on limy ground. What is worse for gardeners, however, is that the practice of budding onto understocks often perpetuates weak-growing varieties that should never have been distributed in the first place and induces overly vigorous, disease-prone growth on cultivars that might otherwise prove healthy.

For garden performance on calcareous ground own-root roses are greatly to be preferred. A vigorous rose on its own roots is far less likely to suffer chlorosis or bouts with disease. Resistance to drought, cold, and heat will likely improve as well. In most cases a rose that grows strongly on its own roots will make a fine, long-lasting addition to the garden.

Several specialist nurseries offer own-root roses, either in containers or bare-rooted in the dormant season. It is a simple matter to root one's own summer cuttings of favorite roses as well, and this is an excellent way to acquire good performers from other nearby

Siren red *Penstemon cardinalis* contrasts effectively with light-colored backgrounds of frothy grey *Artemisia* 'Powis Castle' and white Blackfoot daisy (*Melampodium leucanthemum*). In the far distance a smoky lavender Russian sage (*Perovskia atriplicifolia*) repeats the vertical accent of the penstemon.

Above. Lilac Monterrey sage (*Leucophyllum langmaniae*) makes a compact, drought-resistant companion for the fragrant, creamy, shaving-brush blooms and grassy evergreen foliage of the "coconut lily" (*Schoenocaulon drummondii*).

Left. Hybrid dittany (*Origanum × hybridinum*) makes a fine evergreen groundcover to cascade over dry, chalky banks. Pink summer flowers and edible, oregano-scented leaves provide additional charms.

Opposite. Tiny ruby blooms of miniature China roses (*center*) combine with white lazy daisies (*Aphanostephus* sp.), blue, pink and red salvias, scarlet standing cypress (*Ipomopsis rubra*), the rich green foliage of 'Tuscan Blue' rosemary, and frothy golden tatalencho (*Gymnosperma glutinosum*) for a lush, colorful display on chalk.

Above. Rhodamine purple blooms appear in lavish flushes along the silvery-grey branches of this richly-colored selection of ceniza (*Leucophyllum frutescens* 'Convent') several times each summer.

Left. Jerusalem sage (*Phlomis fruticosa*) makes a first class evergreen shrub for dry, well-drained soils. Bold, golden yellow, whorled blooms tops its leafy branches in late spring.

Above. The scaly, snakelike branches of dwarf spurge (*Euphorbia myrsintes*) offer an unusual foreground accent for a dry border. Companion plants include a dwarf blue sage (*Salvia sinaloensis*) (*right foreground*), pink skullcap (*Scutellaria suffrutescens*), and grey-leaved, creeping *Stemodia canescens.*

Right. Mexican oregano (*Poliomentha longiflora*) flowers tirelessly through the summer and retains its shiny green leaves through the winter months.

Above. Creeping silver germander (*Teucrium cossonii*) makes a surprisingly hardy, drought-tolerant groundcover. Wine-pink blooms appear atop its rosemarylike branchlets in early summer.

Left. Wall germander (*Teucrium chamaedrys*) is a favorite edging shrublet, with boxwoodlike evergreen leaves. Its purplish-pink blooms appear in June.

Opposite. Claret-cup cactus (*Echinocereus coccineus*) is one of the most cold-hardy and easy-growing of cacti, and boasts especially lovely, long-lasting blooms.

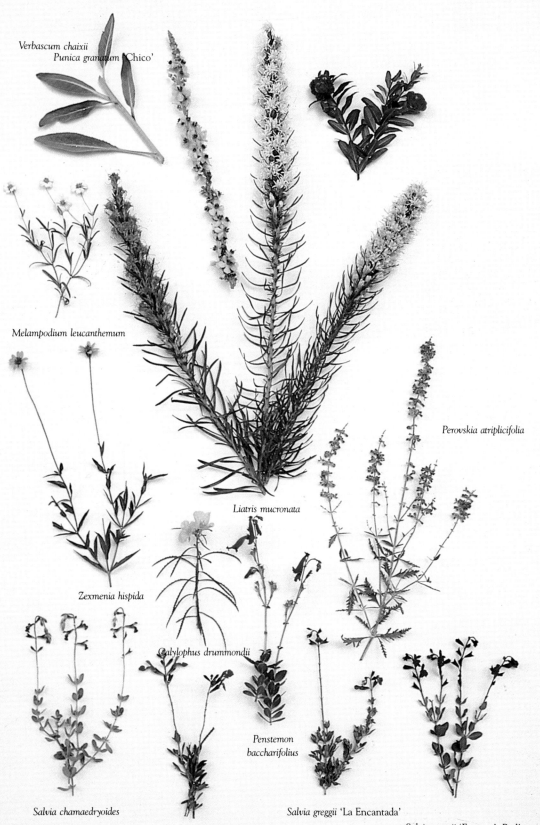

Verbascum chaixii

Punica granatum 'Chico'

Melampodium leucanthemum

Perovskia atriplicifolia

Liatris mucronata

Zexmenia hispida

Calylophus drummondii

Penstemon baccharifolius

Salvia chamaedryoides

Salvia greggii 'La Encantada'

Salvia lyciodes × *greggii* 'Plum Wine'

Salvia greggii 'Furman's Red'

Above. 'Texas Centennial' is a vigorous, easy-growing Hybrid Tea, with sumptuously large, warm-colored blooms.

Right. 'Rosborough' is a flavorful blackberry suited to home gardens in warm climates. It adapts to reasonably deep alkaline soils if irrigated through periods of summer drought.

Above. This silver-leafed form of fluttermill, or Missouri primrose (*Oenothera missouriensis*) enjoys rocky limestone soils, and opens long-tubed, luminous yellow blooms on warm evenings throughout the summer.

Left. Fragrant, night-blooming spiderlily (*Hymenocallis* sp. "Tropical Giant") and river fern (*Thelypteris kunthii*) give a lush, overgrown look to a partially shaded garden corner.

Opposite. The airy white blooms of *Gaura lindheimeri* open at dusk, and contrast with the bold-textured leaves of plume poppy (*Maclea cordifolia*) and bright orange blooms of klondike (*Cosmos sulfureus*).

Above. Queen of the night (*Selenicereus grandiflorus*) is the most celebrated of night-flowering cacti. In frost-prone gardens this tender, vining cactus can best be enjoyed in a hanging basket.

Left. Phlox paniculata 'Mt. Fuji' is a surprisingly vigorous white-flowered summer phlox. It resists mildew, enjoys moisture, and makes a bright show in full or partial shade.

Opposite. The chinese ground orchid (*Bletilla striata*) grows easily in partial shade and makes a charming early spring display.

Above. Tropical sage (*Salvia coccinea*) affords a colorful show for difficult, dry shady positions. This pale-colored strain ('Jone's Pink') shows up well against a dark background of purple heart (*Setcreasea pallida*).

Left. This frost-hardy pink-flowered iceplant (*Delosperma cooperi*) hails from the high mountain country of southern Africa. It enjoys a cool root run along a rocky crevice or under a carpet of mulch.

Above. For moist soil in partial shade the evergreen gold-flowered *Chrysanthemum pacificum* makes a good small-scale groundcover, and a choice complement for annual sweet alyssum (*Lobularia maritima*).

Right. Golden February blooms of shade-loving *Sedum palmeri* enliven a permanent outdoor planter surrounded by grassy winter foliage of oxblood lily (*Rhodophiala bifida*). In its native Mexican home this yellow-flowered succulent prefers rocky, north-facing ledges.

Red-flowered cross-vine (*Bignonia capreolata* 'Rubra') has few rivals among hardy flowering vines.

gardens. Vigorous flowering shoots can be taken in fall or spring, dipped in rooting hormone, and inserted in a sandy compost. These should be sheltered from wind or strong sun either in a shady protected corner or in a pot covered with plastic or glass to hold in the humidity. After three to four months, the cuttings should be ready to transplant to a permanent location. Budded roses obtained from traditional nursery sources should be set in the ground a couple of inches below the graft so that roots may be encouraged to form from the scion or budded variety.

Climbers and Ramblers

As with other shrubs planted on calcareous grounds, garden performance for rose varieties often corresponds to general vigor. Since the ancestors of most roses were vines or scrambling shrubs, it follows that modern bush roses are *de facto* dwarfs with considerably reduced vigor compared to climbers. Although many bush roses thrive on limy ground, climbing roses are the group that seems most truly at home under rugged conditions. For the amateur in search of beautiful, carefree roses, climbers promise fragrant, seasonal delights, and combine readily in a variety of settings.

Mastering familiarity with the many different climbing rose classes would challenge even an experienced botanist, and the many divisions certainly create confusion for rose-lovers. For garden purposes these large-growing roses most conveniently divide into true climbers (those robust enough to train over an arbor or up a tree) and those that merely sprawl (the so-called "pillar" roses). Each of these sections further divides between once-flowering types and repeat-blooming varieties, and among hardy and half-hardy cultivars.

Once-blooming Climbers

Of the once-flowering climbers, the yellow Lady Banks' rose (*Rosa banksiae* v. *lutea*) is a prime choice for regions where winter lows remain above 0° F. The white form of this rose is also good, although somewhat less lavish with its violet-scented blooms. Both varieties produce clouds of tiny double flowers in spring and nearly thornless canes covered in semievergreen foliage. 'Purezza' is a white-flowered banksia hybrid that repeat-blooms in autumn. All of these thrive in brutally arid positions and revel in rubbly caliche as well as on heavy calcareous clay.

Other half-hardy spring-blooming climbers include the ancient Chinese 'Fortune's Double Yellow.' This tough rose is a deliciously blended shade of apricot. Its delicate, medium-sized, semidouble blooms disguise vicious thorny stems.

'Belle of Portugal' and 'Souvenir de Mme. Leonie Viennot' are rampant pink-flowered varieties with large, blousy, fragrant blooms. Vigorous climbing stems enable them to ascend obliging rough-barked live oaks with ease, and they soon sprawl into huge floriferous canopies. In full spring flush scarcely any rose compares with these robust giants. However, they are likely to suffer badly in weather below 10° F.

Although hardier than these, 'Mermaid' is likely to show chlorosis following unusually cold winter seasons, especially when growing on heavy clay soils. Its waxy, single yellow blooms and evergreen foliage enchant many, and 'Mermaid' consistently wins top ratings as a garden rose. Nevertheless, cruel thorny stems and unreasonable bulk are distinct detractions and make training this variety a challenge. If allowed to sprawl unsupported, 'Mermaid' will easily fill a space ten feet high and wide.

In colder regions these large-flowered climbers are replaced by the Tea-ramblers, a valuable class of roses with great vigor, cold-hardiness, and disease resistance. In contrast to the mildew-prone ramblers of the 'Dorothy Perkins' type, which descend from *Rosa multiflora*, the marriage of Tea roses to *R. wichuriana* ramblers results in a class of thoroughly healthy vines and sprawlers with large, delightfully colorful spring blooms.

'Albertine' is the classic large-flowered rambler of this type and remains especially popular in Europe. Its blush-tinted blooms sparkle against glistening, hollylike foliage. Other Tea-ramblers include the buff gold semidouble 'Gardenia,' creamy yellow 'Alberic Barbier,' white 'Silver Moon,' apricot pink 'François Juranville,' and the rosy 'Alexander Girault' and 'Paul Transom.'

Although most of these ramblers are of French origin, one of the most famous of all climbing roses, 'New Dawn,' or 'Everblooming Dr. Van Fleet,' is an American contribution to this group that has sired generations of valuable roses. It holds the first of all patents awarded for an ornamental plant. Unlike most ramblers 'New Dawn' repeat flowers under favorable conditions. In hot-summer regions like Texas, however, this blush pink climber usually blooms effectively only in spring.

Valuable small-flowered hardy climbers include the empurpled "blue rambler," 'Veilchenblau,' and the pink-flowered *Rosa multiflora* 'Carnea.' These are much healthier than the more common *wichuriana* ramblers and adapt well to heavy prairie soils. The rampant, late-flowering Himalayan Musk rose, 'Kiftsgate,' the native American prairie rose (*Rosa setigera*), the European sweetbriar (*R. eglanteria*), and the Southeastern swamp rose (*R. palustris*) adapt to heavy soils as well.

Repeat-blooming Climbers

Truly everblooming climbers are a select group comprised mostly of half-hardy and tender sorts such as Noisettes. Only a few of these achieve really large size. One of the most robust and dependable is the lemon-scented climber, 'Lamarque.' The white blooms of this tough old-timer are accented by touches of yellow at the center and appear tirelessly along vigorous climbing stems.

Even more magnificent, but less cold-hardy is 'Maréchal Neil,' whose nodding, yolk-yellow blooms are renowned for their sweet Tea rose fragrance. This most famous of yellow climbers is treasured in mild-climate gardens along the Riviera. Kipling describes it romantically in *Rikki Tikki Tavi* as a semiwild vine naturalized among Indian jungle trees surrounding English plantations. It makes a wonderful rose to train on a tall post of rustic cedar and envelops any short branches left as support in a short time, creating an everblooming rose tree.

Although liable to freeze back at temperatures below 10° F, 'Maréchal Neil' is remarkably tough and vigorous if a good strain can be secured. Unfortunately, a virus spread from infected rootstocks is common among 'Maréchal Neil' clones offered in the nursery trade (yet another evil result of grafting). Attentive nursery operators are seeking to eradicate such infections, and roses may one day be sold with virus indices to assure health, as is now done for many fruiting stocks.

Pillar Roses

The most popular by far of the small hardy climbers or pillar roses are the cerise-red types such as 'Blaze' and 'Paul's Scarlet.' These dominate the April scene in gardens of many established neighborhoods and practically demand white picket fences in the background to complement their brilliant rosiness. They seem especially at home among displays of spring cottage flowers such as larkspurs or cornflowers. Like most pillar roses, 'Blaze' and 'Paul's Scarlet' are at their best when splayed out fanwise along a fence or trellis, although they may be grown as large, loose bushes, or trained on posts as well.

Such treatments also favor 'Zéphirine Drouhin,' which endears itself to gardeners with sweetly fragrant cerise blooms and welcomely thornless stems. Although often classed among the Bourbons, this famous thornless climber apparently derives from a cross between a Noisette and a Boursalt rose and bears little resemblance to other members of its class. This truly unique variety is tough, fast-growing, fragrant, and beautiful.

A more traditional climbing Bourbon is 'Mme Isaac Pereire.' This fine, heavily doubled flower drips with old rose fragrance and radiates a rich raspberry-lavender hue. Although a demon for black spot fungus during hot, humid weather, 'Mme. Isaac Pereire' endures such attacks and redeems itself with an annual spring show that extends into early summer. It flowers more prolifically if its branches are splayed out horizontally and in Victorian times was often pegged down to induce heavy blooming.

Gardeners accustomed to the large-flowered pillar roses may balk at the modest-sized blooms offered by the old-fashioned 'Russell's Cottage Rose,' but those who appreciate vigor, stamina, and the ability to withstand neglect can readily appreciate this old variety. Its lavender-crimson, quartered double blooms appear over a brief spring season, but are enchanting when mixed with gray-foliaged plants. Its dark blue-green foliage turns to useful coppery shades in the fall.

Although everblooming in temperate climates, most of the large-flowered Hybrid Tea climbers cease blooming during the heat of summer in warm regions. If they rebloom in the fall it is generally only a modest reprise of their April show. Despite this failing, these roses include many of the most desirable small climbers.

For rich, dark red blooms one could hardly envision a finer rose than 'Don Juan.' This enthralling pillar rose often blooms in several flushes through spring and early summer. 'Aloha' is a silvery pink variety with equally luscious blooms and glossy green foliage. 'Alchymist' sports heavily double flowers of a glowing orange blend. 'Joseph's Coat' provides a scattering display of kaleidoscopic blooms that turn from yellow to red as they mature.

Where winter lows regularly fall below 0° F the old dark red *R. setigera* hybrid, 'Thor,' is a fine choice. Its prairie rose ancestry passes on excellent tolerance to heavy soils and good resistance to disease. Large, fully double blooms envelop its canes in spring with rich glowing red.

The more truly everblooming pillar roses fall mostly into the valuable Hybrid Musk class, which was developed early in the twentieth century by the Rev. William Pemberton. These modest climbers may be trained as espaliers against north walls, and include some of the best roses for shady positions. They are equally useful as large, lax shrubs when planted in the open.

'Penelope' is one of the favorites of this group and is particularly generous with its semidouble, soft saffron blooms. 'Buff Beauty' produces luscious creamy yellow flower clusters, but requires several years' establishment before blooming heavily. The white-flowered 'Prosperity,' strawberry-colored 'Cornelia,' delicate pink 'Ballerina,' and rose-colored 'Vanity' are other charming, romantically named varieties of this class.

The delicate pink climbing Noisette, 'Mme Alfred Carrièrre,' is a rose with many of the desirable attributes of the Hybrid Musks and, like them, performs well in shade or as a large shrub. Its quartered, blush-colored blooms appear continuously, and emit one of the finest of rose fragrances. The rosy red 'Fellemburg' and the old white-flowered Persian variety, 'Nastarana,' are additional fine, fragrant Noisettes suited for use as small climbers. These are more cold-hardy than most of their class.

Although usually classed among the large-flowered climbers, 'Golden Showers' shows Hybrid Musk ancestry in its glossy green foliage and everblooming habit. Its semi-double golden blooms unfurl from big, graceful buds. 'Climbing Pinkie' is a Floribunda climber with big masses of pink blooms and Musk-influenced glossy foliage as well. It flowers in successive flushes throughout the growing season and makes a fine shrub as well as a climber.

Tea-scented China Roses

In warm climates the most magnificent of the shrub-type roses belong to the old class of Tea-scented Chinas. These progenitors of modern Hybrid Teas are unique among flowering shrubs adapted to calcareous soil in the size and beauty of their blossoms. In many cases these roses have outstandingly attractive foliage with brilliant reddish tints that would shame a *Photinia*. It is this combination of luxuriant, semievergreen foliage, large size, and bounteous bloom that endows the Tea rose with compelling allure for warm-climate gardeners.

Warm, humid weather sometimes ruins the soft-petaled flowers of the Teas, causing them to "ball," and this can be especially irritating on heavily double varieties. Nevertheless, in the more equitable weather of autumn most of these roses put on shows to rival any camellia, and they afford even humble gardens a season of true magnificence. Heavy, sweet fragrance is another fine property of many of these cherished old varieties.

One of the most satisfactory Teas from the standpoint of resistance to balling is the pink-flowered 'Duchesse de Brabant.' In the cool weather of spring and fall its cupped blooms often nod gracefully, but through summer heat they assume upright positions. "Duchess" is one of the most tirelessly flowering of the Teas.

Another heat-tolerant variety is the thornless 'Mrs. Dudley Cross.' The creamy yellow, fully double blooms of this variety open to wide, flat discs that blush pink in the sun. Its new shoots and leaves are rich, purplish red and complement its rose-tinted yellow blooms.

Other fine Teas include the rich yellow 'Souvenir du Pierre Notting,' pink 'Bon Silène,' white 'Wm. R. Smith,' rose-red 'Mrs. B. R. Cant,' and purple-red 'Mons. Tillier.' Both the warm pink 'Mamon Cochet' and its sport, 'White Mamon Cochet,' are deserving old favorites in warm climates. 'Mme Antoine Rebe' is an attractive single with dark rose, butterfly blooms and red foliage to match. 'Beauté Inconstante' produces a "fruit salad" of delicate warm hues including yellow, orange, and purple. 'Enchantress' is a compelling rich red.

The Tea-Bourbon, 'Souvenir de la Malmaison,' is an especially romantic rose. Its soft-petaled, pearly, quartered blooms were named to commemorate the garden of the Empress Josephine, whose famous collection of roses and other plants was painted by the consummate botanical illustrator, P. J. Redouté.

Although this variety inherits essentially habits from the Tea side of its ancestry, the other portion of its parentage conveys the cherished old rose fragrance and appearance of the Bourbon class. Its creamy white sport, 'Kronprinzessin Viktoria,' is even lovelier than the pink form. Planting in partial shade will help protect the delicate blooms of these roses from continuous balling.

Chinas and Polyanthas

On drier, chalkier grounds and in areas where below-zero weather limits the usefulness of the Teas, the shrub roses to choose are the Chinas and Polyanthas. The blooms of these roses are smaller than those of the Teas and generally lack their delicacy and fragrance, but compensate for this loss with a tireless abundance of blooms in strong, clear colors—especially red.

The ancient silver-pink 'Old Blush' and the double crimson 'Louis Phillippe' are two of the most dependable of this group. They grace the dooryards of many older gardens. Other good Chinas include the pink and rose-colored 'Archduke Charles,' buff-rosy 'Le Vesuve,' and the multicolored "butterfly rose," 'Mutabilis.' This last is famous for its single blooms that fade from creamy yellow to rose-red. It makes an especially attractive bush with coppery leaves, but requires careful placement in the garden, lest its many-colored blooms incite a riot with other colorful flowers nearby.

Modern miniatures in part descend from the tiny China rose, 'Roulettii.' The more vigorous of these *de facto* "hybrid Chinas" sometimes make good garden plants. 'Oakington Ruby' is an older type with garnet-colored double blooms on a small, twiggy bush.

The curious little rose nicknamed "Caldwell Pink" is a ubiquitous, successful feature of many older gardens on lime. Sprays of pink button blooms appear almost continuously along its stems through heat and drought. "Caldwell Pink" easily takes the prize as the toughest, longest-blooming rose of summer and offers an added fall bonus of brilliant orange-red foliage.

'La Marne' is an invaluable Polyantha with glistening green foliage and pink chalicelike clusters of bloom. 'Marie Pavié' possesses small double blooms with a delicate porcelain hue and has a wonderful and unexpected sweet fragrance. 'Margo Koster' is a warm-hued orange blush; 'Summer Snow' a pristine white; 'The Fairy' a prolific pink. 'Gloria Mundi' electrifies the garden with a rare tangerine, but inclines to mildew in humid weather.

Although healthy and generous with bloom, the old-fashioned "sweetheart rose" ('Cécile Brünner') is valueless for garden decoration, as its miniature, scrolled blooms unfurl unattractively if left on the bush. Its popularity rests instead on its ability to generate hundreds of tiny flowers, perfectly sized for boutonnières.

'China Doll' is a deservedly popular Polyantha for its healthy constitution, generous pink bloom, and bright glossy green foliage. Its bloom clusters quickly fade to an unattractive blue-pink in hot weather, however, and hang on the bush in ugly half-wilted masses unless sheared off. Unfortunately, this same fault is common to the dark red Floribunda, 'Valentine,' which otherwise shares 'China Doll's' useful vigor, good foliage, and generosity of bloom.

Floribundas

The Floribunda class is an extension of the Polyantha group with somewhat larger flowers that includes a wide array of useful garden roses. The more vigorous types are best for plantings on calcareous soils.

The semidouble pink 'Kirsten Poulsen' and shrubby 'Simplicity' are two of the toughest and most reliable. These make excellent choices for low hedges to divide areas within the garden, and bloom tirelessly with a minimum of care. Other tough roses of this type include the *R. setigera* hybrids, 'Carefree Beauty' and 'Goldilocks.' These inherit unusual hardiness and disease resistance from their native prairie rose ancestors. They make attractive pink and yellow-flowering shrubs, respectively.

Another rose bred along these lines, with especially choice flowers of clear electric orange, is the old selection, 'Jiminy Cricket.' "J. C." makes a tough, well-foliaged shrub three to four feet tall and wide. Its fluorescent blooms steal the show in any garden and are particularly generous in spring and fall.

Many older Floribundas, such as the single pink 'Betty Prior,' double pink 'Gene Boerner,' and deep red 'Eutin,' are among the most popular and long-suffering garden roses. Along with such well-known varieties as 'Fashion,' 'Pinocchio,' and 'Europeana' they brighten a variety of otherwise dreary garden corners.

American gardeners refer to the taller, larger-flowered Floribundas as "Grandi-floras," and these roses include some of the best types for informal hedging. 'Queen Elizabeth' is a well-known pink-flowered variety. 'Montezuma' and 'Spartan' are geranium-orange cultivars that perform especially well in hot-climate gardens.

'Belinda's Rose' is a shrubby pink type with serrated foliage and huge flowers stuffed to the brim with ruffled petals.

Hybrid Teas

The Hybrid Tea class offers larger, more colorful, less balling-susceptible versions of the flowers found on the Tea-scented China roses, and these are born on bushes with strong upright stems suitable for cutting. These most popular of garden roses perform especially well in temperate climates. In warm areas they are apt to become rather tall and leggy and will require frequent attention to keep them bushy and compact. Yet, the allure of a shrub that provides blooms for both the garden and the table is strong, and a well-chosen Hybrid Tea can be among the most rewarding of garden shrubs.

As with the other classes of roses, it is the more vigorous, coarse-rooted varieties that give best value on alkaline land. Few Hybrid Teas accept thin chalky soils, but for gardens on modestly deep, limy clays there are many successful types from which to choose.

One helpful way to evaluate the potential garden value of rose varieties is offered by the All-America Rose Selections and Proof of the Pudding ratings of the American Rose Society. In these programs recent rose variety performances are rated around the country on a ten-point scale. Although a high rating is no guarantee of success on calcareous soil, it often corresponds to a plant's general vigor and gives some idea of its likely performance. AARS award winners and roses with POP ratings of eight and above usually offer the best garden value.

'Peace' is a famous Hybrid Tea with legendary vigor and enormous flowers of a delightful pineapple-yellow blend. This variety and its several sports are an excellent place to begin a collection of Hybrid Teas. Perhaps even stronger-growing is 'Pink Peace,' a second generation descendent of its famous namesake with delightfully fragrant blooms and an unusually compact, bushy habit. This last character makes 'Pink Peace' a good choice for general garden use, as lanky growth habits are a common failing of the Hybrid Teas.

Older varieties such as the light pink 'La France' and rosy-colored 'Radiance' have strong perfumes that seem rare in more modern selections. However, fragrance is a function of ancestry, rather than date of introduction, and often correlates to bloom color. Most red-flowered types are fragrant; the crimson-red 'Chrysler Imperial,' 'Mirandy,' 'Crimson Glory,' 'Oklahoma,' and 'Mr. Lincoln' come to mind immediately as fragrant roses. Whites such as the old 'K. A. Victoria,' although antediluvian, are in contrast nearly scentless.

One of the most magnificently strong-growing Hybrid Teas is the old 'President Herbert Hoover.' Planted on its own roots it matures to a bush five feet high and wide. Even better is its sport, 'Texas Centennial.' This luxuriant rose produces huge flowers tinted a brilliant cerise-pink, suffused with gold and scarlet.

The well-known 'Tropicana' can be relied upon for generous displays of orange-scarlet under trying conditions. This tough cultivar is a favorite in Europe, where it is known as 'Superstar.' Other strong-growing Hybrid Teas include 'Helen Traubel,' 'Charlotte Armstrong,' 'Tiffany,' 'Talisman,' 'Lowell Thomas,' and 'Katherine T. Marshall.' 'Dainty Bess' is a robust pink with enchanting single blooms.

Old European Roses

After the opulence of the Hybrid Teas, the April-blooming roses of the old Gallica section seem modest, indeed. Their once-flowering habits and propensity to sucker into large clumps have won them few friends in warm-climate American gardens. Nevertheless, for troublesome limy soils they have much to offer, and they are among the best roses to combine in perennial borders. The true rose fragrance of these old types is another compelling reason to plant them.

'Hippolyte' is one of the "bluest" of these roses and adapts to tough situations. It showers itself in lavender-crimson flowers in April. Other *R. gallica* selections come in shades of pink and crimson (such as 'Tuscany Superb'). All of these accept even the thinnest soils over chalk and readily endure long, droughty summers. Although their flowering seasons last only a few weeks, the profuse show of bloom provided by these old Gallicas creates a memorable, eagerly awaited annual garden event.

Just as tough are the varieties of the Damask rose, several of which offer scattering blooms in fall as well as spring. The light pink 'Autumn Damask' and the deep rose 'Rose de Resht' are two that rebloom. Both possess exquisite fragrance. The blousy soft pink 'Blush Damask' is tellingly fragrant as well, but offers its flowers only in the spring. These ancient garden plants of Persia and the Mediterranean tolerate extreme drought and thin, limy soils. Their fragrance and their historical associations make them romantic garden subjects of great value.

Many of the roses classed variously as Bourbons, Portlands, and Hybrid Perpetuals retain the essential features of the Damasks and Gallicas, but with increased size and vigor. In the case of varieties such as 'Louise Odier,' 'Paul Neyron,' and "Maggie" ('Souvenir du Eugene Margottin') excellent reblooming characters are inherited as well. These roses retain the lavender-pink, raspberry, and crimson hues, and the heavy rose fragrances of their forbearers.

Gardeners who enjoy the effect of these globular, heavily double blooms, but prefer more modern colors, may wish to experiment with the so-called "English Roses." These shrub roses have been bred from a diverse parentage that includes Gallicas, Floribundas, and climbers. Although relatively new to American gardens, the most vigorous among them promise to become fine garden shrubs with excellent disease-resistant foliage and uniquely lovely blooms in delicate pastels and warm hues. The apricot 'Abraham Darby,' silver-pink 'Warwick Castle,' and yellow 'Graham Thomas' all succeed on limy clay.

Other miscellaneous roses tolerant of limy conditions include 'Harrison's Yellow,' *R. rugosa* varieties such as 'Blanc Double du Cobert,' and modern shrubs such as 'Bonica.' Although valuable in cooler, temperate regions, these types give only modest, fleeting displays in warm-climate gardens.

The Chestnut Rose

The prize for originality among roses adapted to calcareous ground must surely go to the chestnut rose (*R. roxburghii*). The double form of this rose is an ancient garden plant from the warm parts of China. The English carried it to India at an early date, and its Latin name commemorates the superintendent of the botanical garden at Calcutta, William Roxburgh. The common name of this rose makes reference to this rose's strange prickly buds, which resemble the burs of a chestnut.

As a garden shrub the chestnut rose would be worth planting for its lovely foliage alone. Its leaves are fernlike and fine-textured and give these lax, six-foot bushes a truly graceful appearance. Although shy to bloom in youth, after settling in for a few seasons the chestnut rose produces delightful sputtering displays of cabbagey silver-pink blooms that open well even in the hottest weather. It makes an excellent shrub for heavy clay soils and often marks old gardens in the Southern states.

CHAPTER FOURTEEN

Plants for Shade

In hot climates shade provides unique habitats for plants that otherwise grow only in cooler, northern climes. For the plant lover this qualifies as a resource to be expended wisely on the choice items that require it. Shady positions are usually either continuously moist and boggy or seasonally parched and arid. Each situation favors specific suites of plants, and gardens may be arranged to take advantage of both.

Dry Shade

Although moist shade is easier to garden, it is a less common condition on calcareous soils than seasonally dry grounds. Many shade-providing trees have competitive roots that extract moisture from the soil's surface. This is especially noticeable on heavy clay soils, for they encourage shallow rooting.

Nevertheless, several types of plants actually seem to enjoy such dryish, rooty soils. Members of the shrimp plant family (*Acanthaceae*) such as the familiar fawn-colored shrimp plant (*Justicia brandegeana*) and the orange-red shrimp (*J. tomentosa*) are exceptionally tolerant of dry shade.

The dark violet Mexican petunia (*Ruellia malacosperma*) is also good and accepts both dry and wet conditions. A white-flowered form and the related dwarf, *R. brittoniana* 'Katy,' are choice. In milder regions the prostrate, gray-leaved *R. squarrosa* is a good summer-flowering, shade-tolerant perennial.

Dry shade suits such evergreen shrubs as mahonia, nandina, holly, and pittosporum. English boxwood, viburnums, and bamboos are also good in shady positions. An unusual conifer, the Siberia carpet cypress (*Microbiota decussata*), accepts medium shade and makes a good small-scale groundcover.

A listing of flowering perennials suited to dry shade might well include the old double-flowered soapwort (*Saponaria officinalis* 'Flore Plena'), the orange-red, everblooming Turk's cap (*Malvaviscus drummondii*), and the pink rock rose (*Pavonia lasiopetala*).

Several salvias are ideal for parched, shady conditions. The shrubby, scarlet-flowered royal sage (*Salvia regla*) and the various white, pink, or crimson strains of the tropical sage (*S. coccinea*) give a lush appearance to unwatered garden understories. Tropical sage self-sows vigorously and soon colonizes bare ground. Its blooms open freshly each morning through the summer. The compact, bushy, blue-flowered canyon sage (*S. lycioides*) makes a good low plant for an informal hedge.

Mexican oregano (*Poliomintha longiflora*) is a subshrub similar to salvia that succeeds with dry shade. Lavender-pink blooms appear atop its twiggy branches all summer, and its shiny, aromatic foliage remains evergreen through the winter months.

Native yellow-flowered columbines (*Aquilegia longissima* and *A. hinckleyana*) and the fulvous red *A. canadensis* are fine performers in the root-filled soils found beneath oaks or elms. False gromwells (*Onosmodium bejarense* and *O. helleri*) produce fascinating white, bell-shaped blooms in drooping, unfurling clusters. These graceful cousins of comfrey (*Symphytum officinale*) complement the delicately constructed columbines and flower at the same season. They endure ruggedly dry, shady conditions.

Texas asters (*Aster texanus*) produce clouds of small lavender daisies in delicate sprays. They overwinter with rosettes of heart-shaped leaves and accept both wet and modestly dry soils. The graceful, softly colored blooms of these asters light up shady corners in late October.

White bone set (*Eupatorium havanense*) makes a three- to four-foot shade-tolerant subshrub with white blooms in autumn, and occasionally in spring as well. Its dark green foliage provides a good foil for its flowers.

Frost weed (*Verbesina virginica*) projects a rustic, homely appearance most of the year. In fall this leafy, four-foot perennial redeems itself with big plates of snowy blooms that butterflies find irresistible. In winter juices within the tall stems often freeze and appear as a white, frozen froth. Frost weed is exceptionally tough and tolerant of dry shady conditions.

Dry shade is practically an imperative for success with the ground-hugging ivies (*Hedera* cvs.) and mondo grasses (*Ophiopogon* cvs.). If kept too moist during warm summer weather these popular groundcovers often suffer from leaf and root-damaging fungal diseases. Positioning these plants where tree roots can sop up excess moisture helps to limit such problems.

In addition to the common green mondo grasses (*Ophiopogon japonicus*), tufted dwarf and variegated cultivars may be had as well. The tiny 'Kyoto dwarf' is fancifully known as "dragon's moustache" in its native Japan. Other ophiopogons include the coarse-textured *O. planiscapus* and its strange black-leaved cultivar, 'Arabicus.' This novelty is excruciatingly slow growing and prefers more moisture than other mondo grasses.

Moist Shade

When shade plants come to mind, gardeners usually picture banks of ferns, lush, leafy maples, or thriving, verdant liriopes. These plants have considerable drought tolerance, but grow best in gardens where subsoils remain moist through the heat of summer. Perpetually damp, shady positions often occur near north-facing walls. On heavy, calcareous clays these beds are often constantly waterlogged. A modest effort to improve the soil with organic material and to increase drainage by raising beds will afford homes for a variety of choice plants.

Ferns truly enjoy moist soils, and several specialize in those that contain lime. The most vigorous and easy-growing of these is the Southern river fern, or woodfern (*Thelypteris kunthii*). Its lush, soft green leaves appear all summer above creeping, spreading rootstocks.

Although ethereally delicate in appearance, the wiry-stemmed Venus' maidenhair fern (*Adiantum capillus-veneris*) has an equally tough constitution and spreads thriftily over damp, limy ground. It makes a beautiful, soft-textured edging along a path of limestone flags.

Holly ferns (*Cyrtomium falcatum*) have wholly undeserved reputations as finicky lovers of acid ground. These evergreens thrive even on bare limestone, if kept constantly damp. Winter freezes sometimes damage the holly fern's glossy whorls of foliage, but the plants usually recover to send forth new leaves from their wooly crowns in spring.

The beautiful Japanese silver-painted fern (*Athyrium nipponicum* 'Pictum') seems surprisingly indifferent to lime. Its milk-splashed leaves have a unique metallic sheen. The compact, dwarf habit of this perennial makes it a fine accent for a shady nook.

Plantain lilies (*Hosta* spp.) are favored shade perennials in cool climates, but often perform erratically in warm regions. The most heat-tolerant are selections and hybrids of the moisture-loving *H. plantaginea* and they offer warm-climate gardens some of the largest and most fragrant of hosta blooms. 'Grandiflora,' 'Royal Standard,' and 'Honeybells' are popular cultivars with lush green leaves; 'Sugar and Cream' is a choice fragrant *Hosta* with creamy variegated foliage. All of these thrive on permanently soggy ground and bear tall spikes of sweet-scented, white midsummer flowers.

In mild-winter gardens the Mediterranean bear's breech (*Acanthus mollis*) affords another leafy, moisture-loving perennial. These big plants produce lush fountains of handsomely lobed foliage and were the plants after which the capital designs of Corinthian columns were patterned by the ancient Greeks. Acanthus flower with purple and white bracted spikes in early summer. Like other Mediterranean natives, they are cool-season growers and appear freshest during fall and winter.

The showiest and longest-flowering perennial for moist, shady conditions is summer phlox (*Phlox paniculata*). In warm regions the old magenta-pink strain of this highly bred perennial performs more reliably than the mildew-plagued hybrids. Its three-foot wands of iridescent "phlox pink" dominate garden scenes wherever they are planted and continue in flower from June through August.

Although many plants have white-flowered sports, most are weaker growers than the corresponding colored forms. It comes as a welcome surprise to discover that the white *Phlox paniculata* cultivar, 'Mt. Fuji,' grows nearly as strongly as the common pink forms. Since white is one of the best colors for use in designing plantings in shade, this herbaceous flower deserves wide recognition.

Sweet violets (*Viola odorata*) are sentimental favorites that offer tiny, fragrant, blooms through the cool days of late winter and early spring. In warm regions they need hiding during the heat of summer, when their foliage yellows and suffers from spider mites. Missouri violet (*Viola missouriensis*) holds up better, but lacks the strong fragrance of the sweet violet. Its flowers come in pale blue or white shades instead of the beloved rich purple of *V. odorata*.

Subtropical perennials such as firespike (*Odontonema strictum*), crinums, spider lilies (*Hymenocallis* spp.), and gingers enjoy moist soils and perform with considerable shade. Irises of the Evansia section such as Japanese roof iris (*I. tectorum*) and Burmese bamboo iris (*I. wattii* 'Nada') are additional lilylike perennials suited to moist, shady ground. The fascinating miniature Chinese ground orchid (*Bletilla striata*) is surprisingly tough and easy-growing. Pink or white blooms appear above its neat, pleated foliage in April.

Green dragon (*Arisaema draconitum*), Italian arum (*Arum italicum*), and monarch-of-the-east, or "voodoo lily" (*Sauromatum guttatum*) are bulbous members of the taro family (*Aracea*) with exotic foliage and preferences for moist, shady positions. Their peculiar "jack-in-the-pulpit" blooms follow in autumn with clusters of orange-red berries. In mild regions, the winter-growing callas (*Zantedeshia aethiopica*) make good subjects. Tender cousins of these perennials, the caladiums, are popular tubers for summer bedding, treasured for their showy, colored leaves.

A favorite of Victorian gardens, the cast iron plant, aspidistra, or (*Aspidistra elatior*), produces tongue-shaped leaves from a creeping rootstock. These give a pleasant, informal appearance to shady borders and make a rich, dark-colored background for other flowers. Although famously tough, aspidistras look their best when well-watered and require an annual grooming to remove old, faded leaves. The several variegated cultivars are better appreciated in pots than in the garden.

Unlike the mondo grasses (*Ophiopogon* cvs.), which perform best in dry shade, liriopes enjoy constant moisture. *Liriope spicata* 'Silver Dragon' rates especially highly for shady gardens on lime soil. Its showy ivory-striped leaves display an outstanding silver variegation. Like other *L. spicata* cultivars 'Silver Dragon' lays its evergreen foliage flat on the ground during winter and emerges with fresh new leaves in spring. It spreads rapidly by underground runners.

Other liriopes such as *L. muscari* 'Big Blue', 'Majestic', and 'Monroe White' are worth planting for their attractive lavender or white flower spikes. 'Silvery Sunproof' offers a show from both its creamy yellow variegated leaves and its purplish blooms. Evergreen giant liriope (*L. gigantea*) is a popular clumping perennial for warmer gardens. Its three-foot fountains of green, grassy foliage afford distinguished specimens for large tubs or crevices among rocky boulders.

Gold dust plants (*Aucuba japonica* 'Variegata') are deservedly popular evergreens for moist, shady gardens. Although tropical in appearance, these surprisingly hardy shrubs withstand zero weather without a flinch. Like other members of the dogwood family, aucubas bear male and female blooms on separate plants. When both are present, the females ripen fat clusters of red autumn berries. Cultivars with gold splashes and variegations are most popular; 'Picturata' is a female with gold-edged leaves, 'Crotonifolia' is a gold-flecked male, 'Serratifolia' is a female with dark green foliage.

Another shade-loving shrub with showy berries is spice bush (*Lindera benzoin*). Like the aucubas, both male and female bushes are needed to produce fruit. Spice bushes flower in early spring with quiet traceries of greenish-yellow along their bare branches. In summer they make leafy, suckering shrubs, that proclaim their relationship to the bay-laurels (*Laurus nobilis*) through redolent baylike foliage.

Japanese aralias (*Fatsia japonica*) convey much the same subtropical effect to shade gardens as aucubas, but fulfill the gardener's expectations by freezing when temperatures fall below 20° F. Fatsias are easy growers, however, and usually recover quickly from cold damage. Their glossy, palmate leaves have great architectural value. Rice paper plants (*Tetrapanax papyrifera*) offer similar, gray-felted foliage and return as suckering perennials in frost-prone gardens.

Robust mounds of grapelike leaves make Japanese anemones (*Anemone* × *hybrida*) attractive even when out of bloom. These rugged carpeters soon spread over large areas, if given moist, well-drained ground. Although some Japanese anemone cultivars are shy to flower in warm climates, one of the finest, 'Honorine Jobert', reliably offers its exquisite white blooms each autumn. Other perennial anemones such as the wood anemone

(*A. nemoralis*) may be planted for spring bloom. Like the Japanese types, these perennials are lovely, permanent, and adaptable to shady calcareous soils.

Coral bells (*Heuchera sanguinea* cvs.) are some of the best-loved shade perennials in cool climates, and grow fabulously on lime. However, in hot-summer regions these prostrate carpeters struggle during the summer months and are often short-lived. The fancifully named strawberry begonia (*Saxifraga stolonifera*) is a better choice, and quickly spreads its strawberrylike rosettes along short runners. Strawberry begonias produce airy sprays of white bloom and give a fairy woodland effect to plantings near rustic boulders or old logs.

Images of enchanted forest dells follow the somber, quietly colored hellebores (*Helleborus* spp.). These evergreen perennials are highly regarded and sought after, and a thriving clump is often a mark of pride for a keen gardener. Pale green, fawn, or chocolate bowl-shaped blooms crown hellebores in early spring. Dark green leathery leaves give them a bold architectural presence year-round. These sophisticated Europeans revel in limy ground, but expect a continuous supply of moisture through summer drought.

The Christmas rose (*Helleborus niger*) appreciates extra attention to summer watering in warm regions. Lenten roses (*H. orientalis*) are easier and flower in late winter with varicolored blooms. *H. foetidus* warrants planting for its strange, fingerlike palmate leaves. Most tolerant of drought once established is Corsican hellebore (*H. lividus corsicus*). It matures to a two-foot evergreen subshrub and bears big clusters of green blooms.

Another cherished subject for the shade garden is the shrubby Japanese maple (*Acer palmatum*). Although often said to dislike lime, Japanese maples accept calcareous soils without difficulty when offered shade and continuous summer moisture. The soft, graceful foliage of these leafy understory trees scorches if it is allowed to dry out or is exposed directly to hot sun.

Dark red-foliaged selections and bizarre thread-leaf cultivars of these maples perform poorly in warm regions. Because these varieties are grafted onto seedling rootstocks, they have difficulty transpiring moisture efficiently in the summer. Seedlings of *Acer palmatum*, whether with green foliage or red, are better garden performers. These own-root maples offer an explosively colorful mixture of orange, red, and yellow leaves in the fall.

Most shade-loving flowers enjoy being planted under trees, but there is at least one half-hardy type that likes to be planted *on* the tree. Bailey's ball moss (*Tillandsia baileyi*) is a coarse, grassy epiphyte native to southern Texas and Florida. The Texas populations are surprisingly hardy and withstand 10° F. These exotic relatives of pineapples and Spanish moss flower in late spring with showy six-inch spikes of violet-pink bloom. They give a romantic, disheveled look to gardens when wired to the branches of rough-barked trees.

CHAPTER FIFTEEN

Vines and Groundcovers

❦

Climbing and trailing plants carry with them an air of eminent practicality. Their vigorous, sprawling habits enable them to cover a multitude of sins: unsightly structures or rough ground unsuited to other garden plants. Uninspiring, lifeless edifices acquire charm and grace when softened by bowers of greenery. Rugged, difficult-to-manage garden space can be transformed into neat, pleasant vistas of green or grey when filled with ground-hugging vegetation.

Climbers, sprawlers, and groundcovers are as readily valued for the landscape dilemmas they resolve as for the unique beauty each has to offer. They are truly plants for gardeners with little time or capital to invest in plantings, yet they often offer rewards of flower and fragrance as splendid as any of the most coddled subjects.

Calcareous soils and hot-summer climates challenge this group of plants in the same ways as others and provide especially difficult conditions for low carpeting groundcovers and lawns. Only the toughest types withstand the alternating cycles of heat, drought, flood, and winter cold. The classically manicured, eternally green lawn is all but an impossibility, and burdensome expenditures of time and effort ensue from its pursuit.

Lawn Grasses

Lawn enthusiasts certainly are able to create velvety golf-greens in miniature with such heat-tolerant hybrid varieties as 'Tifgreen' Bermuda and 'Emerald' zoysia. However, these demanding turfs are slow and expensive to establish, and they enslave their admirers to arduous schedules of fertilization, supplemental irrigation, and mowing with expensive reel-type lawn mowers.

For the majority of homeowners turf areas are simply unloved regions that fill the spaces between more cherished plantings and facilitate an occasional autumn scrimmage or summer game of croquet. Although an attractive sward of green is certainly appreciated for its enhancement to the garden's overall appearance, ease of maintenance and establishment are usually the primary criteria used when selecting lawn varieties.

Cool-season grasses such as tall fescues (*Festuca elatior*) are easily established in the fall from seed and make attractive lawns on deep, moist soils. Unless provided with shade in the heat of summer and copious amounts of water, however, fescue lawns often deteriorate into widely spaced clumps and must be renewed by annual reseeding.

For sunny gardens with casual plantings of trees and shrubs, turf-type Bermuda grasses (*Cynodon dactylon* cvs.) are often the most practical. Common Bermuda grass, or improved strains such as 'Sahara,' may be seeded at little cost and readily conquer new ground if provided with modest irrigation and faithful mowing one to two inches high. They thrive on all types of calcareous soils.

If gardens include a number of flower beds, or if sizable trees provide a measure of shade, St. Augustine grasses (*Stenotaphrum secundatum*) are often preferable. These lack the aggressive underground runners of Bermuda grass and are more easily restrained around beds of shrubbery, perennials, or groundcovers. St. Augustine grasses are also generally the most successful lawns in shade. They struggle beneath aggressive, shallow-rooted trees, however, just as do other lawn grasses.

St. Augustine culture on calcareous ground requires attention to the needs and wants of this moisture-loving, subtropical grass. Lawn mowers should be positioned at their highest setting to encourage a thick, rugged turf. Waterings should be well-spaced and lengthy to entice deep rooting. Fertilizers, both organic and chemical, should be applied with caution, for they readily stimulate lush growth that succumbs to freeze damage, insects, and disease.

Because many strains of St. Augustine are susceptible to virus (St. Augustine decline), resistant selections such as 'Raleigh' or 'Flora-Tam' are usually sought when establishing new lawns. If heavily fertilized and irrigated these turfs produce impressively lush summer growth. However, brown patch fungus (*Rhizoctonia solanii*) and winter freezes can devastate these improved varieties literally overnight. Benign neglect produces less lavishly green lawns, but improves resistance to cold and disease.

Regions of lime soil are natural prairies from which several native grass alternatives may be selected. Considering the difficulties of maintaining manicured lawns in warm, semiarid climates, these prairie grasses are of great interest and are especially appropriate for gardens with thin, rocky soil or caliche.

Buffalograss (*Buchloe dactyloides*) and blue grama grass (*Bouteloua gracilis*) are two of these drought-tolerant natives. In their natural, wild forms both make tough, informally attractive turfs or meadows that require little mowing, irrigation, or fertilizing. They can be established from direct seed, grow well on even the thinnest soils, and withstand temperatures from below zero to over 100° F.

However, for those accustomed to the thick appearance and feel of traditional lawns these rough grasses may be disappointing. Such native turfs endure spells of drought and cold by going dormant and off-color. They seldom fill in as solidly as traditional lawns, and very likely will be invaded by weeds or Bermuda grass during seasons of heavy rainfall.

The best use for these wiry grasses seems to be as unmown groundcover, rather than lawn. Both buffalograss and blue grama assume attractive tufted or tousled textures if left unmown (growing about six inches or less high) and produce interesting tiny flowers and seed heads in summer and fall. Stands of these grasses may be overseeded with wildflowers as well.

Some turf-type buffalograsses have been introduced and have slightly more formal appearances and improved tolerance to mowing. 'Prairie' is a female strain that holds its seed heads invisibly below the tops of its leaves. Although neat and dense for a buffalograss, 'Prairie' is easily outcompeted by common Bermuda and remains relatively expensive. For informal, infrequently mown areas seedling buffalograss is less costly, equally appropriate, and more ornamental because of the attractive flowers born by the male plants.

The oriental zoysia grasses have for many years captured the interest of lawn enthusiasts because of their lush, dense textures, hardiness, and drought resistance. If permitted to grow in their natural, hummocky fashion these grasses are among the least demanding, as well, and require only rare mowing or fertilizing.

Considerable time and expense required for establishing zoysia lawns from sod or plugs has limited popularity in past years. For smaller areas, however, these grasses are eminently practical. 'Meyer' is a selection of *Zoysia japonica* with a texture similar to that of bermuda grass; 'Emerald' is a popular hybrid with a dwarf, velvety appearance. These, and a plethora of newer, faster-growing zoysia cultivars, are gaining acceptance and recognition as lawns evolve to smaller dimensions and gardeners seek more drought-tolerant, low-maintenance turfs.

Groundcovers

Where foot traffic is infrequent, groundcovers often prove easier to establish and maintain than these grasses and widen the range of textures available to design into the garden. Varieties can be selected to endure dense shade or grueling drought and to cover rugged slopes or steep embankments where lawn grasses would be impractical at best.

In hot climates the most popular of these is the glossy leaved Asian jasmine (*Trachelospermum asiaticum*). This indispensable trailing vine is ruggedly drought-tolerant when established, yet thrives with abundant moisture as well. It succeeds on both thin, rocky soils and heavy clays, and performs admirably in sun and shade. Attractive dwarf and variegated cultivars are available and especially choice.

If Asian jasmine should be faulted, it is for its susceptibility to freeze damage when temperatures fall below 15° F and for its failure to bloom like its fragrant cousin, the confederate jasmine (*T. jasminoides*). Both Asian and confederate jasmine varieties tend to climb up into nearby shrubs or trees and look neater if excluded from beds of shrubbery. They can be restrained by regular trimming and occasional mowing with a lawn mower raised to its highest setting.

For shady gardens the most popular groundcovers are cultivars of English ivy (*Hedera helix*) and Algerian ivy (*H. canariensis*). Like the jasmines these are tremendously drought-tolerant once established and readily carpet large areas. An enormous number of cultivars, many with attractive variegations or unusually crested leaves, are available from specialists. All enjoy limy soils.

Ivies are slow to establish, but eventually conquer any shady corner they are allowed to invade. ("The first year they sleep; the second year they creep; the third year they leap!") They also climb trees, fences, and buildings and must be restrained where not desired. In addition to their value as groundcovers, ivies make beautiful vines to train up shady north-facing brick or masonry walls. Variegated cultivars such as the large-leafed 'Gloire de Marengo' are especially good for this use.

English ivies are hardy, but Algerian varieties often freeze when temperatures fall below 15° F. Both types resent heavy overhead irrigation during the summer and may suffer from leaf-spotting diseases or root rots during periods of high humidity. Once again, benign neglect is the best recipe for success with these groundcovers.

Another plant of value for shade, especially on rugged slopes that dry out in summer, is the large-leafed periwinkle (*Vinca major*). This trailer is as tough as the ivies and makes a good large-scale groundcover, as well as a pleasant perennial to associate with shade-loving shrubs or flowers. In spring it bears blue-lavender pinwheel blooms. Although the evergreen *V. minor* is often cultivated as well, it seldom persists in hot-summer climates.

In the heat of summer, *V. major* is liable to become partially dormant or deciduous. Upon return of cool weather and fall precipitation, periwinkle puts forth fresh foliage that remains attractive through the winter. The variegated form of this Mediterranean perennial is especially good for lighting up shady corners and shows off its blue flowers to good effect.

Tough, evergreen wintercreeper (*Euonymus fortunei* 'Colorata') deserves consideration for groundcover use, and withstands considerable cold. Like English ivy, it also makes a good slow-growing vine to train on a wall. Wintercreeper tolerates both sun and shade, and turns an attractive plum-purple in the winter months.

The grasslike lily-turfs (*Liriope* spp. and *Ophiopogon* spp.) are dependable and rugged for shaded and partially shaded positions, and accept foot traffic better than most groundcovers. However, liriopes are liable to sunburn if planted in exposed situations and need a steady supply of water to endure the hot months of summer. *Ophiopogon* is more drought-tolerant, but suffers from root rot when moistened during hot, humid weather. Dry shady positions in rooty soil beneath oaks or elms suit these perennials best.

Everblooming groundcovers that enliven landscapes with colorful flowers all season are difficult to find, but a few heroic plants compete in this category. Preeminent among these are the perennial verbenas, most of which originate as hybrids between the South American *Verbena tenuisecta, V. erecta,* and *V. peruviana.* The most rugged types are generally those with deeply divided fernlike leaves. However, even these require well-prepared soils and reliable summer irrigations if they are to fulfill their task of forming dense, weed-suppressing masses of foliage.

Another long-blooming perennial worthy of use as groundcover is the yellow evening primrose (*Calylophus hartwegii*). This tough, roadside wildflower suckers to form bushy clumps of willowy foliage that stay attractively compact and low, and produce large, pale yellow flowers on summer evenings. *C. drummondii* is similar, but has golden-yellow blooms and a less vigorous spreading habit. Baja primrose (*Oenothera stubbii*) creeps aggressively to form low carpets and flowers with rosy blooms.

Japanese honeysuckle (*Lonicera japonica*) is fragrant, long flowering, and readily smothers weeds, but is so rampant that it overpowers other nearby plants and becomes a nuisance. Nevertheless, both the green-foliaged 'Hall's' honeysuckle and the dark-leaved 'Purpurea' are popular for industrial plantings and for rough bank cover. These types, as well as the better behaved, red-flowered coral honeysuckle (*L. sempervirens*) are perhaps more readily appreciated as climbing vines than as groundcover.

Once-blooming, creeping evergreens such as moss phlox (*Phlox subulata*), double-flowered soapwort (*Saponaria officinalis* 'Flore Plena'), Texas betony (*Stachys coccinea*), gray santolina (*Santolina chamaecyparissus*), or St. John's wort (*Hypericum calycinum*) are more practical carpeters. Although not as long-flowering as honeysuckle or verbena, these groundcovers are showy in their season and remain neatly attractive all year long.

Other rugged trailers especially suited to shady positions include *Lamium maculatum, Mazus reptans, Teucrium scorodonia, Chrysanthemum pacificum,* and the colorfully variegated *Houttuynia cordata* clone, 'Chameleon.' Somewhat taller, but also valuable for shady cover are the fall-blooming Japanese anemones (*Anemone × hybrida*) and the semitender, but otherwise indestructible cast iron plant (*Aspidistra elatior*).

An underutilized group of groundcovers of particular merit for gardens on limy ground are the ornamental marjorams (*Origanum* spp.) These fabulous perennials have tough, hardy constitutions and tremendous drought resistance. They make splendid low-growing subshrubs with lush, aromatic foliage and attractive blooms over a long season.

The creeping golden marjoram (*Origanum vulgare* 'Aureum') and the trailing *O. vulgare* 'Humile' form dense mats of leafy herbage that stay low to the ground. 'Herrenhausen' is a European selection with attractive pink summer flowers. Hybrid oregano (*O. × hybridinum*), Lebanon oregano (*O. libanoticum*), Amaragos dittany (*O. calcaratum*), and the *O. rotundifolium* hybrid, 'Kent Beauty,' all produce low shrublets that flower in frothy pink masses through summer heat. *O. laevigatum* becomes a foot or more tall when in bloom, but stays reasonably low at other times. Its tiny flowers are a cheerful lavender-pink and show well against blue-green foliage.

Several germanders (*Teucrium* spp.) have trailing habits that make them equally useful groundcovers for limy soils. The creeping wall germander (*Teucrium chamaedrys* 'Prostrata') makes a tough mat of shiny green foliage that spreads by underground runners. It performs well in dry, partially shaded areas.

Perhaps the finest of all the herb-type groundcovers is the silver germander (*T. cossonii*), whose narrow gray leaves provide a dense silvery carpet. This rosemarylike perennial withstands below-zero cold and endures hot, exposed positions on the poorest soils. Although slower to establish than some other groundcovers, silver germander is among the loveliest when its magenta flowers appear at the ends of its gray branchlets.

As a mat-forming groundcover or edging for rose beds the hazy lavender-gray catmint (*Nepeta faassenii*) is a deserving classic and helps subdue and combine the bright colors of other nearby flowers. The feather-leaved, trailing Mt. Atlas daisy (*Anacyclus depressus*) might be tried in similar situations with equal success. Its yellow-centered, white spring blooms close up at night to tight buds marked primly with red on the exterior of the petals.

The leafy mounding *Geranium sanguineum* is another flowering perennial useful as small-scale groundcover. This wine-pink species grows more thriftily in warm climates than other *Geranium* species and looks good as an edging among boulders or flagstones.

For perpetually dry, sunny positions the trailing silver dalea (*Dalea greggii*) and prostrate rosemaries (*Rosmarinus officinalis* 'Lockwood de Forest' and *R. o.* 'Huntington Carpet') are especially attractive. If kept overly moist and in active growth, however, both are liable to freeze at 15° F.

"Vittadinia" or Mexican daisy (*Erigeron karvinskianus* 'Profusion') provides a frothy mass of tiny white daisy flowers and readily naturalizes and self-sows on arid slopes. *E. myrionactis* trails over dry, limy ground with leathery, paddle-shaped leaves and white daisylike blooms. Both of these endure extremes of heat, cold, and drought.

A diminutive trailing ally of cenizas, *Stemodia tomentosa*, produces similar silvery gray leaves and small lavender flowers. *Stemodia* makes loose carpeting mats of foliage that drape attractively over the driest, rocky lime soils. Although these perennials die back to crowns of foliage in the winter, they quickly ramble about and cover the ground when spring returns.

This is true also of the rugged *Setcreaseas*, or "purple hearts," whose colorful, succulent leaves quickly form lush mats. These may be easily and inexpensively started from cuttings and withstand tremendous heat and drought once established.

For well-drained soils several of the trailing junipers are useful groundcover and may be woven together into a tapestry of varicolored, soft-textured foliage. *Juniperus horizontalis* 'Blue Chip' and *J. h.* 'Prince of Wales' are especially refined and tolerant of poor limy soil and harsh exposures. Blue shore juniper (*J. conferta* 'Blue Pacific') and Japanese garden juniper (*J. procumbens*) prefer well-prepared, fast-draining ground and partial shade. All junipers enjoy mulches of gravel or decomposed granite.

On wet or boggy ground in shade the Southern wood or river fern (*Thelypteris kunthii*) and the Venus' maidenhair fern (*Adiantum capillus-veneris*) are reliable and lush. The golden-flowered trailing buttercup (*Ranunculus repens*), the mosslike *Lysimachia japonica*, and the carpeting bugle-weed (*Ajuga reptans*) are also good for such situations, but suffer if allowed to dry out in late summer. Mock strawberry (*Duchesnea indica*) performs well in partial shade, but bears foliage eternally marred by a curious reddish rust disease.

A curious groundcover useful for damp soil is the sun-tolerant dwarf clover-fern (*Marselia macropoda*). These aggressive spreaders form lush thickets of gray-green, clover-like foliage, which folds up each evening and expands again on the following day. Although tolerant of considerable drought, these dwarf ferns look best with ample moisture and should be sheared over annually to renew their foliage.

Sedums and other carpeting succulents are popular groundcovers in temperate regions, and several types grow aggressively during the cool parts of the year. Few tolerate summer heat without supplemental irrigation or partial shade, however, and their value as groundcover is usually limited to favorable eastern exposures and protected nooks among rocks or flagstones. *Sedum potosinum*, *S. reflexum*, *S. forrestianum*, and *S. palmeri* are some of the most tolerant. Other succulent groundcovers such as the hardy iceplants, *Delosperma cooperi* and *D. nubigenum*, and the Chinese *Orostachys spinosa* enjoy similar coddling.

Vines

Climbing vines adapted to limy ground offer attractive foliage and beautiful flowers and include some of the most desirable of garden subjects. Although most vines are tougher and more vigorous than other types of plants, varieties such as the large-flowered *Clematis* hybrids need and warrant generous, attentive culture. For practical garden purposes these climbers fall into three categories: those that support themselves with aerial roots or attachments, those that twine and can ascend wires or strings, and those that require tying to substantial supports.

The first group includes the ivies and confederate jasmines already mentioned and other evergreens such as the semitender climbing fig (*Ficus repens*). Deciduous vines with the capacity to affix themselves to walls include scarlet trumpet creeper (*Campsis* × *tagliabuana* 'Mme Galen'), Boston ivy (*Ampelopsis tricuspidata*), and its American cousin, Virginia creeper (*Parthenocissus quinquefolia*). These rampant climbers display beautiful blooms in the case of the trumpetvine, and attractive orange-red fall color on the ivy and its relation. Boston ivy and Virginia creeper perform best on walls sheltered from hot western sun.

Clinging vines can damage wood and are best restrained to brick, masonry, or chain link. Even here, however, these varieties present problems if removal becomes necessary, for their aggressive aerial rootlets will have to be scraped away. This is a tremendous chore, but must be performed when tender types like fig ivy or confederate jasmine freeze during a severe winter.

A vine with the unique capacity to ascend masonry walls without such permanent hold-fasts is the hardy cross-vine (*Bignonia capreolata*). This tough, fast-growing evergreen bears big crops of trumpet-shaped blooms in several flushes over the growing season. These are often yellowish-brown, but in the best forms are rich scarlet-orange. The cross-vine's common name derives from the x-shaped pattern of its hollow stems when viewed in cross-section.

Bignonia accomplishes its miraculous climbing feats with clawlike tendrils that grasp any rough surface, yet will not damage wood or brick. Although in many ways an ideal vine with unusual tolerance to cold and drought, cross-vine is a nightmare in nurseries due to its propensity to entangle itself with any plant nearby. It remains relatively uncommon in the nursery trade.

Of the twining vines the evergreen Carolina jessamine (*Gelsemium sempervirens*) has many admirers. Its fragrant early spring blooms and dense, glossy foliage give it an opulent character, and this Southeastern native grows well on moist, heavy clays. On limy soils, however, Carolina jessamine seems to die out mysteriously after five to ten years, and it thoroughly resents drought or thin, rocky ground. *Gelsemium* belongs to the notorious strychnine family, and all parts of the plant are poisonous.

Although tolerant of lime, wisterias often show chlorosis during summer, for these fast growers place tremendous demands for food on the soils in which they grow. Severe pruning on a monthly basis is frequently required to maintain wisteria in its place in the landscape. These vines are best used on tall arbors where their natural vigor can run its course.

Chinese wisteria (*Wisteria sinensis*) is the most fragrant and reliable variety for warm climates, but is often sold as inferior unflowered seedlings. Only vegetatively propagated wisterias can be relied upon to bloom, and the safest course for gardeners is to purchase vines *only* while in flower. The resplendence of a wisteria in full spring dress is a reward worthy of this extra care in selection.

One of the grand favorite vines of hot-climate gardens is the queen's crown or queen's wreath (*Antigonon leptopus*). This tremendously vigorous perennial dies back to a swollen tuber after frost, but returns with summer's heat and may easily top a telephone pole by autumn. In late summer clouds of pink, heart-shaped blossoms drape up and down its lush bowers of green foliage.

In cold-winter regions the white-flowered silver-lace vine (*Polyganum aubiertii*) offers similar charms, and shows an obvious relation to the queen's crown. Both vines are unusually drought-tolerant and remain neat and attractive all season. In the last century they were popular subjects for planting along screened porches to provide shade. This was also a popular use for the succulent-leaved Madeira vine (*Anredera cordifolia*), whose inconspicuous flowers emit a sweet fragrance. Like the queen's crown it dies to a tuber in winter and thrives on heat and drought.

The most robust of all vines for poor, lime soil must surely be the Grecian silk vine (*Periploca graeca*). This eastern Mediterranean native has large, glossy leaves that give it a resemblance to a coarse-textured Asian jasmine. Its flowers resemble those of milkweed, and white sap exudes from its leaves and branches when they are cut. The fruits split to reveal silky masses of fiber, which carry the tiny seeds on the wind. On the thinnest, rockiest ground Grecian silk vine will quickly overpower a sizable arbor and soon suckers to form a forest of stems. Climbing milkweed (*Sarcostemma cynanchoides*) is a drought-tolerant native Southwestern vine of similar character.

For beauty of flower there are few lime-loving vines to compete with the *Clematis*.

In warm regions these are not used as often as they might be, however, for they require more care to establish than other vines. Like many of the most rewarding garden plants clematis exact a measure of time before giving their best; for most varieties three or more years are needed before blooms achieve their full size and abundance.

All clematis enjoy lime, but few endure drought. For the majority a deep, moist root-run is essential. For best flowering these vines need several hours of direct sun, but benefit from afternoon shade. The delicate, wiry stems of clematis are easily broken, and gardeners will do well to set young plants extra deeply to afford a reserve of stem from which the vines may resprout if disaster occurs.

In many gardens the ideal position for a clematis is found along a north or east foundation, where a large, sparsely branched *Philadelphus, Magnolia, Viburnum,* or rose bush can provide a natural scaffold. The twining leaflets of the clematis will then be able to carry its leaves and blooms to the sun, while the roots of the vine remain in the shade of the nurse shrub. The old technique of laying a flat rock over clematis roots to hold in moisture and keep the ground cool is also worth employing.

Robust-growing species clematis such as the scarlet-flowered *Clematis texensis,* the purple leather flower (*C. pitcheri*) and the fall-flowering, semievergreen *C. dioscoreifolia* are easy-growing, but lack the opulent blooms of the large-flowered hybrids. Crosses such as the *C. texensis* hybrid, 'Duchess of Albany,' and various *C. viticella* selections provide compromises between bloom size and vigor. Of the large-flowered class, varieties of proven value in warm regions include the purple 'Jackmanii' and 'Gypsy Queen,' lilac-blue 'Ramona,' pink 'Comtesse de Bouchaud,' white 'Henryi,' red 'Ernest Markham' and 'Ville de Lyon,' and pale blue, double 'Belle of Woking.'

Gardens blessed with moist positions and partial shade can accommodate the evergreen *C. armandii,* which matures to a leathery-leaved vine with attractive coppery new growth. Modest glistening white blooms appear against its dark, lush foliage in March and April.

The showy passion-flowers (*Passiflora* spp.) are another group of lime-tolerant vines with extraordinarily beautiful blooms. Most are semitender perennials, but the Brazilian *Passiflora caerulea* remains evergreen to 15° F or less. 'Incense' is a showy hybrid between the native prairie maypop (*P. incarnata*) and a luxuriant tropical Argentinean species. Although exotically beautiful, cold-hardy, and easy-growing on heavy calcareous clay, this variety suckers frightfully. *P.* × *alatocaerulea* is a slightly more tender but better behaved hybrid with large blue flowers.

Morning glories (*Ipomoea* spp.) are mostly grown as annuals, but a number of varieties develop swollen perennial roots. Nearly all succeed on lime. The luxuriant, large-flowered *Ipomoea tricolor* selection, 'Heavenly Blue,' is a cottage-garden cliché, often draping over whitewashed picket fences where its ivory-centered, cerulean flowers weave a celestial tapestry. The rich purple perennial *I. purpurea* is nearly as common and endures to bloom around many abandoned gardens. A rugged perennial morning glory with a restrained, trailing habit and large lilac blooms is *I. lindheimeri.* This tough variety is especially suited to chalky lime soils and may be propagated from the succulent tubers that form on its roots.

Especially good, too, for poor, limy ground are the annual cypress vines (*I. quamoclit*) and cardinal climbers (*I. lobata*). These have attractive divided foliage and bright crimson, tubular blooms. The cypress vine in particular is unique for its feathery mass of foliage. A white-flowered form of this appears particularly lush and soothing in the summer garden.

Other rugged flowering vines suited to limy ground and hot-summer climates are Mexican flame vine (*Senecio confusus*, an orange-flowered daisy) and potato vine (*Solanum jasminoides*, a semievergreen climber with leathery green leaves and small, white fragrant flowers). In its variegated form the potato vine is particularly showy and worthwhile and tolerates both shade and sun.

Purple hyacinth bean (*Dolichos lablab*), balsam gourd (*Momordica charantia*), and dish cloth gourd (*Luffa aegyptiaca*) are tough vines that are generally grown as annuals. All produce ornamental fruit as well as attractive flowers. Air potato (*Dioscorea bulbifera*) is planted for its handsome green leaves and curious aerial tubers.

Although tender to frost, the pink, trumpet-flowered *Podranea ricasoliana*, the Rangoon creeper (*Quisqualis indica*), the tuberous-rooted *Mandevilla* 'Alice du Pont,' and blue-flowered sky vine (*Thunbergia grandiflora*) are especially heat-tolerant and valuable in warm regions. The strange orange- or yellow-flowered climbing lilies (*Gloriosa* spp.) are other exotic vines suited to a subtropical garden. These withstand considerable cold and return as perennials if mulched heavily for the winter.

Lime-tolerant climbers that require tying to supports include climbing roses and the shade-loving *Fatshedera litzei*. This last is a cross between English ivy and Japanese aralia (*Fatsia japonica*). Its large, scalloped leaves provide a good sculptural effect against a north-facing wall.

The seven-leaf creeper (*Parthenocissus heptaphylla*) is another vine that requires some support. A glossy-leaved relative of Virginia creeper, this small vine is a specialty of the limestone Texas Hill Country. It makes a tough, drought-resistant vine with showy orange-red fall foliage.

Additional vines suited to lime soil include snapdragon vine (*Maurandya antirrhiniflora*), rattan vine (*Berchenia scandens*), Carolina moonseed (*Cocculus carolinus*), Dutchman's pipe (*Aristolochia* sp.), grapes (*Vitis* cvs.), pepper vine (*Ampelopsis arborea*), blueberry creeper (*A. brevipedunculata*), and cow-itch vine (*Cissus incisa*).

CHAPTER SIXTEEN

Treasures of the Sierra Madre

I n the joyous search for suitable plants to perform on limy soils and in summer heat, gardeners soon exhaust the false promises of California and the East. Successful varieties from the West may accept lime, but usually perish in winter cold or on poorly drained ground. Favorites from the East frequently develop chlorosis. Neither group has much to offer in high summer heat.

Gradually, ineluctably, the gardener's attention draws southward, to the botanical treasure-house of North America: Mexico. Perhaps no comparable area on earth offers a greater diversity of floral wonders than the Mexican republic. Mexico combines the botanical provinces of plains and mountains in the north with tropical lowlands, deserts, plateaus, and barrancas in the south, so that each square mile displays an astounding array of species. Many of these grow happily on lime, and a great number accept intense heat and summer rain.

Gardeners have marveled at the floral wonders of this country since pre-Columbian times. Popular vegetables such as tomatoes, corn, squash, beans, and peppers, and familiar flowers like marigolds, zinnias, cosmos, dahlias, and tuberoses derive from plants cultivated by the Aztecs and their predecessors. The gardens of Mexico have generously contributed to horticulture since they were first discovered by Europeans. They still have much to offer!

Like other countries rich in plant life, Mexico attracted plant collectors from Europe and America during the centuries following its conquest by Spain. Early collectors such as Sesse and Mocino saw much of their work lost or destroyed in the political struggles of Europe. Although several later collectors brought out information on and specimens of the flora of Mexico, it was not until the late 1800s that a true picture of the country's rich plant life began to emerge. This came about through the efforts of the most prolific and dedicated of collectors: Cyrus Guernsey Pringle.

Pringle grew up on a New England farm and was inspired by his bucolic experience in youth to pursue a career in horticulture. In 1858 he began his first nursery in Vermont. After enduring persecution during the Civil War for his pacifist beliefs, and after ending his marriage, Pringle sought to devote his remaining career to plant collecting, mostly in the wild back-country of Mexico. This was accomplished on foot, unarmed, carrying water, food, and plant press over rugged mountains and canyons. In thirty-five years of field work he collected over twenty thousand species of plants, of which twelve hundred proved new to science: a feat that has never been, and probably never will be, repeated.

Writing of his collections in the Mexican state of San Luis Potosí, Pringle said, "The most common oak here is *Quercus germana*, which bears acorns two inches long. *Dendropanax arboreus*, symmetrical in form and bearing attractive foliage and fruits, is one of the most interesting trees here; and *Banara mexicana* is pretty when covered with white berries. But to enumerate all the arborescent species of these forests would be tedious, were it possible; and I will only mention *Xanthoxylum pringlei* Wats. and *Clethra pringlei* Wats., as discoveries.

"If it were hardly possible to mention all of the trees of this region, what can I say for the shrubs and endless variety of herbs of Las Canoas and Tamosopo, and of the long canyon connecting these, the pursuit of which has occupied me for many weeks of two summers? I am sensible that the species accessible from the railroad, which has opened a way through mountains and jungles, is far from being exhausted."

In the century since Pringle collected in Mexico, plant discoveries have followed each new road cut into the wilderness, and a host of plant collectors have brought out rare novelties at a regular pace. The journals of societies dedicated to cacti, bromeliads, amaryllids, and other typically Mexican plants are studded with recent findings. With industrialization and population growth, much of the grandeur that Pringle witnessed has fallen to the plow, or to goats, or to urbanization. Each year plants disappear forever, under the pressure of civilization. These may easily equal or exceed in quantity the new discoveries of science and horticulture.

Although only part of the Mexican flora adapts to garden culture in America, these plants are a beautiful heritage and deserve wide appreciation. In spite of increased modernization, Mexico is still a wild country with many back roads and unexplored mountain valleys. For dedicated horticulturists the glorious plants of Mexico beckon to be sought out and brought home so that they may be cherished and passed on to future generations.

As one travels south into Mexico from the river crossing at Laredo, the outliers of the Sierra Madre Oriental soon come into sight. Many of the plants in these mountains have considerable cold-hardiness, and most tolerate lime, for the underlying rocks are often limestone or marble. These rugged, wild mountains rise sharply from less than one thousand feet above sea level to over ten thousand on the highest peaks. In some canyons sheer walls several thousand feet high rise steeply up from the bottom.

One of the trees common on the dry slopes of the foothills is the recently discovered legume, *Myrospermum sousanum*. It has attractive light green leaves and white flowers and ripens pleasantly aromatic wood that has encouraged the nickname of "arroyo sweetwood." *Myrospermum* makes a fine tree for dry caliche soils, hardy to 10° F or less.

On the same dry slopes the yellow-flowered butterfly vines (*Mascagnia macroptera*) provide cheerful notes of color, and agaves, yuccas, and several half-hardy cacti abound. In nooks and crannies among the rocks there are occasional yellow rain lilies (*Habranthus* sp.) and lush rosettes of succulent *Echeveria*. These crevices are also home to the rugged purple heart (*Setcreasea pallida*) and the velvet creeper (*Tradescantia sillamontana*), which thrive in similar rocky settings in the garden.

Like limestone country everywhere, this is a region of springs, and near several old north Mexican towns crystalline blue-green water wells up into deep pools. These oases provide habitats for the graceful Montezuma cypress (*Taxodium mucronatum*) and the yellow Mexican waterlily (*Nymphaea mexicana*). This golden bloom was used by the famous nineteenth-century French breeder, M. Marliac, to create the sulfur-colored hybrid, 'Chromatella,' which even today rates among the most popular of hardy garden waterlilies.

Upon entering the moist, cool canyons of the Sierra itself, full-sized forests of oak and pine make an impressive display. Mexico is the center of distribution for both oaks and pines and boasts more of each than any comparable place in the world.

One of the most desirable of the Mexican oaks for gardens on lime is the evergreen Mexican white oak (*Quercus polymorpha*). These occur throughout the highlands of Mexico and range southward into Guatemala. For hardiness the trees from the eastern Sierras seem most promising. They make massive specimens with ponderous, heavy branches and large, irregularly scalloped leaves. *Q. polymorpha* is attractively pyramidal in youth and withstands frost to 5° F or less.

Another valuable Mexican oak is *Q. canbyi*, a relative of the Chisos red oak (*Q. gravesii*) of western Texas. Canby oak grows rapidly into an upright tree covered in small, glittering green, serrated foliage. These leaves remain evergreen in mild regions, but assume tints of orange and yellow in cool winter weather.

Of the numerous pines of Mexico, the Montezuma pine (*Pinus montezuma*) carries a special measure of enchantment. Its long, bright green needles are carried in lush bundles of five and give the tree a graceful, drooping appearance. Like the yellow pines of North America, Montezuma pines form broad, open canopies with age. Although native over a wide range in Mexico and Central America, trees from the state of Nuevo Leon offer the greatest tolerance to cold and lime.

In the sheltered canyons of the Sierras all manner of woody undershrubs can be seen. Mock oranges, hollies, wild roses, dogwoods, and dwarf evergreen bays (*Litsea* spp.) are common and exquisite. The shade-loving evergreen yew, *Taxus globosa*, lurks in some of the more protected vales. On sunny slopes the cotoneasterlike serviceberry, *Amelanchier denticulata*, sets its showy crops of soft, pink berries.

Two choice mahonias are prime attractions to the plant lover visiting these mountains. *Mahonia gracilis* grows slowly into a suckering shrub with shiny, grass-green foliage and wine-colored stems and new shoots. Its nearly spineless, evergreen leaves withstand full sun and cold to 5° F or less. This rugged, yet elegant shrub presents a lush appearance at all times. The treelike *M. chochoco* comes to resemble a mountain laurel as it matures. Like *M. gracilis*, it tolerates sun, cold, and poor soils. Both species flower with long racemes of yellow midwinter blooms, which later ripen to strands of berries.

Dry, rocky sites are home to several types of half-hardy *Brahea* palms, all of which make choice, slow-growing prizes for limy-soil gardens. *Brahea bella* is the largest and most cold-tolerant and usually retains a single trunk. Other varieties often sucker to form low clumps and vary in leaf color from green to silvery blue.

Along the steep, rocky canyonsides one of the most magnificent of hardy sedums drapes its succulent rosettes. *Sedum palmeri* comes into full flower in mid-February and smothers its gray-green leaves in golden bloom. This shade-loving succulent is a perfect choice for a large planter, from which its pendant branchlets can be allowed to hang down. *S. palmeri* endures frost to 10° F with little damage.

Ghost plants (*Graptopetalum paraguayense*) trade the floral beauty of the sedum for fleshy gray rosettes that look like flowers fashioned of stone. Like *S. palmeri,* ghost plants offer good material for raised planters or containers, but prefer shelter from temperatures below 15° F. Although sorely confused as to origin by early botanists (who thought they came from Paraguay), ghost plants are true natives of northeastern Mexico.

Flowering perennials such as *Salvias, Justicias, Cupheas,* and *Eupatoriums* abound on the rugged slopes and hillsides, and in moist canyons may be found tufts of the orange-flowered Mexican campion (*Silene laciniata*). Succulent manfredas with snaking, undulating foliage make rosettes along low embankments. On dry hilltops the twiggy pink-flowered skullcap, *Scutellaria suffrutescens,* makes dense shrublets covered in tiny bloom. On the arid plateaus and canyons ash-leaved cenizas such as *Leucophyllum zygophyllum, L. laevigatum,* and *L. langmaniae* turn to hazy clouds of blue and lavender following summer rains.

In eastern Mexico a great proliferation of rain lilies (*Zephyranthes* spp.) makes each journey over hill and vale into a voyage of discovery. Near Jacala, Hidalgo these tiny amaryllids appear in shades of yellow, pink, white, crimson, and apricot, all within a few square miles. The variations of the rainbow, save blue, may be found in blossom along the roadside.

One of the most characteristic Mexican flowers often can be found along with the rain lilies, for it enjoys the same rugged terrain. The Aztec lily (*Sprekelia formosissima*) rates as a true treasure wherever it grows and ranges widely across Mexico, as well as Central and South America. These orchidlike, crimson blooms rise like rain lilies from black-coated bulbs and appear in both spring and fall. 'Orient Red' is a good garden strain that performs better than the commercial cultivar, 'Superba,' which often must be dug and stored to induce bloom.

In central, southern, and western Mexico the common summer-flowering bulbs are spider lilies (*Hymenocallis* spp.) and tuberoses (*Polianthes* spp.). Both occur in complex and mysterious variety. The spider lilies range from big, bulky tropical evergreens to tiny, daffodillike miniatures. *Hymenocallis eucharidifolia* is a rare shade-loving species with rosettes of broad green, hostalike foliage. Of the many tuberoses, *Polianthes howardii* is especially easy-growing on lime. It produces Christmas-colored red and green blooms that hummingbirds visit regularly. Colorful hybrids between this species and several other tuberoses also make good garden plants.

Popular images of Mexico are often those of cactus-studded deserts, but one of the most memorable of the country's many landscapes is the high, pine-covered volcanic region that lies to the west of Mexico City. Here, on the slopes of the mountains lush forests gradually give way to expanses of open pine and solid stands of compellingly beautiful grass, *Stipa tenuissima.* This is the same feather needle grass that ranges through the mountains of the Southwest and may be found south to Argentina.

These discussions offer only glimpses of the vast range of Mexican natives with potential for gardens on lime. As with all introductions, new plants require time to prove themselves before they can be safely declared successes. Yet, with the many lovely Mexican flowers already among our garden treasures and the long lists of specimens collected in herbaria, it seems likely that a vast range of worthy plants yet remain to be tried. This enchanting land and its beautiful flora promise to enrich gardens on lime for years to come.

CHAPTER SEVENTEEN

Widening the Range

The challenges inherent in gardening on lime elicit sighs of discouragement from some, but true, hearty plant-lovers are as liable to respond with heightened interest. In the midst of multitudes of beautiful, easy-growing, lime-tolerant flowers, the allure of a delicate runt of a bloom, requiring careful nurturing to bring into flower, sends a siren song to the heart. Eventually, even the most sensible gardeners succumb to desires for adventure and yield to the illicit pleasures of cultivating "forbidden" lime-haters.

The multitudes of illustrated gardening books written for acid soils, and the experiences of gardeners newly transplanted to the limy hills and prairies from other parts of the world provide common starting points for interest in growing calcifuge plants on limy ground. Gardeners can fulfill their desires in two ways: by doing all that is possible to alter soil and microclimate to suit particular plants or by casting about for suitable lime-tolerant substitutes.

Examples of the latter course have already been suggested in other chapters. Perennial lupines afford another example of the method: Russel hybrid lupines are robust perennials with tall blooms of great value in perennial borders. Although popular and easy-growing in cool, acid soil regions, these lupines are short-lived failures on limy soils in hot-summer climates. The annual Texas bluebonnets (*Lupinus texensis*) succeed on lime and have similarly formed flowers, but are much smaller, and therefore fill a different garden niche.

Instead, the heat- and lime-tolerant perennial that most closely approximates lupines derives from the related wild indigo genus, *Baptisia*. The navy blue *Baptisia australis* affords gardeners on lime a leafy shrublet bearing tall spikes of pea flowers in May. These make long-lived, slow-growing perennials and provide many of the same attractions offered by the Russel hybrid lupines. By employing analogous substitutions, allies of many popular lime-haters can be included in gardens on calcareous soils.

With plants such as peonies (*Paeonia* cvs.), cultural problems follow not from soil, but from an intensely hot summer climate. Only a few of the more vigorous, early-blooming perennial types such as the old, fragrant blush pink 'Festiva Maxima' will flower, and even these scorch unattractively in summer heat. Tree peonies (*Paeonia suf-*

fruticosa cvs.) flower in mild-winter regions, but need shade and protection. Although suitably rugged, heat-tolerant peonies exist in the countries along the Mediterranean, they have seldom been used in breeding modern hybrids. Warm climate gardeners must go back to the wild species to find types suited to their own conditions.

The bright pink *Paeonia cambessedessii* makes a modest-sized clump of silvery green leaves with wine-red undersides. This lovely plant hails from the dry, chalky hillsides of the Balearic Islands and would be ideal to try on the caliche soils of America. Similar varieties such as the Corsican *P. russii* v. *reverchonii*, which bears pink blooms atop its brownish-green foliage, and the dark red *P. mascula* of central France would surely be of value as well. The fern-leaf peony (*P. peregrina*) of the Balkans, which was known to Parkinson in 1629 as the "red peony of Constantinople," is sometimes available in America and seems worthy of trial. Its hybrids with common garden peonies are frequently offered as "lobatas."

Intolerance to high pH has legitimately brought about lime-hating reputations for some plants. Just as often, however, failures on calcareous soils seem to follow from lack of humus and consequent exposure to drought. Careful siting, bed preparation, and watering are often all that are required to succeed with several so-called "lime-haters."

The camellia family is one such group. Although intolerant of chalky caliche soils, most camellias will succeed on improved limy clays if properly sited in shade and irrigated through summer heat and drought. A close ally of camellias, the "cleyera" (*Ternstroemia gymnanthera*) is sufficiently easy to have won a position as a popular evergreen hedging plant. It flourishes in partial shade on the limy soils that this family of shrubs is frequently said to abhor.

The autumn-blooming Sasankwa camellias (*Camellia sasankwa*) are also satisfactory on calcareous clays, so long as soils are well mixed with compost or bark to improve drainage and moisture-holding capacity. A slightly raised bed near a north foundation or under the evergreen branches of a live oak affords a suitable home for these graceful evergreens.

'Mine-no Yuki' is a popular variety with willowy, spreading branches and semidouble creamy white blooms. 'Yuletide' has bright red flowers centered with a boss of golden stamens and develops a compact, upright habit. Like all sasankwas, the late fall flowers of these varieties shatter cleanly and fall to the ground as they fade.

The japonicas (*C. japonica* cvs.) are less valuable landscape subjects, as they retain their waning blooms as a sodden, rotting mass. These large-flowered camellias possess the splendor of the family, however, and have slightly more cold-hardiness than *C. sasankwa*. Nevertheless, their glamorous, midwinter blooms require shelter from hard frost if they are to open properly.

'Debutante' is a well-known, vigorous pearl-pink camellia with double, peony-type blooms set against compact, lustrous green foliage. 'Colonel Fiery' ("C. M. Hovey," "Duc du Devonshire") is a strong-growing dark red with a formal, roselike bloom. Both of these are satisfactory on calcareous clay if plenty of humus is incorporated into the soil. Good drainage, steady moisture, and shade from direct sun are other factors critical to success with these flowering evergreens.

The sweet olives (*Osmanthus* spp.) are another group of evergreens that tolerate lime if offered soil well prepared with organic material. The winter-flowering *Osmanthus fragrans* is a favorite specimen shrub of mild regions, as its tiny blooms permeate the garden with powerful fragrance. Temperatures below 20° F are apt to damage this choice evergreen, but *O. fragrans* is otherwise easy-growing on prepared calcareous clay.

Where winter lows prohibit this most fragrant variety, its spring-flowering hybrid, *0. × fortunei,* may be substituted. This sweet-scented shrub inherits modest hardiness and scalloped, prickly foliage from its other parent, the false holly (*O. heterophyllus*). False holly is sometimes cultivated in an attractive variegated form, although these lack the endearing fragrance of the other *Osmanthus* varieties. All of these shrubs appreciate shade and steadily available moisture. Other sweet-scented evergreens that enjoy these conditions include banana shrub (*Michelia fuscata*) and daphne (*Daphne* spp.).

Shade and moisture-loving conifers include Chinese plum yews (*Cephalotaxus fortunei*) and false cypresses (*Chamaecyparis* spp.). The peculiar-looking China firs (*Cunninghamia lanceolata*) and Japanese cedars, or sugis (*Cryptomeria japonica*), accept full or part sun, but require rich, organic soil and shelter from cold wind.

Japanese yew (*Podocarpus macrophylla*) tolerates lime if afforded rich, well-drained soil and a sheltered position. It makes a fine soft-textured evergreen to brush against near a walk, and its upright masses of dense, blue-green leaflets give a relaxed, yet formal accent to mixed plantings of evergreen shrubs. 'Maki' is an especially elegant, compact selection.

Flowering dogwoods (*Cornus florida*) seldom suffer from mildly alkaline pH if soils are otherwise moist and rich in humus. Drainage is also critical for dogwoods, as these small trees are very susceptible to cotton root rot on alkaline ground. A raised bed at least six feet in diameter should be created beneath a high-branched oak, elm, or pecan to give these understory trees the space they need to develop properly. With this attention a well-sited dogwood will produce its opulent white or pink spring blooms for years to come.

The slightly later-flowering Chinese dogwood (*Cornus kousa* v. *chinensis*) is said to have even greater lime tolerance than the American varieties and might also be tried. 'Summer Stars' is an especially fine, long-blooming selection. In addition to showy white flowers, these small, shade-loving trees offer colorful autumn berries and foliage.

Shade-loving perennials such as toad lily (*Tricyrtis* spp.), trillium, and Solomon's seal (*Polygonatum* sp.) are remarkably easy to grow if offered beds of moist, humusy earth. They make excellent companions for acid-loving shrubs and trees. This is also a good position for the moisture-loving evergreen *Bergenia*, which has no dislike for lime if kept steadily cool and damp through the summer.

Transvaal daisies (*Gerbera jamesonii*) are tremendous favorites for their colorful blooms in shades of yellow, orange, and red that make stunning cut flowers. Although they prefer acid soils, these half-hardy perennials generally accept calcareous earth if it is heavily improved with peat and compost. Fast drainage is critical for these rosette-forming daisies, lest they succumb to rotting fungi at the crown. If offered shade and good, loamy ground they are easy-growing and fairly permanent.

The beautiful evergreen *Agapanthus orientalis* cultivars are good growers in summer and give a cooling effect to gardens with their invaluable blue or white flowers. Unfortunately, these types lack winter-hardiness and must be mulched to encourage survival through frost. On limy ground this often results in rotting of the crowns over winter, and these perennials are frequently short-lived unless potted and protected.

More cold-hardy deciduous *Agapanthus* such as the 'Headbourne Hybrids' require rich, peaty ground and unfailing moisture through summer if they are to size up and flower. Partial shade is also welcomed by all *Agapanthus* varieties.

Hydrangeas respond to alkaline soils like litmus paper, by turning from blue to pink. This peculiar capacity can be manipulated by gardeners to achieve varying shades of bloom. By adding a plant food rich in manganese, or acidifying chemicals such as aluminum sulfate or magnesium sulfate (epsom salts), otherwise pink hydrangea flowers may be induced to turn blue. These acidifying materials also alleviate chlorosis on hydrangeas and provide a quick cure for any acid-loving plant that flags when planted on limy ground.

The popular "hortensia" hydrangeas that derive from *Hydrangea macrophylla* and *H. serrata* are easy-growing on limy clays if offered plenty of shade and humus. Unlike camellias and dogwoods, whose delicate fibrous roots require well-aerated soils, hydrangeas enjoy wet feet and thrive along north foundations in rich, eternally damp ground. 'Nikko Blue' is a popular selection with large, dome-shaped flowers. These most often appear light pink when planted on alkaline soils, but may be restored to lilac-blue by diligently excavating an acid bed of pine bark or peat and through annual treatments of acidifying chemicals.

The Southeastern native oakleaf hydrangea (*H. quercifolia*) has a greater tolerance to lime than the hortensias and makes a good understory shrub for naturalistic gardens. Its coarse-textured, lobed leaves turn to showy orange tints in the fall and offer a lush, dark green summer background for its oblong clusters of milky white blooms. 'Snow Queen' is an especially elegant, select form of this shade-loving shrub. The globular, creamy white *H. paniculata* cultivars, 'Grandiflora' and 'Annabelle,' accept improved limy clay as well, if afforded shade and moisture.

For azaleas and gardenias, however, no half measures will do. Only complete replacement of the soil with acid compost will satisfy these finicky lime-haters, and this must be accomplished with care to assure that the roots of these shrubs do not grow significantly into the limy subsoil. Both fibrous peat moss and composted pine bark are suitable materials for building acid beds, but bark is often preferred for its lower cost and longer lasting properties.

Although azaleas require soils that are constantly moist, they must also drain well. For this reason beds for azaleas are best raised above grade. A simple method for constructing these is to mix four parts volume composted bark with one part each peat moss and rotted manure or compost. This may then be formed into a mound raised at least two feet above the surrounding soil so that the bed will retain a significant rise even after several seasons of settling. This mixture should then be dressed with epsom salts or an acid plant food to further improve its acidity, and this can be repeated annually or as needed to maintain the low pH. Acidic mulches such as pine needles, rice hulls, cotton hulls, or bagasse may also be used to help keep the soil in good condition in future seasons.

For azaleas in particular, one more step sometimes assists successful bed preparation. Like madrone trees, azaleas depend on relationships with soil mycorrhizae to obtain nutrients efficiently through their wiry roots. Knowledgeable gardeners obtain small amounts of soil from an established bed of azaleas to inoculate the ground for a new planting.

Azaleas are true woodlanders and thoroughly resent hot, windy positions. Good microclimates often can be found near shady north foundations or under large oaks or elms. Late-leafing shade trees such as pecans are less suitable, as the early blooms of azaleas often appear before the trees can provide shelter.

Robust, easy-growing azaleas for mild regions may be found among the southern indicas (hybrids of *Rhododendron indicum*, *R. simsii* and *R. mucronatum*). These big, sprawling shrubs suffer when subjected to freezes below 20° F, but are otherwise rather forgiving. The rose-purple 'Formosa' and deep pink 'Pride of Mobile' are particularly strong and successful.

Where cold weather rules out these types, the Satsuki hybrids fall next in line for ease of culture. Satsukis include a wide range of oriental cultivars with useful low dwarf or weeping habits of growth and interestingly marked or variegated flowers. The miniature "Gumpo" types belong here also. They should be among the first azaleas attempted in any garden on lime, as they are neat, hardy, easily accommodated evergreens. Their soft pink or white blooms appear in May or June, long after most other azaleas have finished for the season.

The Kurume hybrids that descend from the Japanese *R. kiusianum* and *R. kaempferi* offer breathtaking banks of color when massed under trees and are the electrically colored evergreen azaleas most often attempted by amateurs. 'Hino-degiri,' 'Hino-crimson,' 'Coral Bells,' and 'Snow' have been fancied for decades. Although fairly hardy, these varieties are more prone to suffer from blight and disease than other evergreen azaleas.

The Glen Dale hybrids appear similar to the Kurumes, but have tougher, more resistant constitutions. 'Glacier' is a popular white selection. The coppery orange cultivar, 'Fashion,' provides an added bonus of scattered autumn flowers in addition to its annual explosive spring bloom.

Although the enormous *Rhododendron* genus offers a whole array of lovely plants that might be tried in special acid beds, most are even less likely to repay the gardener's efforts than the varieties already mentioned. Deciduous azaleas and true evergreen rhododendrons are better left to cooler, more temperate climes.

A lime-tolerant ally of azaleas worth trying on well-enriched ground is the winter-flowering Mediterranean heath, *Erica* × *darleyensis*. Unlike the calcifuge heathers (*Calluna* spp.) this delicately constructed evergreen will grow successfully on the limiest soils if offered steady moisture and good drainage. It makes a fine-textured medium green bush with tiny rose flowers from late fall to spring.

Unlike most of these acid-lovers, Cape jasmines or gardenias (*Gardenia jasminoides*) enjoy direct sun and will even tolerate hot, exposed positions if provided with rich soil and plenty of summer moisture. The reward of their fragrant, waxy white blooms is sufficient to justify excavating the special acid bed they require. A raised planting similar to that for azaleas is satisfactory, but should be lined on the bottom with plastic to prevent the gardenia's more aggressive roots from wandering too far into the limy earth beyond.

'Mystery' is an opulently large-flowered gardenia with moderate cold-hardiness. 'August Beauty' trades this grandeur for an abundance of smaller blooms and a tougher, hardier constitution. The dwarf 'Radicans' offers prostrate growth, suited to fragrantly edging a path, but requires a winter mulch to avoid freeze damage. Florist gardenias such as 'Veitchii' flower only in cool fall and winter weather and are best avoided in frosty climates.

Grafting gardenias onto the lime-tolerant G. *thunbergia* often improves their acceptance of alkaline soils, and this is a popular garden technique in south Florida. However, G. *thunbergia* is tender to cold, and a suitably hardy lime-tolerant rootstock has yet to be discovered for frost-prone regions.

Granite Gardens

Although beds of peat or bark appropriately house many acid-lovers, such plantings require steady supplies of moisture through summer, and periodic applications of epsom salts to restore acidity. Eternal vigilance is the price exacted for success with these delicate woodland shrubs, and the careless gardener can easily lose even old, established specimens in a moment of neglect.

Not all acid-lovers require summer irrigations, however, and a great many enjoy sun. For these plants raised beds of decomposed granite or acid sand offer more permanent homes than can be afforded by peat or bark. Such plantings require minimal summer waterings and little attention from gardeners once the plants become established.

Many bulbs enjoy granite beds. Spring star flowers (*Ipheion uniflorum*) are easy and permanent on sand. These low-growing clumpers bear light blue flowers from late winter through spring and make good plants for an informal edging.

Daffodils of the *Narcissus cyclamineus* section such as 'Peeping Tom', 'February Gold', or 'March Sunshine' enjoy sand or crushed granite beds as well. The tiny fragrant *N. jonqilla* is easy and permanent if well watered during its growing season. These are among the most valuable narcissus in warm regions, as they flower early in the spring season.

Other bulbs with affinity for sand include Amarcrinum (*Crinodonna corsii*), Hurricane Lily (*Lycoris aurea*), and the Mediterranean sea-daffodil (*Pancratium maritimum*). This last variety is a native of coastal dunes, and thrives without irrigation if offered similar garden soils.

Many plants that suffer from summer rots when planted on limy clay thrive on raised beds of granite. Such positions are excellent for lamb's ears (*Stachys byzantina*), santolina, or artemisia. This would also be a good place to try the pale blue *Ceanothus* hybrid 'Gloire de Versailles'. This deciduous variety is more easily grown than its evergreen "California lilac" cousins, which are notorious failures in warm-climate gardens. 'Gloire de Versailles' makes a ten-foot shrub and flowers in late summer or early autumn.

Deep-rooted perennials such as butterfly weed (*Asclepias tuberosa*), yellow false lupine (*Thermopsis caroliniana*), or red valerian (*Centranthus ruber*) appreciate the extra drainage and more neutral pH afforded by sandy soils. Granite beds are ideal for many of the same drought-loving plants that thrive on chalky ground or caliche. The South African *Gazania* daisies popular for annual summer bedding often return as perennials if afforded gritty, well-drained soil.

Low carpeting plants such as sedums or pink iceplant (*Delosperma cooperi*) make denser mats of leaves when planted on granite sand and seem to endure extremes of heat and cold better. This is also true for many low-growing junipers, and these invaluable evergreens often grow more robustly and suffer less from foliar blights when planted on raised beds of sand or crushed granite.

Cold-climate garden subjects such as Colorado blue spruce (*Picea pungens*) generally struggle in high summer heat, but may succeed if offered deep, moist, gravelly root-runs. An especially vigorous cultivar worth trying in warm regions is 'Foxtail'.

Granite miraculously seems to improve the hardiness of semitender subjects such as Mediterranean fan palms (*Chamaerops humilis*) or Pindo palms (*Butia capitata*) as well. In marginal areas this allows gardeners to succeed with these plants, though they regularly freeze in adjacent gardens on limy clay.

CHAPTER EIGHTEEN

Fruits and Vegetables for Limy Ground

When it comes to the cultivation of edible crops upon alkaline land, any willingness among gardeners to compromise with the local soil and climate must be weighed against the desired results: abundant, high-quality produce. To achieve success in this endeavor almost any trick is justifiable. Certainly all the techniques of soil improvement, fertilization, and microclimate selection should be utilized, and this is generally the place to pull out the stops on otherwise avoided tasks such as pruning and spraying.

Although a number of gardens successfully raise vegetables and fruits at a savings over what they might cost at market, most home farmers invest effort in their backyards for a return in increased quality and freshness of their homegrown produce, rather than the small savings on its cost. Soft fruits and vegetables taste remarkably better when fresh from the garden. Moreover, gardeners who grow their own are not limited to the small variety of crops offered by grocers and may enjoy fruits and berries that seldom come to market due to poor shipping qualities.

Another priority of many is assurance that vegetables and fruits are free from harmful pesticide residues. In home gardens organic methods of production are eminently practical and result in satisfactorily abundant yields. Where quality of production, rather than cost of production, is the goal, there is little justification for resorting to chemical pest controls. Most home gardens produce enough for both the gardener and the occasional hungry caterpillars, bugs, and birds.

Garden vegetables often thrive on limy soils if generously supplied with organic material. It is the fruit and nut tree groups that are most limited by alkaline lands. These must naturally tolerate lime if they are to produce abundantly when planted on calcareous soils. In spite of this, a wide range may be selected for even the chalkiest sites.

Soft Fruits

Soft fruits are premier crops for home gardens. These are the delicious grapes, berries, peaches, and plums that come infrequently and expensively to market, yet that often grow with ease at home. They repay modest efforts from gardeners with generous fresh fruit and wonderful home preserves.

Of the wide group of plants classed as berries the gardener on limy ground is most likely to succeed with the blackberry and its ally, the dewberry. These are rampant thorny vines that demand at least three feet of space in which to sprawl and quickly take more if allowed. They ask for little else, however, other than an annual pruning to remove old, spent canes, and they make attractive, glossy-leaved shrubs that combine well in informal garden borders.

Where space is at a premium and gardens offer deep, calcareous clay soil, the true erect-caned blackberries are the best values and will produce more per square foot than the sprawling, ground-hugging dewberries. 'Brazos' is especially large-fruited and productive; 'Rosborough' is slightly smaller, but more flavorful. Of the useful thornless types, 'Navaho' and 'Black Satin' are choices for hot-summer regions.

On thin soils over chalk, however, dewberries come into their own and successfully produce where erect blackberries might struggle. 'Austin' is a flavorful variety that ripens several weeks before most blackberry selections. It makes an attractive small-scale groundcover for a naturalistic garden and grows well in partial shade, as well as full sun.

Grapes are another group of fruits that offer tough varieties suited to the heaviest clays, as well as to poor, rocky sites on limestone and chalk. They are also among the most drought-tolerant of fruit-bearers. Like the dewberries and blackberries, grapes make attractive vines to mix in garden plantings of flowers and shrubs. They are particular favorites for planting shady arbors, from which their ripe fruit clusters may hang down in summer.

Gardeners accustomed to the seedless varieties offered at grocery stores are frequently disappointed to discover that the same types fail to flourish at home. Except in parts of California and the desert Southwest, most of the grapes suited to home gardens fall into the seed-bearing class. Although new seedless types such as 'Orlando' are being tried in some areas, their performances on alkaline land have not yet been well tested.

A grape that endures truly harsh prairie soils and rugged climes is 'Champanel,' a hybrid derived from a wild mustang grape (*Vitis champinii*). It makes loose clusters of big, black-skinned grapes well suited for jellies, preserves, or homemade wines. Other tough varieties with breeding to rugged native stocks include 'Lomanto,' 'Ellen Scott,' and 'Extra.' These selections stem from the genius of the famous horticulturist, T. V. Munson, whose work with grapes at the turn of the century helped to save the disease-threatened vineyards of Europe. For this Munson received the French Legion of Honor; he is the only American ever to have received this award.

Other worthwhile grapes for gardens on limy ground include French-American hybrids such as Seibel 9110 (Verdelet). Although this white-fruited grape bears some seeds, these are small and poorly developed, so the fruits approach a "seedless" condition. Seyve-Villard 12309 (Roucaneuf) is a good type to plant on thin chalky soils; it endures severe heat and drought and produces large, loose clusters of tangy, aromatic grapes with a delicate pink blush. Unlike most of the French-American hybrids, S-V 12309 shows resistance to Pierce's disease virus.

Although often reported to fail on limy soils, the muscadines (*Vitis rotundufolia*) seem to have little objection to calcareous clays, so long as they are not unduly stressed by drought. These sweetly flavored Southeastern natives should be trained along fences or wires to encourage formation of their big, fragrant berries. 'Triumph,' 'Welder,' 'Carlos' and 'Magnolia' are self-pollinating varieties and may be planted alone. 'Jumbo,'

'Scuppernong,' and 'Higgins' require other muscadine types nearby to assure pollination.

Plums are among the best soft fruits for home gardens and are usually generously productive. However, on limy soils most of the popular Japanese varieties have limited life spans and suffer from bouts of fungus and bacterial diseases. Nevertheless, these large-fruited types can be productive if well cared for. Plums with native American ancestry generally make more long-lived bushy trees. Although their fruits are smaller than commercial Japanese types, native American hybrid plums make excellent ornamental trees or shrubs to include in edible landscapes. They are just as sweet and flavorful as the standard Japanese varieties.

For small gardens with space for only one plum tree, the Japanese variety, 'Santa Rosa,' is a suitable choice. It is self-pollinating and productive and yields large red plums with a delicious sweet flavor. Leaf diseases are likely to mar the tree's appearance in summer, however, and this type usually expires from bacterial stem canker after about five years of production. Nevertheless, 'Santa Rosa' grows quickly and may easily be replaced with young trees as needed.

Of the American plum hybrids a good self-pollinating type is 'Methley.' This variety makes a graceful, spreading tree with attractive white blooms in spring and an abundance of small, sweet purple-red fruits in late May. It resists drought and tolerates poor, limy soils. If pruned back by one third each season, 'Methley' will bear each year. If left unpruned, these plums often adopt alternate bearing cycles, skipping a year between unusually heavy crops. Thinning the fruit can help increase fruit size when large numbers of plums set on the stems.

'Methley' and other American types descend from native plums originally domesticated by early American pioneers. One of the most interesting of these was the old variety, 'Wild Goose,' which is thought to be a natural cross between *Prunus americana* and *P. munsoniana*. It was introduced in the early 1800s by a Tennessee farmer who claimed he planted a seed found in the stomach of a wild goose he shot for supper!

In addition to 'Methley,' varieties such as 'Morris' and 'Ozark Premier' make good home garden plums. These require another plum variety nearby as a pollinator, however, and perform best where winter temperatures regularly fall below 10° F.

Peaches rank as the most popular soft fruits for home gardens and bear successfully on both heavy calcareous clay soils and thin rocky positions. Although peaches are in general tolerant of lime, some understocks (notably "Nema-guard") may induce chlorosis on alkaline soils. The best course for gardeners with ruggedly limy grounds may be to plant peach strains such as 'South China,' which may be grown on their own roots. Alternatively, one may plant seedlings grown from naturalized lime-tolerant peach trees and then bud these to desired varieties at a later date. Such wild lime-loving peaches are common in central Texas.

In general, however, these measures are seldom required for success. Most minor bouts of peach chlorosis can be cured by maintaining generous mulches of organic material over tree roots, and by carefully pruning during the dormant season to avoid undue stress on the trees. If appropriately sited on well-drained ground, a healthy peach should produce for several seasons before requiring replacement. Although less long lived on heavy clays than on sand or loam, peaches usually have productive lives of about ten years.

For longevity and productivity the old-fashioned cling peaches are among the best to grow and have especially good, sweet flavors. Although they require more effort to slice and clean than freestone types, home gardeners will be rewarded with superior preserves from these varieties. 'Frank,' 'Chilow,' 'Junegold,' 'Dixired,' and 'Indian Cling' are good types for hot-summer regions. Most of the better quality freestone varieties produce well only in regions that regularly receive winter chills below 10° F. 'Redskin,' 'Ranger,' and 'Loring' are some of the best types for warm regions.

For truly mild-winter climates, however, and for home garden use in general there are few peaches that can compete in flavor and quality with the white-fleshed "honey" peaches. These include varieties such as 'Babcock,' 'Belle of Georgia,' 'Luttichau,' and 'Melba,' all with characteristic sweet, cream-colored flesh and dark red skins. Because of their soft flesh these types ship poorly and are rarely offered commercially; they should be the first choices for home gardeners, as they are unsurpassed in quality as fresh fruit. For those who enjoy novelty the doughnut-shaped 'Australian Saucer' is another interesting white peach for the home garden and tastes delicious in spite of its peculiar form.

Apricots are tough, long-lived trees that adapt well to limy soils and endure rugged drought. However, these natives of the arid Middle East require low humidity to ripen fruit properly and produce only erratically in many areas. Brown spot fungus is the culprit usually responsible for poor fruit set and maturation. Chemical control of this malady is generally impractical, so apricots are best appreciated in drier western sections. 'Bryan,' 'Blenheim,' and 'Royal' are some of the better types to try in humid regions, but will probably only bear significant crops in one year out of five.

Subtropical Fruits

In addition to these hardy fruits several subtropical varieties are good producers in warm-climate gardens. Chief among these are the figs. These big shrubby trees make good garden ornamentals, as well as opulent providers of tasty morsels to lay atop slices of dark bread and cream cheese.

Where summers are prone to drought figs benefit from deep mulches to limit moisture fluctuations. This helps to prevent fruit drop. Figs often freeze back during severe winters and are best trained as large, many-stemmed shrubs. Even badly frozen figs are nonetheless able to recover and produce crops the following summer.

The fig "berry" is a strange compound fruit that may be likened in structure to an inside-out blackberry. In nature tiny wasps enter the open "eyes" on the end of the figs to effect pollination. Unfortunately this same route can be used by dried fruit beetles, and these induce fruit spoilage. For this reason figs with closed eyes are the most popular types. Nevertheless, large dessert-quality varieties with open eyes (such as 'Mission') still warrant planting in home gardens, although a goodly portion of their fruits likely will fail to mature.

'Celeste' is a cold-hardy fig with small, sweet fruits that are known locally as "sugar figs." 'Alma,' 'Brown Turkey,' and 'Texas Everbearing' are other good varieties with closed eyes and medium to large fruits. 'White Everbearing' produces large, white fruits with an unusually sweet flavor; it apparently originated as a sport of 'Celeste.'

Oriental persimmmons not only provide luscious orange-red fruits for the table, but do double duty as showy ornamental trees. Their bright reddish fall foliage tones and big rounded fruits create a spectacle that justifies their culture even in gardens where the persimmons will never be eaten.

These big fruits are as tasty as they are attractive, however, and have a pudding-like consistency. Most types are slightly astringent until fully ripened by autumn frost, a character responsible for the well-known "parsimonious" pucker! Ripe fruit may be picked and placed in the freezer to provide a tasty frozen desert. One of the choice home garden varieties, the giant 'Fuyu,' lacks astringency and may be eaten even while young and green. Other popular garden persimmons include 'Eureka,' 'Tamopan,' and 'Tanenashi.' Some selections are seedless if not pollinated by another variety growing nearby.

Like figs, oriental persimmons benefit from a generous mulch around the tree base to prevent moisture fluctuations and consequent fruit drop. They are undemanding small trees, otherwise, and perform well on calcareous clay soils. Because these trees are usually grafted on American persimmon rootstocks they enjoy year-round moisture.

A third subtropical fruit suited to limy soil is the Chinese date, or jujube (*Zizyphus jujube*). Although these plants have little relation to the true date (a type of palm) the fruits of these suckering shrubs look and taste remarkably like their namesakes. Jujubes make attractive small trees with shining green foliage and thrive on the rockiest and most arid lime soils. 'Li' and 'Lang' are two horticultural types that are occasionally offered.

Perhaps the easiest-growing of all these subtropical fruits is the pomegranate, which seems to thrive on heat, lime, and aridity. Although below-zero temperatures may damage these suckering shrubs, they soon recover. Pomegranates bear their orange carnationlike flowers and big fruits on wood of the new year. 'Wonderful' is a popular type for both fruit and ornament, but is not as productive as many of the old unnamed varieties which lurk about farmsteads throughout the Southwest.

Apples and Pears

Few fruits are as well-loved as apples, and gardeners on limy ground frequently attempt these trees at home. In many cases apples fail to produce, however, due to improper selection of varieties, rootstocks, or appropriate pollinators. In truly warm regions only especially adapted apples will flower and produce. Cotton root rot is a serious problem on calcareous clay soils and often prematurely ends an apple tree's life just as it reaches mature bearing size. Many mild-climate apples ripen their fruits in early midsummer and must be harvested promptly and placed in cold storage if they are to retain good eating quality. These summer-ripened apples seldom develop the brilliant colors associated with apples grown in cooler climes.

In spite of these challenges to success, brave gardeners have successfully cultured several apple selections on lime. Heat-tolerant apple varieties have been evaluated by many growers so that several types may be selected for even mild-winter areas. The Israeli varieties, 'Anna' and 'Ein Shemer,' and the Bahamian introduction, 'Dorsett Golden,' produce well in the hottest areas. Where some modest winter chilling can be expected, types such as 'Mollie's Delicious,' 'Holland,' and 'Starkrimson Red Delicious' offer even higher quality fruit and better production.

For home gardens dwarf or semidwarf apple trees grafted to the Malling 9 or Malling 111 rootstock, respectively, are the most desirable choices. Although a few varieties such as 'Ein Shemer' are more or less self-fertile, most cultivars should be combined in plantings of three or more clones to ensure good cross-pollination and fruit set. By selecting dwarf trees gardeners can more readily accommodate several types together.

Another advantage of dwarfs is that they may be readily cordon-trained or espaliered. By tying the branches of these trees to inclined or horizontal wires gardeners can induce early maturation so that even young trees come into production quickly. Such carefully trained trees will also be easier to harvest.

Perhaps the most compelling reason to select dwarf trees is the relative ease with which soil may be adjusted for these miniatures. Generous additions of organic material and sulfur will help keep cotton root rot at bay beneath these small apples, and even on shallow, rocky ground, raised beds can readily be constructed to accommodate a modest row of dwarf trees.

As troublesome as apples can be to cultivate on limy soils, many pears can be sublimely easy. Pears are also long-lived and attractive when in flower or autumn color. As with grapes, however, the best home garden pears are types distinct from the popular supermarket varieties. Because of their susceptibility to bacterial fireblight disease the soft-textured European pears such as 'Bartlett' fail in American gardens. Yet, venerable oriental pear hybrids survive with little care around many old farmsteads. These are generally hard, gritty, canning types such as 'Keiffer' or 'Garber' instead of varieties favored for eating out of hand. Modern selections such as 'Orient' and 'Moonglow' also fall into this category.

A few oriental pears combine fair resistance to fireblight with relatively soft, grit-free fruit. 'Leconte' and 'Ayers' are two of the best-quality types for fresh eating. Although these varieties take several years to mature and bear fruit, they are otherwise easy and adaptable. Most pears require a pollinator for best production. Cordon training or espalier may be used to help induce bearing at a young age, and to accommodate the trees in a smaller garden.

Another exciting prospect is offered by the Asian or "apple" pear clan. These seem to combine the toughness and beauty of the oriental pear tree with a unique crisp fruit that, although not soft-textured, has excellent fresh-fruit flavor. 'Monterrey' is a curious pear that seems to inherit characters of both the oriental and Asian types and thrives on rugged, limy soils. 'Twentieth Century,' 'Shiseki,' and 'Hosui' are popular Japanese selections of Asian pear.

Nuts

Pecans are by far the most popular nut trees for gardens on lime, and are generally productive and long-lived. Although many named varieties have been introduced for commercial production, home gardeners who wish to avoid heavy pesticide use will usually find seedling trees more satisfactory. 'Desirable' is an excellent, commercially available pecan that may be planted as a nut where a tree is wanted.

Walnuts are possible for gardens on limy soil, but require suitable lime-tolerant rootstocks and scions selected for production in the local climate. Most commonly available English walnut varieties (e.g. 'Carpathian') are only marginally productive in humid areas. The black walnut makes a passable nut tree for prairie gardens. 'Thomas' is a commonly available selection with relatively thin-shelled nuts.

Other popular nut varieties such as filberts, hazelnuts, and chestnuts prefer acid soils. Almonds and pistaches favor calcareous ground, but require a mild, arid climate to fruit properly.

Vegetables on Lime

Vegetables planted on calcareous soils, as on other types of garden earths, respond well to additions of humus. Most limy clay soils are naturally rich in minerals and become wonderfully productive if well-manured and enriched with organic debris. Nitrogen-bearing grass clippings are especially beneficial for this purpose.

There are, of course, a few vegetable types that object to calcareous soils, although it is generally the heavy clay texture they dislike rather than the alkaline pH. Sweet potatoes are one of these crops that prefers sandy soil and produces poorly on even the most ameliorated limy clays. Peanuts also prefer light soils.

Nevertheless, vegetable objections can usually be resolved by selecting more appropriate varieties. Although long-rooted carrots require sandy soils to mature properly, the shorter strains such as 'Danver's Half-long' and 'Scarlet Nantes' produce abundantly on amended clays and were selected precisely for their good performances on heavy ground.

Chemical fertilizers and overly rich manures should usually be avoided for legume crops such as snap peas, beans, and Southern peas. These plants are able to manufacture their own nitrogen, but will fail to do so if oversupplied with artificial fertilizers or heavy manures. Most other vegetables respond well to generously enriched soil and enjoy applications of commercial fertilizers as well as lavish additions of compost.

The remaining challenges to successful vegetable culture come primarily from climate and revolve around timing crops to evade seasons of severe heat or cold. A few types endure such vicissitudes and may be left in the ground most of the season. Okra, Southern peas (blackeyes and crowders), jicama, chayote squash, New Zealand spinach, eggplant, and both sweet and hot peppers produce over the length of the summer. Leeks, shallots, asparagus, and Jerusalem artichokes remain as perennials that grow through fall and spring as well.

Most other vegetable crops lack endurance to the worst bouts of winter cold and summer heat and perform best when scheduled to mature during either spring or fall. For this reason warm-climate gardeners often divide the growing season into spring and fall plantings and select early-maturing vegetable varieties to take advantage of these favorable seasons.

Tomatoes, beans, peas, squash, cucumbers, and most root and leaf vegetables perform best with these split seasons. Vegetables that need long periods of equitable weather, such as head lettuces, should be abandoned in favor of their faster-maturing leaf lettuce relations.

With tender crops such as tomatoes, early-maturing, determinate varieties may be started indoors to afford a head start on the season. The young plants can then be set out on, or just prior to, the average last date of frost for the region. Protective cloches of translucent cloth or plastic can be positioned over the young plants to ward off frost on cold nights. This early coddling will be repaid by added weeks of production in the summer, for once nighttime temperatures rise into the high seventies few fruits will set, so most spring-planted tomatoes finish bearing in mid- to late June.

Fall gardens also begin several weeks before optimum temperatures arrive. Tender crops such as tomatoes and peppers must be set out by mid-July if they are to mature before autumn frosts arrive. Temporary shade structures can be of great assistance in establishing the young transplants through high summer heat.

Although the majority of vegetable varieties can be grown during both the spring and fall seasons, many types mature higher quality produce during the cool weather of autumn. This is particularly true for frost-tolerant vegetables such as carrots, cauliflower, broccoli, and cabbage. However, snap peas, potatoes, corn, cucumbers, and squash usually provide their best yields during the spring season.

Onions occur in both short- and long-day variants whose plantings must be appropriately timed if large bulbs are to form. Short-day onions such as 'Granex' or '1015' may be planted in mild regions from late fall to winter for harvest in May. Long-day types like 'Yellow Sweet Spanish' are better suited to cold-winter areas and require early spring planting.

Because of the tremendous heat of high summer and the natural droughtiness of calcareous soils, careful attention to arranging and positioning crops benefits home gardens. The technique of alternating rows of tall vegetables such as corn or okra with vining or sprawling types such as beans, Southern peas, or squash is an ancient tradition of warm climates. Such "intercropping" allows vegetables to benefit from the alternating sun and shade of the variously tall and short rows and helps enrich the soil by maintaining a diverse planting including nitrogen-fixing legumes. This mixing also helps to discourage massive attacks of insect pests by spacing host plants at distance around the garden.

Careful mulching to discourage moisture-thieving weeds and crusting bare earth is another critical measure for successful vegetable culture. In general, a layer from one to three inches thick of straw, dried grass, or other debris should be maintained over plantings throughout the summer. Artificial materials such as plastic or old newspaper may be used as well and are favored by some gardeners. All of these substances help to retain soil moisture and keep the ground cool during summer heat.

Care should be exercised when laying on mulches during early spring, however. Because a mulch prevents the soil's warmth from rising on cool evenings, it can aggravate early season frosts. When surrounded by heavy mulches, otherwise frost-tolerant vegetables such as onions and snap peas can be damaged by winter cold. For this reason gardens should not be mulched until danger of frost has safely passed.

Exotic Crops

Immigrants from warm climates often bring with them exotic vegetables from their homelands, and an increasing array of curious, subtropical produce has accompanied migrants from Southeast Asia, India, and the Middle East in recent years. Many of these are fascinating and productive in home gardens.

Malabar spinach is an odd tropical vine that produces edible leaves through hot weather. Kiwanos or African spiny melons make tough, drought-tolerant vines with colorful, spiky cucumberlike fruits. Both of these are unusual crops well suited to warm weather.

Guinea peas are shrubby, perennial legumes from India whose pealike seeds may be shelled out for inclusion in rice dishes or curries. The great appeal of Guinea peas is their drought resistance and perennial habit; they produce almost indefinitely with little input from gardeners and accept tough, limy soils and grueling heat.

Island Gardens

A primitive, but elegantly sophisticated technique with which gardeners can modify intemperate climate and drought-prone soil is the ancient Amerindian concept of gardening on *chinampas,* or floating islands. Vegetables such as beans, corn, squash, tomatoes, and peppers were first domesticated on these raised platform gardens, which are well-known and continue to produce today in the Mexican district of Xochimilco.

Native Americans used the moderating influence of the waterside environment to successfully cultivate vegetables even in torrid heat and used natural organic debris from aquatic plants to help improve their garden soils.

Chinampa gardens are raised platforms built up above a shallow lake or pond. These beds remain perpetually soggy at depth, and vegetables grown atop such raised ground require minimal irrigation, as their roots penetrate down to the waterline eighteen inches or more below. This constantly available moisture, along with the evaporating water from the nearby pond, assures optimum growing conditions and helps moderate summer heat and ward off winter frost.

Because the green algae that flourish in fresh water fix nitrogen, continuous harvests of seaweed, rushes, and other bog plants can be taken from the nearby waters and applied as nutritious mulches to the garden. This ancient technique has been shown to be outstandingly productive and in warm climates often exceeds in value the most modern agricultural systems. Apparently, chinampa culture renews and enriches the land indefinitely.

Although a bit grandiose for home gardens, a modest platform bed might be constructed by excavating a 20′ by 20′ square, which could be lined with impermeable plastic. Then layers of straw, compost, and soil may be alternated to build the raised bed inside, leaving a two-foot-wide surrounding moat. After packing soil on the sides of the garden platform, water-loving bog plants such as Louisiana irises, sweet flag (*Acorus calamus*), or pickerel weed can be established to help stabilize and hold the artificial shore. A garden hose may then flood the plastic-lined basin to ready the chinampa for planting.

Water-filled tubs or barrels brimming with waterlilies or water hyacinths might be positioned between vegetable rows in smaller gardens. These miniature ponds cannot irrigate beds like a true chinampa, but they can ameliorate the adjacent microclimate, and they also provide ready sources of nutritious herbage to incorporate into the garden soil, as well as a wonderful excuse to cultivate a collection of beautiful waterlilies.

Herbs

Ideal garden edibles for limy ground may be found among the herbs, and these should be among the first plants included in any garden on lime. Many types relish dry, calcareous soils and thrive in home gardens with ridiculous ease. Their fresh flavors are joyous revelations compared to the withered remains offered at grocery stores.

Most herbs are at their best in a fresh condition, and one of the great luxuries of the home herb garden is having their flavorful leaves available only a few steps from the kitchen door. Leafy types like parsley, basil, and cilantro are used almost exclusively while fresh. Sweet marjoram is one of the few whose flavor actually improves on drying. An annual homegrown harvest may be hung and dried for use the following season, and will be far superior to commercially available seasonings.

Chalk-loving perennials such as sage, rosemary, lavender, and thyme prefer raised beds of limy rubble over traditional garden soils. These herbs remain evergreen and may be harvested year-round. Sweet marjoram also enjoys dry, chalky soil, but usually freezes and must be grown as an annual.

Although upright rosemary cultivars are the most cold-hardy, they can be slow-growing, and often need a year or two to size up before taking significant harvest. The prostrate cultivar, 'Lockwood de Forest,' is a more vigorous producer of leaves for the table, and is one of the best-flavored rosemaries. Where winter temperatures fall too low for this type, it may be accommodated in a large pot on the patio for the summer and shifted to a protected room for winter.

When oreganos are considered warm-climate gardeners may select from several true *Origanum* cultivars, as well as the "Mexican oreganos," *Poliomintha longiflora* and *Lippia gravolens*, to provide pungent leaves for the table. *Lippia* retains its sweetly spicy flavor when dried and grows easily on a chalky bank. *Poliomintha* accepts either chalk or good garden soil, as do most *Origanums*. The evergreen Greek oregano (*Origanum vulgare* v. *heracleoticum*) is particularly flavorful and productive.

Annual herbs such as sesame, basil, and summer savory may be planted along with the vegetables in well-prepared limy ground. Those herbs that belong to the carrot family (*i.e.* parsley, cilantro, dill) and German chamomile are best seeded in the fall. They will grow over the winter before flowering the following spring. Such perennial herbs as chives, garlic, shallots, and salad burnet also enjoy prepared garden soils.

Mints require an unfailing supply of moisture, and their underground runners must be restrained if they are not to spread and take the garden. A special bed near the outflow of the washer or a downspout from the gutter is a good solution.

French tarragon usually fails to prosper in warm regions and seldom returns after its first season. Mexican marigold or *yerbanis* (*Tagetes lucida*) has quite similar flavor, however, and grows with ease on limy soils. Its yellow, late-season flowers are a welcome bonus. These can best be enjoyed by locating this bushy perennial near a south-facing wall to offer shelter from early frosts and prolong the season of bloom.

One of the most valuable and characteristic of lime-loving herbs is fennel. The rocky Plain of Marathon in Greece is named for this rugged perennial, which grows there in abundance. Fennel resembles dill, but has a distinctive anise-like pungency of its own that is found in both leaves and seeds. Its ferny foliage and flat yellow blooms make it attractive as an ornamental. A showy bronze-leafed form is often cultivated in chalky flower borders.

For the table, however, the favorite strain of this herb is the Florence fennel, or *finnochio*. This type develops a bulbous, swollen stem that may be braised and eaten as a delicious vegetable. Fennel grows easily on limy garden soils and, like its cousin, dill, often proliferates by self-sown seed. It is a delightful, self-perpetuating herbal vegetable.

EPILOGUE

That gardeners on lime, alkaline clay, or caliche should choose plants well suited to their soils may seem commonsense. Yet, as simple as this may sound, for even modest plantings on calcareous ground this assertion obliges a fair measure of sophistication. Not only (or necessarily) native plants, but an array of garden subjects from around the world will need to be investigated and considered. The factors influencing their success or failure will follow not only from their inherent adaptability to soil, but also from mysterious and subtle climate tolerances and from the gardener's care, preparation, and choice of particular sites.

Even assiduous, experienced planters, armed with stacks of notes, plans, and careful lists, will be likely to suffer occasional setbacks. In practice, watchful experimentation and dedicated observation will help gardeners puzzle out the needs of various plants more often than adherence to theory or accepted gardening wisdom. The most successful will be those who delight in unravelling the mysteries and challenges offered by each plant placed in their care. Over time their careful attention will grow into that intuitive sense celebrated as a "green thumb."

The challenges presented by limestone, alkaline clay, and caliche soils are admittedly profound, but these grounds will quickly educate any who persist to garden upon them. By observing other gardens on lime and adding experience, gardeners will begin to discover many possibilities. Eventually, even difficult soil situations and exposed aspects will seem to afford limitless potential. With each new success, gardeners on lime will contribute to the diversity and beauty of their plantings and feel the satisfaction inherent in participating in the world of growing things. The living legacies of gardens and the sharing pleasures of exchange with other gardeners will be the worthy achievements and rewards for the extra effort invested in gardening on difficult soils!

SOME USEFUL ADDRESSES

Plant Sources

American Ornamental Perennials
P.O. Box 385
Gresham, OR 93070–0054
Ornamental grasses

Andre Viette Farm & Nursery
Route 1, Box 16
Fishersville, VA 22939
(703) 943-2315
Perennials

The Antique Rose Emporium
Route 5, Box 143
Brenham, TX 77833
Old garden and shrub roses, perennials

Botanicals
219 Concord Road
Wayland, MA 01778
(508) 358-4846
Perennials and rockery plants

Bluebird Nursery, Inc.
P.O. Box 460
Clarkson, NB 68629
Perennials

Carol Gardens
P.O. Box 310
Westminister, MD 21157
Woody ornamentals and perennials

Coastal Gardens & Nursery
4611 Socastee Boulevard
Myrtle Beach, SC 29575
(803) 293-2000
Perennials

Daffodil Mart
Route 3 Box 794
Gloucester, VA 23061
(804) 693-3966
Narcissus species and hybrids

David Austin Roses
Bowling Green Lane, Albrighton
Wolverhampton, WV7 3HB
United Kingdom
Old garden and shrub roses

Forestfarm
990 Tetherhof Road
Williams, OR 97544
Woody ornamentals and perennials

Hastings
1036 White, S.W.
P.O. Box 115535
Atlanta, GA 30310–8535
Warm climate fruits and vegetables

J. L. Hudson, Seedsman
P.O. Box 1058
Redwood City, CA 94064
Wide and varied list of plant seeds

John D. Lyon, Inc.
143 Alewife Brook Parkway
Cambridge, MA 02140
(617) 876-3705
Miniature and rockery bulbs

Louisiana Nursery
Route 5 Box 43 (Highway 182)
Opalousas, LA 70576
(318) 948-3696
Woody ornamentals, perennials, and bulbs

Mesa Garden
P.O. Box 72
Belen, NM 87002
(505) 864-3131
Hardy and half-hardy cacti and other succulents

The Natural Garden
38W443 Highway 64
St. Charles, IL 60175
(708) 584-0150
Prairie wildflowers and grasses

Plants of the Southwest
1550 Pacheco Street
Santa Fe, NM 87501
*Southwestern wildflowers, grasses, and
    vegetables*

Siskiyou Rare Plant Nursery
Department 1 2825 Cummings Road
Medford, OR 97501
(503) 772-6846
Woody ornamentals and perennials

TyTy Plantation
Box 159
TyTy, GA 31795
(912) 382-0404
Subtropical bulbs and perennials

Wayside Gardens
1 Garden Lane
Hodges, SC 29695–0001

Western Hills Rare Plant Nursery
16250 Coleman Valley Road
Occidental, CA 95465

William R. P. Welch
Garzas Road
Carmel Valley, CA 93924
(409) 659-3830
Tazetta narcissus

Woodlanders
1128 Colleton Avenue
Aiken, SC 29801
Woody ornamentals, southeastern native plants

Yucca-Do Nursery
Peckerwood Gardens
P.O. Box 655
Waller, TX 77484
(409) 829-6363
*Woody ornamentals, perennials, southwestern
    natives*

Plant Societies

American Horticultural Society
Box 0105
Mount Vernon, VA 22121

International Bulb Society
U. C. I. Arboretum
University of California
Irvine, CA 92717

American Rock Garden Society
P.O. Box 67
Millwood, NY 10546

Native Plant Society of Texas
P.O. Box 891
Georgetown, TX 78627

Royal Horticultural Society
Vincent Square
London SWIP 2PE
United Kingdom

BIBLIOGRAPHY

Adams, William D. *Shrubs and Vines For Southern Landscapes*. Houston: Gulf Publishing Company, 1979.

Affleck, Thomas. *Hedging and Hedging Plants in the Southern States*. Houston: E. H. Cushing, 1869.

Bailey, Liberty Hyde, and Ethel Joe Bailey. *Hortus Third*. New York: Macmillan Publishing Company, 1976.

Berrisford, Judith. *Gardening on Chalk, Lime, and Clay*. London: Faber and Faber, 1978.

Brady, Nyle C. *The Nature and Properties of Soils*. 8th Edition. New York: Macmillaan Publishing Co., 1974.

Correl, Donovan Stewart, and Marshall Conring Johnston. *Manual of the Vascular Plants of Texas*. Richardson, Texas: University of Texas at Dallas, 1979.

Cox, Paul W., and Patty Leslie. *Texas Trees*. San Antonio: Corona Publishing Company, 1988.

Davis, Helen Burns. *Life and Work of Cyrus Guernsey Pringle*. Burlington, Vermont: University of Vermont Press, 1936.

Egolf, Donald R. and Anne O. Andrick. *The Lagerstroemia Handbook/Checklist*. American Association of Botanical Gardens and Arboreta, Inc., 1978.

Eliovson, Sima. *South African Flowers for the Garden*. Cape Town: Howard Timmins, 1957.

Enquist, Marshal. *Wildflowers of the Texas Hill Country*. Austin: Lone Star Botanical, 1987.

Gorer, Richard. *The Development of Garden Flowers*. London: Eyre and Spottiswoode, Ltd., 1970.

Harrison, Charles R. *Ornamental Conifers*. New York: Macmillan Publishing Company, Inc., 1975.

Howard, Sir Albert. *An Agricultural Testament*. New York: Oxford University Press, 1943. Special Rodale Press Edition, 1974.

Hume, H. Harold. *Hollies*. New York: The Macmillan Company, 1953.

Johnson, Hugh. *The International Book of Trees*. New York: Crown Publishers, Inc., 1973.

Johnson, Hugh. *The Principles of Gardening*. New York: Simon and Schuster, 1979.

Land Publishing. *Sunset Western Garden Book*. Menlo Park: Lane Publishing Company, 1988.

Lawrence, Elizabeth. *The Little Bulbs*. New York: Criterion Books, 1957.

Lundell, Cyrus Longworth. *Agricultural Research at Renner, 1944–1966*. Renner, Texas: Texas Research Foundation, 1967.

McEachern, George Ray. *Growing Fruits, Nuts, and Berries in the South*. Houston: Gulf Publishing Company, 1978.

Parnes, Robert. *Organic and Inorganic Fertilizers*. Mt. Vernon, Maine: Wood's End Agricultural Institute.

Peattie, Donald Culross. *A Natural History of Western Trees*. New York: Crown Publishers, Inc., 1953.

Phillips, Roger, and Martyn Rix. *Shrubs*. New York: Random House, 1989.

Readers Digest. *Field Guide to the Trees and Shrubs of Britain*. London: The Reader's Digest Association, Ltd., 1981.

Rollins, Elizabeth D. "Origanum: Beauty of the Mountains." *Pacific Horticulture*. Vol. 52, No. 2, Summer 1991.

Scruggs, Mrs. Gross R., and Margaret Ann Scruggs. *Gardening in the Southwest*. Dallas: Southwest Press, 1932.

Sinnes, A. Cort. *All About Perennials*. San Francisco: Chevron Chemical Co., 1981.

Sperry, Neil. *The Complete Guide to Texas Gardening*. Dallas: Taylor Publishing Company, 1982.

Standley, Paul C. *Trees and Shrubs of Mexico*. In *Contributions from the United States National Herbarium*. Vol. 23. Washington,

D.C.: Government Printing Office, 1920–26. Germany: J. Kramer Reprint, 1982.

Stern, Sir Frederick C. *A Chalk Garden*. London: Thomas Nelson and Sons, Ltd., 1960.

Stout, A. B. *Daylilies*. Milwood, New York: Sagapress, Inc., 1986.

Taylor's Guide to Annuals. Boston: Houghton Mifflin Company, 1986.

Thomas, Graham Stuart. *Perennial Garden Plants*. London: J. M. Dent and Sons, Ltd., 1982.

Treseder, Neil G. *Magnolias*. London: Faber and Faber, Ltd., 1978.

Welch, William C. *Perennial Garden Color*. Dallas: Taylor Publishing Company, 1989.

Wilder, Louise Beebe. *Adventures With Hardy Bulbs*. New York: Macmillan Publishing Co., 1990.

Wills, Mary Motz, and Howard S. Irwin. *Roadside Wildflowers of Texas*. Austin: University of Texas Press, 1969.

INDEX